Inside Roman Libraries

STUDIES IN THE HISTORY OF GREECE AND ROME

Robin Osborne, James Rives, and Richard J. A. Talbert, editors

Books in this series examine the history and society of Greece and Rome from approximately 1,000 BC to AD 600. The series includes interdisciplinary studies, works that introduce new areas for investigation, and original syntheses and reinterpretations.

Inside Roman Libraries

Book Collections and Their Management in Antiquity

GEORGE W. HOUSTON

The University of North Carolina Press   Chapel Hill

This book was published with the assistance of the H. Eugene and Lillian Youngs Lehman Fund of the University of North Carolina Press. A complete list of books published in the Lehman Series appears at the end of the book.

Manufactured in the United States of America
Designed by Kimberly Bryant and set in Miller types
by Tseng Information Systems, Inc.
The paper in this book meets the guidelines for permanence and durability
of the Committee on Production Guidelines for Book Longevity of the Council on
Library Resources. The University of North Carolina Press has been a member
of the Green Press Initiative since 2003.

Jacket illustration: Marble relief of a doctor reading, from a fourth-century
sarcophagus (detail on front of jacket; full image on back of jacket). Gift of
Mrs. Joseph Brummer and Ernest Brummer, in honor of Joseph Brummer, 1948
(48.76.1). The Metropolitan Museum of Art, New York. Image from
Art Resource, New York, © The Metropolitan Museum of Art.

Library of Congress Cataloging-in-Publication Data
Houston, George W.
Inside Roman libraries : book collections and their management
in antiquity / George W. Houston.
pages cm — (Studies in the history of Greece and Rome)
Includes bibliographical references and index.
ISBN 978-1-4696-1780-0 (cloth : alk. paper) — ISBN 978-1-4696-1781-7 (ebook)
1. Libraries—Rome—History—To 400. 2. Manuscripts (Papyri)—Collectors and collecting.
3. Manuscripts, Greek (Papyri)—Italy—Herculaneum (Extinct city) 4. Manuscripts,
Greek (Papyri)—Egypt—Bahnasa. 5. Books and reading—Rome. I. Title.
Z722.H68 2014
027.037'63—dc23
2014017087

18 17 16 15 14   5 4 3 2 1

For Jean

Contents

3. The Villa of the Papyri at Herculaneum, 87

4. The Book Collections of Oxyrhynchus, 130

Illustrations

Preface

This is a book about book rolls, collections of book rolls, assemblages of ancient volumes that were thrown out together or buried in the eruption of Vesuvius, or that are known to us, however partially, in some other way. It is not a study of library buildings, although we will meet some of them in passing; rather, our focus throughout will be on collections of book rolls and on the equipment and staff needed to organize and maintain them. The ultimate goal is not to recreate a typical Roman book collection or library, but to explore the possibilities: what kinds of book collections can we find, or recreate in our mind's eye, along a spectrum from very small to large, complex, and expensive? To answer these questions, we will exploit whatever evidence we can find: papyri, inscriptions, material remains including archaeological finds and ancient depictions, and texts of all sorts, literary, legal, and documentary. As we will see, papyri constitute the single most important type of evidence for the questions we want to ask, and I hope that my treatment of this material will be of interest to the papyrologists whose work has made it possible; but my chief hope is that the book will be useful to classicists and library historians generally, and to that end I have included definitions and information that papyrologists may find elementary.

It is a pleasure to recall the process of writing this book and to acknowledge the help I have received in that process. T. Keith Dix of the University of Georgia first suggested I look into the material in Egypt to see what could be learned about libraries there, and that suggestion ultimately led to the focus of the present volume, on book collections rather than on libraries as institutions. I did much preliminary work in the Papyrology Room in Duke University's Perkins Library, where the late John Oates welcomed me and facilitated my work. The University of North Carolina has provided me with superb facilities and full library privileges both before and after my retirement, and the Department of Classics has supported my work in numerous ways; in particular, Kim Miles, Cinnamon Weaver, and Karna Younger have all given me invaluable assistance.

I owe thanks to many colleagues here in Chapel Hill: Robert Babcock, Donald Haggis, Jerzy Linderski, James O'Hara, William Race, James Rives, Philip Stadter, William West. All have listened to oral versions of parts of the book, answered specific questions, read sections, or provided advice or critiques, and all have helped to improve the book.

Numerous papyrologists have been wonderfully generous with advice and help as I have tried to navigate my way through their field, an area of classical studies that was previously unfamiliar to me. David Blank, Mario Capasso, Maria Clara Cavalieri, Maria Rosaria Falivene, Nikolaos Gonis, Richard Janko, Kathleen McNamee, Dirk Obbink, Rosa Otranto, Peter Parsons, and Kent Rigsby all have helped me by responding to queries, sending me copies of their work, discussing particular problems, or in some other way helping me understand the papyri. I thank all those who helped me obtain photographs of papyri: Bernhard Palme and Sophie Kovarik (Vienna); Olga Filippova (St. Petersburg); Rainer Thiel (Jena); Dorota Dzierzbicka and Tomasz Derda (Warsaw); and Patricia Spencer, Christopher Naunton, and Joanna Kyffin (P.Oxy.). Many classicists who are not papyrologists have answered queries, sent me copies of their recent publications, and discussed particular problems with me. At the risk of forgetting to include some, I would certainly like to thank Ewen Bowie, Alberto Ciampi, and Peter White.

Several people have read parts of this book or listened to papers in which I tried out some of my ideas, and I am grateful for their comments and criticisms. I presented early versions of parts of the book at the Universities of Cincinnati, Pennsylvania, and St. Andrews, and I thank the audiences for their perceptive comments and helpful questions. Lucia Criscuolo, Giovanni Geraci, Kerr Houston, and William Johnson read part or all of the manuscript (or of earlier versions) and provided me with many helpful comments. The readers for the University of North Carolina Press read the draft with great care, saved me from many errors, and asked questions that led to major rewriting and adjustments in the draft, and I am very grateful for their help. It goes without saying that I alone am responsible for whatever mistakes or misjudgments remain.

I thank Chuck Grench, Paula Wald, Heidi Perov, and Lucas Church of the University of North Carolina Press for their patient help and guidance; Shirley Werner for her exceptionally careful copyediting; and Richard Talbert for his encouragement and advice.

Above all, I thank my wife, Jean Houston. She proofread the entire book and earlier versions of parts of it twice or more, and commented on matters both small and large. She encouraged me, patiently, for the several years it took to complete the project. I dedicate the book to her with love and gratitude.

Abbreviations

Besides the following abbreviations, titles of journals are abbreviated as in *l'Année philologique*, and ancient authors and works as in the *Oxford Classical Dictionary* (4th edition). Authors and texts not in the *Oxford Classical Dictionary* are abbreviated as in *Der Neue Pauly*, vol. 1, or (for the works of Galen) R. J. Hankinson, *The Cambridge Companion to Galen* (2008). Papyri are cited as in Oates and Willis et al., *Checklist of Editions of Greek, Latin, Demotic, and Coptic Papyri, Ostraca and Tablets*, online at library.duke.edu/rubenstein/scriptorium/papyrus/texts/clist.html.

AE	*L'année épigraphique* (Paris, 1889–).
ANRW	*Aufstieg und Niedergang der römischen Welt: Geschichte und Kultur Roms im Spiegel der neueren Forschung* (Berlin and New York, 1972–).
*CAH*³	*Cambridge Ancient History*, 3rd edition (Cambridge, 1970–).
CGFP	*Comicorum Graecorum fragmenta in papyris reperta*, edited by C. Austin (Berlin and New York, 1973).
CGL	*Corpus glossariorum Latinorum* (Amsterdam, 1965).
CIL	*Corpus inscriptionum Latinarum* (Berlin, 1862–).
CLA	*Codices Latini antiquiores: A Palaeographical Guide to Latin Manuscripts Prior to the Ninth Century* (Oxford, 1934–66).
CLGP	*Commentaria et lexica Graeca in papyris reperta* (Munich, 2004–).
CPF	*Corpus dei papiri filosofici greci e latini: Testi e lessico nei papiri di cultura greca e latina* (Florence, 1989–).
CPP	*Catalogue of Paraliterary Papyri*, edited by M. Huys (online at http://cpp.arts.kuleuven.be).
CPS	*Corpus dei papiri storici greci e latini* (Pisa, 2008–).
Diz.Epig.	*Dizionario epigrafico di antichità romane* (Rome, 1895–).
DNP	*Der Neue Pauly* (Stuttgart and Weimar, 1996–).
FGrHist	*Fragmente der griechischen Historiker*, edited by F. Jacoby (Berlin, 1923–).

Galen, *Ind.*   Galen, *De indolentia* = *Galien, Ne pas se chagriner*, edited
                 by V. Boudon-Millot and J. Jouanna (Paris, 2010).
IG   *Inscriptiones Graecae* (Berlin, 1873–).
IGRR   *Inscriptiones Graecae ad res Romanas pertinentes* (Paris,
                 1901–8).
IGUR   *Inscriptiones Graecae Urbis Romae* (Rome, 1968–).
IK Ephesos   *Die Inschriften von Ephesos*, vol. 11.1 of *Inschriften
                 griechischer Städte aus Kleinasien* (Bonn, 1979–).
ILS   *Inscriptiones Latinae selectae* (Berlin, 1892–1916).
Insc.Ital.   *Inscriptiones Italiae* (Rome, 1931–).
LDAB   *Leuven Database of Ancient Books* (online at http://www
                 .trismegistos.org/ldab/index.php).
LIMC   *Lexicon iconographicum mythologiae classicae*
                 (Zurich, 1981–).
MP³   Mertens-Pack database of papyri, 3rd edition (online at
                 http://promethee.philo.ulg.ac.be/cedopal/index.htm).
MRR   T. R. S. Broughton, *Magistrates of the Roman Republic*,
                 3 vols. (New York, 1951–52 and 1984).
PCG   *Poetae comici Graeci*, edited by R. Kassel and C. Austin
                 (Berlin and New York, 1983–).
PIR²   *Prosopographia imperii Romani*, 2nd edition
                 (Berlin, 1933–).
PME   H. Devijver, *Prosopographia militium equestrium* (Leuven,
                 1976–80).
PSI   *Papyri greci e latini*, Pubblicazioni della Società italiana
                 per la ricerca dei papiri greci e latini in Egitto, 15 vols.
                 (Florence, 1912–57).
RE   Pauly-Wissowa, *Real-encyclopädie der classischen
                 Altertumswissenschaft* (Stuttgart, 1893–).
SEG   *Supplementum epigraphicum Graecum* (Lyons,
                 Amsterdam, Leiden, 1923–).
TLL   *Thesaurus linguae Latinae* (Leipzig, 1900–).
TrGF   *Tragicorum Graecorum Fragmenta* (Göttingen,
                 1971–85).

Inside Roman Libraries

Introduction

There is no lack of interest in, and scholarly study of, ancient book collections. Even in antiquity, the library at Alexandria entered the public imagination and became a virtual myth; and in modern times the royal library at Pergamum, the carbonized rolls from the Villa of the Papyri at Herculaneum, and the great imperial libraries in the city of Rome are all well known and much studied. In general, interest has centered on these collections as institutions, on their building histories and architecture, and on their functions.[1] Much less attention has been paid to the actual collections of book rolls, the titles and authors represented in them, the age and condition of the rolls, and the interests of the owners implied by the nature of their collections. These are the sorts of questions that most interest me and that I propose to explore in this study. We will begin with a brief description of the ancient book roll and its characteristics, then consider a number of specific Roman-era book collections, and finally turn to the equipment and personnel needed to tend such collections. Our subject, in short, is everything that one might find inside a Roman library. These matters have seldom been studied in detail, and no single study has considered them together.[2]

My hope is to obtain a better understanding of several matters. How did Roman-era book collections come into existence, and how long did they stay together as coherent bodies of material? When we can identify specific ancient book collections, what do we find? Did all collections include a more or less predictable range of works in Greek and Latin, or were there different sorts of collections, some general, others specialized? To what extent are the tastes and interests of individual collectors evident in the books they brought together? Did collectors care if there were mistakes in their

---

1. We will come across specialist studies that touch on these topics and libraries in the course of our study, but here we may note a few more general items. On Alexandria: Canfora (1993); Bagnall (2002); Berti and Costa (2010), 49–159. Pergamum: Coqueugniot (2013). Villa of the Papyri: Sider (2005), Houston (2013). Rome: Fedeli (1989), Dix and Houston (2006). Ancient libraries in general: Blanck (2008), 181–303. Among the many studies of the architecture of libraries, we may note here those of Callmer (1944) and of Strocka, Hoffmann, and Hiesel (2012). Note also Nicholls (forthcoming), on all aspects of Roman public libraries.

2. The papyrological materials that provide much of the evidence in chapters 2, 3, and 4 have not previously been exploited systematically in the context of library history. Much of the literary evidence has been studied repeatedly, but not from the point of view that I will adopt.

book rolls? How concerned with economy were they, or with elegance? How were books stored and retrieved from storage, and who was responsible for protecting, repairing, and maintaining them? These are the sorts of problems I will explore in this book. As we will see, many of our questions can be answered, at least in part, but there are also important aspects of book collections and libraries that, at least for now, remain mysteries, completely dark to us.

Preliminary definitions are needed. By "Roman world" I mean, somewhat arbitrarily, the geographical area of the Roman Empire and the four centuries from Cicero to Constantine. Most of our evidence comes from Italy and Egypt, but useful materials appear elsewhere as well. I will not attempt to describe variations in local practice because our evidence across time, space, and discipline is largely consistent: the ways men assembled, managed, and used collections appear to have been similar throughout the Empire during these four centuries. What we find in the Greek papyri from Egypt, for example, is similar to what we learn about libraries in Rome and Italy from Latin authors such as Aulus Gellius. The library of Celsus at Ephesus, despite its location in the Greek-speaking East, is very much a Roman creation in design, source of funding, and purposes, and I accordingly regard it as a library of the Roman world.

As for date, I will occasionally range backward in time to the second and third centuries BC, but the great bulk of evidence on all of the central questions posed in this book dates from the period that begins roughly in the middle of the first century BC and extends through the third century AD to the time of Constantine. The beginning point is clearly marked by the appearance of two important bodies of evidence: the letters of Cicero and the collection of manuscripts found in the Villa of the Papyri. Before this, we know very little. The end point is not as sharply defined, but over the period of about two centuries, beginning in the second century AD, there are significant changes in library history that collectively suggest a stopping point for this study. The book roll gave way to the codex, with consequences for storage, retrieval of texts, and durability of manuscripts.[3] Christian texts began to replace classical Greek and Latin literature, affecting the contents of collections. Equally important for the modern scholar, papyrological and epigraphical evidence on collections of classical Greek and Roman authors (as opposed to Christian libraries) becomes very scarce from the fourth cen-

---

3. Roberts and Skeat (1983), 37; Cavallo (1989b), 173. Codices seem to have become standard for classical Greek texts by the fourth century AD.

tury on, and after about AD 200 references in literature to contemporary collections are few in number and as a rule uninformative.[4] My study is thus limited, with only a few exceptions, to the period from Cicero to Constantine.

I do not include every known assemblage of papyrus rolls or codices. The eight or nine hundred rolls found in caves at Qumran in Israel (the so-called Dead Sea Scrolls) fall within our period, but they belong to a different tradition, neither Greek nor Roman, and I have omitted them;[5] so too the Coptic codices found together in a jar at Nag Hammadi in Egypt.[6] Manuscripts recovered from mummy cartonnage at Al Hiba in Egypt cannot yet be traced to particular owners,[7] and a potentially useful library from Antinoopolis was published by its excavator only in general terms, making it difficult to analyze.[8] I will occasionally refer to these and other collections on particular points, but to analyze them fully, with all of their problems and scholarly controversies, would require a far longer book than this one. It is my hope, rather, that the present study will provide a kind of baseline, a set of Roman-era materials that other scholars can build on and exploit as they work on ancient libraries and book collections.

I avoid, but do not completely exclude, the terms "public" and "private" library. I do this not because the ancient Romans had no concept of "public" libraries—they did[9]—but because in the modern mind these terms carry connotations that are often not appropriate when applied to the ancient world, and because the situation is more complex than this simple twofold division suggests. For the modern reader, "public library" is likely to suggest a library that is supported by public funding, usually from public tax receipts, and used by a broad spectrum of society, including children and women. By contrast, Roman "public" libraries, so far as we can tell, were

4. Papyri and ostraca do, however, provide important evidence on collections of Christian texts and small collections of texts in Coptic right through the early medieval period until at least AD 800. Examples are given in Harrauer (1995), 70–72.

5. Introductions to the Qumran texts and to some of the numerous scholarly controversies surrounding them will be found in Magness (2002), Tov (2002), and Hirschfeld (2004).

6. For a concise description of the Nag Hammadi find, see Robinson (1996), 10–25.

7. In a series of very useful articles, Maria Rosaria Falivene has contributed greatly to our knowledge and understanding of these texts, which date from the third to the first centuries BC. For a summary of the evidence on them as one or more collections, see Falivene (2003).

8. Johnson (1914). What can be done with the Antinoopolis texts has been done by Menci (1998).

9. This is clear from the terminology applied to libraries, as when Isidore (*Etym.* 6.5.2) states that Asinius Pollio created the first public library at Rome: *primum autem Romae bibliothecas publicavit Pollio.* ("Pollio [was the] first [who] made libraries in Rome available to the public.") For perceptive discussions of the concept of "public library" and its implications, see Dix (1994) and Nicholls (2013).

seldom if ever supported by municipal tax receipts,[10] and they seem to have made no provision for children.[11]

Moreover, in antiquity, as in modern times, there was a wide range of libraries of various types, some overlapping in function, others representing subcategories within larger groups. Some of the large "private" libraries— the late Republican library of Lucullus, for example—seem to have functioned in ways that are indistinguishable from those of the great "public" libraries in the city of Rome of the first three centuries A D : collections, staff, and usage are all virtually identical, so far as we can tell.[12] Some libraries, such as those in gymnasia, were neither "private" collections nor open to the public at large. Libraries of imperial date were often situated within temple precincts. This is not at all surprising in the ancient world, but a religious context hardly springs to the modern mind when someone mentions a "public library."[13] And it is still not entirely clear exactly who used, or was entitled to use, the libraries modern scholars class as "public."[14] In the Roman world, in short, there were many variations on the theme of library, and one of the goals of this book is to explore those variations.

The reader will already be aware of one assumption I make: I believe that there is considerable continuity between different types of collection, from personal collections of a few dozen rolls, through municipal collections such as the library of Celsus in Ephesus, to the great imperial libraries in Rome, and that all of these collections resemble one another in important respects and can be discussed within a single framework. We will find smaller collections being absorbed by larger ones, the result being that the great collections consist, to some degree, of assemblages of smaller ones and share some or many of their characteristics.[15] Moreover, the work involved in the assembling and maintenance of small- and medium-sized collections, in a world where every manuscript is an individually handwritten product, is similar in nature if not in scale to the effort needed to establish a large one.[16]

10. Where we have evidence on the funding of municipal libraries, the funds come from endowments established by wealthy citizens of the town.

11. No ancient source ever mentions a woman or a child in a library, but the interest Octavia, sister of the emperor Augustus, took in founding a library in honor of her son Marcellus certainly suggests that women were allowed in libraries. We know of several other women, too, who provided funding for libraries.

12. Houston (2002), 141 and 147–48.

13. One example of many would be the library in the Sanctuary of Asclepius in Pergamum, paid for by a woman, Flavia Melitine, and containing a statue of the god Hadrian. See section 5.7 on the statue.

14. Dix (1994) considers the evidence in detail.

15. Several examples are cited in section 1.11. More could be added.

16. Scribes make new copies of works using the same or similar techniques regardless of the size of

A SHORT INTRODUCTION TO THE ROMAN BOOK ROLL

How we store and identify our texts, how we retrieve them from their places on shelves or in containers, and how we use them, is determined in part by their physical form. Throughout the period we are concerned with, the typical form of a book was the papyrus roll.[17] (See Figure 1.) To create a book roll, individual sheets of papyrus were glued together with a slight overlap, thus forming continuous long sheets. In Egypt, the individual sheets tended to be some 25 to 33 cm high, while in manuscripts discovered at the Villa of the Papyri in Herculaneum the sheets average some 19 to 24 cm in height. The heights of sheets—and consequently the width of rolls—may thus have varied either from place to place or at different periods or both.[18] The text was written in columns perpendicular to the length of the roll, and ordinarily on only one side of the roll. This side (to omit the technical details) is generally now termed the recto, and the reverse, ordinarily left blank, is called the verso.[19]

The columns were usually some 5 to 7 cm wide in prose texts, wider and more variable in verse.[20] In many carefully written papyri from both Egypt and Herculaneum, each successive line in a column begins slightly farther to the left than the one above it, so that the column appears to lean to the right. This phenomenon is called "Maas's Law" by papyrologists, and its presence can be taken as a sign that the writing was done by a professional or by a carefully trained scribe.[21]

For storage, the papyrus could be rolled up, either by itself or around a wooden dowel. Lengths of papyrus rolls varied greatly, the length ordinarily being determined by the nature of the contents. A book of poetry of 900 lines might require a papyrus only 3 or 4 m long, while a long book of

---

the collection that acquires the new roll; all rolls, in whatever kind of library, must be protected against theft, damp, and insect larvae; and so on.

17. Given the extensive modern literature on papyrus and the book roll, we need only a brief account here. For full details, see Turner and Parsons (1987), 1–23. Also: Leach and Tait (2000), 231–39 (manufacture of papyrus sheets and rolls); Johnson (2009), 256–62 (dimensions and characteristics of the papyrus roll); Blanck (2008), 58–77 (other writing materials, including wax tablets).

18. Egyptian papyri: Johnson (2004), 141–43. Herculaneum: Cavallo (1983), 48. The Herculaneum papyri seem to have shrunk some 5 to 10 percent due to the heat produced in the eruption of Vesuvius, so the difference in sizes may not be quite so marked as at first sight appears. See Capasso (2007), 77, for the shrinkage.

19. For a full discussion and more precise definitions, see Turner (1978).

20. Column widths: Johnson (2004), 101–8 for prose, 115–19 for poetry. Columns of verse were often wider, in the range of 9 to 13 cm, because they had to preserve the lines of poetry.

21. On Maas's Law in general, see Johnson (2009), 261; in manuscripts from Herculaneum, Janko (2000), 72.

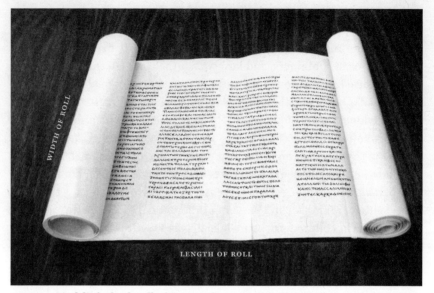

Figure 1. Model of a book roll of Roman date containing a small part of Thucydides, Book 2 (including some scribal errors). The text runs left to right, so one would gradually unroll the text on the right. This roll is about 28 cm wide and 12 m long. Model by author.

Thucydides or Livy might fill a roll of 15 m or so. Papyrus rolls of all lengths ranging from 3 to 15 m are attested in significant numbers at Oxyrhynchus, and some seem to have exceeded 20 m.[22] This variation in length means, of course, that the diameters of the rolled-up manuscripts must have varied greatly as well.[23]

Occasionally a roll was reused, and in this case the roll is sometimes called an "opisthograph," or roll with writing on both sides. Such a roll might have, for example, documents on both sides, or two different literary texts, one on the recto and the other on the verso.[24] For our purposes,

22. Johnson (2004), 217–26, table 3.7A, with discussion at 143–52. At Herculaneum, manuscripts have been found that range from 6.5 m to more than 20 m in length: Janko (2000), 114.

23. Johnson (2004), 150, estimates that a papyrus 5 m in length would have a diameter when rolled up of 5.2 cm, while a papyrus 15 m in length would have a diameter of 9 cm. Sève (2010), 24–25, reached very much the same conclusion (diameters of 5 to 8 cm as the norm). These figures are important when we consider the capacities of various storage facilities: see below, sections 5.2 and 5.4.

24. The word "opisthograph" derives from a Greek word that was taken over into Latin. Rare in both languages, it has been used with a number of slightly different meanings in both ancient and modern times. For a discussion, see Manfredi (1983). I use the word, rather more freely than Manfredi's technical definition would allow, as Pliny the Younger used it: to indicate papyrus rolls that have writing on both sides (Plin. *Ep.* 3.5.17); but I will regularly state what kinds of text (documents or literary work) are on each side.

by far the most important and the most numerous opisthographs are those in which a roll of documents ceased to be of value and was turned over and reused, a literary text being copied onto the verso. At least 182 such texts have been identified among the papyri from Oxyrhynchus. Some of these are students' practice work, but some are quite handsome texts that may have been copied by professional scribes. Most seem to be copies of works of literature made either by private individuals for their own use or by professionally trained scribes.[25] Since a reused roll should cost less than a new one, it is reasonable to assume that the presence of opisthographs in a collection is ordinarily a sign of an economy-minded collector who hoped to save money by using or buying less expensive materials.

ANNOTATIONS

Ancient readers, so far as we can tell, almost never wrote their own personal reactions or observations in the margins of their book rolls, but they sometimes added—or had scribes add—variant readings, aids to the understanding of a text, or both. Roughly 5 percent of the papyrus fragments published so far contain annotations of some sort, but if we had more of each original book roll, and more papyri from the great centers of learning as opposed to smaller towns, the percentage of manuscripts that included annotations might well turn out to be substantially greater.[26] The annotations were sometimes copied right along with the main text by the principal scribe, but more often they seem to have been added by a second hand, either as part of the original production process or soon after the copying of the text. A few manuscripts contain marginal comments in several hands.[27] The annotations generally consist of variant readings or of explanatory material that had been excerpted or condensed from the scholarly commentators who worked in Alexandria and other centers of learning in the first three centuries BC. The explanatory comments include paraphrases, definitions, notes to help the reader understand strange words or dialectal forms, and comments on such things as mythical, historical, and geographical references.[28] Most of the marginalia that survive appear in the manuscripts of

25. Lama (1991): elegant texts, 94–101; students' texts, 106–9; texts meant to be kept and read by individuals, 104–5 and 115–18.

26. McNamee (2007), 2–3. She notes that at Oxyrhynchus, which was a town of considerable importance, some 10 percent of all the papyri published so far contain annotations: McNamee (2007), 11.

27. Ibid., 26–28.

28. Ibid., 130, lists thirty-three different categories of content. The last two are "quasi-personal notes," the others being textual or exegetical additions of some sort.

poets; annotated texts of prose authors are much less frequent. Very few of the published manuscripts from Herculaneum include marginalia, presumably because almost all of the Herculaneum texts are prose, and because very few of them are likely to have been studied intensively by scholars and critics in the period between the time of their creation—mostly in the second and first centuries BC—and the eruption of Vesuvius.

END TITLES AND INITIAL TITLES

Titles, authors, and whatever other identifying text there might be, such as the number of the book within the work (e.g., *Iliad* Δ = *Iliad*, Book 4), were regularly written at the conclusion of the text, either beside the last column (the usual place) or just below it, and in at least some and perhaps most cases were entered at the beginning of the text as well.[29] These ancient equivalents of our title pages are known as end titles, final titles, or *subscriptiones* when they appear at the end of a text, and as initial titles, front titles, or *inscriptiones* when they appear at the beginning. Like modern title pages, initial titles seem generally to have been written in a script that was larger, and sometimes more elegant, than the script of the main text.[30] Wherever they appear, titles that have survived in ancient book rolls differ in at least one crucial respect from modern title pages: they do not include information about the production of the roll.[31] The name of the scribe, the place and date of copying, the person who commissioned the copying: none of this information is included in titles known to us.[32]

Although we have no direct evidence that such information was included in ancient manuscripts, it is possible that at least some manuscripts did in-

---

29. Cavallo (1983), 22, for such titles at the ends of texts from Herculaneum. End titles were regularly placed to the right of the last column of text, not below it: Capasso (1982b), 57–60.

30. For initial titles in decorative scripts, see Capasso (2001a); Caroli (2007), 55, n. 179.

31. Schironi (2010) analyzes the *subscriptiones* at the ends of books, primarily those in Egyptian papyri containing hexameter verse. The *subscriptiones* in her database include the author (unless the author is Homer, in which case no author is specified), title, and book number, but no other information.

32. There are just a few possible exceptions. *P.Lond.Lit.* 97 (second century AD), a fragment of Herodas's mimes, is signed on the reverse "Heracleides copied this from the library of Praxias," ἐκ βιβλιοθή(κης) Πραξί(ου?) / Ἡρακλείδης ἀ[πέγραψεν]. The *subscriptio* of *P.Mil.Vogl.* 1.19 (*MP*[3] 1197; Tebtunis, second century AD) ends with the word σωσύου, which could possibly refer to the Sosius brothers, copyists at Rome known to us from Horace: Turner (1980), 51. The date in this case gives one pause: would a copy shop continue in existence, under the same name, for close to two centuries? Below the final column of text in *P.Herc.* 1426 is written "Of Poseidonax, son of Biton." Poseidonax could be a copyist, a bookseller, or a former owner of the manuscript. I think him most likely a former owner. See below, section 3.8.

clude it. In a recently discovered treatise of Galen, the *De indolentia*, Galen mentions several specific groups of book rolls that had been stored in the Palatine libraries and destroyed in the fire of AD 192.[33] He refers to the groups by name and clearly expects them to be recognizable: "Callinia, Atticiana, and Peducaeana, and even Aristarcheia."[34] It is possible that Galen is referring to discrete, identifiable collections that were kept in specific spaces—perhaps their own cabinets, for example—within the Palatine collection. But it is also possible that the Atticiana volumes, and the other groups, had in their *subscriptiones* some sort of identifying marks, such as the names of the scribes who prepared them, or of their previous owners.[35]

SILLYBA

In the case of both end titles and initial titles, the author's name and the title of the work would be hidden once the papyrus was rolled up. In a few known cases, the title and author were written also on the verso, that is, on the outside of the roll, so that the volume could be identified without being unrolled.[36] More commonly, it seems, manuscripts were provided with a title tag, or *sillybon*.[37] This was a strip of papyrus or parchment, roughly 3 by 8 cm, on which were written the author and title. It was glued to the edge of the roll but extended out from the edge so that, when the papyrus was rolled up, the *sillybon* protruded from one end of it, thus enabling the reader to identify the contents of the roll.[38] It is not known how common

33. For a description of the new work by Galen, discovered in 2005, see section 1.2 with n. 1.

34. Gal. *Ind.* 13. The satirist Lucian, writing about AD 170, also referred to carefully prepared volumes that were associated with men named Callinus and Atticus (Lucian *Ind.* 2 and 24). These men seem to be identical with the Callinus and Atticus implied in Galen's text. For discussion, see Jones (2009), 391–93; Roselli (2010), 137–39; and Jouanna in Boudon-Millot and Jouanna (2010), 50–51. The names (Callinia, etc.) are corrupt in the manuscript, and there has been much discussion of the proper spelling. I will use the names as above for convenience, with no claim that these are certainly the correct spellings.

35. It is not likely that the name of the copyist was supplied in the manuscript, given the low status of the profession of scribe. More likely, the names Atticiana, Callinia, and Peducaeana refer not to scribes but to men of higher rank who had commissioned the volumes, or to whose specifications the volumes had been copied.

36. At least seven cases of titles on the outside of rolls are known from Egypt, and at least one and perhaps three from Herculaneum. See Caroli (2007), 23–28 and 133–73, for a list.

37. Various forms of the word—*sillybos, sittybos,* and *sillybon*—appear in ancient texts, and all may have been in use. For the neuter form *sillybon*, which for consistency I will use throughout except when I am quoting an ancient source, see Pintaudi (2006), 205–6. Caroli (2007), 28–52, provides full information about the *sillyba*. Romans seem sometimes to have called these labels not *sillyba* but (confusingly for us moderns) *indices*. Thus Suet. *Calig.* 49.3 and perhaps Suet. *Gram. et rhet.* 6.3. On the latter passage, see the note of Kaster (1995), 114–15.

38. *Sillyba* may have been added not by the copyist or bookseller but by the owner of the book,

sillyba were.[39] In the absence of an external title or *sillybon*, and if the previous reader had rerolled the volume after use (or had a slave roll it back up), the reader would need to unroll the first twenty or thirty centimeters of the papyrus and identify the text from the initial title or the opening lines.

STICHOMETRIC COUNTS

Many papyrus manuscripts from Herculaneum, and some from Egypt, include stichometric (line) counts. Typically, the count appears at the end of the text, usually just below, or forming part of, the *subscriptio*, and it gives the number of standard-length lines (*stichoi*) in the text.[40] Sometimes the number of columns is included as well, and in many manuscripts a running count is kept in the margins, with a dot indicating every tenth or twentieth *stichos*, or, in some cases, a number count every hundred or two hundred *stichoi*. Sometimes we find both a running count in the margin and a summary number of lines at the end of the text, and stichometric counts may appear even in literary texts written on the verso of documents.[41] The purpose or purposes served by these counts remains uncertain and may have varied over time and from place to place, but it is likely that they were intended, at least originally, to help in calculating the copyist's fee, with the scribe being paid so much per, say, hundred lines.[42] If this was the purpose of the counts, then, the presence of a stichometric count could be taken as

---

either in some cases or regularly: Turner and Parsons (1987), 13; Holtz (1997), 472. Examples of surviving *sillyba* are shown in Turner and Parsons (1987), plates 6, 7, and 8.

39. At least ten survive on literary works. Dorandi (1984), 195–99, published seven; to these may be added Stephens (1985), 6–8, no. 2; Hanson (2004); and *P.Oxy.* 72.4853. Pintaudi (2006) published the first known example of a *sillybon* attached to a roll of documents rather than to a work of literature. No *sillyba* seem to survive from the Villa of the Papyri, where they would have been highly vulnerable to the superheated mud, but they appear in at least three wall paintings from Pompeii (Caroli [2007], tables 5b, 6c, and 7).

40. The *stichos* was a conventional measure. It was the equivalent of a line of hexameter verse, and thus some sixteen syllables or roughly thirty-four letters. Scribes tended to write prose in columns about twenty letters wide, so that one *stichos* was equal to about a line and a half in a prose text. There is an extensive bibliography on stichometric counts. For a useful recent summary and discussion, see Del Mastro (2012c), 38–48.

41. Stichometric counts in the papyri from Herculaneum: Capasso (1991), 210–12; below, section 3.8. Counts in literary texts written on the verso of a document: Lama (1991), 109–11.

42. Thus *P.Lond.* 2110, discussed by Turner (1952b), 90, is a statement, submitted by a scribe in Oxyrhynchus, of the fee for the copying of three classical Greek plays; the fee is based on a rate of twenty-eight drachmas per ten thousand lines. Also, as has often been noted, Diocletian's price edict (Graser [1940], 342, on 7.39–40) specifies the amount to be paid scribes per one hundred lines of two different qualities of writing, *scriptura optima* and *sequens scriptura*.

evidence that the manuscript had been copied by a professional scribe, and I will in general accept that as a reasonable inference.[43]

Such, then, are the basic physical characteristics of a papyrus book roll in our period.

CONVENTIONS

It may help the reader if I set out the conventions I follow in the presentation of material.

When dealing with individual Greek words or short phrases, I have chosen to be pragmatic at the expense of consistency. When the original Greek word is needed, I supply it, but elsewhere I may simply transliterate or provide an English translation. In dealing with lists of authors and titles (especially in chapters 2, 3, and 4 and in the appendices), I use the standard English translations of works that are well known to modern readers (Aristophanes's *Birds*, for example, rather than Aristophanes's *Ornithes*), but for works that are not well known, I simply transliterate the titles (Diocles's *Thalatta*, not Diocles's *The Sea*).

I follow the traditional principles of transliteration as used, for example, in Lesky (1966).

When dealing with the fragments of manuscripts found in the Villa of the Papyri, I use a plus sign to indicate that a given book roll consists of one or more fragments assigned to each of two or more *P.Herc.* numbers. Thus *P.Herc.* 336 + 1150 means that a single original roll contained the fragments now called *P.Herc.* 336 and *P.Herc.* 1150.

All translations are my own unless otherwise indicated.

---

43. There are, however, complicating factors and several additional ways such counts could have been used. Del Mastro (2012c), 43–46, sets out and provides evidence for a range of uses of stichometric counts.

1

Assembling a Collection

1.1. INTRODUCTION

We must begin at the beginning, with the creation of a book collection. How do book collections come into existence? What options did ancient Romans have when they wished to acquire texts, and how much choice—in variety of title, in quality of manuscripts—did they have? In this chapter, we will look in some detail at the different methods by which Romans acquired and built up their collections. For the most part, these are predictable, even obvious—they include purchase, gift, inheritance, and so on—and they are reasonably well attested in our sources. Others, such as confiscation, are not so well attested and may have been more important than our sources would suggest. Some aspects of this material, including the physical production of texts, release of texts to the public, and sale of both new and older book rolls, have been dealt with carefully by earlier scholars. In such cases, I make no attempt to include every available item of evidence, and I will limit the discussion to a summary of what is relevant to our central concern (the nature of Roman book collections), cite particularly useful or interesting items of evidence, and point the reader to fuller discussions. I will provide full discussions of new evidence and of classes of evidence, such as papyri, that have not previously been exploited in this context, and of topics that have been treated less fully in the literature.

This chapter, like the subject itself, can be thought of as divided into two main parts: acquiring volumes one or a few at a time, thus gradually building up a collection (sections 2 to 10); and acquiring large numbers of volumes and even whole libraries at one time (sections 11 to 14). These are, of course, artificial distinctions, and I employ them simply as a convenient way of organizing and controlling the vast amount of information available. Much of the chapter is concerned with collections acquired by individuals, rather than the libraries that were in any sense public. This is partly because much more evidence on personal collections survives, and partly because most collections that could be called "public" were very likely personal collections in origin, included book rolls that had previously formed part or all of a private collection, or grew through the same processes as personal collections. We begin, then, with the simplest method of acquiring a personal collection.

1.2. MAKE YOURSELF A COPY OF A MANUSCRIPT

Individual book rolls could be acquired in many different ways. You could, of course, simply copy out a text yourself, and even an eminent scholar might occasionally do this, as we learn from Galen. In a treatise that was discovered in 2005 and first published in 2007, Galen described the destruction caused by the fire of AD 192.[1] In the course of his narrative, he referred to "the writings of the ancients that I had copied in my own hand,"[2] and later in the same treatise he refers to book rolls in one of the imperial libraries—probably the one in the great villa at Antium—which, he tells us, he had copied for his own use.[3] Galen also knew, or thought he knew, that several earlier collectors had acquired particularly accurate copies "either by copying them [i.e., in their own hand] or by having them copied."[4] Fronto tells us that a number of scholars of Republican date, among them Octavius Lampadio and Lucius Aelius Praeconinus, had made their own copies of works of other authors, although he does not say that they had done so in order to acquire the volumes for their own use.[5]

It is impossible to estimate how common this practice was. In the pa-

1. This new treatise is extraordinarily important for Roman library history and has already occasioned a considerable bibliography. Its title in Greek was Περὶ ἀλυπίας, or roughly "On the Avoidance of Grief." It is known by a Latin version of the Greek, *De indolentia*, or *Ind.* for short, and I will refer to it as Galen, *Ind.* The story of the discovery is in Boudon-Millot and Pietrobelli (2005), 498–500 and 510; the *editio princeps*, with a provisional translation into French, is Boudon-Millot (2007b). There are now at least three editions of the work. I will use the Budé text, edited by Boudon-Millot and Jouanna (2010), unless otherwise specified; details on the various editions and the title of the work are conveniently set out in Rothschild and Thompson (2012).

2. *Ind.* 6: διὰ τῆς ἐμῆς χειρός.

3. *Ind.* 19. The verb is ἐγγράφομαι. Since in this case Galen does not say "in my own hand," it is possible that he had a slave do the copying, but that does not seem to be the implication. Cicero fairly often says of a text, "I am copying [it]" (*describo*), but that probably means not that he copied the text in his own hand, but rather that he gave orders to a slave to copy it: McDonnell (1996), 482–85. On the passage in Gal. *Ind.* 19, see also Stramaglia (2011), 138.

4. *Ind.* 13: ἢ ἔγραψαν ἢ ἀνεγρέψαντο. For the identities of the collectors, see Jones (2009), 391–93. In all probability, they include Atticus, the friend of Cicero, and Sextus Peducaeus, a younger contemporary of Cicero.

5. Fronto *Ep.* 1.7.4: *Lampadionis . . . aut Aelii manu scripta*. The passage is controversial. Many scholars have doubted that the manuscripts Fronto cites were genuine, but see McDonnell (1996), 477–82, for a defense of their authenticity. The new evidence from Galen provides additional support for the thesis of authenticity, since it shows clearly that scholars sometimes copied out works of other authors in their own hand.

pyrological record, the vast majority of literary texts seem to have been copied not by individuals for their own use, but by trained scribes who copied texts for a living.[6] It may well be, however, that at least some advanced students copied out works of literature for their own use in their studies, then kept them in later life as basic works for their library. We find, for example, comedies of Menander made in "fluent but somewhat unprofessional handwriting," and it is quite possible that other authors read by advanced students were copied by the students themselves.[7] Doing your own copying would have certain clear advantages. For the less wealthy, it was a cheap way to acquire a text; for those, like Galen, who did not need to worry about expense, it meant that you could control the level of accuracy of the copy. On the other hand, it was time-consuming and boring work, and we may reasonably assume that the normal procedure, for anyone who could afford it, was not to copy a text yourself, but to have a slave or a team of slaves copy it for you.[8]

1.3. HAVE A SLAVE MAKE A COPY FOR YOU

A wealthy man might own one or more professionally trained slave scribes. The classic example is Cicero's friend Atticus, who owned, Cornelius Nepos tells us, first-rate readers and many scribes. Atticus thus would have been able to produce copies of texts in-house for his own library or for the libraries of his friends.[9] Cicero too owned slave scribes, at least in some periods of his life. In 46 and 45 BC we find him referring to scribes (*libra-*

6. Johnson (2004), 160, notes that the great majority of published surviving papyri from Egypt show the characteristics of book rolls prepared by trained scribes. Copyists never or almost never identified themselves on the manuscripts they copied, leaving us very much in the dark on this question. On scribes and their work there is very useful information in Parsons (2007), in particular 263–64. For the varying levels of skill and professionalism of scribes, see Mugridge (2010), 575–80.

7. Cribiore (2001), 200, with n. 74; cf. 201–4, where she notes a number of authors and works who were read by advanced students, among them Aristophanes, Callimachus, Pindar, and the speeches of Isocrates. Students at that level of training would be experienced enough in writing to create copies worth keeping, and the texts they were working with were ones they might well want to keep.

8. On the drudgery involved in copying a text, and the avoidance of such work by wealthy Romans, see McDonnell (1996), 477. Libanius mentions making notes in his own hand, but he preferred those in the hand of his assistant (probably a slave), since the assistant's writing was clearer than his own: Lib. *Or.* 1 (= *Autobiog.*) 232.

9. Nep. *Att.* 13.3: *anagnostae optimi et plurimi librarii. Anagnostae* were highly trained readers (cf. Gell. *NA* 18.5.2–5). Because of their skill, they could have served as readers when copies were being made by dictation (although no extant source shows them doing this), or as proofreaders and correctors. Earlier generations of scholars considered Atticus a kind of publisher, but recent scholarship has stressed the fact that he was by no means a publisher in the modern sense. For a useful assessment of Atticus's activity, see Iddeng (2006), 63–65.

rii) who were apparently members of his own *familia*; they were preparing texts of works he had written recently.[10] An emperor, of course, might have access to a large number of scribes and so be able to have many texts copied in a short period of time. Thus Domitian, concerned to rebuild and restock one or more libraries that had been destroyed by fire, sent men, presumably professional scribes, to Alexandria to make and double-check replacement copies.[11]

On the other hand, many less wealthy readers, and in all probability many wealthy men too, may well have owned no trained scribes. The case of Atticus was clearly exceptional, and it is precisely because it was unusual that Nepos describes it. Slaves who were fully trained as professional scribes were expensive,[12] and for men who owned smallish libraries it was probably not worth owning such a slave. Even Cicero did not have trained scribes in his *familia* at all times. In the fall of 54 we find him perplexed as to how to fill out and improve his and his brother's libraries. You cannot find high-quality texts in the book markets, he complains, and to have a good copy made would require an experienced and careful scribe.[13] The clear implication is that neither Cicero nor his brother owned any such scribe at that time; suitably trained scribes might have seemed something of a luxury even to the Tullius brothers, or perhaps no well-trained scribes had come on the market recently.[14]

In the absence of trained scribes, you might copy a work yourself, or have some literate slave in your household copy a text. When Nepos tells us

10. Cic. *Fam.* 16.22.1: Tiro is supervising the work of two or more *librarii* in the summer of 46. See also *Att.* 12.14.3, of March 45, and *Att.* 13.21a.2, of June 30 or July 1, 45. Scribes who could make copies of your own works (as here) could also, of course, make copies for you of texts written by others. We can probably infer the presence of copyists in Cicero's *familia* also in 59 BC, because Cicero's brother Quintus evidently expected Cicero to be able to produce copies of Quintus's latest work at that time: *Att.* 2.16.4. There is a full discussion of Cicero's staff in Dix (1986), 133–37.

11. Suet. *Dom.* 20. On this passage, see further below, n. 37. Suetonius does not tell us the number of scribes involved. The men were not necessarily all library staff. The imperial administration employed many scribes, in various offices, in drafting and copying official documents, and Domitian may have reassigned some of them temporarily to this task.

12. Marshall (1976), 254, citing Sen. *Ep.* 27.6–7.

13. Cic. *QFr.* 3.4.5: *Confici nisi per hominem et peritum et diligentem non possunt.* The same thought and implication recur in *QFr.* 3.5.6, written a few weeks later. In the latter case, Cicero makes it clear that it is book rolls of Latin texts that are causing him problems. On this passage and the interpretation of it, see most recently P. White (2009), 273–74.

14. Cicero may have had no trained scribes in 56, either: at *Att.* 4.4a.1 we find him writing to Atticus to request some scribes (*librarioli*) to help with his library. The tasks he specifies in this letter do not include copying, but that may well have been understood. Ordinarily, Cicero employed slaves with a variety of backgrounds and levels of training, not necessarily training as scribes, in his library: Dix (1986), 133, 135.

that even the *pedisequi* (unspecialized servants) in the household of Atticus were literate, the implication seems to be that Atticus was willing, at least on occasion, to have virtually any slave who could read and write undertake a copying job.[15] A famous example of a text copied by individuals or slaves who did not have formal training as scribes is preserved in *P.Lond.Lit.* 108 (*LDAB* 391), Aristotle's *Constitution of Athens*. Four different scribes were at work in the making of this copy, all of them inexpert.[16] One of the four seems to have been the most important and may have supervised the work of the others; he corrected errors and filled in gaps left by the other three, and it is possible that he used a second exemplar for the corrections.[17] The variable quality of the copying shows that the copy was not made by professional scribes, even though there was a clear desire for an accurate text.

1.4. BUY A READY-MADE TEXT FROM A DEALER

If you did not copy a text yourself, or have one of your own slaves copy it, you could turn to the commercial trade in book rolls. During the period of the principate, we hear of dealers who sold used book rolls,[18] recently copied texts,[19] and what either were, or purported to be, valuable editions of famous or rare texts.[20] You could also commission a scribe to make a copy of a particular text you wanted. In a letter found in Oxyrhynchus (*P.Oxy.* 18.2192, second century) and containing several separate messages written by at least three different people, one of the writers reports that Demetrius the bookseller has certain texts the writer is looking for. Demetrius, he implies, might either sell the manuscripts outright or make copies of them on commission; from the letter, we cannot tell which procedure was the one expected in this case.[21] Since all books were copied out by hand, books never

---

15. Nep. *Att.* 13.3; cf. Dix (1986), 134.

16. For a discussion of this text, and the ways in which it differs from a professionally prepared text, see Johnson (2004), 157–58.

17. Modrzejewski (2011), 429 (supervisor) and 432 (second exemplar).

18. Gell. *NA* 9.4.1–5 (set in Brundisium). Starr (1990) doubted that there was any significant trade in used book rolls, but see now P. White (2009), 268–82.

19. The production of book rolls and the market in them have been much studied. Dorandi (2007) (especially chapter 5) and Kleberg (1992) provide full and detailed accounts. For an excellent discussion of the bookstalls in the city of Rome, see P. White (2009), 277–82.

20. The question of rare texts has been treated repeatedly, especially the matter of "autograph copies," or a text said to be, for example, in Vergil's own hand. Particularly useful here: Dorandi (2007), 47–64; McDonnell (1996), 477–82; Kleberg (1992), 69–73.

21. Johnson (2010), 180–83, discusses this letter in detail. Note that, when seeking a particular text, one might look for it in the collection of a friend or of a dealer (Demetrius). The possibility of

went out of print, and it really made no difference if you bought a book roll that a dealer had recently copied on speculation (that is, in the hope that someone would walk in and buy it), or if you commissioned the dealer to make you a copy. Either way, you acquired a book roll that had recently been copied by hand.[22]

1.5. PRESENTATION COPIES, GIFTS, AND PURCHASES FROM FRIENDS

There were several further ways in which individuals acquired books one or a few at a time. Authors gave presentation copies, with special dedicatory phrasing, to friends and patrons.[23] The emperor, of course, was the ultimate patron, and we might expect authors to send copies of whatever they wrote to the reigning emperor, but specific dedications to emperors, while frequent, are not as common as dedications to other patrons and friends.[24] You might give a copy of any text (not just one you had written yourself) as a gift. In his short poems describing *apophoreta* (party favors), Martial mentions, as possible gifts, copies of more than a dozen authors, including Homer, Menander, Vergil, Cicero, and Propertius (Mart. 14.183–96). In most cases, he makes it clear that these are special editions, on parchment, say, or in small print for easy transport, but there is no reason to doubt that ordinary books, too, were often presented as gifts. Presumably, individuals might buy one or a few book rolls directly from another individual, but how often friends sold single copies to one another is not known and may have been more common than is reflected in our sources.

So far, most of the means of acquiring books we have noticed involved the making of a new copy of an existing work. The quality of any such copy would depend, among other things, on the level of accuracy of the exemplar; and finding a high-quality exemplar was by no means easy. For many less demanding readers this was perhaps not a concern, but serious scholars were, it seems, willing to go to considerable trouble to acquire accu-

---

looking in a library—municipal or otherwise—for the texts in question is not considered by the writers of this papyrus.

22. On the question of ready-made versus commissioned texts, see Johnson (2004), 154–60.

23. Thus Catullus 1.1, where he dedicates his book of poems to Cornelius Nepos and at the same time gives Nepos a physical copy of the book, *dono* being used in the double sense of "I dedicate" and "I give this physical object." So also Gal. *Lib.Prop.* 14.9, 10 (= Boudon-Millot [2007a], 165–66; 19.10 Kühn); other examples in Kleberg (1992), 68–69.

24. Ambaglio (1983), 32–39, gives examples of dedications dating from the time of Tiberius to that of Domitian.

rate texts. Galen, for example, copied out at least some works by hand in order to be sure that they were free of copyists' errors (*Ind.* 14). Assuming you were such a serious reader, how would you go about locating a trust-worthy exemplar? There were a number of possibilities, as becomes clear from an anecdote in Galen. Galen was searching, he tells us, for a particular text by Archigenes, a physician who had practiced in Rome in the time of Trajan. Galen tells us where he went in search of the volume: "I went run-ning round to all the libraries, all the booksellers, and all the doctors [pre-sumably Galen's friends] who I knew were students of his works, in order to get hold of this book."[25] Taking Galen's list as our guide, we may consider the evidence for each of these possible sources of exemplars. I deal with them in a slightly different order: friends, libraries, and dealers.

1.6. BORROWING COPIES OF BOOKS FROM FRIENDS

So far as we can tell, it was at all times and in all places common to borrow a text from a friend. We find Cicero doing this repeatedly, although we can-not always tell if he borrowed a text to have a copy made or simply to read and make excerpts. We need not list all of the books Cicero is known to have borrowed; a list limited to the volumes he borrowed from Atticus will give an idea of their range and character: a book by Serapion; books by Alexan-der of Ephesus; an oration of Q. Celer; a book *de concordia* by Demetrius of Magnesia; a book by Tyrannio; a work of Brutus; works of Cotta; *On the Gods* by Phaedrus; eulogies of M. Varro and Ollius.[26] Several of these (and many of the other items Cicero borrowed) are relatively obscure items, and from that we may perhaps infer that Cicero owned all or most of the stan-dard texts, and that Atticus's library by contrast included a considerable range of less common texts, Latin as well as Greek.[27] We know, in addition, that Cicero borrowed books from his brother Quintus, from Sextus Fadius, and from Marcus Lucullus.[28] In the second century AD, we find the future emperor Marcus Aurelius lending a book—an old copy of Ennius—to his teacher and friend, Fronto, who had a scribe make a new copy of the text.[29]

---

25. Gal. *Loc.Aff.* 3.5 (= 8.148 Kühn).

26. The list was compiled by Dix (2013), 220, with references in n. 48.

27. Dix (2013), 221, makes this point, noting that the volumes Cicero borrowed tended to be rare or unusual texts.

28. Quintus: Cic. *Att.* 2.3.4 and 13.8. Fadius: Cic. *Fam.* 7.20.3. Lucullus: Cic. *Fin.* 3.2.7. Cf. Dix (2013), 220, nn. 49 and 50.

29. Fronto *Ep.* 4.2.6. Borrowing with a different motive (plagiarism or simply to avoid buying a copy) is implied in Mart. 1.117.

Outside of the city of Rome, borrowing from friends is almost certainly part of the scenario to be reconstructed from a famous letter found in Roman Egypt, *P.Oxy.* 18.2192.[30] One of the correspondents who appears in this papyrus wanted to have copies of two books of Hypsicrates's *Characters in Comedy* made and sent to him. He advised the recipient that the items in question could be found among the books of a certain Polion. Later in the letter, a second writer, also searching for certain books (not named), says that Diodorus and his friends might have some of them. While it is possible that Polion and Diodorus were book dealers, it is much more likely that they were scholars and perhaps friends or acquaintances of the men who wrote the various parts of the letter.[31] We can probably assume that the texts in question were to be borrowed from Polion and Diodorus (or others), copied, and returned to their owners.[32]

In late Republican Italy, we find scholars not only borrowing individual volumes, but also visiting the libraries of their friends, either simply to read and take notes or, at least in one case, to locate and take away certain texts, presumably on loan. Cicero and Cato visited and used the library of Lucullus, as did a number of unidentified Greek scholars, and Cicero seems to have felt free to borrow volumes from that library, which he could then either read and excerpt or give to a slave to copy.[33] Cicero also mentions enjoying the library of Faustus Sulla on the Bay of Naples, and in May of 54 BC we find him requesting permission to use Atticus's library in Atticus's absence.[34] Both Tyrannio and a number of unidentified scribes, we are told, gained access, at least partly by underhanded means, to the library of Aristotle once it was brought to Italy and installed in Sulla's house.[35]

---

30. On a different part of this letter, see above, section 1.4.

31. Turner (1952b), 92, showed that both Polion and Diodorus are almost certainly identifiable scholars, not book dealers.

32. We have what may be a sort of address label written to accompany a book as it was being sent from one person to another. *P.Turner* 6 reads "To Isidore. The *Thais* of Menander." The tag does not seem to have been a *sillybon*. See Roberts (1981), 30, and Dorandi (1994), 231.

33. Cato: Cic. *Fin.* 3.2.7, the dramatic date of which is the late 50s; at that time, Lucullus had died and the library belonged to his son, the younger Lucullus. Greek scholars in the library of Lucullus during his lifetime: Plut. *Luc.* 42.1–2. See on all of this the excellent discussion in Dix (2000), 444–46 and 457–58.

34. Faustus's library: Cic. *Att.* 4.10.1. Requesting permission to use Atticus's: Cic. *Att.* 4.14.1. As Dix (2000), 458, pointed out, it was evidently more difficult to gain access to Atticus's library than to Lucullus's.

35. Strabo 13.1.54 C609 and Plut. *Sull.* 26.1: when what remained of Aristotle's library was installed in Sulla's house, the booksellers in Rome allegedly smuggled in copyists to transcribe the texts and so were able to put them out for sale.

1.7. THE PUBLIC LIBRARIES

The custom of using friends' libraries and allowing friends and scholars to use one's own collection, apparently common in the late Republic, provided a model for the way in which the public libraries of imperial Rome might function. So far as we can tell, the public libraries, beginning with the library in the Atrium Libertatis created by Asinius Pollio sometime between 39 and 28 BC, operated on very much the same principles as the grand private libraries of the Republic. They were, either in actual legal fact or for all intents and purposes, the book collections of the emperors, and it was his friends (that is, men of the senatorial and equestrian orders) and other scholars who must have formed the bulk of the users.[36]

Until recently, however, it could only be assumed, not demonstrated, that copies of texts from public libraries were at least sometimes used by individuals as exemplars for the creation of new copies, as had been the case in the Republic. Now, though, we have clear proof of the use of texts from imperial libraries as exemplars. In the newly recovered treatise of Galen, *De indolentia*, or *On the Avoidance of Grief*, Galen talks about making copies of works that he had found in various of the imperial libraries. In *Ind.* 19, he tells us that book rolls in some library, probably the one in the imperial villa at Antium, had been severely damaged by damp; that had caused the successive layers of some papyrus rolls to stick together, he says, so that the volumes could not be unrolled. These books he had earlier been in the habit of copying for his own use. In *Ind.* 13 and 14 he names both collections and specific texts that had been housed in the libraries on the Palatine hill before the fire of AD 192, states that those valuable old texts had been destroyed in the fire, and implies that he had earlier made copies of some of them, but that those copies too had been destroyed. Thus at least one question concerning the public libraries of Rome has now been definitively answered: scholars did seek out volumes in them specifically to make copies. Similarly, Domitian, in restocking fire-damaged libraries, sent copyists to many locations, including Alexandria, in search of exemplars.[37] In this case,

---

36. On the continuity between late Republican personal collections and the imperial collections: Houston (2002), 151–52 and 172–74. On the uncertain legal status of Asinius Pollio's library, see Houston (2002), 157.

37. Suet. *Dom.* 20: *exemplaribus undique petitis, missisque Alexandream qui describerent emendarentque.* ("He looked everywhere for exemplars and sent men to Alexandria to copy and correct [the texts].") The Domitianic search for exemplars from which copies could be made may well have included bookstalls in Rome and private collections of scholars and wealthy men of Rome and Italy. On the fire, see further Dix and Houston (2006), 686, 688, and 694.

we have on a grand scale what Galen did on a personal level: where Galen had searched for and copied texts himself, Domitian restored the imperial collection by sending out men who searched for exemplars in many places, among them Alexandria, and copied the texts that were needed.

1.8. FINDING EXEMPLARS IN DEALERS' COLLECTIONS

As we have seen, Galen mentioned the bookstalls of Rome as one of three places to look for a copy of a given text. We can see this process in some detail in various texts, both literary and papyrological. Writing probably in the 170s or 180s, Gellius tells us about the scholar Antonius Iulianus renting a desired text (in this case a copy of Ennius's *Annals*) from a dealer. Iulianus had rented, Gellius says, a very old copy, which was said to have been corrected by Octavius Lampadio (a scholar of the second century BC). Iulianus was very eager to consult the manuscript and paid a high price in order to check a single verse.[38] Although in this case Iulianus had rented the text just to check it, it is reasonable to assume that he could have made a copy of it instead or in addition, perhaps for a higher fee. Renting manuscripts from dealers is attested in letters from Egypt as well. In one of these, of the second century AD, a son is writing to his father from Ptolemaios Hormou and informs him that "when Deios was with us, he showed us the six parchments. We did not take any of them, but we made collations against eight others, and paid one hundred drachmas for that."[39] Deios was presumably a bookseller, perhaps itinerant. He had a number of texts in stock, ready to sell (the "six parchments" and perhaps the "eight others"), and customers could buy those ready-made texts if they chose. In this case, however, the writer of the letter chose not to purchase, but simply to rent eight volumes in order, it seems, to correct texts he already owned.

Purchases needed to be made with care, and both complaints of inaccuracy and suspicions of forgery appear in our sources. Writing to his brother Quintus in 54 BC, Cicero complained that he could not find high-quality copies of Latin texts; the book rolls that were being offered for sale, Cicero said, were full of errors.[40] A generation later, Strabo voiced the same complaint. Book dealers in Rome and Alexandria, he said, employed bad scribes and did not have the newly produced copies checked against reliable ex-

38. Gell. *NA* 18.5.11. The verb is *conducere*, the standard term for "to rent."

39. *P.Petaus* 30, second century. The "parchments" (*membranai*) were codices, not book rolls: Van Haelst (1989), 22. My thanks to Rosa Otranto for this reference.

40. Cic. *QFr.* 3.4.5; *QFr.* 3.5.6; cf. n. 13 above.

emplars.[41] Careful buyers might, it seems, seek professional advice. Gellius tells us of a buyer who brought a *grammaticus* along with him to assess the manuscripts being offered for sale (*NA* 5.4.1). Galen tells a similar story: he had been looking on as potential customers in a bookshop in Rome debated whether a text labeled "Galen's *Doctor*" was really by Galen. One of them read the first few lines and declared it not by Galen. He was, Galen leads us to believe, correct.[42] In Galen's *De indolentia*, the difficulty of finding accurate texts is implicit in his anguish over the loss, in the fire of AD 192, of many book rolls that *were* accurate: "It is now not possible to find what is rare and cannot be found anywhere else, [namely texts that] are demanded [or highly prized] because of the precision of their writing."[43]

Book collectors also needed to be wary of unauthorized and potentially misleading copies of works they wanted to acquire.[44] Galen tells us various ways in which such versions could come onto the market, and his information is corroborated by references elsewhere, in both Greek and Roman sources. Galen and other scholars and authors wrote some treatises purely for the use of their students or friends, or to be read within their literary circles, rather than for the general public, but some of these informal texts were, against the author's will, copied and circulated, in some cases widely. Or so Galen claims; and there is no reason to doubt him. In *On the Order of His Books*, he brings the matter up at least twice,[45] and in *On His Own Books* he tells of an even more elaborate scenario: there were certain works he had given, without titles, to friends or students; some of those persons had died; their heirs, in some cases, had given lectures based on Galen's material, presenting it as their own. Other students had copied out Galen's texts, book by book, making some changes and then presenting the texts as their own creations.[46] The lament in its simple form—the general distribution of what was never intended to be public—was not uncommon, and

---

41. Strabo 13.1.54 C 609: βιβλιοπῶλαί τινες γραφεῦσι φαύλοις χρώμενοι καὶ οὐκ ἀντιβάλλοντες. Strabo begins by referring to new but inaccurate copies of texts found in the library of Aristotle (brought to Italy by Sulla), and then goes on to say that the same shoddy practices are characteristic of many booksellers in Rome and Alexandria.

42. Galen *Lib.Prop. praef.* 1–2 (= Boudon-Millot [2007a], 133–34, 176–77).

43. *Ind.* 13. In the following chapter, Galen stresses the care he had himself taken to produce error-free copies. It is clear that he perceived such careful copies as being very hard to find.

44. There were, of course, complete fabrications as well, books written by one person but purporting to be by someone else. For a full discussion of them, see Speyer (1971).

45. At *Ord.Lib.Prop.* 1.2 (= Boudon-Millot 2007a, 88), Galen explains how he had written certain treatises for friends and dictated others to students. But some of these, he tells us at *Ord.Lib.Prop.* 1.5 and 1.11 (= Boudon-Millot 2007a, 89 and 90, respectively), had now been disseminated widely.

46. *Lib.Prop. praef.* 6–7 (= Boudon-Millot 2007a, 135).

V. Boudon-Millot in her recent edition of these works cites enough similar passages, from Plato, Cicero, and Tertullian, that she can characterize the claim as "en quelque sorte un topos."[47] Topos or no, Galen's account is specific and circumstantial enough to be convincing. From a book collector's point of view, this was, needless to say, disconcerting: how could you be sure that you were acquiring a text that the author regarded as authoritative?

1.9. EVIDENCE OF CARE IN THE PREPARATION OF TEXTS

Despite the appearance of a freewheeling, not to say chaotic, book market that emerges from such sources, there are clear indications also of attempts both to obtain and to provide authoritative texts in reliable copies made according to generally accepted professional standards. Hellenistic scholars, especially those associated with the library at Alexandria, had developed methods of analysis to help them distinguish genuine lines in the Homeric poems from interpolated ones.[48] Applied subsequently to Hesiod, the Greek tragedians, and other Greek poets, these techniques were available to Roman scholars, and we occasionally catch glimpses of scholars, such as Gellius and Galen, employing them.[49] Even when they were not involved in textual criticism, scholars might expend considerable effort in an attempt to obtain sound texts. Galen tells us explicitly the trouble he went to in hopes of acquiring sound texts to use as exemplars: "I copied out [some] texts to serve as my own exemplars, free of words that were unclear and mistakes in writing," he says, and continues by noting that he wanted "to get it just right, so there would be nothing added and nothing left out, not even a single or double *paragraphe* or a *coronis* incorrectly placed in the middle of a text, not even [an incorrect] period or comma."[50] A different sort of care is implicit in the manuscript of Aristotle's *Constitution of Athens*, *P.Lond.* 131 verso. The text here does not begin at the beginning of the work, and the archetype evidently lacked the beginning. Accordingly, the scribe left a

47. Boudon-Millot (2007a), 103. We may add to her list Quint. *Inst.* 1 *praef.* 7 and 7.2.24. For a full discussion of this matter, see Dorandi (2007), 65–68 and 93–94.

48. The work of the Alexandrians is treated at length by Fraser (1972), 447–79. See also Speyer (1971), 112–28, on scholarly work aimed at establishing the authority of specific texts.

49. Gellius's scholarly work: Holford-Strevens (1988), 115–25. Gellius's scholarship only occasionally shows any direct influence of Alexandrian critical method. Galen describes an occasion when an unnamed Roman scholar used stylistic characteristics, as the Alexandrians had done, to judge the authenticity of a work: *Lib.Prop. praef.* 1–2 (= Boudon-Millot 2007a, 134 and 176–77). More generally on Roman-era scholars, Speyer (1971), 122.

50. *Ind.* 14. The text is not certain at all points.

blank space about a column wide, apparently in hopes that the missing beginning could be found somewhere and entered later.[51]

From the point of view of Roman-era book collectors, the work of the Hellenistic scholars had several consequences. First, the information they brought to bear on their texts—lexicographical, historical, ethnographic, and the like—was occasionally condensed into notes or glosses on unusual words or expressions, and those notes could then be added, in the form of marginal or interlinear annotations, to the texts.[52] They might then be carried along from one copy of the text to the next. Second, the Hellenistic scholars created a range of reference works called "subliterary" or "paraliterary" works by modern papyrologists. These included lexicons and glossaries, plot summaries and biographies of authors, and commentaries incorporating a wide variety of material intended to elucidate such matters as obscure mythological references, geographical and technical terms, and historical events.[53] All of these reference works were available to book collectors of our period, provided they could find an exemplar to copy, and we might therefore expect such reference works to turn up as part of the contents of particular collections. Finally, and most obviously, Roman scholars could and did apply such techniques to Roman authors who wrote in Latin. Much effort was expended on Plautus, for example.[54]

There is now considerable evidence for the existence of widely accepted professional standards and for attempts (admittedly not completely successful, and occasionally not successful at all) to ensure the preparation of texts that were correct and accurate. William Johnson has shown that many literary papyrus rolls surviving from Egypt reveal clear signs of having been prepared by trained scribes. They share features—length of line and column, size of margins at top and bottom and between columns, and a movement of each successive line to the left as the column descends the page—that point very strongly to a conventional, agreed-upon set of standards.[55] As we will see in chapter 3, the papyri from Herculaneum reveal a similar set of standards, slightly different from those discernible in papyri from

51. Modrzejewski (2011), 428.

52. McNamee (2007), 37–41, discusses such corrections, all of which demonstrate a desire for a correct text. She identifies three specific types: revision in the form of queries in the margins; verification of readings; and variant readings attributed to other scholars or sources. We will see such annotations in the manuscripts from Oxyrhynchus in chapter 4.

53. Ibid., 32–36, describes these reference works. Galen refers to a glossary that he himself had compiled. It included all (unusual?) words "in all of the ancient [Greek] comedy," but it was destroyed in the fire of AD 192: *Ind.* 23.

54. Speyer (1971), 122.

55. Johnson (2004), 85–160, with a summary, 155–60.

Egypt but demonstrating a similar care for consistency and a considerable interest in accuracy. Illustrations could be added to texts where appropriate, for example in works on geometry or botany, and those, we know, were done at least in some cases by people who specialized in illustrations as opposed to text.[56] In such a case, the book collector, if commissioning a text, might need to order first the text and then, from a second professional, the illustrations. The specialization, and the resulting logistical complications in completing a manuscript, both argue for careful attention to the quality of manuscripts.[57]

In the introduction we noted the presence in texts from both Egypt and Herculaneum of stichometric, or line, counts. In general, such counts can be taken as a sign that the text was copied by a professional scribe, as opposed to an individual who wanted to make a copy for himself or a slave who happened to have a clear hand but was not a professionally trained copyist. While professional scribes did not always produce first-rate work, they were probably more reliable than most amateur copyists, and papyri from both Egypt and Herculaneum show that the work of professionals was regularly corrected, either by the original copyist or by a second hand.[58] In some cases, there is evidence that a copy was checked against a second exemplar, evidently in an attempt to provide as accurate a copy as possible.[59] There was, in short, at least some concern for accuracy among many of those who were involved professionally in the production of books. We also noted that stichometric counts may have served to help scribes determine if their exemplars were complete, and, if not, how much was missing. Both of these possible uses of line counts—to determine a copyist's pay, and to reveal lacunae in the text—are important, for they both imply care in the preparation of the text: a professional copyist has been hired, or attention has been paid to the integrity of the exemplar being copied, or both.

56. Thus *P.Yale* inv. 1318, published and discussed by Parássoglou (1974), 364–66. In this papyrus, which dates to the fourth or fifth century AD, we are told of a manuscript handed over to an illustrator for the addition of pictures (εἰς κόσμησιν). Cf. a letter in Coptic of the fifth or sixth century concerning illustrations (Harrauer [1995], 69, no. 18).

57. Horak (1992), 42–52, sets out the evidence for illustrations in papyri. Rare in literary works, they are common in works on mathematics and geometry, and they appear also in botanical, astronomical, and magical texts. In a few cases, it is clear that the copyist left a space for an illustration to be added: Horak (1992), 44, 48. More succinctly: Blanck (2008), 141–54.

58. Details in Turner and Parsons (1987), 15–16.

59. Thus *P.Oxy.* 17.2102 (= *MP*[3] 1400.1), Plato's *Phaedrus*, and *PSI* 11.1195 + *P.Oxy.* 57.3882 (= *MP*[3] 1509), Thucydides 1, both of which come from the collection I call "Breccia + GH3" in chapter 4 below. Turner and Parsons (1987), 16, take such collation as often carried out by the owners of manuscripts rather than by the original copyists.

1.10. WRITE YOUR OWN BOOK

In addition to the volumes they bought, inherited, or were given, authors both talented and otherwise might well, over time, accumulate considerable numbers of their own works in various stages of preparation—notes, drafts, final copies—and of various types. In a few cases, we have at least some information about an author's collection or the materials that might be found in it. In a passage that we will discuss further below, Aulus Gellius tells us that Terentius Varro lost many of his own compositions when his villa was plundered and his libraries confiscated.[60] The implication is clear: Varro's library contained many volumes of his own work; or, to put it the other way round, Varro's own compositions may have constituted a significant part of his library.

The personal library of Pliny the Elder included, at the time of his death, 160 volumes of notes. Pliny the Younger, who tells us this fact, remarks that the volumes were written on both sides and in a very fine hand. Thus they seem to have been the equivalent of more than 300 ordinary book rolls (160 rolls times two sides).[61] We can also make the reasonable assumption that Pliny the Elder had copies of his own finished works, which amounted to some 105 volumes.[62] If that is so, then Pliny's own creations, if we count both notes and final versions, will have been the equivalent of something over 400 book rolls, a number high enough to make them an important section of his library.

The physician Galen certainly kept copies of all or many of his own works as part of his book collection. He tells us that many manuscripts he owned were destroyed in the fire in Rome of AD 192, and that among the volumes destroyed were copies of several specific items he had written: Books 1 and 2 of his work *On the Composition of Medications by Type*; numerous medical treatises that he had written in the period from the spring of AD 169 to the fall of 176; an unspecified but probably large number of works that he had composed for his own use; a glossary of words used in ancient comedy; and a summary, in six thousand lines (or about two book rolls), of an earlier dictionary by Didymus.[63] These are the items he happens to men-

---

60. Gell. *NA* 3.10, 17. See further section 1.13 below.

61. Plin. *Ep.* 3.5.17; cf. Dorandi (2007), 30–36. The "160 volumes of notes" seem to have been papyrus rolls (*volumina*), with the notes (*commentarii*) copied into them from tablets (*pugillares*): Roberts and Skeat (1983), 12.

62. Plin. *Ep.* 3.5.3–6 lists the titles and the number of volumes in each.

63. Books 1 and 2: *Comp.Med.Gen.* 1.1 (= 13.362 Kühn). Medical treatises: *Lib.Prop.* 3 (= Boudon-Millot [2007a], 143, with n. 1 on pp. 197–98). Galen seems to have composed close to three dozen

tion, and there may have been other volumes, too. Taken together, they may well have constituted an important part of Galen's no doubt substantial book collection.

Philodemus, the Epicurean poet and philosopher of the first century BC whose works were found in the Villa of the Papyri at Herculaneum, seems to have saved at least some of his notes and drafts, although we cannot know how long he himself maintained possession of them. The clearest example is *P.Herc.* 1021, an early draft of Philodemus's work on Plato and his school. It contains a collection of notes and excerpts arranged in a more or less logical sequence, with subsequent revisions, corrections, and additions, some of which were entered on the verso.[64] There may be other examples. *P.Herc.* 339 appears to be an early draft of Philodemus's history of the Stoics, and *P.Herc.* 152 + 157 a draft of *On the Gods*.[65] Similarly, Dioscorus of Aphrodito, a sixth-century AD lawyer, notary, and poet, kept draft copies of many of his own compositions. Along with his collection of the classics (including the *Iliad*, Menander, and probably works of Old Comedy) were found codices containing his own works. These include draft copies of poems that Dioscorus sent to prominent persons as flattering prefaces to petitions, drafts of legal documents, a Greek-Coptic lexicon written out by Dioscorus himself, and other items.[66] Gellius, writing in the second century AD, tells us that he had tracked down a copy of the *Commentarium de proloquiis* of the great Republican scholar, Lucius Aelius Stilo, finding it after a long search in the library of the Temple of Peace. When he did find it, he was disappointed: "I did not find there anything very instructive, nor was it written clearly in order to be helpful in teaching. Aelius seems to have composed the volume more as notes for his own use than to teach anyone else."[67] Gellius is quite clear: Stilo's notes (*commentarium*) were just that—informal notes—and, we may infer, an autograph copy.

We may draw a brief and simple conclusion. When we imagine Cicero (or

---

treatises in the seven years from AD 169 to 176: Bardong (1942), 633–37. Works for his own use: *Lib. Prop.* 14.9 (= Boudon-Millot [2007a], 166); cf. *Ind.* 29. Glossary: *Ind.* 20 and 23. Summary of Didymus: *Ind.* 24. Discussion of Galen's losses, and of the place where he stored his books: Tucci (2008), 137–40 and 134; Houston (2003).

64. *P.Herc.* 164 may be a later version of this work: Cavallo (1984), 13–17.

65. What seem to be more polished versions of these works survive as well, although there is some uncertainty in each case. On *P.Herc.* 339, see Cavallo (1983), 34 and 51–52; on *P.Herc.* 152 + 157, Cavallo (1983), 36 and 52.

66. Poems attached to petitions: Fournet (1999), 369–458, poem nos. 1 to 24. Cf. nos. 32–37, *epithalamia* sent to important persons. The lexicon: Bell and Crum (1925) (= MP^3 354.01).

67. Gell. *NA* 16.8.3: *Sed in eo nihil edocenter neque ad instituendum explanate scriptum est, fecisseque videtur eum librum Aelius sui magis admonendi, quam aliorum docendi gratia.*

any other prolific author) entering his library, we may want to imagine him finding that a significant part of it is his own work. In cases where scholars or authors worked in their libraries, there might be a mixture of materials, everything from editions, elegant or not, of classic authors to one's own notes, some on rolls and others on loose sheets or wax tablets, as well as preliminary drafts, revisions, and notes from lectures.[68]

1.11. BUYING PART OR ALL OF A PREEXISTING COLLECTION

It was sometimes possible to buy whole collections or large numbers of books at one time. In the first century AD, the senator Larcius Licinus made an offer to buy the notebooks of Pliny the Elder, apparently the equivalent of three hundred rolls or more, but Pliny refused, instead bequeathing them, it seems, to his nephew, Pliny the Younger.[69] About a century later, Lucian advised the ignorant book collector (the subject of one of his satires) to sell his books, apparently all of them at once, to some scholar who might actually be able to read and profit from them.[70] The few such purchases we hear of may be representative examples in a long and continuous tradition, one that can be traced well back into the classical Greek world. Plato, we are told, bought the collection of Philolaus, and Aristotle purchased Speusippus's collection.[71]

For a more detailed picture of such block acquisitions, we must turn to the letters of Cicero. Not long before the middle of February, 67 BC, Cicero wrote to Atticus, who was then in Greece, asking him to see about procuring a library for Cicero and reminding Atticus that he had promised to do so.[72] Such a library would consist, of course, primarily or exclusively of texts in Greek. By May, it seems, Atticus had purchased an appropriate collection of books, informed Cicero of his purchase, and told Cicero how much the

---

68. It is worth recalling at this point that while in modern times published books are quite distinct in appearance from notes, drafts, and the like, that was not the case in antiquity: notes gathered into a roll (as were Pliny the Elder's), first drafts, and final versions intended for sale would all be written by hand on papyrus rolls and thus more or less indistinguishable as they sat on a shelf. Wax tablets and other writing materials, obviously, would be a different matter.

69. Plin. *Ep.* 3.5.17. We do not know how many rolls were in the collection when Larcius made his offer. Pliny the Younger says that he inherited 160 rolls of notebooks from his uncle, but that there had been considerably fewer at the time of Larcius's offer. On Pliny the Younger as heir: Dix (1996), 89, with n. 13.

70. Lucian *Ind.* 24.

71. Plato: Diog. Laert. 3.9, Gell. *NA* 3.17.3. Aristotle: Diog. Laert. 4.5, Gell. *NA* 3.17.3.

72. Cic. *Att.* 1.7. On Atticus's role as purchaser of books and on the availability of book collections in Greece in this period, see Dix (2013), 212–13.

books would cost; this can be inferred from a letter of Cicero's in which he asked Atticus not to promise the library to anyone else and told him that he was gradually assembling the funds to pay for it.[73] Three months later, Cicero wrote again to Atticus, asking him to keep the book rolls and stating that Atticus had said he would do so.[74] We do not hear anything further of this collection and so cannot be sure that Cicero acquired it, but there is no good reason to doubt that he did.

On another occasion, some twenty years later, Cicero wrote to his freed-man Tiro, telling him that he was sending a collection of books to his villa at Tusculum. Cicero did not say how large the collection was, nor how he had acquired it, but he did ask Tiro to put the volumes in their cabinets and to make an inventory (*index*) of them, thus indicating that this was a new acquisition and that it constituted at least a useful, and perhaps a substan-tial, addition to the library in that villa.[75] It is of interest that Cicero wanted an inventory of these materials. Perhaps he simply wanted to make sure he had received everything he had paid for. More likely, he had made a block purchase of manuscripts, possibly a collection related to the work he was then doing or planned to do, and now wanted to have a complete inventory of exactly what was included.[76]

A passage in Galen's *De indolentia* may indicate that such bulk acquisi-tions, however acquired, could be kept together (at least in part) as coher-ent and recognizable collections. In chapter 13 of that work, Galen men-tions the loss of several specific collections of particularly accurate copies that were destroyed in the fire of AD 192. These included, Galen tells us, the "Callinia, Atticiana, and Peducaeana."[77] It is quite possible that Galen has in mind discrete and identifiable collections, ones that had been acquired en bloc and that had been stored separately as coherent collections.[78] The

73. Cic. *Att.* 1.10. 4: *Bibliothecam tuam cave cuiquam despondeas . . . nam ego omnis meas vinde-miolas eo reservo.* ("Don't promise that library you've got to anyone . . . for I'm setting aside all my little profits for [it].") Thus Atticus had himself bought the collection and expected Cicero to pay him for it. On these transactions see Dix (2013), 210.

74. Cic. *Att.* 1.11.3.

75. Cic. *Fam.* 16.18.3 and 16.20, both written in the fall of 47 BC: *libros compone; [fac] indicem.* ("Put the book rolls away and make a list of them.") We will return to this incident in section 2.1 below.

76. Cicero published several works on the art of rhetoric (*Brutus, Orator,* and *De optimo genere oratorum*) in the year following this acquisition, and in 45 and 44 turned to philosophy. Note, how-ever, that Cicero does not say that he had purchased this collection just recently. He may have bought it with other projects in mind.

77. On the spelling of these names, which are corrupt in the Greek, see introduction, n. 34, above; Stramaglia (2011), 120–21.

78. It is also possible that these books were to be found here and there in the libraries, each within its appropriate genre (or other organizing group), and that they could be identified by information in

"Atticiana," for example, may have been what remained of a collection of book rolls that had belonged to Cicero's friend Atticus or had been prepared at his direction (or both; the two were by no means mutually exclusive).[79] Whatever the precise origins of the three collections, the important point in the present context is that they may have constituted well-known groups of book rolls that had been acquired in bulk, were known by the names of their original owners, and could still be identified as specific collections long after the deaths of those owners.[80] There was precedent for this in the Greek world, where, Strabo tells us, Theophrastus's library included Aristotle's.[81] In short, book collections could and did grow by absorbing other collections, and in some cases the earlier collections, or parts of them, continued to be identifiable by name.

1.12. BEQUEATHING AND GIVING COLLECTIONS

When the poet Persius died, he included in his will a provision that his mother should give his teacher, the Stoic Cornutus, a sum of money and Persius's entire library, which included, we are told, some 700 volumes, all of them works of Chrysippus.[82] As we have seen, Pliny the Younger inherited the 160 volumes of notes of his uncle, Pliny the Elder, and it is reasonable to assume that he inherited the rest of the elder Pliny's library as well.[83] In 61 or 60 BC, Servius Claudius left what appears to have been a substantial collection of manuscripts to his *"frater"* (brother, half-brother, or cousin) Lucius Papirius Paetus, and Paetus in turn gave them as a gift to Cicero. Claudius was most likely residing in Greece when he died, and that is where his book rolls seem to have been, for Cicero wrote urgently to Atticus, who was in Greece at that time, asking him to secure the collection, make sure nothing was lost, and arrange to have it sent to Cicero. According to Cicero,

---

their front or end titles or by the addition of a note, e.g. "of Atticus," in the margin. Such additional notes, however, are unlikely: see above, in the introduction, on titles and *subscriptiones*.

79. Atticus may also have edited the volumes Galen has in mind. Galen states explicitly that it was the correctness of the readings (γραφῆς ἀκρίβεια) that had made these volumes so valuable, and we know that Atticus did some editing, for example of Cicero's work.

80. So Nicholls (2011), 132–33, with suggestions on how the collections might have entered the imperial collections.

81. Strabo 13.1.54 C608.

82. *Vita Persi*, in Clausen (1956). There were various reports of the amount of money, and we need not place much trust in the figure of seven hundred books or in the statement that they were all by Chrysippus. The important thing for us is that the author of the *vita* thought it reasonable that a person might inherit another person's library.

83. Plin. *Ep.* 3.5.17. It is possible that the elder Pliny's books formed the core of the collection in the library that Pliny the Younger created at Comum: Dix (1996), 89.

the collection certainly included Latin texts, and he suspected that it contained certain Greek texts as well.[84] He wanted them all.

Beyond these specifically attested inheritances, we may surely assume that book collections regularly passed from parent to child, from friend to friend, or from teacher to student, along with other property.[85] A body of law grew up around such bequests, and we find the jurists concerned with a number of book-related questions. How do we define "book"? How can we distinguish that from a person's notes or accounts? If a person bequeaths his "library" to someone, does that mean the cabinet by itself, or the books within it, too? Do blank papyrus rolls count as part of a collection of "books"? A chapter of the *Digest* devoted to these and similar questions quotes opinions of at least six jurists and clearly implies that there were many such cases and numerous disputes arising from them.[86] Also, as we will see when we study what remains of manuscript collections from Egypt (chapter 4), there is good reason to suspect that book collections frequently retained their essential shape and character over a period of two or three generations, and the most likely mechanism for such a phenomenon would be inheritance, either within the family or by a friend or student.

1.13. CONFISCATIONS OF ENTIRE LIBRARIES

At the end of an extended essay on the scholar Marcus Terentius Varro and Varro's use of the term *hebdomades*, Aulus Gellius reports a comment of Varro: Varro claimed, says Gellius, that he had written, to that point in his life, some 490 volumes, but that a considerable number of these had been lost, since his libraries had been plundered when he was proscribed.[87] Varro had been proscribed by the triumvirs in 43 (or possibly later) and took refuge with his friend Fufius Calenus, thus saving his life but not, evidently, his property or his books.[88] We cannot be sure what happened to Varro's manuscripts, but it seems very likely that some or all of them were seized by Mark Antony, passed on Antony's death to his wife Octavia, and were given by her to the library she helped found in the Portico of Octavia.[89]

---

84. Cic. *Att.* 1.20.7, written after May 12 of 60; *Att.* 2.1.12, of early June. On all of this, see Dix (2013), 217.

85. We hear of several cases of teacher-to-student bequests in the context of the earlier Greek philosophical schools: thus Aristotle to Theophrastus (Strabo 13.1.54 C608), Theophrastus to Neleus (Diog. Laert. 5.52), and Epicurus to Hermarchus (Diog. Laert. 10.21).

86. *Dig.* 32.52. The jurists are Ulpian, Gaius Cassius, Sabinus, Nerva, Pomponius, and Labeo.

87. Gell. *NA* 3.10.17.

88. App. *B Civ.* 4.47.

89. Antony had occupied Varro's villa at Casinum for a period shortly after the assassination of

Although this seems to be the only instance of confiscation of books that is explicitly mentioned in our sources, it was almost certainly just one in a long series of such incidents beginning well before, and extending for centuries after, Varro's time.[90] From at least the middle years of the Republic, when an individual was convicted of a crime against the state, his property (*bona*) was seized by the state and sold at auction.[91] This was a process that could readily be adapted for use against one's political enemies, as happened in the period of Sulla's proscriptions, during the civil war of 49–46, and in the proscriptions of 43 and later.[92] Under the Empire, as Fergus Millar has noted, there were two important developments in the treatment of *bona damnatorum*: first, confiscation of property as a penalty was extended "to all major criminal convictions," and secondly, there was "large-scale retention, rather than sale, of the property by the ruler."[93] Confiscation of property after trials for *maiestas* was notoriously common in the first century. A list of such criminal trials, many but not all of which will have involved the seizure and sale of the condemned man's property, is hardly necessary here; the *maiestas* trials under Tiberius and events under Caligula, Nero, and Domitian are well known.[94] What has not been noted previously

---

Caesar, and so knew of its contents (Cic. *Phil.* 2.104–5). Moreover, at least one statue in the Portico of Octavia—a Cupid by Praxiteles, once owned by Verres—had been inherited by Octavia from Antony, and the library of Varro may have followed the same route through Antony to Octavia and thence to the library in the Portico of Octavia. See Dix (2000), 460–61. Tucci (2013), 289, suggests an alternate route: from Stilo to his student Varro; from Varro to Asinius Pollio's library in the Atrium Libertatis (which included a statue of Varro); and from that library to the library in the Templum Pacis. Tucci's thesis may be supported by the appearance in the Templum Pacis library of a copy of the notes of Aelius Stilo (Gell. *NA* 16.8.3; cf. above, n. 67). Stilo was a teacher of Varro, and he may have bequeathed some or all of his materials to Varro. From Varro, they could have gone to Asinius Pollio's library in the Atrium Libertatis, and thence to the Templum Pacis library.

90. Some or many of Cicero's book rolls may have been confiscated when he was exiled in 58. Cicero claims that movable property (*instrumentum* and *ornamenta*) in his Tusculan villa was taken by the consul Gabinius, and that columns from his Palatine house were removed by the other consul, Piso (Cic. *Dom.* 62). At least part of Cicero's book collection was damaged or diminished during the period of his exile (Cic. *Att.* 4.4a.1–2), and it is possible that Piso or Gabinius (or Clodius) made off with some of Cicero's books. See Dix (1986), 112–13; Dix (2013), 222–23.

91. The procedure (*publicatio bonorum*) involved the taking of the property by the state and its sale at auction: Livy 25.4.9; Suet. *Aug.* 24.1; pre-Sullan instances in *RE Suppl.* 10, 101–7, s.v. *publicatio bonorum* (Waldstein).

92. For a detailed discussion of the proscriptions and confiscations of the first century BC, see Hinard (1985). Hinard gives lists of the proscribed (128–33, 275–92, 329–411, and 415–552). His lists include 235 men, virtually all of senatorial or equestrian rank, of whom 77 are known to have been executed promptly. There can be little doubt that many, and probably most, of these men owned book collections small or large, and that those book collections were often or always among the *bona* sold at auction. As for the Caesarian civil war, see Caes. *B Afr.* 90.1, 97.1: Caesar had spared the lives but sold the property of his enemies, claiming that they had taken up arms *contra populum Romanum*.

93. Millar (1977), 165–74.

94. For the gradual extension of the use of the procedure and numerous specific examples, see Mil-

is that such trials and their consequences almost certainly had a significant impact upon book collections, especially but not only in Rome and Italy.

Since virtually all of the men who were proscribed or tried on a charge of *maiestas* (or similar capital charges) were wealthy and in all probability highly educated, it is more than likely that they possessed collections of book rolls, and in many cases substantial ones. Those manuscripts were part of their property, and there would need to be a process for dealing with them. The basic procedure, of course, would ordinarily be the sale at auction of the condemned person's *bona*, with the proceeds of the sale being divided between the prosecutor and the state.[95] From our point of view the question concerns not the *bona* in general, but the condemned man's manuscripts: in the case of large collections, were they sold en bloc? Or item by item? We cannot answer this question in any detail, but there is some evidence for a preliminary sorting of the *bona* before their sale. In the *Digest*, for example, we read that handwritten documents and papers pertaining to the condemned man's private affairs could be returned to those who so requested, presumably his relatives or heirs.[96] This seems to imply a sorting of the *bona* prior to the disposition of the property. Similarly, when Philo discusses the confiscation of the property of Flaccus, he mentions "cups, clothing, blankets, utensils, and whatever other beautiful things were in the house," as though some sort of inventory had been taken.[97] This in turn suggests the possibility that at least some book rolls—perhaps just the most valuable ones—might be auctioned individually, or separated out and retained by the emperor.[98]

The implications of this information for libraries and book collections in the late Republic and early Empire are clear enough, even if we cannot know the details. In cases where the emperor did *not* keep possession of the confiscated book rolls, the collection could have been sold en bloc, and in this case entire libraries might change hands. It is also possible that some

---

lar (1977), 165–74; or *RE* 23.2, 2497, s.v. *publicatio bonorum* (Fuhrmann). On the financial rewards granted to *delatores*, see Rutledge (2001), 39–44.

95. In cases of *maiestas*, for example, the prosecutor ordinarily received one-fourth, the state (whether *aerarium* or *fiscus*) three-fourths: Rutledge (2001), 39.

96. *Dig.* 49.14.45.4 (= Paul. *Sent.*, third century): *Ex his bonis, quae ad fiscum delata sunt, instrumenta vel chirographa, acta etiam ad ius privatorum pertinentia restitui postulantibus convenit.* Note that book rolls containing works of literature are not mentioned. They were presumably sold along with the rest of the property or were retained by the emperor.

97. Philo *In Flacc.* 148.

98. Beginning late in the second century AD, we hear occasionally of a *procurator ad bona damnatorum* or the like, and the existence of such an official seems to imply that considerable attention was paid to confiscated *bona*: Pflaum (1960–61), 604 and 644–46, nos. 228, 239, and 240. Some books, of course, were particularly valuable.

or many volumes in a given collection entered the used-book market, either because the new owner found they duplicated what he already owned, or because he was simply not interested in those particular volumes.[99] In those cases where the emperor *did* retain possession of the condemned man's estate, we can posit several possible fates for the book rolls. They might stay in the confiscated *domus* or villa as part of its furnishings; some or all could be given to some nearby estate or to friends of the emperor; and some or all of the manuscripts could be brought to Rome or to one of the emperor's villas elsewhere, to be lodged with other volumes in one or another of the great imperial libraries.

In short, political and criminal trials, with the punishments consequent upon them, may have played a significant role as a mechanism for the dispersal of manuscript collections or a change in their ownership. At certain times—one thinks of the aftermath of the Pisonian conspiracy under Nero, when the philosopher Seneca and his brother Annaeus Mela, the poet Lucan, Petronius, Calpurnius Piso himself, and numerous other wealthy and cultured men were condemned—a very considerable number of books may have changed hands, either as whole libraries or as individual volumes put up for sale.[100] From the emperor's point of view, such retention of property could be an important source of wealth in general and manuscripts in particular. If we assume that emperors did retain at least some of the manuscripts so confiscated, that would help to explain the appearance, every generation or so, of new library buildings in Rome: they would be needed to house the book rolls that had accumulated over the years, in part through gifts and the like, and in part through the confiscation of book rolls that had previously formed important private collections.

1.14. BOOK COLLECTIONS AS BOOTY

Entire libraries could be acquired as the result of conquest in war. We cannot here deal in detail with the laws regarding booty (which are not entirely clear), and a brief summary will suffice.[101] All booty won in war, it seems,

---

99. It is easy to imagine other scenarios as well: dealers buying part or all of some collections; books being bought at auction and then given away as gifts; and so on.

100. Pisonian conspiracy, with names of the men who were condemned: Rutledge (2001), 166–70. Not all condemnations resulted in confiscation. In many cases, suicide before conviction would avoid confiscation of one's estate: Rutledge (2001), 42–43. There were, though, so many men condemned and executed that tens of thousands of book rolls must have been auctioned off over the course of the first and second centuries.

101. On the treatment and legal status of booty, see Bona (1960) and Churchill (1999). Summaries of the general's control and responsibilities are at Bona (1960), 148–49, and Churchill (1999), 109–10.

became the property of the Roman people, but the victorious general was allowed considerable latitude in deciding how the booty might best be put to use. He could use it to reward his soldiers and officers, he could send booty or proceeds from its sale to the *aerarium*, and he could use it to fund projects that were in the public interest, such as the building of temples. He was not, however, allowed to keep booty for his own personal use or treat it as his own property.

Ancient sources tell us of four occasions when the Romans seized book rolls as booty. In 168 BC, Aemilius Paullus defeated King Perseus of Macedon, and the king's collection of books formed part of the booty. Paullus allowed his sons—Fabius Maximus Aemilianus and Cornelius Scipio Aemilianus—to choose for themselves volumes from the royal book collection.[102] In 89 BC, during the Social Wars, Pompeius Strabo captured and sacked the Italic town of Asculum, and again the booty included manuscripts.[103] As Sulla returned from Asia to Italy in 84 BC, he stopped in Athens and "took for himself" the collection of book rolls that had belonged to an Athenian bibliophile and general named Apellicon.[104] Finally, L. Licinius Lucullus is said by Isidore to have acquired an important collection of volumes "in the booty from Pontus" (*e Pontica praeda*).[105] Although Isidore gives no further details, we know that Lucullus defeated Mithridates, the king of Pontus, in 70 BC, and it is likely that Mithridates had a collection of Greek manuscripts in his capital city, Sinope. Those volumes, and perhaps some from other cities, probably formed the "booty from Pontus" that Isidore refers to.[106] There were no doubt other generals, too, who acquired some or many volumes through conquest, legally or otherwise, especially as most Roman commanders were highly educated, and many of them were Hellenophiles who would have coveted such manuscripts. We hear of several campaigns in which works of art were seized as booty, and in each case manuscripts could have been included in the *spolia*. Among these we might note Fabius Maximus's capture of the city of Tarentum in 209, Fulvius Nobilior's capture of Ambracia in 187, and Lucius Mummius's sack of Corinth in 146.[107]

Such acquisitions are important for Roman book collections in two ways. First, the book rolls thus acquired might be maintained more or less intact

---

102. Plut. *Aem.* 28.6.

103. Oros. 5.18.26.

104. "Took for himself" (ἐξεῖλεν ἑαυτῷ) is the way Plutarch puts it, *Sull.* 26.1–3. See also for the incident Strabo 13.1.54 C608–9.

105. Isid. *Etym.* 6.5.1.

106. On Lucullus's library, see Dix (2000), especially in this connection 441–44.

107. See Miles (2008), 68–69, for Tarentum, 69–70 for Ambracia, and 73–76 for Corinth.

in the general's house in Rome or in a villa outside the city, or added to the general's own preexisting collection, and in such cases they may well have constituted extensive collections that could serve as virtual public libraries. Secondly, they added to the variety, and probably the quality, of manuscripts that were available in Italy. Perseus's book rolls, for example, being a royal collection, were presumably of generally high quality.

The clearest example of a collection kept together, at least for a while, is the library of Lucullus. Lucullus apparently installed the volumes that had belonged to Mithridates in his villa at Tusculum, where, as an educated man, he had no doubt already assembled a considerable collection.[108] Here, Plutarch tells us, Greek scholars and writers flocked to read and debate.[109] Lucullus died by 56, but the collection passed to his son, and he too evidently kept the library intact and accessible to scholars. Cicero, for one, went there frequently, as he himself tells us, and on one occasion in the late 50s BC he found Cato the Younger there, reading Stoic texts.[110] We can trace a similar, but slightly less certain, history for the collection that Sulla brought back from Athens. Apellicon's collection, now Sulla's, seems to have included works of Aristotle, Theophrastus, and a substantial number of other authors. It is very likely that Sulla kept the collection together and housed it in his villa on the Bay of Naples,[111] and after his death in 78, the property, including the manuscript collection, passed to his son Faustus. Subsequently, we hear of it attracting the attention of the Greek scholar and philologist Tyrannio, probably in the late 60s or early 50s; and, despite several uncertainties, it is very likely this collection that Cicero was referring to when, in 55 BC, he wrote Atticus from Cumae and mentioned that he had been "feasting on the library of Faustus."[112] In these two cases, then, the importation of whole libraries that had been acquired as the result of war had a considerable impact upon the intellectual and literary life of Rome.

Theoretically, the texts won in war might be sold off, given away, or in

---

108. Dix (2000), 443–44, discusses the likelihood that Lucullus was a lifelong buyer of book rolls.

109. Plut. *Luc.* 42.1.

110. Cic. *Fin.* 3.7. This was written in 45–44, but the dramatic date is 52 BC.

111. Our sources are not clear on where the collection was housed, but see Rawson (1985), 41, with n. 8; D'Arms (1970), 31–33 and 177; Dix (2004), 67–68.

112. Tyrannio: Strabo 13.1.54 C609; Christes (1979), 29, for the date of Tyrannio's activities. Cicero using the library: Cic. *Att.* 4.10.1. The texts Tyrannio worked on were subsequently made available to Andronicus of Rhodes, who compiled a catalog and may have disseminated copies of some of them. A Ptolemy (otherwise unknown) put together a condensed version of Andronicus's catalog, and an Arabic translation of Ptolemy's list survives: Hein (1985), 416–39. No authors other than Aristotle and Theophrastus appear in the list, so if the collection itself included other works, as seems probable, they were omitted by Andronicus, Ptolemy, or the Arabic translator. Gottschalk (1987), 1090–97, provides the details.

some other way dispersed, rather than kept together. The manuscripts that Pompeius Strabo took from Asculum may be an example. When Pompeius Strabo died, the books came into the possession of his son, Pompey (later the Great); in 86 or 85, a lawsuit was brought against the younger Pompey, apparently claiming this booty for the state; but Pompey was able to show that the book rolls had been stolen from the house of the Pompeys by agents of Cinna and so could not possibly be given back to the state.[113] We do not hear of these books again, and it is possible that Cinna's men sold them on the used-book market, since the younger Pompey seems to have believed (or claimed) that they were unrecoverable. In this case — and we are admittedly dealing with many uncertainties here — they may have added to the number of Greek texts for sale in Rome.

One thing that, rather surprisingly, is not attested in our sources is the seizure by generals of manuscript collections which they then used directly to establish libraries that belonged to the Roman state.[114] It is possible that some book collections acquired as booty were given to the people in the form of libraries that were housed in temples, or that captured book rolls were stored in warehouses along with other booty, or in buildings that housed state archives and documentary materials, where the existence of some sort of shelving would make the storage of book rolls easy. But if such was the case, we never hear of it.[115]

1.15. CONCLUSION

It will be immediately evident that the ways in which books were produced and acquired determined, to a significant degree, the nature of the resulting collections and libraries. Here, by way of summary, we can venture some

113. Plut. *Pomp.* 4.1. There is doubt about the precise nature of the case. I follow the analysis of Bona (1960), 163–64, and Churchill (1999), 107, but see also Alexander (1990), 62, no. 120, and Shatzman (1972), 194–95.

114. This may of course be due to the lacunose nature of our sources. It is possible that Asinius Pollio, who rebuilt the Atrium Libertatis *ex manubiis* and established a library within that building, stocked the library with book rolls he had seized as booty. His victory, however, had been over the Parthini, a tribe of Illyria, and, as Dix noted in Dix and Houston (2006), 679, the Parthini seem unlikely to have had collections of book rolls worth seizing. Under the Empire, we hear of one library specifically seized as booty, and that is the temple library at Jerusalem, captured by Titus in AD 70. The book rolls taken from the Temple may have been placed in the Temple of Peace in Rome, but they seem to have been sacred texts, not literature.

115. For the possibility of book collections captured in war becoming temple libraries or parts of them, see Affleck (2013), 124–26 and 129–31. Some book rolls, Affleck notes, might have been included in the booty from battles in Italy well before the time of Aemilius Paullus; small collections would very likely have been ignored in the sources that tell us about war and booty.

preliminary guesses as to what collections built up in the ways we have identified might look like. As we move deeper into the material, we will be able
to correct, modify, and deepen this first portrait of Roman book collections.

We might expect any given collection to have some mix of personally, in-
formally, and professionally copied texts. There will be extremes: some less
wealthy readers might have owned just a few book rolls, all or most of which
they had copied out themselves; very wealthy men might strive for collections of volumes that were valuable because of their elegance or their rarity
or, perhaps, both.[116] Most collections, in all likelihood, fell in between these
extremes, at some point along a spectrum from all home-copied to all professionally produced, and one of our continuing concerns, as we examine
the physical remains of book rolls from Herculaneum and Egypt, will be to
see what evidence exists concerning precisely this question.

There might be duplicates in any collection. You could be given or inherit a second copy of a book roll you already owned, or, if you purchased
a collection, as we have seen Cicero doing, it might contain texts that you
already owned. On the other hand, you might never succeed in acquiring all
the books in a multivolume work, for some books in, say, Homer's *Odyssey*
seem to have been much less popular than others, and finding an archetype of a less popular book could well be difficult.[117] This would be even
more true of works or authors who were less popular. A collection strong in,
say, Epicurean philosophy might lack the works of the early and important
Epicureans Polyaenus and Hermarchus simply because exemplars were not
available. Gifts and inherited items could distort the nature of a collection,
too, for they might introduce authors, works, or types of material that were
otherwise not of interest to the owner but, despite that lack of interest, were
now represented in the collection. If the only available exemplars of a certain work, or the only volumes of it offered for sale, were of low quality, an
otherwise strong collection might include inaccurate texts, no matter how
carefully they were prepared from the archetype. And, of course, any collection might include unauthorized versions of a text, or one or more variant versions, or complete forgeries. In short, heterogeneity is probably to be
expected as the norm. It would take an exceptionally experienced, knowl-
edgeable, and wealthy collector to gather a fully coherent and consistently
trustworthy collection of book rolls.

116. Lucian's ignorant book collector, a fictional character but presumably in some way based on
reality, is an example of the wealthy collector (Lucian *Ind.*, especially 1–2 and 25).

117. Mertens-Pack[3] currently lists only three papyrus rolls of *Odyssey* 13 (*MP*[3] 1109.1, 1109.2, 1110),
whereas there are dozens of surviving papyri of *Iliad* 1 and *Iliad* 2.

2
Lists of Books Preserved
on Papyrus

2.1. INTRODUCTION

In the autumn of 47 BC, Cicero wrote from Rome to his freedman Tiro, who was at Cicero's villa in Tusculum. Tiro was not feeling well. Cicero sent him best wishes, advice, news, and instructions, and also mentioned that he would soon be sending along a *horologium* (presumably a sundial) and some books. Soon thereafter, he wrote a follow-up note: Tiro was to put the books away, but wait until he felt better before preparing a list (*index*) of them.[1] Cicero's offhand remark gives Tiro no specific instructions, and that omission provides useful information about what he and Tiro took for granted: first, they both assumed that, if you had a collection of books, you would want to make a list of them; and second, they were agreed upon what such a list would include. It would be good to know what they expected the list to be: authors and titles, presumably, but would there be anything else? Would it be arranged by language—Greek or Latin—or by genre, or chronologically? Would it include other information, such as the physical condition of the book roll or the total number of rolls in a given work? Cicero and Tiro, we may safely infer, knew the answers to all these questions, because from long experience they knew what such a book list would and should include.

Book lists seem to have been common by Cicero's day, although they varied in physical form and, to some degree, in the information they provided. A famous list from Rhodes, dating to the later years of the second century BC, was cut in stone, and so was presumably intended to be *the* list, once and for all, of a certain collection.[2] Most of one column and part of

---

1. Cic. *Fam.* 16.18.3; *Fam.* 16.20. The relevant text in the follow-up note is *Libros compone; indicem cum Metrodoro libebit, quoniam eius arbitratu vivendum est.* ("Put the books away, and compile the list when Metrodorus [the doctor] tells you it's OK, since you have to live by his instructions.") Shackleton Bailey (1977), ad loc., takes *compone* as meaning "put the books away (in their cupboards)," but it may just mean "store the books somewhere (for now)."

2. First published by Maiuri (1925), 14–15; improved text in Segre (1935).

another survive and give us the titles of some thirty works by nine different authors. Following each title is a number, usually "one" but once "five." This is probably the number of book rolls contained in the work. The authors in each column are listed alphabetically, but the titles under each author's name are in no discernible order, neither alphabetical nor chronological, and the alphabetical order of author's names seems to begin over again on the second column. Other such lists are known, among them a similar fragmentary list on stone from the Piraeus, containing works by dramatists, the historian Hellanicus, and the orator Demosthenes.[3] We need not here review all of the evidence for these early lists, since it has been set out clearly by Rosa Otranto.[4] The point is simply that when the ancients, from at least Hellenistic times on, saw a collection of books, they seem to have felt that it would be useful to draw up a list of the items it contained.

No such list survives for any of the great imperial collections in Rome, but we do have lists on papyri from Egypt that can tell us a good deal about the lists that the ancients made of their book collections, the information they chose to include, and, thus, something of the state of library science in antiquity. Also, and even more importantly, they give us specific information about the content, size, character, and coverage of the book collections themselves. Those collections and their contents are what I ultimately hope to recover. My goal in this chapter is to explore the lists on papyri from Egypt, which have not previously been exploited in the context of library history, and to see what we can learn from them, not just about ancient lists of book rolls, but about Roman-era book collections.

2.2. BOOK LISTS ON PAPYRUS

Some nineteen book lists of widely differing types, dates, and quality have been found so far, and these have been conveniently gathered and republished as a group by Rosa Otranto.[5] Several of the lists Otranto includes are clearly not of use to us in the present context. Otranto number 4 (= *P.GettyMus.* acc. 76.AI.57), for example, is a letter in which the writer

---

3. *IG* II/III² 2363; cf. Burzachechi (1963), 93–96.

4. Otranto (2000), xi–xv. Callimachus's famous *pinakes* are closely related to these lists, but there are differences. Callimachus, it seems, did not attempt to list every book in the collection of the Alexandrian library, and he gave more bibliographical information than is usual in the lists of collections, including material to assist in identifying the author. See Otranto (2000), xvi–xvii; cf. Jacob (2013), 77. For more detail: Fraser (1972), 1: 452–53.

5. Otranto (2000). A more expansive list, extending well into the early medieval period but not including the texts themselves, is provided by Harrauer (1995).

lists several Epicurean texts he has sent to the addressee, but we have no way of knowing if these volumes derived from a particular collection of books or what part of any such collection they might represent.[6] Some of the lists are clearly not inventories but rather bibliographical lists (Otranto number 2), others are letters discussing books (Otranto numbers 11, 19), and a few are too problematic in too many ways to be reliable as evidence (Otranto number 18).

Other lists may well be inventories of specific collections. There is a problem, however: no known list has a title or any other explicit indication of its purpose, at least none that survives. How then can we tell if a list was an inventory of a real collection of books? A list of titles or authors might serve any one of a number of different purposes. It might be an inventory of an actual collection of books, but it could also be a list of books some person hoped to buy, borrow, or have copied; it could be part of a scholar's or a student's list of the works of some author, drawn up as part of a biography, as a school exercise, or for some other reason; it might be a person's own future reading list. If a list was an inventory of real book rolls, it could be a personal collection of books, the books in a collection that had been given to a town or an institution, the inventory of the texts on hand or on order in a copyist's or scribe's shop, or an inventory of a collection made on the occasion of a sale or the passing down of a collection as part of an inheritance. What we are hunting for, of course, are inventories of actual physical collections of books, so for us the critical question is this: does a given list represent a collection of actual, physical book rolls, or is it a list of, say, desiderata?

2.3. INDICATORS OF REAL COLLECTIONS

As they have worked on the lists, papyrologists have noticed a number of characteristics that help distinguish inventories of real book rolls from lists of books that existed in the compiler's mind, such as a scholar's list of what a particular author had written. We can summarize these characteristics as follows:

1. If all or almost all of the book numbers in a given work are enumerated, we are probably dealing with an inventory of real

---

6. Neither the writer's nor the recipient's name survives. Although we cannot draw useful inferences from this letter about book collections, it does refer to actual book rolls, is not just a list of recommended reading, and contributes to our understanding of the sharing of texts in Roman Egypt. Otranto no. 5 (*P.Mil.Vogl.* 11) is similar: a letter in which the writer reports sending six Stoic texts to the addressee.

book rolls. A person wanting to acquire a copy of the *Iliad*, for example, would not be likely to list all of the books one by one, nor would a teacher (unless he was assigning certain specific parts of the *Iliad*) or a scholar list the books one by one.

2. If a list includes the title of a given work more than once, that is probably an indication that the collection contained duplicate copies of the work. This then would be an inventory of real book rolls.

3. If one or more book numbers is omitted from a list of the books in a given work such as Hesiod's *Catalog of Women*, that may indicate that the list is an inventory of a real collection, since it implies a counting of actual volumes. (Alternatively, however, it might be a list of particular books that someone wanted to acquire, especially if it is a short list.)

4. If items seem to be entered as opisthographic volumes, they are probably real book rolls. A teacher, for example, would not be likely to give an assignment to students that specified "Plato's *Meno*, with the *Alcibiades* on the reverse."

5. Some lists contain problem titles that can best be explained on the assumption that the compiler of the list is looking at a damaged book roll—one that lacks a *sillybon* or title, for example—and in that case the list must be an inventory of real book rolls.

6. In some cases, one or more of the types of lists of nonreal volumes can be ruled out. A very long list would not be a teacher's assignment; a list containing a variety of works would not be a scholar's bibliography of the works of a given author; and so on. I will comment on such as we come to them in the lists.

If we exclude items that are clearly not inventories of real book collections and include those lists that seem, on the basis of one or more of the criteria just enumerated, to be inventories, we are left with about a dozen of Otranto's lists. Four of these are so short that we cannot know the purpose they were intended to serve. Otranto number 8 (*P.Oxy.* 35.2739), for example, is a small fragment of papyrus containing the titles of six comedies which, as is known from other sources, were written by Cratinus. This might be a section of an inventory of real book rolls, but it could just as easily be part of a list of the works of Cratinus included in or attached to a biography of Cratinus. We cannot assume it represents part of an inventory of real physical book rolls, and I will omit it.[7] Ultimately, we are left with

---

7. For the same reason I omit Otranto no. 7 (*P.Oxy.* 25.2426), Otranto no. 9 (*P.Oxy.* 27.2462), and Otranto no. 10 (*P.Oxy.* 27.2456).

a group of eight lists that have good reason to be considered inventories of actual collections.[8] In this chapter, I will describe and analyze these lists, five in detail and three more briefly. The five I have chosen for close analysis will illustrate a number of the problems that one faces in trying to exploit this material and, at the same time, provide a representative sample of the diverse range of collections they represent.[9] The three lists that I describe briefly provide additional evidence on a number of points that we will consider in the discussion. The material is organized as follows. The basic five lists are presented and discussed in sections 2.6 to 2.10; they are numbered list 1 to list 5. Greek texts, English translations, and a limited commentary on each will be found in appendix 1, with the same numbers, while photographs of the five are in Figures 2 to 6. The three lists I treat briefly are described together in section 2.11 and numbered list 6 to list 8.

2.4. CHARACTERISTICS OF THE LISTS ON PAPYRUS

Typically, the lists that survive include very limited information about the manuscripts. They provide authors and titles; the authors' names, or the titles, or both, may be listed alphabetically, but that is by no means universal.[10] The lists often include the numbers of the books present in the collection ("*Iliad*, Books 1, 2, 3," etc.), or indicate the total number of book rolls in a work ("Xenophon, *Anabasis*, 8 [rolls]," for example). Occasionally, they provide summary counts of the number of rolls in a section of the collection: "20 dialogues," for example, or "142 of philosophers." In one (list 4), the number of opisthographic rolls is counted up and recorded. In lists 2 and 8, two or more of the titles are checked off, perhaps indicating that the titles in the list were being checked against the volumes in the collection, with those volumes that were found (or missing) being noted.

---

8. An actual physical collection might itself be any one of a number of things: a personal collection; the collection of a municipal or institutional library; the stock in hand of a scribe or bookseller. While we are primarily interested in collections that endured for some time, as opposed to collections of books for sale, even a bookseller's stock can be useful as an indication of the characteristics and content of collections. There are some ways to identify libraries as opposed to a bookseller's stock, but, as we will see, it is generally impossible to know the exact nature of a given collection.

9. The three likely inventories of actual collections that I do not discuss in detail are *PSI Laur.* inv. 19662 verso (= Otranto no. 16), which I analyzed in Houston (2009); *P.Vindob.* inv. G 39966, column 1 (= Otranto no. 3, column 1), which is similar to my list 1; and *P.Turner* 9 (= Otranto no. 18), which may have been part of a codex. I will refer to each of these from time to time in the discussion. Texts of all are available in Otranto (2000).

10. Alphabetization in the lists is generally what is called "single-letter" alphabetization, meaning that it does not extend beyond the first letter of a word. Thus Aeschylus will precede Bacchylides, but Diocles might precede Demosthenes. This is typical of ancient alphabetization: Daly (1967).

It is worth noting what is *not* included in these lists. Naturally, they provide no publication information. In no case do we find any information on the age of the book roll, when it was copied, or where or by whom. The compiler of the list would ordinarily have had no way of knowing this, since this information was either never or only very rarely written into a book roll.[11] Only if a compiler was listing a collection of brand-new rolls would he be likely to know the scribe's name or the date of copying, and so far as we can tell the compilers of lists did not choose to include that information. More surprising is the omission in our lists of a physical description of the roll, since the number of *stichoi*, and sometimes the number of columns, was recorded in the *subscriptio* and could easily have been transferred onto the list. Presumably the compilers saw no reason to record this information.[12] The compilers also do not explicitly describe the physical condition of a roll.[13]

No list known to us includes any sort of catalog or index number for the volumes it lists. The lists thus gave the person consulting them no specific information on where—which shelf, set of shelves, or container—to find the manuscript. Modern historians of libraries have often referred to Greek or Roman library "catalogs," but that word should be avoided in the ancient context, because for the modern reader it carries specific connotations, including publication information and a call number that tells the reader exactly where to find the book. This information is not provided in the *indices* of the Roman world. Lists are what we find, not catalogs, and "lists" or, for the sake of variety, "inventories" is what I will call them.

Beyond the names of authors, titles of works, and some additional information, the lists provide us with limited information on how the compilers conceptualized or organized their collections. Poetry is often, but not always, kept distinct from prose, and in several lists there are indications of an organization by genre or subject matter.[14] Lines or spaces are occa-

---

11. On the contents of *subscriptiones* and initial titles, see above in the introduction.

12. This may be an argument against the use of stichometric counts as bibliographic aids. If they had functioned as a way of identifying specific versions, and if it was at all important for collectors to know which version of a work they owned, we would have expected stichometric counts to appear in inventories. But they have not appeared in the lists discovered so far.

13. Sometimes there is one indication of the physical condition of a given work, and that is the listing of the specific books of the work that were to be found in the collection. Thus in list 1, the compiler noted the presence of Books 1, 2, and 5 of Hesiod's *Catalog of Women*, but omitted Books 3 and 4, which were, we may infer, absent from the collection.

14. We know that genre was a factor in the organization of Greco-Roman libraries from a source independent of our lists and collections. Herennius Philo, whose floruit was ca. AD 100, wrote a work Περὶ κτήσεως καὶ ἐκλογῆς βιβλίων ("On Buying and Collecting Books"). This work was in twelve books, of which the ninth was devoted to works by physicians and medical treatises. It is an easy inference that Herennius organized his study of libraries by genre and expected collectors to do the same with

sionally used, it appears, to distinguish between different parts of a collection, separating, say, the works of Xenophon from those of a series of poets. Clearly, though, many of the lists are not very well organized. Often the authors and titles are presented in no discernible order: not alphabetical, nor chronological, nor by genre. Authors who wrote in Latin are rare, but when they appear (as in list 3, lines 11 and 12, and in list 2, column 2, line 15) they seem to be mixed in with Greek. The probable inference to be drawn from this is that most of the collections were small, and no elaborate or systematic organization was needed. You might keep the book rolls of the *Iliad* in one container, but other, smaller works could be mixed together; to find what you wanted, you could just riffle through your collection.

2.5. WORKING WITH THE LISTS: PROBLEMS AND PAYOFFS

Several problems arise from the physical properties of the lists. They are fragments of papyri, often quite small and almost always damaged, and accordingly there are sometimes gaps in the surviving text, or letters that are present but difficult to read. Thus we often cannot know the name of an author or the title of a work, even though they were present in the original list. More importantly, we lack the beginnings and endings of most such lists. This means that we cannot tell the exact size of the original collection, and we have no evidence on the titles and authors it contained apart from those titles that survive in the list.[15] These shortcomings, being obvious, can generally be accommodated. We must simply use what we do have and avoid drawing inferences based on what is lacking.

More perplexing challenges arise not from the physical nature of the lists, but from the practices and intentions of the compilers. In several lists the compiler has left spaces, sometimes of a whole line (thus after line 10 in list 1), sometimes of a few letters.[16] In general, spaces of this sort seem to correspond to changes of author or genre in the list, but that is not always

---

their actual libraries. For the sources, see *RE* 8.653–54, s.v. Herennios 2 (Gudeman). We will see several indications of the use of genre as an organizing principle in our lists.

15. Lists 1, 3, and 6 are probably complete or nearly so, but they are very short. List 5 may represent a collection of several thousands of volumes. In list 4 we are given numbers of volumes—"142 philosophers," for example—that seem to represent subsections of the whole collection.

16. In list 1 there seems to be a space of some eight letters at the very beginning of the first line, before the name of Homer. What or who could possibly have taken precedence over Homer? (If the list were chronological, it might be Hesiod; but the list was not arranged chronologically.) We cannot know, since the letters are lost in a lacuna. Puglia (1998), 81, noted the problem and pointed out that something must have been written in this space, for a trace of one letter survives. Perhaps it identified the collection in some way, giving its location or the owner's name.

the case. In list 1, there appears to be no significant change of genre from line 10 to line 11, despite the blank line left between them. Perhaps such gaps were in some cases purely casual, or left in order to allow space for later insertions. We cannot assume that all gaps or spaces had the same function.

Few of the compilers of the lists that survive seem to have felt any need to be consistent in how they presented their material. In list 1 a change of title seems to be signaled in line 2 by a vertical stroke that follows Book 24 of the *Iliad* and precedes the *Odyssey*.[17] Elsewhere in this list, though, no such strokes appear, and whole authors simply follow one another with no sign of separation at all (lines 3, 4, 12) or perhaps, in some cases, with spaces left as indicators of change, as in lines 6 and 10. As a result, we will need to be cautious in basing conclusions upon assumptions of consistency. This becomes important when we apply some of the critical tools articulated by Enzo Puglia.[18] Three of these are of particular interest in this context and can be summarized as follows:

1. The inclusion of individual book numbers of a title probably means that the collection did not include a copy of every book in that work (Puglia [1998], 80). If the collection had contained every book, there would have been no need to enumerate the books.
2. When we find the title of a work in the genitive case, that probably indicates that book numbers followed, and so (in accordance with principle number 1) not all of the books in that work were present in the collection.
3. If a title appears in the nominative, it is likely that the work was present in its entirety in the collection.

These principles are logical and reasonable, but they cannot be relied on absolutely, because we must allow for inconsistencies and carelessness. If we find the title of a work in the nominative followed by a lacuna, we cannot be absolutely sure (in accordance with principle number 3) that the collection contained the entire work, because it is possible that in this case the compiler deviated from the usual and logical practice, putting the title in the nominative and then adding the book numbers of whatever books the collection contained. The lacuna would prevent us from knowing this.

17. Sijpesteijn and Worp (1974), 330, on line 10, call it a "horizontal dash," but in the photograph it appears clearly as a vertical stroke.

18. Puglia (1996a, 1996b, 1997a, 1998, 2000) has studied several of these lists in detail and with great acumen. I am very much in debt to his careful work.

We are, in short, dealing with probabilities rather than certainties; but in general these will be assumptions that have a high degree of probability.[19]

We must also note that we cannot know for sure if any given list was a preliminary and perhaps rough draft, or a final more polished draft, or the one and only draft.[20] In the first instance, we might imagine the compiler (or the compiler and an assistant) working through the collection shelf by shelf or container by container and writing down titles and book numbers as they came to them. In this case, if books were out of order on the shelves, they would be recorded out of order in the inventory, and perhaps left that way. But it would also be possible, once this first inventory had been made, to prepare a second, more orderly, list, with all books present in the collection listed in a sequence that the compiler regarded as logical and proper. In that case, the order of books in the inventory might not correspond to their organization on the shelves (or in containers) at all.

The three principles I outlined above, following Puglia, will hold true in the case of second drafts more reliably than in the case of first drafts, because as he revised his list and prepared a second draft of it, the compiler would know if he had found all of the books in a given work, and he would be able to list books in their proper order and sort the various titles according to some organizing principle such as genre or chronology. The compiler writing out the first draft, by contrast, would be dependent, to some extent, upon the ordering of the physical volumes in the collection, and he might list items out of order, miss some volumes, not attempt to arrange the titles in any systematic way, and so on. He could leave all of that for a revision, if he planned to do a revision. Thus first drafts will probably tell us more about the status of the physical collection—its arrangement or lack of it—while revised drafts are more likely to be consistent in following such principles as that of using the genitive of a title only when not all of the books of that title are present.

It is, of course, impossible to be sure if we are dealing in each case with a first or a revised list, but we can make reasoned guesses. List 1 appears to be informal and is most likely a first draft compiled directly from the collection of books, not from a preliminary list of them. The writing is erratic

---

19. Puglia (1998), in his reconstruction of list 1, seems to violate one of the principles that he had articulated. As he noted in his discussion of line 4, the addition of the numbers of individual books suggests that the collection did not include every book in the work. In lines 1 and 2, however, where the compiler listed the individual books of the *Iliad*, Puglia assumes that the collection did include every book in the work. Despite this, Puglia's observations in general seem valid and useful, and inconsistencies such as these are no doubt to be expected in our lists.

20. I owe this observation to Ann Kuttner.

in size and thickness, there are inconsistencies, and the list is written on a sheet of papyrus that contains several other documents as well. Similarly, list 4 is a wonderfully wild document, almost certainly a first draft drawn up during a survey of the physical books. (See Figure 5.) The script varies but is always informal; there are abbreviations, numbers are crossed through, and at one point two lines are squeezed together into the space of one line; large looping parentheses seem to be employed to distinguish parts of the collection. On the other hand, disorder in and of itself is not proof that the list is a preliminary draft, because we cannot assume that an ancient compiler would strive for the same kind of order that we do. This is clear from the formal lists of book collections in some late antique monasteries: the lists are carefully drawn up and clearly not first drafts, yet they may seem to us to present the monastery's holdings in a disorganized way.[21]

Another potential limitation on the utility of the lists arises from their provenance. All of these lists come from Egypt. Are inferences drawn from them valid for the rest of the Roman Empire, and in particular for Rome and Italy? The technology of the book roll—its physical characteristics and manner of production—was very much the same in Italy and in Egypt, to judge from the manuscripts found at Herculaneum and papyrus rolls known from Egypt. Also, readers and book collectors in Italy and Egypt seem to have behaved in very similar ways, as we saw in chapter 1: the concerns and practices of Cicero, Pliny, and Galen are reflected in those of the individuals we meet in the papyrological record. Thus, literary culture in general seems to have operated in very much the same way in Egypt as it did elsewhere, and there is no reason to believe that book collections and libraries in Egypt were different in any significant way from those in Italy and other areas.[22] I therefore take it as a given that any reader from Rome or Italy, looking through an Egyptian book collection, stepping into a library in Egypt, or reading a list of the contents of a collection, would immediately have recognized it for what it was, understood the ways in which it might have come into being and how it functioned, and felt perfectly at home.

21. See, for example, Coquin (1975), a catalog in which there are some logical groupings such as New Testament texts, but in which the same groupings reappear at more than one place in the list, while unrelated texts are intermingled with them. Another example is Crum (1893), 60–62, no. 44, in which the texts are, as Crum remarked, "not arranged according to their contents." Both of these lists are in Coptic.

22. Obviously, there is a difference in language. Most texts in Egyptian collections were in Greek, with a few in Latin or Coptic. Collections in Italy no doubt contained a higher proportion of texts in Latin than did collections in Egypt; but even here, Greek texts may have outnumbered Latin, at least in large scholarly collections, simply because so much more was written in Greek. Cf. Horsfall (1993), 59–60, for the period of the late Republic.

It is time to look at individual collections. They are of great interest, both individually and collectively, because they give us, despite the problems they present, a chance to look directly at book collections of the Roman period, and they provide us with information that is available from no other source. I will present and analyze in detail five lists as examples of variations on the theme, outline three additional lists more briefly, and then consider a number of topics—opisthographs, indications of organization, duplicate copies, and the like—which are best studied together rather than list by list. We begin with an example of a general collection of literature.

2.6. LIST 1: A GENERAL COLLECTION

List 1, *P.Vindob.* inv. G 39966, column 2 = Otranto number 3,
column 2 (Figure 2); Arsinoite nome, mid-first century AD

This is list 1 in appendix 1. It was written on the same reused scrap of papyrus as *P.Vindob.* inv. G 39966, column 1, a slightly shorter list that included only poetry.[23] List 1 included the following works:[24]

Homer, *Iliad*, possibly complete but more likely missing one or a few
books. The book numbers of Books 14–16 and 20–24 survive in the
papyrus.

Homer, *Odyssey*, possibly complete but perhaps missing one or more
books. There may have been two copies each of Books 3 and 4.

Hesiod, *Catalog of Women*.[25] Books 1, 2, and 5 are listed as present in
the collection. There may have been two copies of Book 5.

Hesiod, *Theogony*.

Hesiod, *Works and Days*.

---

23. For details on the physical properties of this papyrus, see the appendix. The list in column 1 is described briefly below as list 6. The two lists are quite different. Column 1 includes Pindar and probably Sappho but probably no or very limited prose, whereas column 2 includes a good deal of prose, but neither Pindar nor Sappho. It is possible that column 1 recorded a collection of rolls that existed at a certain time, that the collection evolved and changed, and that column 2 was a record of a later version of the same collection. Possibly the two lists have no relation to one another at all, each being the inventory of, say, a separate block purchase or inheritance.

24. The lines here do not correspond to the lines in the original Greek text. Here I arrange the material in a way that will make the authors present in the list readily apparent.

25. Many modern scholars assign the *Catalog of Women* to a period later than the time of the Hesiodic poems and thus to a different but unidentified poet, but the ancients took the *Catalog* as by Hesiod, and I will do the same. Similarly, I will not ordinarily take up discussions of authorship, as for example of Aristotle's (or the Aristotelian) *Constitution of the Athenians*. My concern is to see what texts the ancient collections contained and to treat them as their owners saw them, not to debate their authenticity.

Figure 2. P.Vindob. *inv. G 39966, column 2 = list 1. List of authors and works including poets and relatively obscure prose works. This list is in an upper corner of a papyrus that contains several other documents as well (not shown here). Image reproduced by permission of the Austrian National Library, Vienna.*

Callimachus, *Aetia*. Book 1 is listed. A lacuna follows, so we do not
know how many of the four books of the *Aetia* were present in the
collection.

Callimachus, *Hymns*.[26]

Callimachus, *Epigrams*.

Callimachus, *Hecale*.

Selections of (or from) the orators (or rhetoricians).[27]

A lexicon in at least thirteen books by an unknown author. Books 1–3,
6–8, and 10–13 are listed. The collection seems to have lacked Books
4, 5, and 9.[28]

Dionysius, an unknown work.

Ailianos = Aelianus (?), an unknown work.[29]

Peri epimones. Nothing is known of this work. It might be a treatise
on rhetoric, a speech, or a philosophical essay. It may be mentioned
twice in the list, either by mistake or because the collection
contained two copies of it (lines 9–10 and 13; in the latter case the
end of the author's name, -rius, survives), or perhaps there were two
distinct works bearing the same title, and the collection included
one copy of each.

Aeschines, *Against Ctesiphon*.[30]

Peri epimones. A second copy?

Demosthenes, *On the Crown*.

There can be no serious doubt that this is the inventory of some real collection of papyrus rolls. Individual books are counted, and some are found
missing. Others may be present in duplicate copies. The presence of a substantial number of obscure works almost certainly rules out the possibility
that this is the inventory of a merchant who prepared new copies of texts,
for it is difficult to imagine a scribe or bookseller preparing, on speculation,
most but not all of the books in a long lexicon, one and perhaps two copies
of a work *Peri epimones*, or works by Dionysius and Aelianus. It is, however,

26. Callimachus wrote six hymns, totaling something over a thousand lines. They could all have
fit in a single book roll.

27. It is not clear if this is a particular work—an anthology of passages from speeches, for example—or a heading inserted by the compiler to indicate the nature of what follows in the list.

28. The author's name ended in -doros. There is some uncertainty about exactly which book numbers survive.

29. The name of the author is very uncertain. Sijpesteijn and Worp (1974), 330, noted that one
could possibly read Ae[o]lidae instead.

30. This title, the second *Peri epimones*, and *On the Crown* are all separated from the earlier part
of the list by a space the height of one line. It is possible that they constitute a list of a small collection
of manuscripts that was distinct from, or stored apart from, those listed in lines 1–10.

possible that a bookseller had bought all or some of these volumes en bloc and was taking inventory of his purchase. In this scenario, too, we would have a collection of real books.

I take the list, then, as reflecting part or all of a collection of real books, and it is a very interesting collection. The three poets, Homer, Hesiod, and Callimachus, are classics and among the most popular authors in Roman Egypt; so far as we can tell, the collection included no obscure poets and no poets of the second rank.[31] The owner of the collection was able to gather most of the works of Hesiod and Callimachus and either all or almost all of the *Iliad* and *Odyssey*. The prose works in the collection, however, are strikingly different in nature. If the owner of the collection had gathered works of prose authors as well known and popular as the poets in his collection, he would have acquired copies of, say, Plato, Demosthenes, Thucydides, Herodotus, and Isocrates.[32] Apart from Demosthenes's *On the Crown*, however, none of these authors appears in this collection. Aeschines's *Against Ctesiphon* was well known,[33] but apart from that speech and *On the Crown*, all of the prose works in the collection are little known, problematic, or impossible to identify. They include a reference work (the lexicon), perhaps an anthology, works by Dionysius and perhaps someone named Aelianus, and one or two treatises entitled *Peri epimones*. In terms of period, the datable works are mostly archaic to classical (Homer, Hesiod, Aeschines, Demosthenes), but the Hellenistic period is represented by at least Callimachus, and, if the reading Aelianus is correct, we probably have a Roman author. At least five genres are represented: epic, short epic (Hesiod and Callimachus's *Hecale*), elegiacs (Callimachus's *Hymns*), orations, one or two reference works, and perhaps a philosophical work, the *Peri epimones*. In short, this is an eclectic collection, with absolutely standard choices on the poetry side and almost equally nonstandard works in prose.

The compiler seems to have divided the list into three sections. The first certainly consists of works of poetry (Homer, Hesiod, and Callimachus), and is separated from the second section by a blank space, some eight letters in length, that follows Callimachus's *Hecale* in line 6. The second section consists, so far as we can tell, entirely of prose works.[34] It may con-

---

31. Krüger (1990), 214, lists them as the first, second, and third most frequently attested poets at Oxyrhynchus.

32. These are the five most frequently found prose writers at Oxyrhynchus: Krüger (1990), 214.

33. At least twenty-seven copies of Aeschines's *Against Ctesiphon* survive in papyri from Egypt (MP^3 9.02–18.04).

34. It is not known for sure that the *Peri epimones* and the treatises by Dionysius and Aelianus were in prose, but the identifiable works after Callimachus's *Hecale* are all prose, and any work of

tinue until the end of the list, but there is a second break, this time of a full line, following the first mention of the *Peri epimones* in lines 9 and 10, and that break may indicate that what follows in lines 12 to 14 constituted, in the compiler's mind, a third and distinct group of manuscripts. Perhaps the last three works—Aeschines, a *Peri epimones*, and Demosthenes— were all speeches, while the works in the second group were not themselves speeches but rather treatises and reference works dealing with rhetoric: one or more lexicons, an anthology, and the unknown works of Dionysius and Aelianus.[35] It is also possible that this division of the list into three sections reflects a physical division of the manuscripts in the collection, with each group stored, for example, on a separate set of shelves or in its own container. In any case, the collector was presumably a serious reader, for he was willing to seek out, acquire, and perhaps consult a lexicon that ran to at least thirteen rolls.

2.7. LIST 2: A FOCUSED COLLECTION

List 2, *P.Ross.Georg.* 1.22 = Otranto number 15 (Figure 3); Memphis, first half of the third century A D

This is list 2 in appendix 1. It is arranged in two columns, and there may have been further columns preceding, following, or both. Written on the recto, with the verso left blank, the list was set out and copied with care. The margins at the top and between columns are fairly generous, the cursive script is regular and generally clear, there are few abbreviations (even the genitive case endings being written out in full), and there is only one probable mistake.[36] For each work, the compiler recorded the author's name and then the title of the work, generally entering only one title on each line. In two cases—lines 1.8 and 1.21—specific book numbers are added. Given the careful formatting, it would seem that the person who prepared the list, or who had it prepared, thought of it as being worth some time and trouble.

In light of this careful preparation, it is surprising to find that the list is poorly organized. Aristotle, Chrysippus, and Theophrastus all appear in both column 1 and column 2. Works that one would expect to find listed

---

which the title begins with *peri* is almost certainly prose. It is an easy inference that this part of the list consisted entirely of prose works.

35. In this case, the *Peri epimones* in lines 9–10 might have been a rhetorical work on the figure of speech that consists of "persisting with a particular point," while the *Peri epimones* in line 13 was, like the items that precede and follow it, a speech. See the commentary in appendix 1 for these possibilities.

36. In line 1.13 (i.e., column 1, line 13), πολιτεία (*politeia*) was written as the genitive πολιτείας (*politeias*).

Figure 3. P.Ross.Georg. 1.22 = list 2. Fragment of a papyrus with a list of authors and their works, arranged in two columns. Most of the right-hand column has been lost. Image reproduced by permission of the National Library of Russia, St. Petersburg.

together, such as Aristotle's two constitutions (1.12, 1.22) or the three writers (or titles) classed as "Socratic" (1.14, 1.19, 1.23) are not grouped together. Authors are not arranged alphabetically, as they often are in other lists, and they are not organized chronologically, by philosophical school, or in any other discernible order. It will be worth our while, then, to do our own organizing. If we arrange the authors chronologically and omit those who cannot be identified at all, the contents of the collection appear as follows.

Author	Title	Date	Line
Crito, Socratic	?	400S BC	1.14
Simon, Socratic	?	400S	1.19
Cebes, Socratic	?	400S	1.23
Hippias	?	400S	2.11
Aristotle	*Constitution of the Athenians*	300S	1.12
Aristotle	*Constitution of the Neapolitans*	300S	1.22
Aristotle	?	300S	2.22
Theophrastus	?	300S	2.10
Theophrastus	*On Wisdom*	300S	1.10
Chrysippus	*Handbook of Arguments and Moods*, Book 1	200S	1.20
Chrysippus	?	200S	2.19
Chrysippus	?	200S	2.21
Archimedes?	?	ca. 287–218	2.18
Diogenes (of Babylonia?)	*On Avoiding Grief*	240–150	1.16
Posidonius	*On Anger*, selection(s) from Book 1	130–50 BC	1.8
Pseudo-Aristotle	*On Virtue*	100 BC–AD 100	1.7
Dio (of Prusa)	*On Distrust* = Speech 74	AD 50–110	1.11
Apion	rhetoric?	1st cent. AD?	2.1
Theodas	*Basic Principles*	100–150	1.9
Incertus	(. . .)estius's selections of Socratic letters	200S	1.1–2
[N]igrinus (?)	*Apologies*	?	1.15
Incertus	Talks (or Speeches) to the Tyrians	?	1.17
Aelius	?	Empire?	2.15

From its very first publication, the list was identified as philosophical in character, and it is easy to see why. Four famous philosophers—Aristotle, Theophrastus, Chrysippus, and Posidonius—appear, and at least three of the great philosophical traditions are represented, namely the Academics, the Peripatetics, and the Stoics.[37] We find forms that are typical of philosophical literature: there are dialogues (1.14, 1.19, 1.23), letters (1.1–2), speeches (1.17), and treatises on such traditional topics as wisdom, grief, anger, virtue, and mistrust. The few nonphilosophical works included— medicine (Theodas, 1.9), Aristotle's two accounts of city constitutions (Athens, 1.12; and Neapolis, 1.22), perhaps rhetoric (Apion, 2.1), and possibly mathematics (Archimedes, 2.18)—are all closely related to philosophy, and all are prose. No poetry has crept into the collection, or at least into the part of it that survives.

For all of its focus on philosophical works, however, the collection is remarkably wide-ranging in dates, topics, and character. Although more than half of the titles are certainly or probably to be dated in the fifth, fourth, or third centuries BC, later periods are represented as well, for Posidonius was active in the second and first centuries BC, Dio of Prusa in the first and second centuries AD, and Theodas in the second century AD.[38] There are treatises on abstract concepts, but there are also Aristotle's two semihistorical works in political science, a medical treatise, and perhaps works on mathematics or physics (2.18). There may be a novel (1.5–6).[39] The owner acquired (knowingly or not) at least two spurious works, the pseudo-Aristotelian *On Virtue* of line 1.7 and the collection of Socratic letters (1.1–2), and at least one condensed version of a larger work, the selections from Book 1 of Posidonius's *On Anger* (1.8).

Although there are several great names, we have in this part of the list no major work of any philosopher, with the possible exception of Aristotle's *Constitution of the Athenians*.[40] Other than that, the works inventoried here are not famous now, and they were not famous in the third century. A

37. Academy: Letters of Socratics, and probably the works listed as by Crito, Simon, and Cebes. Peripatetics: Aristotle, Theophrastus. Stoics: Chrysippus, Diogenes.

38. In addition, the Apion mentioned in line 2.1 may be the Apion we know from the first century AD, and the "Letters of the Socratics" (lines 1.1–2) have been dated to the second and third centuries AD, although the owner of the collection may have thought of them as much earlier in date. The Aelius of line 2.15 was probably also Roman imperial in date.

39. On these problematic lines, see the commentary in appendix 1. It is also possible that these lines referred to a geographical work.

40. The ancients may have valued this work highly. It is cited by several ancient sources (Kenyon [1892], viii–ix), and there appears to have been a commentary on it, indicating scholarly interest (*MP*[3] 163.1). Two papyrus copies are known, *MP*[3] 163 and 164).

significant number of them are known to have been short, or parts of larger works. Dio's *On Distrust* survives and is a brief treatise of a dozen pages or so. The collection had only one book each of Chrysippus's *Handbook* and Posidonius's *On Anger*, not the complete works. The works, perhaps Socratic dialogues, of Crito, Simon, and Cebes (if these are rightly taken as authors) were, it seems, short, since between three and seventeen of them could fit in a single papyrus roll.[41] In fact, nothing prevents us from taking every item on this list as quite short, occupying a part of a roll or at most a single roll, and there are no indications of the presence of multivolume works, with the possible exception of Theodas's medical work.[42] This, then, is a list of particular interest: its owner had a broad range of interests that extended to less important authors and relatively obscure works. He sought such works out and, it seems, acquired them. In this respect, he is quite different from most other ancient collectors known to us.[43]

2.8. LIST 3: A LIST THAT EMPHASIZES THE PHYSICAL NATURE OF THE ROLLS AND OTHER OBJECTS

List 3, *P.Jena* inv. 267 = *P.Turner* 39 = Otranto number 14 (Figure 4)

This is list 3 in appendix 1. Despite its brevity, this is a very interesting inventory. It consists of three fragments of papyrus, two of which are very small. Together, they provide a list of book rolls and domestic objects. One of the two small papyrus fragments, which cannot be placed in any certain relation to the main fragment, mentions "two volumes" (τόμοι β'). Whether these two volumes were blank rolls ready for use, or used rolls for which the compiler simply chose not to record the contents, is not certain.[44] In the largest surviving fragment, the compiler listed: an unknown work by a Philemon (perhaps a comedy, or a grammatical work, or other; several Philemons are known); a commentary by Eratosthenes on some aspect, presumably geographical, of the *Iliad*; a lexicon of Plato (either the phi-

---

41. If those names are taken as titles rather than as authors' names, we would apparently have three dialogues, each perhaps a book roll in length.

42. We know of three works by Theodas. Galen wrote commentaries on two of them, one in five books, the other in three. That would seem to imply that at least those two treatises of Theodas were multivolume works. References in *RE* 5A.2:1713–14, s.v. Theodas (W. Capelle).

43. Needless to say, he may well have owned the standard works—Homer, Euripides, Plato, and so on—as well. They may have appeared in a part of the list that is now lost. But the contents of the list that survive clearly show him moving well beyond the classics.

44. Since the compiler later duly records the contents of two rolls that contained registers of taxes and (perhaps) citizens, it may be best to take these two rolls as blank.

Figure 4. P.Jena *inv. 267* = *list 3.*
Three fragments from one papyrus,
containing a short list of book
rolls and domestic objects. Image
reproduced by permission of the
Friedrich-Schiller Universität,
Jena, from http://www.uni-jena
.de/Papyrussammlung.html.

losopher or the playwright); a commentary on the poetry, probably epic, of a certain Priscus, who may be a Roman author contemporary with Ovid; and an encomium on an unknown subject by a Rufus, again perhaps a Roman author, to judge from his name. Immediately after these five works of or pertaining to literature, the compiler recorded a register of payments and a register of the inhabitants (?) of Dios[polis]. He then left a space of two lines, and following that entered "cellaria," which may mean storerooms or containers, "iron knife," and "tin containers."

At least three types of materials are mentioned in this papyrus: literary or paraliterary texts, documents (the two sets of "registers"), and domestic objects. Our primary interest is in the collection of texts, which despite its brevity is quite distinctive in character. With two commentaries and one or two lexicons, it centers on aids to reading or understanding, rather than on works of literature themselves. It is a remarkably wide-ranging collection given its size, pointing to an owner of eclectic tastes who was interested in Homer, Latin poetry, Greek geography, Roman-era encomiastic literature, probably drama, and perhaps philosophy.

The nonbook objects are of interest as well. The knife—useful for trimming and repairing papyri—and the tin containers, protection against insects and mice, can readily be taken as useful in the maintenance of book rolls or papyrus documents.[45] Before these items the compiler recorded κελλάρια (= *cellaria*), a loan word from Latin with a wide range of meanings: it might refer to shelves; it might also mean more generally cabinets or ceramic jars, and it could even mean storerooms.[46] Finally, the "two volumes" entered in one of the small detached fragments could obviously be relevant to the work of a scribe. It is possible, but far from certain, that the whole inventory consists of items produced or used by a person who was active in copying, whether for his own or someone else's use.

The papyrus as a whole also shows a connection to or interest in things Roman that is unusual in Egypt: among the book rolls, both Priscus and Rufus are Roman names, and in the second half of the list we have two Latin loanwords, *salarium* ("payments," line 13) and *cellaria* in line 15. The

---

45. So Puglia (2000), 196–97. I have found no other examples of a tin container used to protect book rolls in a library or book collection, but the word ἀγγεῖον appears in a papyrus of the second century AD (*P.Tor.* 1 and 4) with the meaning of receptacle or box. Extended discussion of this phrase: Casanova (2001), 236–37, with n. 49.

46. Shelves: Puglia (2000), 195–96; cabinets: Poethke (1981), 165. Both Poethke (1981), 164, and Otranto (2000), 76, remarked on the inclusion (unique to this papyrus) of three types of materials. For *cellaria*, see also appendix 1.

inventory may have been prepared in the context of an inheritance, perhaps as a partial listing of assets.[47]

2.9. LIST 4: A SPECIALIZED COLLECTION IN AN INFORMAL INVENTORY WITH SEVERAL UNIQUE FEATURES

List 4, *P.Vars.* 5 verso = Otranto number 17 (Figure 5);
Arsinoite nome, third century AD

This is list 4 in appendix 1. A single strip of papyrus, 31 cm high, contains a column of text, much of which is lost. The list provided, on the left, the names of authors in the genitive case and, on the right, numbers corresponding to each name, evidently the number of rolls of that author's work (or of the particular title) in the collection. Few of the authors' names survive intact, and most are lost entirely. In the lower half of the list, the format changes, and we apparently have summary sections that provide total numbers of rolls, the numbers of rolls that are opisthographs, and, it seems, some distinction between rolls stored in one place and those stored in another.

There can be no reasonable doubt that we are dealing with real physical manuscripts: both the individual and summary numbers of book rolls and the attention paid to exact counts of opisthographic texts make that clear. But it is also clear that this is a rough inventory, not an elegant catalog. (See Figure 5.) There are numerous abbreviations: the word opisthograph (always spelled opistograph in this list) is abbreviated as ὀπιστογρ (*opistogr*) in lines 20, 22bis, 24, and 26a; the final sigma is omitted in the genitive forms of the names Glaucon (20), Xenophon (21), Themison (26b), and Harpocration (33); and, in line 22, the word γίνεται (*ginetai*) is abbreviated to just the gamma. Mistakes are crossed through in lines 18 and 24, and in line 28 the number 266 was corrected to 296. The apparent insertion of lines 26a and 26b into an existing space, the crowding in of line 22bis, and the use of encircling parentheses to separate off whole sections of the text are consistent with what one might expect a provisional list to look like. The list also changes in appearance and to some extent in content at about line 20, as we will see.

Lines 1–18 seem to be straightforward in form. On the left, the compiler listed a series of names of authors, most of which are now lost, and to the right of the names he added one number for each name, presumably

47. As suggested by Puglia (2000), 198. How or why the owner obtained and kept a record of the residents (or some other countable element) of the town of Dios[polis] we cannot know.

Figure 5. P.Vars. *5 verso = list 4. A long, highly fragmentary list of, it seems, philosophical and medical writers. Note the encircling lines and parentheses and, in general, the disorderly nature of the list. Image reproduced by permission of the Department of Papyrology, University of Warsaw.*

the number of book rolls by that author present in the collection. Two of the names that survive in these lines (Diogenes of Babylonia and Hierocles) are those of philosophers, Geminus could be a philosopher, and in line 19 there is a summing up that counts 142 books "of philosophers." We may safely conclude that the section of the inventory that extends from line 1 to line 19 dealt with the works of philosophical writers.

Lines 20–22 have been variously interpreted. Manteuffel, Manfredi, and Otranto, noting the names of the medical writers Thessalus, Erasistratus, and Themison in lines 23 to 26b, took the authors named in lines 20–22 also as medical writers.[48] In that case, the sum of "142 (rolls) of philosophers" in line 19 would end the first section of the inventory, and from line 20 on would be medical writers. Puglia, however, noting that lines 20–22 begin with the word "opisthographs" and seem to be set off from the preceding and following material by the encircling parentheses, suggested that these lines, like line 19, contain a summary of what preceded, but that in this case it is a summary not of all the rolls of philosophers, but of those rolls that were opisthographs. If Puglia is correct, the authors named in lines 20–22 are philosophers, not medical writers, their names must have occurred earlier in the list as well as here, and the total of fourteen volumes given in line 22 would be the number of opisthographs found among the 142 philosophical texts.[49] I am inclined to agree with Puglia, but the matter is far from certain, and these lines should not be regarded as certain evidence for the identity of the authors represented in the collection.

At this point—that is, after line 22—the list changes in form and to some extent in content. We no longer have a simple list of names on the left and numbers on the right, and the main column of text shifts to the right, so that more of it is preserved. Surviving names, as we have seen, include Thessalus, the author of one roll (line 23), Erasistratus and Themison in lines 26a and 26b, and Harpocration in line 33. All of these men were certainly or possibly medical writers, and the fragments of other names that survive in this section could also be those of medical writers.[50] We have, thus, a sec-

---

48. Manteuffel (1933), 372–73; Manfredi in *CPF* I.1*, p. 104; Otranto (2000), 102–3. Otranto (2000), 102, provides a convenient discussion of the medical writers with whom the men named here might be identified. There are several possibilities each for Xenophon and Chrysippus.

49. Puglia (1996a), 28–29, pointed out that the fragmentary name]ους in line 21 might be the genitive of a name that in the nominative ends in -ης. The person named here therefore could be Hierocles, who appeared earlier in line 11 as author of nine opisthographic volumes, precisely the number mentioned in line 21. Also, Xenophon could be the author whose name is lost in line 12, and Chrysippus in line 17. In both of those lines opisthographic texts are mentioned. All of the names could be those of philosophers, but they could also be those of medical writers.

50. For the identifications, see Otranto (2000), 103.

ond part of the book collection, dedicated to medical treatises rather than to philosophers, but it was apparently organized in the same way as the list of philosophers was earlier: first, names of authors, with the number of volumes and opisthographs of each (lines 23–25); then a sum total of the number of volumes (perhaps thirteen, line 26), and finally a recapitulation and summary count of the opisthographs (perhaps 11, lines 26a-26b).[51]

Line 25 begins with uncertain letters, probably a -κο, and then gives us νάρθηξ, "narthex."[52] The editors of *CPF* took this in its meaning of "container," so that this line would say something like, "of such and such an author, one container full of books." This is, as Puglia pointed out, an oddly imprecise way of inventorying books in a list which elsewhere is very precise, providing specific numbers for each author and work and for the opisthographic volumes. "Narthex" is used elsewhere as the title of pharmacological works, and Puglia accordingly suggested that we should take it here as a title.[53] That is the most likely explanation for the word, but the matter must remain uncertain, because no other title appears anywhere in what survives of this list.[54]

In the latter part of the list, we find what may be a reference to different places of storage of volumes. The rolls are divided between those that are "present"—προκ(είμενα) in line 27, προκειμένων in line 30—and "others" (ἕτερα, line 31); these "others" may be volumes stored elsewhere and therefore not "present." It is also possible, however, that they were simply inventoried separately. In either case, we have here an indication of some sort of organization of the collection in addition to the division between philosophical and medical works.

In contrast to most of our lists, not much can be learned about the specific authors and titles included in the collection beyond the obvious fact that it included substantial numbers of philosophical, and at least some

51. The numbers are quite uncertain. Puglia, following Manteuffel, read line 26 as a gamma, and supplied an iota before that to give the number 13, that is, a total of thirteen volumes on medical matters. The total of opisthographic volumes among these is not preserved in the fragment of the papyrus, but Puglia (1997a), 133, reckoned it at eleven. That would mean that only two of the medical volumes were not opisthographs.

52. Puglia (1997a), 133–34. If the letters that survive before "narthex" are -κο, they may be all that survives of a name that ended in -κος or -κου, with the last letter omitted in abbreviation.

53. We know of pharmacological works entitled *Narthex* by Heras, Cratippus, and Soranus. See Puglia (1997a), 134; cf. Marganne (2004), 122–27.

54. Marganne (2004), 122–27, discusses the term in the medical context. It was used of small cases for medical instruments or drugs, and thus it came to be applied also to collections of recipes for medications. Otranto (2000), 103, emphasizing the absence of titles in the list, takes "narthex" as a small carrying case or, perhaps, a codex. So, too, Casanova (2001), 237. This list, however, is a particularly disorganized one, and the inclusion of one title is not impossible.

medical, texts. Excluding the authors named in lines 20–22 and 33–34, because they cannot be identified with any certainty, and arranging the remaining writers in chronological order insofar as possible, we have the following.

Line	Name	Subject	Dates of Author's Life	The Author Is Probably to Be Identified with …
26a	Erasistratus	Medicine	4th–3rd centuries BC	Erasistratos 3, *RE* 6.333–50 (Wellmann)
3	Diogenes of Babylonia, 1 roll	Philosophy (Stoic)	ca. 240–150 BC	Diogenes 15, *DNP* 3.60 (Inwood)
2	Geminus,[55] 1 roll	Philosophy?	1st century BC?	Geminus 1, *RE* 7.1026–50 (Tittel)
26b	Themison (of Laodicea), 9 rolls	Medicine	late 1st century BC	Themison 7, *RE* 5A.1632–38 (Deichgräber)
23	Thessalus (of Tralles?), 1 roll	Medicine	1st century AD?	Thessalos 6, *RE* 6A.168–82 (Diller)
11	Hierocles, 9 rolls	Philosophy (Stoic)	2nd century AD	Hierokles 17, *RE* 8.1479 (Von Arnim)

In addition, a "Socratic" writer is listed in line 5 as author of one book roll; Zeno of Tarsus (a Stoic) and Zeno of Citium are probably to be restored in lines 9 and 10 respectively; and an unidentifiable Harpocration appears in line 33.[56] We thus have a collection that ranged widely in date (the authors represented cover a period of more than five hundred years) and that clearly included a substantial number of philosophical texts and at least some writers who were not particularly famous.[57] This list, however, is of interest not so much for the authors it names as for other matters.

55. This may be the Geminus who wrote extensively on mathematics and natural history and was an associate of Posidonius. If so, he would date to the first century BC.

56. Otranto (2000), 101, surveys the earlier suggestions for lines 9 and 10. The two Zenos seem reasonably secure. Harpocration is not: Otranto (2000), 104, cites one philosopher and two medical writers by that name.

57. It is possible that well-known philosophers were present as well. As Puglia (1996a), 30, noted,

First, consider the large numbers that stand by themselves: "142 of philosophers" in line 19; "296" in line 28; and "59" in line 36. The first of these, 142, can reasonably be taken as a reckoning up of all the book rolls of philosophical works. The second, 296, seems to give the number of all the book rolls inventoried to that point and present, it appears, in some particular place or collection.[58] The last number, 59, which follows a reference in line 31 to "others" (i.e., other book rolls) and the names of at least three writers, would thus seem to be not a part of the collection of 296, but a separate collection of some sort. Thus the whole collection may have consisted of at least 296 plus 59 book rolls, for a total of 355.

Another conclusion emerges from the figure of 142 rolls "of philosophers" in line 19. As Puglia noted, the total number of book rolls listed in lines 1 to 17 is not 142 but 118, meaning that 24 rolls of philosophical works must have been listed on a preceding column or papyrus sheet. We can perhaps go further. Those 24 rolls cannot have taken up a whole column, given that our one surviving column runs to at least 35 lines and probably more. Perhaps, then, the preceding column began with works in a different subject or genre—rhetoric, say, or history—and then turned to the philosophical works. We may, then, have a collection of 296 manuscripts: 142 "of philosophers" (lines 1–17), of which 14 were opisthographs (lines 20–22); 13 of medical writers (lines 23–25, summed up in line 26), of which 10 or 11 were opisthographs (lines 26a-26b); and 141 of other subjects or genres, listed in a preceding section of the inventory that is now lost.[59]

All of the scholars who have worked on this papyrus have remarked on how markedly it differs from other lists of book rolls. Titles are not given after an author's name, the one possible exception being the problematic "narthex" in line 25, and specific book numbers are omitted as well. Instead, we are given the total number of rolls of an author's work(s) present in the collection. Clearly, exactly which books of which works were present

---

Plato might have appeared in line 15 as the author of the thirty-two rolls counted there. Also, Aristotle could have appeared earlier in the list, where some twenty-four rolls were written by authors whose names began with the letters alpha, beta, or gamma.

58. Otranto (2000), 100, noted that the figure of 296 might refer just to the collection of medical texts, but that is unlikely. If we assume that every numeral that appears in lines 20 to 27 gives a count of medical volumes, that no volumes are counted twice (once in an original listing and a second time in a summing-up figure), and that after Xenophon we should read not 2 or 2 corrected to 3, but 23, then we arrive at a total of 71 volumes, far short of 296. It is possible that some numbers have been lost in these lines, but it is highly improbable that they could have totaled 225 volumes. The number of 296 must surely be the cumulative count of all volumes in all subjects to this point.

59. In assessing the list this way, I accept the principal hypotheses of Puglia (1996a and 1997a). He too arrives at a figure of some 141 manuscripts not accounted for in what survives of the inventory: Puglia (1997a), 134.

was not important to the compiler of the list. Instead, as several scholars have remarked, it is the physical nature of the rolls that seems to have been paramount in the compiler's mind: exactly how many rolls are there? How many manuscripts are there in each of the subject categories? How many of them are opisthographs? And how many are "present here," and how many "others" are there? These are the questions he seems to have been asking and trying to answer. This has suggested to some that the list may represent not a personal collection of manuscripts, but rather the stock in hand of a bookseller or scribe, but that is unlikely. If these were books ordered by a customer, why are there no titles? And why would a customer specify that certain works, and not others, should be opisthographs? Nor is it likely that any book dealer would prepare manuscripts of these relatively obscure authors on speculation. If a dealer did have such texts copied by his scribes, surely he would want his inventory to include the titles of the works he had on hand.[60] We cannot know the exact circumstances under which, or the purposes for which, this inventory was prepared, but it may well be some sort of first assessment of a newly acquired collection on the occasion of, say, an inheritance or the bulk purchase of a collection.[61] One can imagine that the *index* that Tiro created for Cicero, with which we began this chapter, might have looked something like this list when Tiro first compiled it. The new owner perhaps wanted a quick count and a rough idea of the contents and quality of the collection: hence the raw numbers, the organization by subject, the indication of opisthographs, and the messy nature of the list itself.

60. Otranto 2000, 104, noted that the counts of opisthographic rolls, which presumably differed in price from nonopisthographic ones, suggest that the list was drawn up with the needs of a bookseller in mind: the two counts would help him determine the value of the rolls. A dealer, however, would need much more information than that before determining the cost of a roll. He would probably want to know the title of the work(s), and he would certainly need to know how long the roll was and how many lines of text were in it. The absence of any stichometric counts or the like in the figures given in the papyrus weakens the argument that the list was intended to help a dealer as he priced the collection.

61. The collection, which was, as we have seen, divided into the volumes "present" and "others," may have come in two parts or have consisted of two separate groups of manuscripts, or simply have been housed, permanently or temporarily, in two separate spaces.

2.10. LIST 5: A BOOK LIST THAT MAY COME FROM A MUNICIPAL, INSTITUTIONAL, OR VERY LARGE PRIVATE LIBRARY

List 5, *P.Oxy.* 33.2659 = Otranto number 6 (Figure 6);
Oxyrhynchus, second century AD

This is list 5 in appendix 1. What survives in *P.Oxy.* 33.2659 is part of a list of writers of Old Comedy, with one writer, Ararus, who is usually now assigned to Middle Comedy.[62] The list was copied out with considerable care: the script is clear and uniform, the left margin of column 2 is straight and even, and there are few mistakes and corrections.[63] (See Figure 6.) It seems to be too long, and too carefully drafted, to be a list of desiderata or a teacher's assigned reading; it is almost certainly not part of a scholarly work on, say, comedy, since numerous titles that would have been known to any ancient scholar are here omitted;[64] and it seems to be too long and too complete to have served as the inventory of a dealer's or scribe's stock in hand. In addition, three works of Epicharmus are named twice, so that the collection probably included some duplicates: in column 2 *Harpaga*[?] appears in line 35, *Harpaga.*[?] in line 37; plays probably named *Dionysoi* occur in lines 41 and 42; and *Epinic(ius)* is entered in both lines 44 and 45.[65] The available evidence, that is, points to this being the book list of a substantial library, and that is how the papyrologists have taken it.[66]

62. Ararus was neither prolific nor well known, and he is not assigned to Middle Comedy by any ancient source (see Nesselrath [1990], 58–63), although his dates are consistent with Middle Comedy. He was the son of Aristophanes, who follows in this list, and so perhaps he was associated with him and for that reason included in the list. It is also possible that Ararus's inclusion is a reflection of where his manuscripts were stored (that is, his manuscripts might have been on the same shelf as those of, say, Apollonius and Apollophanes), or that he is listed here simply by mistake.

63. Rea, ad *P.Oxy.* 33.2659, noted one possible mistake, or carelessness in writing, in column 1, line 5.

64. Details are in Otranto (2000), 33–36. Titles of plays by Apollophanes, Archippus, Diocles, and probably Aristophanes and Dinolochus are omitted. At column 1, line 40, the compiler entered "Plutus A," and so clearly knew that a *Plutus B* existed but did not mention it. That is a strong indication that this is an inventory of real book rolls, not a bibliographical list or a list attached to a biography. See also Rea, ad *P.Oxy.* 33.2659, 70.

65. There is room for doubt that these are duplicate copies. The *Harpaga[e?]* in column 2, line 37, is out of alphabetical order and so might just be a mistake (so Rea, ad *P.Oxy.* 33.2659), and the endings of the titles of the plays *Dionys-* and *Epinic-* are missing, so we cannot be absolutely sure that the titles were identical. It is also odd that in a collection containing, so far as we know, no other duplicates, we have here three pairs of duplicates in eleven lines. There may be some factor or problem of which we are not aware, but it is easier to assume duplicates in the collection than to explain the repetitions in any other way.

66. Otranto (2000), 37, with n. 17.

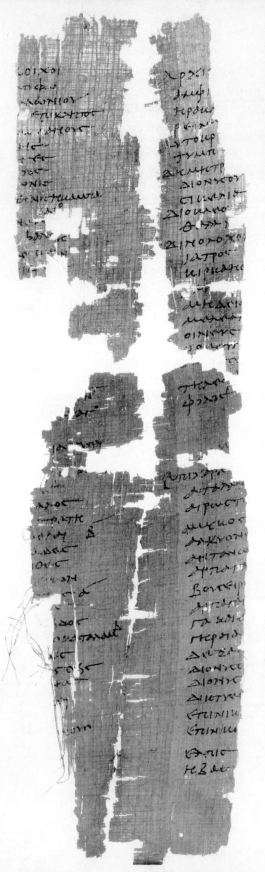

Figure 6. P.Oxy. 33.2659 = list 5. List of writers of comedy and their works, in alphabetical order. Compare the careful, neat organization here to the list in Figure 5. Photograph courtesy of the Egypt Exploration Society. Digital image courtesy of The Imaging Papyri Project, University of Oxford.

Since neither the beginning nor the end of the list survives, we cannot know exactly what it contained nor how long it was, but it is well worth comparing the authors' names in the list to a list of all those writers of Old Comedy whose names begin with the letters alpha through epsilon and would, if they were included in this list, fall between Amipsias and Epicharmus, the first and last authors mentioned in the surviving fragment. We can compile a list of Old Comedy authors from *Poetae comici Graeci*, volumes 1, 2, 4, and 5; in the list I give below, the names of authors who appear in *P.Oxy.* 33.2659 are printed in **bold**, while the names of those authors who are known from some ancient source but are not mentioned in *P.Oxy.* 33.2659 are in *italics*. The resulting list:

Amipsias
Apollonius
Apollophanes
Ararus
Arcesilaus
Archippus
Aristagoras
Aristomenes
Aristonymus
Aristophanes
Autocrates
Demetrius
Dinolochus
Diocles
[Diop]ithes
Ecphantides
Epicharmus
Epilycus

Of the eighteen known authors of Old Comedy in this part of the alphabet, eleven (if we include Ararus) appear in our list. Of the seven who do not, Epilycus is of uncertain date,[67] Arcesilaus is known only from a reference in Diogenes Laertius (4.45), we have the title of only one play by Aristagoras,[68] and [Diop]ithes is known only from an inscription, although he was at least a prize-winning poet.[69] The other three—Aristomenes, Aristonymus, and

---

67. *PCG* 5.170–73. Kassel and Austin assign him to the fifth or fourth century BC.
68. *PCG* 2.558–59, the *Mommacuthus*.
69. *IG* II² 2325.51, in a list of the victors at the Dionysia. Cf. *PCG* 5.43.

Ecphantides—are somewhat better known, with five, two, and two attested titles, respectively.[70]

We can also compare the totals of known titles by Aristophanes and Epicharmus to those in *P.Oxy.* 33.2659. Aristophanes first: twenty-four titles of his plays are present in the papyrus, and eleven or twelve more would have fit in the lacuna in column 1, for a total of about thirty-five. Thus more than three-quarters of the forty-four plays traditionally ascribed to Aristophanes were present in this collection. The case of Epicharmus is similar. Of the fifteen comedies whose titles fall alphabetically between the *Agrostinus* and the *Hebas [Gamos]*, only two are missing in the list of *P.Oxy.* 33.2659: *Bacchae* and *Heorta*.

In short, what we might call the coverage of Old Comedy in this collection was excellent. It is possible that this was a specialist's collection, owned by a scholar or wealthy individual who took a particular interest in comedy. Certainly specialist collections existed: we have just looked at a papyrus that recorded a substantial collection of philosophical volumes, and the Villa of the Papyri at Herculaneum provides archaeological evidence for a collection that included many works on ethics and aesthetics. But it is also possible that this is part of the inventory of a much more comprehensive collection, one that included not only comedy but tragedy and the other genres of poetry, and not only poetry but prose as well. If that is the case, and if we assume that other genres and subject areas were as fully represented in the collection as we know Old Comedy was, we can readily postulate a collection extending to several thousand volumes. *P.Oxy.* 33.2659 may well be part of the book list of an institutional, municipal, or unusually large personal collection.

Such a possibility is consistent with the physical characteristics of *P.Oxy.* 33.2659. (See Figure 6.) First, the list was organized and drafted with considerable care, as we noted above. John Rea, in his comments on *P.Oxy.* 33.2659, noted that it was written "in a small fluent hand, which used cursive letter forms . . . but wrote without any excessive speed and very clearly." The authors' names are alphabetized even, in most cases, beyond the first letter, making it easy for anyone consulting the list to determine if the author he was seeking was present in the collection. There are very few abbreviations and hardly any mistakes. This is not a hastily prepared, informal inventory like lists 1 and 4 in our catalog. Instead, everything points to its being a list prepared with the user's convenience in mind. And although *P.Oxy.* 33.2659 is written on the verso of an older document, that docu-

---

70. Aristomenes: *PCG* 2.562–68. Aristonymus: *PCG* 2.571–73. Ecphantides: *PCG* 5.126–29.

ment was not very old when the book list was written. Rea, who edited both texts, dated the Greek-to-Latin glossary of the recto to the "first or early second century," and the book list to the second century. Thus the compiler of the list may have purposely chosen a book roll that was still relatively new and in good shape. Glossaries such as the one on the recto of this roll were sometimes very long, and there could easily have been sufficient space on the verso of this one for a book list that contained several thousand titles.[71] This list is almost certainly the closest thing we have to the book list of a municipal or institutional library from antiquity.

2.11. LISTS 6–8: BRIEF DESCRIPTIONS

In this section, I describe and comment briefly on three further lists. I hope to provide the reader with a clear idea of the physical condition and content of these papyri, but I will not analyze the lists in detail, and for the most part I will leave papyrological problems aside.[72] For ease of reference in the discussion that follows, I give each list a number, continuing the numeration from the lists we have already studied.

List 6, *P.Vindob.* inv. G 39966, column 1 = Otranto number 3,
column 1= *MP³* 2089.1 = *CPP* 0347; probably from Arsinoite nome,
mid-first century AD, now in Vienna

This list was written on the same reused scrap of papyrus as list 1 above; see appendix 1, number 1, for details. List 6 was placed in the upper left corner of the papyrus, about 20 cm from list 1. We probably have both the beginning (Homer) and the end of this list, since nothing follows it on the papyrus.

Contents of the list: Homer's *Iliad*, with each book enumerated; Homer's *Odyssey*, with each book enumerated; Callimachus's (title lost), and perhaps his *On Birds*;[73] Pindar's (title lost), *Encomia, Processional Odes*, (another

---

71. Similar glossaries are known from medieval manuscripts and often fill dozens of modern pages. Thus the *Hermeneumata Einsidlensia*, which, like the glossary in *P.Oxy.* 33.2660, has rubrics for plants and fish (among many others), covers fifty-six pages: *CGL* 3.221–79 (fish at 256–57). In any case, a book list need not have been restricted to a single volume, and perhaps this one extended over two or more volumes.

72. All three papyri have been carefully dealt with elsewhere. A good starting point for each is the entry in Otranto (2000).

73. For the title *On Birds* (περὶ ὀρνέων), see Puglia (1998), 80. If correct, this would be the only title of a prose work in what survives of the list, but the text is very lacunose, and other prose works may have been listed but are now lost.

title lost), and possibly his *Hyporchemata*; Hesiod's *Catalog of Women*, at least Books 3 and 5; *Works and Days*; *Theogony*; Sappho's (title or book numbers lost).

List 7, *PSI Laur.* inv. 19662 verso = Otranto number 16 = *MP*³ 2087 = *CPP* 0386; Oxyrhynchus, third century AD, now in Florence

This papyrus contains a list of real-estate properties on the recto and our list of authors and titles on the verso. Both texts have been dated on paleographical grounds to the third century AD. The papyrus, about 13 cm wide by 18 cm high, is broken on all four sides. The list, with modern line numbers at the left:

> 1   *Symposium*
>   Dialogues 20
>   *Sophist* 1
>   *Against Callicles* 3
> 5   *Protagoras* 1
>   *Euthydemus* 1
>   *Parmenides Anacharsis*[74]
>   *Charmides*
>   *Alcibiades* or (?) *Lysis*
> 10 *Meno Menexenus*
>   *Hippiases* 2 and *Eudemus*
>   *Timaeus*
>   *Politicus*
>   *Cratylus*
> 15 *Alcibiades*
>   *Philebus*
>   *Phaedo*
>   *Laches*
>   *Alcibiades*
> 20 *Gorgias*
>   *Protagoras*
>   *Philebus*

---

74. Lines 7, 10, and 11 each contain the name of two or more dialogues. These rolls were probably opisthographs, with a dialogue of Plato on the recto and another work copied on the verso. Alternatively, there may have been more than one dialogue on the recto. That would have resulted in very long rolls, but such long rolls are attested at Oxyrhynchus. On the problem, see Puglia (1996b), 55–56.

Xenophon's *(Cyro)paedia* 8
Anabasis
25   *Agesilaus*
Cynegeticus
Symposium

Homer, whatever is available[75]
Menander, whatever is available
30   Euripides, whatever is available
Aristophanes
Cratinus's (?)[76]
. . .
(?)inus's

For a full analysis of this list, see Puglia (1996a); Otranto; Carlini in *CPF* I.1*, pp. 94–98; Houston (2009), 234–37. Here, I comment on only a few of its basic aspects. There is a good chance that some lines have been lost before (Plato's) *Symposium*, and it is reasonable to suppose that those missing lines contained Plato's name in the genitive and some of his other compositions. Line 2 contains not a specific title but a generic term ("dialogues") and a number, "twenty." Since there then follow twenty lines, each of which contains the title of one or more dialogues (lines 3 to 22), most scholars have assumed that the number "twenty" means not twenty dialogues but twenty book rolls containing dialogues. Thus the first part of the list included dialogues, most but not all by Plato. (The *Eudemus* was by Aristotle.) The titles are not arranged alphabetically, and some repeat: *Alcibiades* in lines 15, 19, and probably 9; *Philebus* in lines 16 and 22; *Protagoras* in lines 5 and 21. These can perhaps most easily be taken as duplicate copies.

Following a break marked by a horizontal line (*paragraphus*), we have a section arranged not by genre but by author, specifically Xenophon (lines 23 to 27). Following a second break that consists simply of a blank space, the list ceases to provide titles, instead naming authors in no discernible order (certainly neither alphabetical nor chronological): Homer, Menander, Euripides, Aristophanes, and, probably, Cratinus. The first three of these certainly, and the others possibly, are followed by a phrase that seems to in-

75. The Greek that I translate as "whatever is available" is ὅσα εὑρίσκεται.

76. All that survives of line 32 is .[. . .]εινου. As Carlini in *CPF* I.1*, pp. 97–98, noted, this could perhaps be supplemented to read Κ[ρατ]είνου, or "Cratinus's." In line 33, virtually nothing can be read, and in line 34 all that survives are the last three or four letters, -ινου, or "-inus's." The supplement Cratinus was suggested to me by a reader for the University of North Carolina Press.

dicate all of the authors' extant and available works, ὅσα εὑρίσκεται. Whether this means that those works were in the collection, or part of the collector's desiderata, is not known.[77]

List 8, *P.Turner* 9 = *P.Berol.* inv. 21247 = Otranto number 18 = *MP*[3] 2090.2 = *CPP* 0344; Hermupolis Magna, early fourth century AD; now in Berlin

List 8 is preserved on a composite fragment of papyrus, the main piece being 9.4 cm wide by 17 cm high, the other two very small. The text consists of a single column, 19 lines long, listing authors and titles. The first seven lines are very fragmentary but appear to list a series of commentaries: on Archilochus, Callimachus, Aeschines, Demosthenes, Homer's *Iliad* (?), and Demosthenes's judicial speeches. Following four lines too fragmentary to permit reconstruction, we have at least seven works of prose, one work per line, arranged in no particular order. The authors' names are in the genitive, so we can assume that titles followed them even in lines 12 and 14, where no titles survive. Book numbers might also explain the genitive, but titles seem to be more likely given their presence in lines 15 to 18.

12   // Herodotus's
     // A manual?[78]
     // Xenophon's
15   // Aristotle's *Constitution of the Athenians*
     Thucydides's *Histories*
     Xenophon's *Paideia*
     Callinicus's *Various (Treatises?)*

Down the left edge of the papyrus is a series of small holes which, as Otranto (ad loc.) noted, are very much like those one finds in the margins of codices where pages have been sewn together. It thus may be that this list of books was bound in a codex, and it may have served as a table of contents, or more exactly—since the works listed in it would almost certainly have filled more than one codex—as a permanent record of the contents of a collection that was contained in several codices. This inventory of the works in the collection would presumably have been bound in at the front of the first codex.

---

77. The phrase, along with the interpretation of the whole list, has occasioned much discussion, and its exact meaning is not yet clear. An instructive list of possible ways of interpreting the list is in Carlini, *CPF* I.1*, p. 96; see also Puglia (1996b), 59–60.

78. The Greek is τ[έχ]νης μ[?].

Lines 2, 3, and 5 to 15 all begin with two forward slash marks, perhaps an indication that the list had been used to take inventory of a collection, and that works were checked off when they were found to be present (or missing?). It is not possible to tell if the check marks were in the same hand or ink as the body of the list.

2.12. REFLECTIONS OF THE PROCESSES OF PRODUCING AND ACQUIRING

The eight lists we have considered so far will, I hope, give the reader an idea of the possible contents of such lists, the great diversity of collections represented in them, and the problems involved in using and interpreting them. We will continue to keep such matters in mind, but I want now to redirect our attention and focus not on individual papyri but on a series of questions and topics. We will draw evidence concerning each topic from one or more of our book lists.

Certain aspects of the lists reflect, with varying degrees of clarity, the processes of producing volumes or acquiring a collection. Most obviously, any such list might itself be an element in the collecting process. Lists 1, 4, and 6 appear to be rough drafts of specific collections and can readily be interpreted as inventories of block acquisitions, whether by purchase, inheritance, or some other means. These three lists are sorted into very rough groupings—poetry and prose, say, or philosophy and medicine—and they concentrate on the physical nature of the volumes, such as the number of opisthographs (list 4), or the particular books of Homer, Hesiod, and other works present in the collection (lists 1 and 6). Similarly, list 7 is oddly organized, in large groups, but with no consistency of treatment from group to group, and no systematic use of alphabetization. As Puglia (1996a), 63, noted, this lack of consistency and variation in level of detail is compatible with the hypothesis of an owner preparing a rough list of what he had for his own use. Such a list might well be desirable as an inventory of a newly acquired collection, whether we imagine a collector making a purchase or receiving an inheritance, or a dealer buying a collection that he intended to resell. The list would not be of much use to someone seeking to locate a particular item within the collection unless he was already familiar with its physical arrangement.

In list 8, most lines are preceded by two forward slash marks. The marks have generally been taken to mean that someone was checking the rolls in a collection against the list, and that he put slash marks by titles as he found them. It is also possible, as Kathleen McNamee has pointed out to me, that this is a list of desiderata, and that, as items were either commissioned or found and purchased, they were checked off.[79] In this case, we could see the assembling of a collection in process: a list is drawn up, and the books are then sought out, found or created, and brought together.

We saw in chapter 1 that finding an exemplar of a given text could be difficult, and problems of that sort could have resulted in gaps in collections. This may be reflected here and there in the lists. In list 1, Books 3 and 4 of Hesiod's *Catalog of Women* may have been lacking, as well as Books 4, 5, and 9 of a lexicon in at least thirteen books; some of Thucydides's history may have been missing from the collection enumerated in list 8, since Thucydides's name appears in the genitive case (line 16); the collection in list 2 contained only the first book each of Posidonius's *On Anger* (line 8) and of Chrysippus's *Handbook* (line 20), although the latter consisted of five books.[80] The very fact that each book in the *Iliad* and the *Odyssey* is listed separately in lists 1 and 6 may be due to the difficulty involved in assembling a complete set of Homer: you could not assume that you had, or could acquire, the complete work.[81] The number of certain instances of gaps or missing volumes, however, is not high, and the general impression one gets from these collections is that the collectors were remarkably successful in assembling complete texts of at least those major authors that interested them. Less popular authors, of course, might be quite a different matter.

Collectors could acquire two or more copies of a text through any one of a number of means, and our lists probably reflect a few such duplications.[82] In the collection represented by list 1, there may have been two copies each of *Odyssey* 3, *Odyssey* 4, Hesiod's *Catalog* 5, and (remarkably) the otherwise unknown work *Peri epimones*.[83] The list of Plato's dialogues in list 7

79. Personal communication, May 22, 2009. If this is correct, then the titles in this list could represent not an entire collection, but items that the owner of a collection hoped to add (and in most cases was successful in adding, to judge from the check marks) to his library.

80. The total number of books in Posidonius's *On Anger* is not known, but it was evidently two or more, since the compiler here specified Book 1.

81. It is possible that certain books in a given work were missing for reasons other than the difficulty involved in locating exemplars. An owner might have owned a complete set of Homer at one point, but had lost one or more rolls, or given them away. He may not have liked some books and so never bought them. And book rolls could be destroyed by careless or heavy use, dampness, insect larvae, and so on.

82. You might acquire duplicates by gift or inheritance, or if you bought a collection and it contained a copy of a text you already owned. Or you might have certain favorites and deliberately acquire two or more copies of them.

83. For the problems with the Homer and Hesiod, see the commentary in appendix 1. The *Peri epimones* is certainly named twice, but it is possible that there were two different treatises by this name.

mentions the *Philebus* and *Protagoras* each twice and the *Alcibiades* two or three times, and it probably refers to the *Gorgias*, or to some part of the *Gorgias*, twice.[84] Among the works of Epicharmus in the long inventory of comedies (list 5), there may be three duplicates, the *Harpaga*[?], *Dionys*[?], and *Epinic*[?]. One, some, or all of these sets of duplicates may thus reflect one of the results of book collecting, namely the acquisition, whether deliberate or accidental, of duplicate copies of some items.[85]

Several of the collections contained works that to the modern observer may seem anomalous or somehow out of place. A certain Callinicus, for example, appears twice in list 8 (lines 8 and 18). This is a list that otherwise seems to be composed exclusively of classical prose and poetry, texts or commentaries or both, and authors of very high rank. Callinicus, in striking contrast, cannot be identified with certainty. Otranto (2000), 110–11, suggested he might be identical with Callinicus of Petra, a sophist and historian of the third century A D. If that is correct, it means he lived some five hundred years later than any of the other authors in the list, and in any case he is certainly far less well known. An anomaly, in short. The list that Callinicus appears in clearly reflects the interests of a serious reader, and perhaps a scholar, since it seems to begin with a series of commentaries, and it certainly concentrates on important works.[86] It dates a generation or two after the floruit of Callinicus of Petra, and it is worth considering the possibility that Callinicus and the scholarly man who first assembled this collection were friends, and that the copies of Callinicus's works entered the collection as presentation copies.[87]

Another aspect of collecting is reflected in the presence of opisthographs. In list 4, opisthographic volumes are explicitly designated as such, and there are several dozen of them (forty-six in line 29). These are probably papyrus rolls, originally documents, that have been reused.[88] In the list of Plato's

---

84. On the *Gorgias* (the third and last part of which may be represented by the entry in line 4, *Against Callicles*), see Puglia (1996b), 52–54 and 58–59. The *Alcibiades* is also problematic but certainly listed at least twice.

85. We will see duplicates of certain books of Epicurus's *On Nature* below, in the collection from the Villa of the Papyri.

86. Otranto (2000), 197–99, took lines 2 to 7 all as commentaries, supplying all or almost all of the word ὑπόμνημα in each line.

87. On this theory, the man to whom Callinicus gave presentation copies could be a grandfather or a teacher of the man who compiled the list.

88. It is impossible to know for sure what sense of the word "opisthograph" the compiler of the list had in mind. Perhaps he was thinking of book rolls containing texts that continued from the recto to the verso, like Pliny the Elder's notebooks (*commentarii*, Plin. *Ep.* 3.5.17), or rolls that contained different works of the same author on each side. Actual papyri of the latter sort, however, are very rare. It would be surprising to find a collection with several dozen such book rolls, and it is probably best

dialogues (list 7), opisthographs—here in the sense of rolls containing literary text on both sides—can be inferred with some confidence from the presence of two titles on single lines (lines 7, 10, 11, and possibly 9). Two of these rolls are of particular interest: the one mentioned on line 7 apparently contained Plato's *Parmenides* and Lucian's *Anacharsis*, and the one on line 11 contained Plato's two *Hippias* dialogues and Aristotle's *Eudemus*. This was clearly a collection of Platonic dialogues, and we may safely assume that these rolls were acquired not because the owner wanted copies of the *Anacharsis* or the *Eudemus*, but because he wanted the Platonic works *Parmenides*, *Greater Hippias*, and *Lesser Hippias*. Since it is very unlikely that any bookseller or copyist would prepare rolls on speculation with these particular combinations of material (*Parmenides* and *Anacharsis*, for example), it is most likely that some previous owner had turned rolls containing Platonic dialogues over in order to have copies of the other works made.[89] That in turn implies that the person who assembled this collection acquired some of the volumes through a used-book market of some sort, or at least secondhand.[90]

2.13. PERSONALITIES OF COLLECTIONS

The collections represented by our lists often seem to reflect the particular interests of the persons who assembled or acquired them, and they thus acquire a kind of personality.[91] List 4 included a substantial collection of philosophical, plus some medical, works, and it is not difficult to see in this collection a professional interest. It seems to have included a broad range of authors and, in some cases, many works of those authors.[92] Both broad

---

to assume, with Manfredi (1983), 51, that by "opisthograph" the compiler here means reused rolls of documents.

89. Puglia (1996b), 57–58, citing Petrucci, noted that Greek and Roman book rolls never, so far as we know, included a miscellany of works by more than one author when they were first made. He argued that the volume mentioned in line 11 contained the two *Hippias* dialogues on the recto, and that the *Eudemus* was added subsequently. It must be admitted, however, that we cannot be sure which dialogue or dialogues were on the recto, since the collector was obviously interested in Plato and might well have listed the Platonic works first, regardless of which was on the recto and which on the verso.

90. There is another possible scenario. The collector of Platonic works could have acquired rolls containing the *Eudemus* and the *Anacharsis* and, not caring much about those works, had Platonic dialogues copied onto the reverse sides of them. In this scenario, the owner of the collection of Plato was willing to include reused rolls in his collection.

91. We must allow, of course, for the fact that the lists are incomplete, but lists 1, 2, and 4 are almost certainly close to complete, and there is little reason to believe that list 2 (philosophy) extended much beyond what we have.

92. At least thirty-two volumes of one author—Plato, if we accept the attractive suggestion of Puglia (1996a), 30—appear in line 15.

and deep in coverage of its chosen areas of philosophy and medicine, it may well be a specialized collection similar to the one known from the Villa of the Papyri. List 2 also focuses largely on philosophy, but the titles present in this collection are certainly or probably among the shorter and less significant works of the authors represented. Thus this collection might have been a professional or specialized one, but it might also have been the collection not of a scholar, but simply of a serious reader whose tastes ran to philosophy and closely related subjects.

In contrast to such specialist collections, there are general collections with a broader range of subjects and genres represented. List 1 includes a range of poetry and prose, although it is peculiar in containing major poets (Homer, Hesiod, and Callimachus) but mostly obscure prose (Dionysius, Aelianus, and a work *Peri epimones*, in addition to the well-known Demosthenes and Aeschines). Perhaps the closest we have to a broadly based and representative selection of Greek literature is list 7.[93] Here we have what at first sight appears to be another philosophical collection, since it begins with the *Symposium* (presumably of Plato) and continues with some eighteen of Plato's dialogues, three of which are present in two or three copies. The collection, however, was not just philosophical, for it included several works by Xenophon—history, biography, didactic—and, if the works listed in lines 28 and following were present in the collection, it also included epic, comedy, tragedy, and perhaps other genres. The very small collection in list 3 (*P.Turner* 39), which also lists a knife and a tin container, is unlike any other list in several respects. It is the shortest list, with only five titles; of the titles, three are reference works (two commentaries and a lexicon); and it seems to include works in Latin (Rufus's encomium and an unidentified work by a Priscus). Given the presence of other materials that could be taken as related to scribal activity, it seems possible that these five titles were works that a scribe had copied on commission, perhaps for several different customers.[94]

Given the tendency of these collections to emphasize particular subject areas, it is somewhat surprising to note how few reference works there are; one might have expected serious students of a topic to gather lexicons, commentaries, biographical works, and the like. But we do not find that. Apart from the very brief list 3, which consists almost entirely of paraliterary rather

93. For a more extended analysis of list 7, see Houston (2009).

94. If this is the explanation of this list, then it should, strictly speaking, be omitted from my catalog. I include it, however, for a number of reasons. It seems unlikely that a scribe would receive commissions from several different people for works all of which were obscure. Thus the books may well have belonged to, or been commissioned by, one person after all.

than literary works, the only such materials clearly attested are in list 1, which includes a strong collection of poetry but also at least eleven rolls of a lexicon and what is probably an anthology of rhetoric or speeches; and in list 8, a collection of historical prose with at least one manual (τ[έχ]νη) and, probably, several commentaries on specific authors. No reference works appear in two of the collections of philosophical works (lists 4 and 7), and only a few, mostly "selections," in list 2.[95] We will want to keep this in mind as we look at the collection from the Villa of the Papyri in chapter 3.

2.14. SPECULATING ON SIZES

Despite the fact that none of our lists is complete, it is possible to make useful observations about the sizes of the collections they represent. To anticipate: the impression one gets is that these collections were, by modern standards, small; but given that they belonged to a pre-Gutenberg world, at least two of them were probably quite substantial. That ancient collections were small by our standards is not surprising; the advantage of looking at the lists is that they allow us to be much more exact about what we mean by "small."

I start with list 1 (*P.Vindob.* inv. G 39966, column 2) and its close cousin, list 6 (column 1 on the same papyrus), because in both of these cases we almost certainly have the end of the list and probably have the beginning as well, allowing us to make unusually close estimates of the number of rolls in each collection. For list 1, the authors or titles listed, with the probable number of book rolls in each case, are

Aelianus (?), between one and four rolls.[96]
Aeschines, one roll.
Callimachus, *Aetia*, up to four rolls.
————, *Epigrams*, one roll.
————, *Hecale*, one roll.
————, *Hymns*, one roll.
Demosthenes, *On the Crown*, one roll.
Dionysius, not more than about five rolls, and perhaps just one.[97]

---

95. These are selections from Book 1 of Posidonius's *On Anger* (line 8) and a set of collected letters of the Socratics (lines 1–2). There is also a handbook (probably; the title is mostly in a lacuna) by Chrysippus in lines 20–21.

96. The number 4 appears at the beginning of the line that follows the name of Aelianus (?) and may indicate that some four books of his or of that work were present.

97. The lacuna after Dionysius's name corresponds to about seven characters in the line above and

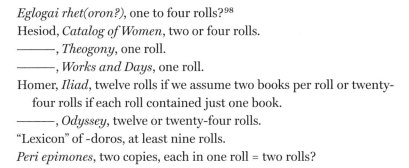

Eglogai rhet(oron?), one to four rolls?[98]

Hesiod, *Catalog of Women*, two or four rolls.

————, *Theogony*, one roll.

————, *Works and Days*, one roll.

Homer, *Iliad*, twelve rolls if we assume two books per roll or twenty-four rolls if each roll contained just one book.

————, *Odyssey*, twelve or twenty-four rolls.

"Lexicon" of -doros, at least nine rolls.

Peri epimones, two copies, each in one roll = two rolls?

Thus the total number of volumes in this collection seems to have been somewhere between fifty and ninety. A similar analysis of list 6 gives a figure for that collection of at least fifty book rolls (assuming two books per roll for Homer and the presence of all or most of Sappho), and perhaps as many as seventy-five rolls if we assume that the *Iliad* and *Odyssey* were written out one book to a roll.

In list 4 (*P.Vars.* 5 verso), as we have seen, the compiler himself reckoned up the numbers of rolls in various subgroups of the collection. The numbers the compiler gives are[99]

Of philosophers, 142 (line 19)

Of those 142, 14 are opisthographs (line 22)

Medical writers, some 13 rolls (line 26)

Of those 13, about 11 are opisthographs (lines 26a and 26b)

296 rolls "present" (lines 27–8)

Of those, 46 are opisthographs (line 29)

59, probably the number of "others" (lines 31, 36)

In sum, we have a collection of at least 296 rolls, and very probably of 355 (296 plus 59) or more, and it may have been physically divided between two different locations, as indicated by the qualifiers "present" and "others." There may have been even more volumes, since the category "of philosophers" could have been preceded by other categories, such as historians or dramatic poets. Thus we cannot know the size of the entire collection, but

---

presumably included the title of a work (perhaps in abbreviated form) as well as any book numbers. Perhaps the whole work was contained in a single book roll.

98. The number of books in the *Eglogai*, if this was a title, is uncertain. The lacuna to the right of this is not large enough for more than about eight characters.

99. The numbers of opisthographs given in lines 22, 26a, 26b, and 29 are what we have if we accept the interpretation of this papyrus provided by Puglia (1996a and 1997a). If one interpreted the list differently, one would end up with slightly different totals.

the figures of 142 rolls of philosophy and 296 "present" rolls put it in the same order of magnitude—hundreds but not thousands of rolls—as, say, the collection from the Villa of the Papyri at Herculaneum.[100] This was a substantial collection. Potentially even larger was the collection represented by list 5, the list of Old Comedy, which may be a part of the formal book list of an institutional, municipal, or unusually large personal library. The collection it represents may have numbered several thousand volumes.

None of the other collections is likely to have included more than some dozens to a few hundred volumes. The very disorganization of list 2 implies a relatively small collection, one you could easily search all the way through for a given title. List 7, of which we seem to have the end and something close to the beginning, certainly represents a substantial collection: the surviving papyrus fragment mentions (Plato's) *Symposium*, twenty rolls of dialogues, roughly a dozen rolls of Xenophon, probably twenty-four or forty-eight rolls of Homer, some dozens each of five dramatic poets,[101] and, since we have probably lost some titles at the top, some further works of Plato.[102] Nothing in what we have, however, indicates that this was a collection extending beyond several hundred volumes. List 8 is difficult to assess. Commentaries, if that is what we have in lines 2 to 7, might be short, with several in one book roll, or long, with a single commentary running to several book rolls. Of Herodotus, Thucydides, and Xenophon, it is not clear if we have one book, a selection of books (or a selection of passages), or the complete works. We do have more than one title, it seems, of Xenophon and Callinicus. Perhaps the best we can do is guess that this was a collection of some dozens of volumes.[103] And list 3, finally, includes only five rolls as it stands, but this papyrus is fragmentary and might have included additional volumes.

In sum, the sizes of collections implied by these lists are consistently within the range of several dozen to a few hundred rolls, with the exception

---

100. See below, section 3.5, for the size of the collection in the Villa of the Papyri.

101. The number of rolls of each of the tragedians and comic writers is uncertain because of the phrase ὅσα εὑρίσκ(εται) = "whatever is available." Just how many titles of these authors were available in the third century is not known.

102. We almost certainly have not lost a significant amount from earlier in the list. To the left of the surviving column of titles are traces of letters at the level of lines 3, 7, and 11. These are in a hand different from that of the scribe who wrote our list, so presumably our list did not begin in this previous column.

103. As we saw earlier (section 2.11, on list 8), this papyrus shows signs of having been bound in a codex, and that raises the possibility that the whole collection consisted not of book rolls but of codices. A codex held much more text than a book roll did, so if this was a collection of codices, we might posit a relatively small number of them. If we had one codex per author, for example, we would have a collection of ten codices.

of list 5 (possibly thousands of volumes) and list 3 (five volumes). So far as we can tell, and again with the possible exception of list 5, these were apparently personal collections, and they would have been assembled volume by volume through commissions, gifts, individual purchases, or the making of one's own copies.[104] Such processes were not likely to result in very large collections.

2.15. POSSIBLE INDICATIONS OF PHYSICAL ARRANGEMENTS

A few words and phrases in the lists, and some aspects of the visual presentation of the lists on the papyrus, may reflect the physical organization and methods of storage of the book rolls themselves. These indications are in all cases problematic, and they never prove how the actual physical books were organized, but they can alert us to possibilities that we might otherwise overlook or not even imagine.

Separate storage areas or containers may be implied or specified in some cases. The *cellaria* in list 3, line 15, may refer to storerooms, storage vessels, shelves, or cabinets, and it is possible to imagine book rolls stored in them.[105] In this same list, tin containers are inventoried at line 17 and may refer to boxes in which book rolls were stored. The *narthex* in list 4, line 25, may be a storage container of some sort; it might have contained the thirteen rolls of medical treatises that appear just before it in the list. If so, it could have been used to keep these medical volumes together and distinct from the preceding philosophical collection.[106] An implicit organization of the physical rolls in groups appears in list 1, where a blank space in line 6 seems to indicate a change from poetry to prose, and again in line 11, where a full line is left blank, although the exact nature of the change is not clear in this case, since we find rhetoric and other prose both before and after the break. So too in list 7: a *paragraphus* after line 22 indicates a change from Platonic dialogues to the works of Xenophon, and a blank space after line 27 signals a change from Xenophon to poetry. The question, of course, is whether such groupings are just ways of organizing the inventories them-

---

104. It is possible, of course, that one might have been able to purchase a complete set of, say, Homer's *Iliad*. But in general, the titles included in the lists were probably procured one roll at a time.

105. If we take *cellaria* as storerooms, they would seem to refer to rooms where objects other than book rolls were kept, since the objects listed after the word *cellaria* are not book rolls. That, though, implies that some other location for the book rolls was specified in the now lost part of this papyrus.

106. Puglia (1997a), 133–34, argued that "narthex" here is the title of a work and does not indicate any kind of container. This is probably correct. See above, section 2.9. Contra: Otranto (2000), 103.

selves, or whether they represent the physical arrangement of book rolls: certain shelves or containers for Plato, others for Xenophon, still others for Homer and the poets.

Elsewhere, there are indications that rolls could be separated into groups by genre or subject, with the various groups stored in different containers, rooms, or buildings. In list 2, line 3, we have the letters that have been restored as [ἐ]ν οἰκίᾳ ("in the house"), and if the restoration is correct, this collection may have been divided between the "house" and a separate building, perhaps a storage room.[107] Some such arrangement may also be indicated in list 4 by the division of book rolls into τὰ προκ(είμενα) ("the ones that are here") and ἕτερα ("others") in lines 27 and 31 respectively.

The lists do not ordinarily suggest that the individual book rolls were carefully sorted and arranged, whether in containers or on shelves. To be sure, we regularly find categories and genres separate and distinct from other categories; thus we find a distinction between poetry and prose in list 1, philosophy and medicine in list 4, and dialogues, Xenophon, and poets in list 7. But the situation changes when we move to the level of individual rolls: only two of the lists, lists 5 and 4, employ alphabetization; in lists 2 and 8 the authors are not listed in any discernible order whatever; and in at least three of the lists works likely to have been in Latin are commingled with Greek texts.[108] It seems a reasonable inference from this that the collections, or at least the various subgroups in the collections, were not of great size, and that it was possible to find the volume you were seeking without the aid of, say, alphabetized authors. All you needed to do was check through the piles, shelves, or containers of rolls, or have a slave check for you.

2.16. CONCLUSION

We know from papyrus fragments found in Oxyrhynchus that the men and women of that town read, or at least had access to, a wide range of literary works. Fragments of the works of at least 119 different authors had been identified by 1990, and there are no doubt more now. We also know that Homer was by far the most popular author. He is known from 236 fragments, compared to 76 for Hesiod, the second most popular. Texts of

---

107. Galen stored some of his books in an *apotheca*, or warehouse, on the Via Sacra in Rome: Gal. *Comp.Med.Gen.* 1.1 (13.362 Kühn); cf. Houston (2003).

108. Thus list 1, line 8 (a work by Aelianus); list 2, column 2, line 15 (an Aelius); list 3, line 11 (the lexicon of Priscus); and perhaps the Callinicus of list 8, lines 8 and 18.

Cicero, Livy, Sallust, and other Latin authors were also present in Oxyrhynchus, although in small numbers of copies.[109] What we cannot tell from such statistics, of course, is how the texts were combined in collections. Did people always own a copy of one or more books of the *Iliad*, if they owned any book rolls at all? Did they strive for broad representative collections of Greek and Latin literature, or did they tend to collect texts focused on one genre or topic? Did their collections have some sort of internal consistency? The lists we have been examining enable us to begin formulating answers to these and similar questions: no, Homer was not present in every collection; yes, collections were often focused on, say, philosophical works, or poetry. Some appear to have been so specifically focused and so thoroughly developed that we may consider them professional collections, but we also find collections that range across various genres, from dialogues to history to epic and drama.

Each of the lists we have looked at is thus of interest in its own right, considered as an individual collection. In these lists we see parts of specific collections as they were inventoried at specific times by eight different owners. Taken as a group rather than one by one, the lists provide us with at least some evidence on what a personal collection of book rolls might look like, the range of possible sizes and balance and contents. This is useful, for just such collections might find their way, through gift, purchase, or bequest, into larger collections and ultimately into municipal or institutional libraries. It is possible that the collections we have identified resembled, in size or content or idiosyncrasies, the groups of volumes mentioned by Galen, *Ind.* 13—the Callinian, Atticianan, and Peducaean—and, if so, they may help us define the constituent elements of the imperial collections themselves.[110]

As we have seen, however, there is a great deal we would like to know but cannot learn from the lists of books. The lists do not tell us how old the book rolls were, nor what their condition was (torn? moth-eaten? pristine?); they tell us nothing about the quality of the text, its accuracy, how thoroughly it had been corrected, or the presence or absence of marginal notes; and the lists give us no information on the number of lines or columns, and none on

109. Krüger (1990), 214–15, gives the statistics.
110. If Jones (2009), 391–92, is correct in taking the "Callinian" as a collection that descended from the book rolls belonging to the philosopher Callinus of Hermione, then the Callinian volumes might well be largely philosophical (specifically, Peripatetic or Aristotelian) in focus, similar to list 7 with its collection of Platonic dialogues or list 4 with its 142 books of philosophers, or to the collection in the Villa of the Papyri (chapter 4).

the arrangement of text on the writing surface. For information of this sort, we will need to look at collections of book rolls that have survived physically, either in whole or in part. That will be our concern in chapters 3, on the Villa of the Papyri at Herculaneum, and 4, on collections from the town of Oxyrhynchus in Egypt.

3
The Villa of the Papyri at Herculaneum

3.1. INTRODUCTION

From lists, we turn to the physical remains of book collections. Known from archaeology, these materials will help us explore not only the authors and titles in particular collections, but the physical nature of an ancient collection. What condition were the book rolls in? How old were they? Do we find any evidence in the surviving manuscripts that might help us learn something about how the ancients managed their collections, how they sorted and stored the volumes and recovered them from storage? We will look primarily at two types of remains. One class of evidence—concentrations of literary papyri found together in Egypt—will form the focus of our study in chapter 4. The other class, the one we turn to now, consists of the many volumes that were covered in the eruption of Mount Vesuvius in AD 79 and that have been recovered from the grand Roman house in Herculaneum now called the Villa of the Papyri. Even in their ruinous state, these carbonized volumes give us a great deal of information about the collection in the Villa. Chapter 3 will be devoted to an analysis of this material.

3.2. THE VILLA OF THE PAPYRI

When Mount Vesuvius erupted in AD 79, it buried not only the towns of Pompeii and Herculaneum but also numerous estates and villas, among them the elegant seaside residence now known as the Villa of the Papyri.[1] Buried under a deep layer of volcanic materials, this villa was rediscovered in 1750, and in the period from 1750 to 1764 one level of it was explored by means of a network of tunnels, permitting the reconstruction of its plan on

---

1. The date traditionally given for the eruption of Vesuvius, August 23–24, has in recent years been called into question, especially by volcanologists. They posit a later date, sometime in the autumn of 79. See Rolandi, Paone, et al. (2007).

that level. It has never been fully excavated, but there has been some important recent work. In the late 1980s two of the old tunnels were reopened for a brief period, in the period from May 1996 to May 1998 a part of the villa close to the sea was cleared, and in the period from July 2007 to March 2008 archaeologists carried out limited further explorations, preservation work, and a review of what is known. This recent work revealed that the Villa was built not on just one, but on three or four levels, and that it was probably not built until the third quarter of the first century BC, or about a generation later than previously thought. For the most part, the newly discovered levels have not yet been explored.[2]

As the tunnelers of the eighteenth century worked through the Villa, they discovered the remains of hundreds of book rolls, clearly the surviving (and fragmentary) part of a large book collection. Book rolls were found in at least four different rooms: a small room with shelves marked "V" on the plan drawn by the architect Karl Weber; the "tablinum"; the small peristyle; and the room now called room XVI. In room V, the rolls were found stored in cabinets, but in other rooms some volumes were in portable wooden cases, some in small piles on the floor.[3] Unfortunately, we do not know which of the surviving rolls were found in each of these locales, nor, in any detail, which rolls were found together.[4]

The book rolls were not in good shape. The volcanic gases, steam, and mud had carbonized them, darkening and deforming them and rendering them fragile and extremely difficult to read. The processes developed to unroll the volumes and read the surviving texts often damaged them further. The outer layers were naturally the most badly damaged in the eruption, and they were sometimes peeled off by later scholars in order to be read and drawn. Scholars cut some rolls into two halves and sliced some down the middle from one end to the other, producing a series of slightly curved

2. The story of the Villa, the eruption of Vesuvius, the tunnels, and what was found in them are all set out fully in Capasso (1991), 29–39; Sider (2005), 10–23; and Delattre (2007), lvii–lxii. For the work of the 1980s, see De Simone and Ruffo (2003), 281; of the 1990s, De Simone and Ruffo (2002); and for the work in 2007–8 and reassessment of the date of the Villa, Guidobaldi and Esposito (2009).

3. Details: Longo Auricchio and Capasso (1987). Of the wooden cases, only the metal fittings have survived. On room V and its shelving, see section 5.3 below.

4. Both Greek and Latin texts seem to have been found in room V and perhaps in the tablinum: Capasso (1992), 227. Capasso (2011), 22, notes that most of the book rolls found in room V were in Greek, but that about eighteen Latin rolls were found in that room, in addition to the Greek ones. We do not know why some of the book rolls were in movable containers. Perhaps the owners were trying to save them from the eruption. Perhaps the Villa was undergoing renovations (for which there is other evidence as well), and these volumes were in temporary storage. Perhaps these volumes were always stored in boxes. (See section 5.2 below.)

pieces.[5] The fragments that survived these procedures were given numbers (*Papyrus Herculanensis*, or *P.Herc.*, numbers) and placed in protective
trays.[6] All but a few of the surviving fragments are now in storage in the
Centro Internazionale per lo Studio dei Papiri Ercolanesi in Naples.

Despite the problems posed by the nature of these fragments and partial
rolls, scholars have from the very first been able to read parts, and sometimes substantial parts, of many of them. It quickly became apparent that
what survives consists of a collection of works that deal primarily with aesthetics, ethics, rhetoric, and related topics, with an emphasis on texts of
Epicurean writers. Eight books of Epicurus's *On Nature* have been identified, some in multiple copies, and there are many works by Philodemus of
Gadara, a poet, philosopher, and critic of the first century BC.

In part because of the presence of so many of Philodemus's works, many
scholars have thought that the Villa was owned, during the middle years of
the first century BC, by Marcus Calpurnius Piso Caesoninus, the consul of
58 BC. We know from Cicero that Caesoninus was a patron of Philodemus,
and it has always seemed possible that Philodemus lived and worked in the
Villa sometime during the period from about 70 to 40 BC.[7] There are, however, problems. There is no way, so far, to know exactly who owned the Villa
at any point in its life.[8] Recent exploration and analysis of the building technique and sculptural program in the Villa suggests that the building dates
from the third quarter of the first century BC. If that is correct, the Villa is
not likely to have been the spot where Philodemus lived and worked, and
it may have been built very late in Piso's life or after his death. The whole
structure may have been built for, and have been the property of, someone
other than Piso.[9]

In this study, with its focus on book collections, the identity of the owner
of the Villa 120 years before its destruction is not crucial, although it is
obviously a question of interest. What is crucial is the book collection that

---

5. Sider (2005), 16–57, provides a full account of what happened to the papyri in the Villa during
the eruption, how they were unrolled, and what this means for modern attempts to reconstruct the
contents of the rolls.

6. Although considerable efforts were made to keep all of the fragments from each roll together
in one or a series of trays, there are thousands of fragments, and some confusion has been inevitable.
Fragments from more than one roll may be stored together; fragments may be stored out of sequence;
some fragments have simply deteriorated and no longer survive. For details, see Delattre (2007), lxiii–
lxxix; Sider (2005), 47–59; or Janko (2000), 15–26.

7. For discussions, see Capasso (1991), 43–64, or Sider (2005), 5–8.

8. Porter (2007), 99, lists the uncertainties.

9. We will return to this topic in section 3.10 below.

existed in AD 79, and recent work, aided by technical advances including multispectral imaging, has greatly expanded our knowledge of both the collection in general and its individual texts.[10] It should be emphasized, however, that many fragments remain unread, unidentified, or both, and, as has often been noted, there may be additional rolls still buried in the unexplored areas of the Villa.[11] It is not known who owned the Villa and its collection of manuscripts when Vesuvius erupted.

3.3. THE MANUSCRIPT COLLECTION: GREEK AUTHORS AND WORKS

As a first survey of the Villa's collection, I list here in alphabetical order the authors and works found in it, so far as is known at present. I divide the list into two parts—first, Greek authors and works, and then (below in section 3.4) Latin authors and works—and I provide a brief summary of the works and the condition of the rolls. For a complete list of the authors and titles attested in the collection, with their *P.Herc.* numbers, see appendix 2.

Carneiscus (Epicurean, third or second century BC). One roll of one work—*Philistas*, Book 2—has been found. It is an elegant roll, carefully copied, with generous spacing between columns, and it was probably produced in Greece or the eastern Mediterranean. The copy is dated to the late second century BC.[12]

Chrysippus (Stoic, ca. 280–207 BC). The collection included at least three titles by Chrysippus, and at least two further rolls may be by him. All of the manuscripts of Chrysippus are dated after about 50 BC.[13]

Colotes of Lampsacus (younger contemporary and friend of Epicurus, lived ca. 310–260 BC). Two rolls survive, each containing a response to a dialogue of Plato (the *Euthydemus* and the *Lysis*). Both were copied after ca. 50 BC, and thus at least two hundred years after Colotes's death.[14]

Demetrius Laco (active ca. 120–90 BC). Six fragments of his mathematical treatise *On the Aporiae* ["perplexing problems"] *of Polyaenus* have

---

10. Delattre (2007), xci–cvii, provides an excellent summary of work on the papyri from 1970 on.

11. Janko (2002), 40–41, argues that a man wealthy enough to own this villa would be likely to possess "a much larger and more diverse collection of books than this," and suggests that more general collections of Greek and Latin literature may yet be found. Sider (2005), 43–45, speculates on specific authors we might find in such collections.

12. Cavallo (1983), 40, 54, 59; Capasso (1988), 140–44, 149–50. All dates of manuscripts in this collection are based upon paleographical grounds.

13. The two manuscripts tentatively assigned to Chrysippus are *P.Herc.* 1020 and 1384. For 1020, see Capasso (1982a), 456–57; for 1384, see Dorival (2008) or Antoni (2012), 24–25.

14. Cavallo (1983), 44, 46, 56–57. The two manuscripts were not copied by the same scribe.

been identified. Of these, one is from Book 1, one from Book 5, and the others are from unidentified books. Four of the six rolls were copied in the second century BC, all by the same scribe (Cavallo's scribe number 4), two a good deal later, probably in the first century BC.[15] In addition, the collection included at least nine other works by Demetrius. Titles of four survive in *subscriptiones* or can be reconstructed, and the subjects of five others can be inferred from what is known of the contents.[16] The rolls containing these nine works were copied in the second century BC, with the exception of *P.Herc.* 1006 (*On Some Topics for Discussion Concerning the Manner of Life*), an expensively produced manuscript of the first century BC; *P.Herc.* 1055 (*On the Form of the Divine?*), a handsome copy with generous spacing made in the first century AD; and possibly *P.Herc.* 188 (*On Poems*, Book 1), 1014 (*On Poems*, Book 2), and 1786 (probably on ethics), all of which date in the late second or early first century BC. The Villa collection thus included a substantial number of Demetrius's works, ten or more titles in at least twelve rolls dealing with a wide range of subjects: mathematics, geometry, music, literary criticism, ethics, physics, and theology.

Epicurus (born on Samos, 341 BC; taught in Mytilene, Lampsacus, and, from ca. 307, Athens; died in Athens, 270). The Villa collection is known to have included a good part of Epicurus's most important work, *On Nature*. Of the thirty-seven books in that work, the Villa possessed at least eight: two copies of Book 2, two copies of Book 11, one copy each of Books 14 and 15 (both by the same scribe), one copy of Book 21, three copies, by three different scribes, of Book 25, and one copy each of Books 28 and 34. The collection probably also contained an otherwise unknown work, *Echelaus*, the title of which Gianluca Del Mastro has recently been able to read.[17]

Most of the copies of *On Nature* were made in the second century BC by a number of different scribes, but there are some important exceptions. A single scribe (Cavallo's scribe number 1), who is to be dated, it seems, in the third century BC, made one of the copies of Book 2 (*P.Herc.* 1149 + 993)

---

15. The earlier fragments: Cavallo (1983), 30, 45, 56–57. The two later rolls: Cavallo (1983), 44, 46, 56 (on *P.Herc.* 1258); Capasso and Dorandi (1979), 41–43 (*P.Herc.* 1822). Cavallo suggested that some of the manuscripts may have been copied early in the first century AD, but that is not certain. See, for example, Parsons (1989), 360. The dating of some of the later manuscripts continues to be a matter of debate. Three of the manuscripts (*P.Herc.* 1061, 1642, and 1822) contain geometrical figures.

16. Secure titles: *On Geometry, On Music, On Poems* (Books 1 and 2 are both present), *On Some Topics for Discussion Concerning the Manner of Life*. In the last case the meaning of the Greek title is uncertain. Less certain titles, inferred from the content: *Textual and Critical Problems in Epicurus, On Rhetoric, On the Size of the Sun, On the Form of the Divine,* and an uncertain work, probably on ethics. See appendix 2.

17. Del Mastro (2011–12).

as well as one of the copies of Book 25 and the copies of Books 28 and 34 (*P.Herc.* 1191, 1479 + 1417, and 1431, respectively).[18] It may be, then, that these rolls were originally created as part of a set of all or most of the *On Nature*.[19] Another very early manuscript is *P.Herc.* 1413, from an unidentified book, which was probably copied in the first half of the third century, and so perhaps during Epicurus's lifetime.[20] At the opposite end of the chronological scale, a few book rolls of *On Nature* were copied in the first century BC or possibly the first century AD, and the Villa's copy of Epicurus's *Echelaus* (*P.Herc.* 566) has been dated to the end of the first century BC.[21] One of the manuscripts of Book 25, *P.Herc.* 1420 + 1056, was copied in the second century BC, but it seems to have been badly damaged or deemed inadequate not long thereafter, since it was repaired before the end of the century.[22]

Metrodorus of Lampsacus (Epicurean, born ca. 331, died 278). The Villa collection included at least two rolls, each with a different work, of Metrodorus. One is very early and was probably copied in the middle of the third century BC. Its title is uncertain.[23] The other roll, a copy of Metrodorus's *On Wealth*, was made in the first century BC, probably late in the century.

Philodemus of Gadara (Epicurean, student of Zeno of Sidon, lived ca. 110 to ca. 40 BC). Far more of Philodemus's works are present in the Villa collection than of any other author. We know the titles of some nineteen of his treatises from *subscriptiones* that are complete or can be restored with a reasonable degree of confidence, and the subjects of at least fifteen more

18. Cavallo (1983), 28, 45, 50; cf. Laursen (1995), 16–18; Janko (2002), 40; and Leone (2012), 364.

19. As suggested by Leone (2002), 28–29, following Cavallo. Leone (2005), 25, noted that *P.Herc.* 1149 + 993 is a high-quality copy. Even so, it contains more mistakes, including some uncorrected ones, than the more recent copy of the same book from the Villa collection, *P.Herc.* 1783 + 1691 + 1010: Leone (2012), 366–69. There may have been continuing efforts over time to assemble as accurate a set of *On Nature* as possible.

20. Janko (2008), 89. Del Mastro (2011) assigns three fragments of *P.Herc.* 1416 *cornice* ("frame") 5 to this same roll and accepts the early date. Other early manuscripts are *P.Herc.* 335 and 989, for which see Janko (2008), 59, and Cavallo (1983), 28 and 50, respectively. Neither can be assigned to a specific book.

21. Books of *On Nature* copied in the first century BC: *P.Herc.* 459 (Book 25), 362 (unknown book). Possibly first century AD: *P.Herc.* 1199 and 1398, for which see Cavallo (1983), 44, 46, and 56, and 37 and 53, respectively. Del Mastro (2011–12), 20, noted that the script of *P.Herc.* 566 is very similar to that of *P.Herc.* 1589, which both he and Cavallo (1983), 53, would assign to late in the first century BC.

22. Puglia (1997b), 40–42, discusses the repairs in full; Del Mastro (2010a), 40–47, reaches very much the same conclusions.

23. Spinelli (1986) suggested *Against the Dialecticians*, Tepedino Guerra (1992) *Against the Sophists*. For the date, see Cavallo (1983), 44, 46, and 57–58. Five fragments have been assigned to this roll. Janko (2008), 56, identified four additional fragments that may be by the same third-century hand and could come from this roll.

can be inferred from the contents of the surviving fragments. Several of these works filled more than one book roll. *On Music* and *On Death* each contained at least four books (in four rolls), *On Poems* at least five (with Book 5 being so long that it filled two rolls), and *On Rhetoric* at least seven and probably ten books.[24]

Each individual book within these long multivolume works was given, as usual in antiquity, a book number. In addition, however, some of the individual books in certain of the long treatises seem to have been given their own titles, which we might think of as subtitles, as well as numbers. In the initial title of *P.Herc.* 222, for example, we read περὶ κακιῶν καὶ τῶν ἐν οἷς εἰσι καὶ περὶ ἄ, α′, ὅ ἐστι περὶ κολακίας, or *On Vices and on Those in Whom They Are Found and What They Are Concerned with, (Book) 1, Which Is "On Flattery."*[25] Thus there was a general work, *On Vices* (etc.), that contained a number of books, and at least Book 1 had a title of its own. Book 2 also seems to have had a subtitle. What survives of it is fragmentary but has been plausibly restored as [Περὶ τῶν] κολ[ακείαι ὁμοειδῶν], "On the (Vices) Similar to Flattery."[26] Similarly, the *subscriptio* of *P.Herc.* 1471 informs us that it belonged to a multiroll ethical work, entitled *Epitome of Characters and Lives from Zeno's Lectures*, and that this particular book had the subtitle Περὶ παρρησίας, or "On Frank Speech."[27] Scholars have accordingly suggested that each of the books (or possibly groups of books) in *On Vices*, and in at least some of the other long works by Philodemus, had its own subtitle, and they have inferred titles from the surviving content. The text in *P.Herc.* 1424 (Book 9 of *On Vices*) may have been titled Περὶ οἰκονομίας, "On Property Management," and that in *P.Herc.* 1008 (Book 10 of *On Vices*), Περὶ ὑπερηφανίας, "On Arrogance."[28] In *Characters and Lives*, in addition

24. The *subscriptio* of *P.Herc.* 1497 reads "Philodemus's *On Music* 4"; of *P.Herc.* 1050, "Philodemus's *On Death* 4"; *P.Herc.* 1538, "Philodemus's *On Poems*, Book 5, the second of two," where "Book 5" is in the (partitive) genitive. Not all of the books implied by these numbers have been found yet. Thus no copies of *On Music* 1, 2, or 3 are known, although a fragment of *On Music* 4 survives. For the division of *On Rhetoric* into seven rolls, see Dorandi (1990b); into ten rolls, Longo Auricchio (1996).

25. Capasso (2001b), 180, translates τῶν ἐν οἷς εἰσι as "des choses en quoi ils consistent," but both Sider (2005), 88, and Monet (2001), 197–98, take this phrase as referring to people, as I do. The title appears in various abbreviated forms in other manuscripts. See Capasso (2010a), 98, for a list of all the variants.

26. *P.Herc.* 1457. See Capasso (2001b), 187–88, cf. 194, accepted by Monet (2001), 200. Whatever the exact title was, the book does seem to have had its own title, part of which was the word "Flattery."

27. Title: Gigante (1979), 336. Discussion: Konstan, Clay, et al. (1998), 6, n. 15.

28. For the title, see Tsouna (2012), xlii. Other subtitles within *On Vices* have been suggested, for example "On Avarice" (*P.Herc.* 253 + 1090) and "On Calumny" (*P.Herc.Paris.* 2 = Gigante and Capasso [1989], 3 and 5). In both of these cases, the subtitles are inferred from the content.

to "On Frank Speech," the subtitle "On Conversation" (*P.Herc.* 873) has been inferred from the content of its text, and "On Gratitude" (*P.Herc.* 1414, with subtitle surviving) has also been assigned to this work.[29]

Another large work is Philodemus's Σύνταξις τῶν φιλοσόφων, or *History of the Philosophers*. In this case, we know the general title not from any surviving manuscript, but from Diogenes Laertius 10.3, and we have no rolls explicitly assigned to it in a *subscriptio* or initial title, but several rolls that may have formed a part of it: *P.Herc.* 1021 and 164 (two distinct copies of a treatise on Plato and the Academy); *P.Herc.* 1018 (the Stoics); *P.Herc.* 1508 (Pythagoreans); *P.Herc.* 327 (Eleatics and Abderites); and *P.Herc.* 1780 (Epicurus and the Garden).[30] A fourth possible large work is a conjectured *On the Passions*. The *subscriptio* of *On Anger* ([Πε]ρὶ ὀργῆς, *P.Herc.* 182) is highly fragmentary but seems to have contained the name of a comprehensive work of which *On Anger* formed a part. Some scholars assigned this to the multivolume Περὶ ἠθῶν καὶ βίων (*On Characters and Lives*), but others noted that anger is not an ἦθος ("character") but a πάθος ("passion"), and so they posited a multivolume *On the Passions* and suggested that titles such as *On Hubris* (*P.Herc.* 1017; the title is inferred from the content) and *On Envy* (*P.Herc.* 1678; another conjectural title) may have formed part of it.[31]

In assigning subtitles to these multivolume works, caution is advisable. We seldom have both the name of the comprehensive work and of an individual volume within it.[32] Only two subtitles are actually attested, and in the case of some treatises that scholars have assigned to large comprehensive works, where the *subscriptio* is otherwise both complete and full, there is no subtitle at all: thus in the first *subscriptio* of *P.Herc.* 1675, written in the hand of the scribe who copied the text, and in the *subscriptio* of *P.Herc.* 1424, written in a different hand, there are no subtitles. In both cases we

29. So Delattre (2007), xlviii. In the case of "On Gratitude," the subtitle survives, but not the title of the multivolume work. It is possible that "On Gratitude" was an independent ethical work, not part of any multivolume work. Earlier, Delattre (2006), 137, had also assigned *On Wealth* (*P.Herc. 163*) to the *Characters and Lives*. Wilke (1914), vii and 1, following Scott, argued that *On Anger* belonged to *Characters and Lives*.

30. Giuliano (2001), 45, took a biographical work on Socrates (*P.Herc.* 495 and 558, probably two copies of a single work) as part of the *History*, but see Gallo (2002), 61–62. Gallo takes it as an isolated biography, like the life of Philonides.

31. Thus Delattre (2009), 72, rejecting the suggestion that *On Anger* could have formed any part of *On Vices* or *On Characters and Lives*. Delattre (2007), xlix, also assigned *P.Herc.* 57 (with a title, *On Madness*, inferred from the contents) to *On the Passions*, but Tepedino Guerra (2008), 103, has recently shown that we have no idea what the title of *P.Herc.* 57 was. There is still much uncertainty concerning the organization and content of these works.

32. Note the caution of Indelli (1988), 36–37, in connection with the hypothetical comprehensive work *On the Passions*: "Given that we have no mention of it . . . prudence is obligatory."

have only book numbers.[33] Subtitles such as chapter headings are familiar to us but were rare in antiquity, and there is sufficient variation in the way titles are handled just within *On Vices* to suggest that there may have been variation in subtitles: perhaps some books had them, others did not.[34] We will return to this question below in the discussion of the content of *subscriptiones*.

Many of the Villa manuscripts that cannot be certainly identified (because neither *subscriptio* nor initial title survives) have been assigned to Philodemus, in some cases with a high degree of probability. If these were all by Philodemus, they would increase the number of texts by him substantially.[35]

At least eight of Philodemus's works were present in two or more copies in the Villa collection. The titles known to have existed in multiple copies are

> *On Flattery*: *P.Herc.* 222 and 1457
> *On the Gods*, Book 1: *P.Herc.* 26 and 1076
> *On Poems*, Book 5: *P.Herc.* 1425 and 1538
> *On Rhetoric*, Book 2: *P.Herc.* 1674 and 1672
> *On Rhetoric*, Book 3: *P.Herc.* 1506 and 1426
> *On Rhetoric*, Book 4: *P.Herc.* 220 and 1007 + 1673 + 224 + 1077a +
>   1114 + 1677a
> *Sketches of Epicureans*: *P.Herc.* 239a + 1787 and 1418[36]
> *On the Stoics*: *P.Herc.* 155 and 339
> ? *On Plato and the Academy*: *P.Herc.* 1021 and 164[37]

It has been suggested that in at least some of these pairs one copy was less formal and perhaps a preliminary draft, while the other copy was a more formal one. Tiziano Dorandi argued that it was Philodemus's practice to circulate a draft of his treatises among his friends and associates, then to revise in light of their comments, and finally to issue a revised and more

33. In addition, the *subscriptio* of *P.Herc.* 1008 provides only a book number; but here the title is very brief in any case: Περὶ κακιῶν ι΄, or *On Vices*, (Book) 10.

34. On subtitles: M. Terentius Varro wrote a multivolume work called *Logistorici* (or *Logistoricon libri*). It consisted of seventy-six separate rolls, each of which had its own title (e.g., "Catus de liberis educandis"; "Tubero de origine humana"). See Chappuis (1868), 1–7. There are probably other examples, but in general in antiquity book numbers, not subtitles, were employed.

35. Many of the papyri with conjectural titles in the list in Gigante (1979), 49–52, would fall in this category.

36. This work is often called *Memorie Epicuree* in the modern literature. Janko (2008), 42–43, discusses the contents and date of *P.Herc.* 239a + 1787.

37. *P.Herc.* 1021 could be, but is not necessarily, an early draft of the text represented by *P.Herc.* 164. See Cavallo (1984), 13–17, and above, section 1.10.

polished version of the text for general distribution.[38] The practice seems reasonable and can be paralleled in Galen, but there are several uncertainties. First, as we will see in chapter 4, duplicates are common in Roman book collections, and their presence in a collection does not in itself imply the existence of a progression of versions, from draft to finished product. Second, it is not always clear, given the poor state of preservation of many Villa manuscripts, which of a given pair might be the more polished one.[39] Third, we do not have any direct evidence that Philodemus circulated his drafts, either regularly or occasionally; that must for now remain an assumption. What we can say is that the owner of the collection was happy to preserve duplicates, and that some of them might represent successive drafts of works.[40]

Finally, we know of at least four works by Philodemus—*On Marriage, On Praise, On Beauty,* and *On Diction*—that have not yet been identified among the rolls from the Villa but are likely to have formed part of the collection.[41] In sum, the Villa collection included at least thirty-four and probably forty or more works by Philodemus, some in at least two copies (or copies of successive drafts), and many consisting of from two to ten book rolls.

Polystratus (Epicurean, succeeded Hermarchus as head of the school ca. 240). A roll of the late second century BC containing Book 1 of Polystratus's *On Philosophy* and a late first-century BC volume containing his *Against Irrational Doubters* have been identified.[42]

Zeno of Sidon (born ca. 150; Philodemus and Cicero heard him lecture ca. 80). One roll, containing Zeno's *Response to the "On Geometric Proofs" of Craterus* and dated to the first century BC, has been identified.[43]

Incerti. In addition to the rolls that can be assigned with some confidence to specific authors, the Villa collection includes at least nine rolls by

---

38. Dorandi (2007), 68–77.

39. Cavallo (1983), 57, for example, took *P.Herc.* 26 as part of a preliminary draft, but Delattre (2006), 77, takes it as a formal copy. In a number of cases, it is not clear whether the differences between two manuscripts of the same work are due to author's revisions or to scribal errors: Blank (1998).

40. We do know of one manuscript—*P.Herc.* 1021—that was certainly not a final version, but rather notes and short drafts preparatory to writing. For manuscripts that have been interpreted as drafts for discussion, see also below, section 3.8, on the term *hypomnematicon* in *subscriptiones*.

41. They are known from references to them in extant works or fragments of Philodemus.

42. *P.Herc.* 1520 and *P.Herc.* 336 + 1150, respectively. For dates, see Cavallo (1983), 32, 45, and 51 (on *P.Herc.* 1520); and Cavallo (1983), 43 and 56 (on *P.Herc.* 336 + 1150). The copy of *Against Irrational Doubters* includes a carefully centered *subscriptio*, and a name, M(arcus) Octavius, is written below the final column and may be that of a previous owner of the manuscript. See Capasso (1995), 188–89, and Houston (2013), 192–93.

43. *P.Herc.* 1533. See Kleve and Del Mastro (2000).

unknown or uncertain authors that are well enough preserved for papyrologists to date them, determine something of their contents, or both. Listed in approximate chronological order—that is, in the order in which they were copied, not necessarily composed—these are as follows.

P.Herc. 439. Middle of the third century BC. A treatise perhaps on physics as the Epicureans understood it, involving atoms.[44]

P.Herc. 176. Second century BC. Biographical sketches of Epicureans, with quotations from their letters.[45]

P.Herc. 1158. Second century BC. Possibly Stoic rather than Epicurean.[46]

P.Herc. 118a. Before Philodemus, and so probably second century. This manuscript seems to quote passages from letters of Epicurus or other Epicureans, and it could be an anthology or a history of the school.[47]

P.Herc. 831. Probably early first century BC. Subject uncertain. Perhaps by Demetrius Laco.[48]

P.Herc. 1041. Middle or late first century BC. The surviving fragment describes the final illness of someone, presumably an Epicurean.[49]

P.Herc. 1570. A treatise, perhaps of the first century BC, that deals with poverty, wealth, and related subjects.[50] Perhaps by Philodemus.

P.Herc. 1111. This short fragment is an undated selection of passages from a series of Epicurean works.[51]

P.Herc. 696. An undated manuscript, perhaps on ethics.[52]

3.4. THE MANUSCRIPT COLLECTION: LATIN AUTHORS AND WORKS

The Villa collection, or at least the part of it that survives, seems to have included sixty to eighty rolls in Latin.[53] Something is known about several of them, although in most cases only very small fragments have been recov-

---

44. Janko (2008), 64–65.

45. Cavallo (1983), 44, 57, and 60; Militello (1997), 49–56.

46. Cavallo (1983), 31, 45, and 50; Puglia (1993), 39–43.

47. Militello (1997), 82–83, with earlier bibliography.

48. Date: Cavallo (1983), 38 and 54. A reader for the University of North Carolina Press has informed me that a date ca. 100–80 BC appears likely. Author: Delattre (2006), 78.

49. Date: Cavallo (1983), 34 and 51–52. Content: Crönert (1906), 73–74.

50. Ponczoch (2009).

51. Obbink (1996), 300–301.

52. Capasso and Dorandi (1979), 37–41.

53. Sixty: Del Mastro (2005b), 188–89. Eighty or more: Capasso (2011), 23–24. The two figures are reasonably close, given the many uncertainties.

ered. The best preserved Latin manuscript is a poem that included a narrative of the Battle of Actium, the so-called *Carmen de bello Actiaco* (*P.Herc.*
817), by an unknown author who cannot have been writing before the date
of that battle and thus not before 31 BC. Three manuscripts contain the texts
of speeches: *P.Herc.* 1067, which appears to have been addressed to one of
the emperors and so must date late in the first century BC or in the first century AD; *P.Herc.* 1475, probably a judicial oration; and *P.Herc.* 238a, probably a political speech.[54]

In addition to these more or less securely identified fragments, Knut
Kleve thought that he could identify a number of fragments from Book 6 of
Ennius's *Annales* (*P.Herc.* 21), and others from a *subscriptio* that he took to
be Caecilius Statius's *Obolostates sive Faenerator* ("The Usurer") (*P.Herc.*
78).[55] Kleve also argued that he had found fragments of Book 2 of Lucretius's *De rerum natura*, and possibly of Books 1, 3, 4, and 5.[56] In recent years,
however, scholars have become increasingly skeptical of Kleve's identifications, and I do not include them in appendix 2.[57] Two other manuscripts
contain unidentified Latin texts copied in the first century BC. They are
P.Herc. 1491 (prose) and *P.Herc.* 1558.[58] Lucretius's poem would, of course,
be a logical title for inclusion in the Villa's collection, and it may well turn
up in future discoveries.

3.5. ESTIMATING THE SIZE OF THE COLLECTION

We can estimate the size of the collection in two ways, first by working from
the number of fragments found so far, and second by considering the authors and works that have been identified. In both cases, we are dealing
with the largely philosophical collection that has emerged to this point. It
is possible that general collections of Greek and Latin literature were stored

---

54. *P.Herc.* 1067: Costabile (1984), 593–95; Capasso (2011), 61–62. The *subscriptio* contains the
letters L · M, which have been restored as L(uci) M[anlii Torquati]. If that is correct, then Manlius
Torquatus, a praetor in 49 BC, might have been the author. See further Costabile (1984), 597–99, and,
for a corrected reading of the *subscriptio*, Del Mastro (2005b), 191–92. *P.Herc.* 1475: Costabile (1984),
595–97. *P.Herc.* 238a: Janko (2008), 35–40; cf. Capasso (2011), 62.

55. Caecilius Statius: Kleve (1996). Ennius: Kleve (1990).

56. Kleve (1989 and 2007). Beer (2009), expanding upon the work of earlier scholars, has shown
that no clear evidence of the presence of a copy of Lucretius's poem has been found in the Villa. Kleve
(2012), 74–77, responds to Beer.

57. Radiciotti (2009), 105, rejected all of Kleve's hypotheses. On Lucretius in particular, see Beer
(2009). Capasso (2011), 63–86, in a detailed review of the evidence and the scholarly debate, also rejected Kleve's claims.

58. *P.Herc.* 1491: Kleve (1994), 318, and Radiciotti (1998), 365–70. *P.Herc.* 1558: Radiciotti (1998),
357, 365–70.

elsewhere in the Villa, and the discovery of any such materials would obviously change our conception of the contents and size of the Villa's collection of manuscripts. Such a discovery, however, is not likely to alter significantly the conception of the professional collection, centered on the works of Philodemus, that we already have.

Marcello Gigante's catalog of the papyri found in the Villa listed 1,826 items, a total which has now been increased to 1,850.[59] This does not mean that there were 1,850 book rolls in the collection, for many of Gigante's catalog entries are but parts of rolls or even small fragments, and we know that in some cases many *P.Herc.* numbers all come from a single original book roll. Thus no fewer than ten fragments, each a separate *P.Herc.* entry, come from one roll, Book 4 of Philodemus's *On Music*, and some nine *P.Herc.* numbers are all part of the first roll of *On Piety.*[60] The 1,850 *P.Herc.* entries, in short, represent many fewer full rolls, possibly as few as six or seven hundred.[61] Even if we accept higher estimates—1,000 book rolls, for example, or 2,000—the point is that this collection was a significant one, hundreds rather than dozens of volumes, but that it did not run to several thousands of book rolls.

What happens, now, if we look not at numbers of fragments, but rather at the authors, titles, and distinct works that are known to be present in the collection? At present, some sixty-nine different Greek and Latin works have been identified either by a *subscriptio* or initial title, or by conjecture from their contents. They are listed in appendix 2, column 1. Many of them were multivolume works. Epicurus's *On Nature* filled thirty-seven books, at least eight of which were in the Villa collection. Demetrius Laco's *On the Aporiae of Polyaenus* filled at least five rolls, of which two are represented in the Villa collection, and Philodemus's *On Death* ran to four or more rolls. Philodemus wrote at least two comprehensive works on ethics that required ten or more volumes, with each of the ten constituent volumes having its

---

59. Gigante (1979). Additions: Capasso (1989), *P.Herc.* nos. 1827 to 1838; and Del Mastro (2000). Del Mastro did not assign *P.Herc.* numbers to the fragments he catalogued.

60. *On Music*: Delattre (2006), 22. *On Piety*: Obbink (1996), 62–73. One of the copies of *On Rhetoric*, Book 4, consists of at least four *P.Herc.* numbers (*P.Herc.* 224, 1007, 1114, 1673) and perhaps five others as well: Janko (2008), 48. There are numerous instances of manuscripts that certainly or probably come from a given work and are all in the same scribal hand, and as scholars produce editions of those works it is likely that many individual rolls will be found to have been divided among two or more *P.Herc.* numbers.

61. Litta, cited by McIlwaine (1988), 64–65, argued for just over 600 rolls, Delattre (2006), 22–24, for some 650 to 700. Janko (2000), 4, reckoned that "somewhere between 800 and 1,100 books were originally retrieved from the Villa." Radiciotti (2009), 103–4, estimated 2,000 book rolls in the entire collection (120 of them in Latin), and Del Mastro and Leone (2010), 315, estimated some 1,100 rolls.

own number and perhaps a distinct subtitle, but not all ten of the compo-
nent books have yet appeared among the Villa's book rolls. We can thus be
confident that the Villa collection included far more than the sixty-nine
titles that can be specifically identified at present. If we assume that there
was a complete set of every multivolume work, we would have a total of
about 180 to 190 book rolls in the Villa collection.[62]

Surely, though, there were more than 190 book rolls in this collection.
We know of some duplicates, we can assume there were others, and there
must also be titles as yet completely unknown to us.[63] If we were to assume
that only half of the titles in the Villa collection have been identified so far,
we might double this figure, to 380; and if there was on average a duplicate
copy of every volume (which is highly unlikely), that figure would double,
to 760. This is, of course, speculation. It has, however, some value: like the
numbers of fragments we calculated above, it suggests that this collection
was substantial but not enormous, hundreds but not thousands of volumes.
Both methods of reckoning size lead us to similar conclusions.

Let us consider, for a moment, some of the implications of these figures.
If we have a collection of some 600 to 1,100 volumes, and if 58 percent of
those volumes are by Philodemus, as is indicated by the surviving *subscriptiones*, then the book rolls by authors other than Philodemus will number
between approximately 275 and 460.[64] This means that the collection cannot have included anywhere near all of the volumes by the major Epicurean
writers. In Book 10 of his *Lives of the Philosophers*, Diogenes Laertius provides a list of what he takes to be the seventeen chief Epicurean writers and
informs us that the works of Apollodorus alone filled 400 rolls, those of Epicurus 300. He gives the titles of twenty-two works by Metrodorus and characterizes Zeno as a prolific author. And there were works by thirteen others
as well, so that we have as a minimum 750 rolls, and probably many more.
This is a considerably larger number than our estimated size of the non-

62. This figure comes from adding all of the numbers of books in column 3 of appendix 2, adding
known duplicates, such as Epicurus's *On Nature*, Books 2, 11, and 25, and allowing for some ten to
twelve as yet unrecognized volumes in the comprehensive sets *On Vices* and *Syntaxis* (*History of the
Philosophical Schools*). There are uncertainties throughout, hence the approximate total (180 to 190)
rather than an exact number.

63. Scholars continue to identify new works among the manuscripts. Zeno of Sidon's work on
geometry was first identified in 2000: Kleve and Del Mastro (2000). A previously unknown work that
seems to deal with poverty and wealth and could be by Philodemus has recently been partially deci-
phered by Ponczoch (2009). Del Mastro (2011–12) recently read the title of a work by Epicurus, *Echelaus*, in the *subscriptio* of one of the Villa rolls. More works will appear in the future.

64. For these figures (slightly rounded off), and the data upon which they depend, see Houston
(2013), 184–85.

Philodemean collection in the Villa (275 to 460 book rolls). The collection, then, must have had significant gaps. That is indicated also by the authors present. Of the seventeen Epicurean writers listed by Diogenes, one or more works of only six—Colotes, Demetrius, Epicurus, Metrodorus, Polystratus, and Zeno—have been found in the Villa so far.[65] In short, the Villa collection of Greek texts is a useful reminder of a basic fact of book collections: they are selective. Owners make choices. Even in the context of such wealth as is manifest in the Villa of the Papyri, works that we might have expected to find may be absent.

3.6. ASSESSING THE NATURE OF THE COLLECTION

The Villa collection as we know it has long been characterized as a specialized collection with a particular emphasis on Epicurean texts.[66] We can, however, make a series of observations that will sharpen that picture considerably. In its focus on philosophy (broadly defined), the Villa collection is similar to the one represented by *P.Ross.Georg.* 1.22 (section 2.7 above), and like that collection it includes a variety of materials. We have in the Villa works by eight different Greek Epicurean writers, one Stoic (Chrysippus), a number of Roman public speakers, and the author of what may have been an epic poem centered on the conflict between Mark Antony and Octavian Augustus. A broad range of subjects, including geometry, mathematics, and literary criticism, is represented, and there are strong interests in theology, aesthetics, and ethics.[67] Most striking is a particular interest in rhetoric and oratory. When the Villa was destroyed in AD 79, it contained copies of at least four and probably all ten of the books of Philodemus's *On Rhetoric*, duplicate copies (perhaps earlier drafts) of at least three of those books, and the texts of three or more speeches in Latin: *P.Herc.* 1067, addressed

65. Philodemus is not in Diogenes Laertius's list. We must, of course, allow for future discoveries, but it is not at all likely that the unidentified rolls and fragments will reveal the presence of 300 or more additional Epicurean titles. Dorandi (1997), 48, made the attractive suggestion that so few texts of Zeno have been found in the Villa because the compositions of Philodemus himself reproduced, to a considerable degree, the lectures and thought of Zeno.

66. Detailed lists of the contents of the collection are presented in Delattre (2007), xlviii–lii, for the works of Philodemus, and in Houston (2013), 197–208, for the works by authors other than Philodemus. A checklist of the entire collection is included here as appendix 2.

67. For theology, see Delattre (2006), 91–92. In aesthetics, we have works on poems, music, and rhetoric. In ethics, there are Philodemus's studies of various vices and virtues, character, and (the proper) life, as well as Carneiscus's *Philistas* (on friendship) and Metrodorus's work on the proper use of wealth. These groups of works are well summarized by Delattre (2006), 87–89 (ethics) and 89–90 (aesthetics), and their Epicurean content is analyzed by Sider (2005), 84–92. Tsouna (2007) analyzes Philodemus's work in ethics.

to an emperor; *P.Herc.* 1475, probably judicial; and *P.Herc.* 238a, probably a political speech.[68] In all, some fifty-three fragments, in at least ten different hands, have been assigned, some with certainty thanks to a *subscriptio*, others conjecturally, to Philodemus's *On Rhetoric.*[69]

There are numerous manuscripts of Epicurus, but almost all of those identified so far come from his great work *On Nature.* Of his other works, only one, *Echelaus*, has been found.[70] Yet Epicurus was a prolific writer. Diogenes Laertius gives us the titles of forty of his treatises and says they totaled about three hundred book rolls.[71] From a papyrus found in Egypt, we know that at least some of Epicurus's numerous works were extant and circulating in the first century AD (when Vesuvius erupted), and we might well have expected the Villa collection to include at least the three great letters of Epicurus—the ones to Herodotus, Pythocles, and Menoeceus— since Diogenes quoted those letters in full, we know the Epicureans valued letters, and Philodemus had referred in his own works to seventeen different letters to or from Epicurus.[72] Some of this material may yet turn up, of course, but for now it is reasonable to suggest that the owner of the Villa collection was much interested in Epicurus's *On Nature*, but not much concerned to collect his other works.

Given that the collection seems to be, and is generally regarded as, a professional collection, it is useful to recall that Philodemus was not only an Epicurean scholar. He was also a poet. Close to three dozen of his epigrams survived and entered the manuscript tradition (while none of his

68. See appendix 2 for the *P.Herc.* numbers of *On Rhetoric.* The duplicates are *P.Herc.* 1427 (Book 1), 1674 (Book 2), and 1506 (Book 3). *P.Herc.* 1067: Costabile (1984); cf. Del Mastro (2005b). *P.Herc.* 1475: Costabile (1984), 595–97. *P.Herc.* 238a: Janko (2008), 35–40.

69. For the fragments and possible reconstructions of the whole of Philodemus's *On Rhetoric*, see Dorandi (1990b) and Longo Auricchio (1996). Several of the fragments have been dated to late in the first century BC or early in the first century AD, and, if those relatively late dates are correct, they may indicate a continuing interest in rhetoric. Thus *P.Herc.* 1114, 1693, 238b, 1015 + 832, 1001, 232, and 473, as well as many of the fragments of Book 4. These fragments were dated by Cavallo (1983), Janko (2008), or both. Dating on purely paleographical grounds is difficult, however, so the continuing interest in rhetoric cannot be proven.

70. On this work, which is otherwise totally unknown, see Del Mastro (2011–12). We do not know who Echelaus was, and not enough of the papyrus (*P.Herc.* 566) survives for us to tell anything about the content of the work. Del Mastro notes, however, that *P.Herc.* 566 and *P.Herc.* 1589 may belong to the same roll. If that is true, we may someday learn more about Epicurus's *Echelaus.*

71. Diog. Laert. 10.27–28.

72. The papyrus from Egypt is *P.GettyMus.* acc. 76.AI.57 (= Otranto [2000], 17–21), a private letter. It named at least two and perhaps four of Epicurus's works. Diogenes (10.34–116 and 122–35) quotes the three letters because, in his opinion, they presented the essentials of Epicurus's thought. On the value the later Epicureans placed upon the correspondence of Epicurus and his immediate successors, see Daroca and López Martínez (2010), esp. 23–24, or Militello (1997), 76. Delattre (1996), 147–50, lists the references to works of Epicurus by Philodemus.

prose works did), and he wrote a treatise *On Poems* in five books, substantial parts of which survive in the Villa collection, but nowhere else.[73] A fragment of a papyrus from the Villa seems to show that Philodemus knew and was probably a friend of Vergil and several other Roman poets.[74] It is somewhat surprising, then, that none of Philodemus's poetry—no poems, no drafts, no working copies of poems—has yet been discovered in the Villa. At present, we can say that the owner of this collection was certainly interested in Philodemus and collected many of his prose works (or retained them, if he inherited the collection); but so far as we can tell he had no interest at all in Philodemus's poetry.

In the lists of books preserved on papyrus that we looked at in chapter 2, we noticed that there were often what we might call reference works of one sort or another. We found a lexicon in at least thirteen books in list 1 (*P.Vindob.* inv. G 39966, column 2) and a lexicon of Plato in list 3 (*P.Turner* 39); in list 2 (*P.Ross.Georg.* 1.22), there may be two handbooks, the *Basic (Medical) Principles* of Theodas and Chrysippus's *Handbook of Arguments and Modes*; and list 8 (*P.Turner* 9) probably includes several commentaries as well as a handbook (τ[έχ]νη) on an unknown subject. The Villa collection, too, contained such works, although no lexicons have been found yet. There are biographical works, for example Philodemus's *Sketches of Epicureans* (*P.Herc.* 1418 et al.) and the *Life of Philonides* (*P.Herc.* 1044), and there are anthologies of passages (thus *P.Herc.* 1111, a series of passages excerpted from Epicurean works), and works that served in various ways as commentaries. Demetrius dealt with textual and critical problems in a series of passages from the works of Epicurus (*P.Herc.* 1012), Zeno commented on and responded to a work on geometry by Craterus (*P.Herc.* 1533), and Philodemus related the contents of some, and perhaps many, of Zeno's lectures.[75] We might also note Philodemus's multivolume work on the histories of the various philosophical schools, which could well have served not only as a work of philosophical exposition, but also as a reference work of historical information.[76]

73. For Philodemus's epigrams, which have come down to us in the Palatine Anthology, see Sider (1997). Books 1, 3, and 4 of *On Poems* have been edited by Janko (2000) (Book 1) and Janko (2011) (Books 3 and 4).

74. *P.Herc.Paris.* 2, first read in 1986–87 and published by Gigante and Capasso (1989). There is further useful discussion in Sider (1997), 19–21.

75. Three of Philodemus's works declare themselves, in their *subscriptiones*, to be derived from Zeno's lectures: *P.Herc.* 1003, 1389, and 1471. *P.Herc.* 1258 may be a fourth.

76. Philodemus's work on the Stoics (*P.Herc.* 155 and 1018) is certain thanks to its surviving *subscriptio*. The titles of other works, which may have included books on Plato and the Academics, the Eleatics and Abderites, and the Pythagoreans, are inferred from their content. The organization by philosophical school suggests a handbook.

There is strikingly little overlap between the volumes found and identified in the Villa and those cited by Philodemus in his written work. In 1996, Daniel Delattre published a list of the authors and titles cited by Philodemus and noted which of those works had been identified as present in the Villa collection.[77] A summary of what he found follows.

Epicurus. Philodemus cited eleven or twelve treatises of Epicurus and mentioned letters to or from seventeen different correspondents. Of all of these, only *On Nature* has turned up in the Villa so far.

Hermarchus. Philodemus cites five works by title and one by "pseudo-Hermarchus." No work by Hermarchus is known from the Villa.

Metrodorus of Lampsacus. Philodemus cites seven works by title, plus a letter to Colotes. Of these, only *On Wealth* has been found so far.

Polyaenus. Philodemus refers to three works by title, plus letters and two works of doubtful authorship. No work by Polyaenus is known from the Villa.

Zeno of Sidon. Philodemus cites two of Zeno's works by title and gives a further list of Zeno's works that includes seven titles. None of the named works has been found in the Villa yet.

Other Epicurean writers. Philodemus mentions Antiphanes, Bromius, and Timasgoras as sources, without giving titles. He refers to "selected lectures" (ἐπίλεκται σχολαί) of Diogenes of Tarsus. No work of Antiphanes, Bromius, Timasgoras, or Diogenes of Tarsus is known from the Villa collection.

Non-Epicurean writers. Delattre found references in Philodemus to fifty specific titles that are not known to have been present in the Villa collection. These include works by eleven Stoics, four from other philosophical schools, and various works of Greek poetry (epic, tragedy, and comedy) and prose (speeches, historical works, and criticism).

The contrary is true as well. A number of treatises have been found in the Villa but are never referred to by Philodemus, so far as we know at present.[78] Of the twenty treatises known from the Villa by authors other than Philodemus and Epicurus, Philodemus cites two or perhaps three: Metrodorus's *On Wealth* and Chrysippus's *On Divination*. Put another way, Philodemus does not cite seventeen, or 85 percent, of the known texts by authors other than himself and Epicurus.[79]

---

77. Delattre (1996). Additional works cited by Philodemus could probably now be added.

78. I do not count the manuscripts in Latin here, since most of them postdate Philodemus and so could not have been cited by him.

79. Of the manuscripts found in the Villa that have been identified so far, Philodemus does *not* cite or refer to Carneiscus's *Philistas*, Chrysippus's *On the Elements of Propositions* and *Problems of Logic*, Colotes's *Against Plato's "Euthydemus"* and *Against Plato's "Lysis,"* any of the ten treatises by Deme-

If we were to assume that the Villa collection was, at one point, Philodemus's working library, we could explain this discrepancy in various ways. First, of course, we might guess that the volumes Philodemus cites are still buried and waiting to be found, and that, as more of his works are read, we will find that he cited more of the volumes that have been found. Perhaps volumes present in the library in Philodemus's day, and cited by him, were given away or sold after his death. He might have borrowed book rolls from friends, or been granted access to other collections, whether in Rome or on the Bay of Naples or elsewhere. He may have cited earlier authors not directly but through an intermediate source, or simply from memory.[80] The owners of the Villa in AD 79 may have taken book rolls with them as they fled the eruption. As usual, there are many uncertainties, but one conclusion that does emerge from the difference between the works Philodemus cites and those found in the Villa is this: the collection as we know it does not seem to have been shaped by Philodemus with a view toward what he might find useful, either in his philosophical or in his poetic work. Perhaps it was not shaped by Philodemus at all, but by some later collector.

3.7. THE BOOK ROLLS AS PHYSICAL OBJECTS

The manuscripts discovered in the Villa of the Papyri are, as we would expect, almost exclusively papyrus rolls; there are no examples of ostraca, parchment, or codices.[81] The eighteenth-century tunnelers found roughly thirty wooden boards—seven in the tablinum, twenty-three in room V— that may have served as the wooden backing of wax tablets such as were used for writing notes, drafts, and short compositions. The tablets, which have not survived, may originally have been tied together to form one or more polyptychs, and it is conceivable, though not likely, that they contained literary or scientific texts.[82] We know nothing more about them, and they can be omitted from our study.

---

trius Laco known from the Villa, Polystratus's *Against Irrational Doubters* and *On Philosophy*, or Zeno of Sidon's *Response to the "On Geometric Proofs" of Craterus*. It is not clear if he refers to Metrodorus's *Against the Sophists* (or *Dialecticians*) or not.

80. For intermediate sources, especially in cases where Philodemus is citing the earliest Epicureans—Metrodorus, say, or Epicurus himself—see Delattre (1997), 115. Note also Sedley (1989), 104, suggesting that Philodemus's knowledge of the debates between Stoics and earlier Epicureans derived not from direct knowledge, but from the lectures of Zeno that Philodemus had attended as a young man.

81. Codices were probably not used, or used very rarely, for literary texts before the second century AD (Roberts and Skeat [1983], 24–37), so it is not surprising that no codices have been found.

82. The tablets are known from eighteenth-century descriptions: Capasso (1990). The tablets found in the Villa were about twice as tall as the tablets customarily used for documents (cf. *CIL* 4,

The papyrus rolls from the Villa appear to have been generally of good quality. Many of them have numerous scribal errors, but the mistakes were regularly corrected by the original scribe or, in some cases, a second hand.[83] Most are some 19 to 24 cm high, with the columns of text occupying ¾ to ⅘ of that height, or roughly 15 to 18 cm.[84] Columns average 5 to 6 cm in width, intercolumnar spaces 8 to 12 mm. The size of letters, and thus the number of lines per column, varies markedly: the columns in *P.Herc.* 1676 contain about 28 lines, those in *P.Herc.* 1021, 1424, and 1497 each about 40.[85] Rolls could and did vary greatly in length, because the texts they contained varied in length, and examples ranging from 6.5 m to more than 20 m in length are known, with many some 9 to 12 m long.[86] The diameter of the manuscripts, when they were rolled up, varied within a range of about 4 to 9 cm.[87] None of the manuscripts found so far is illustrated, but at least three contain geometrical figures.[88] The ends of texts, and sometimes ends of sections within a text, were regularly marked by a *coronis*, a decorative and sometimes elaborate punctuation mark. These vary greatly in size and form, but scribes do not seem to have developed their own individual *coro-*

Suppl., p. 277 [Zangemeister]; Camodeca [2002], 272–75), suggesting that they may have served a different purpose. Hence the possibility of their use for nondocumentary texts.

83. Delattre (2006), 65–66. Delattre takes the second corrector as a professional proofreader, or *diorthotes*.

84. Cavallo (1983), 48–49. The heat of the eruption of Vesuvius may have caused the book rolls to shrink some 5 to 10 percent: Capasso (2007).

85. Cavallo (1983), 18–19. Papyrus rolls known from Egypt seem to have been, on average, somewhat larger, most often 25 to 33 cm high, with columns regularly 14 to 24 cm high and 4.5 to 7 cm wide: Johnson (2004), 141–42, 101, and 119, respectively. Delattre (2006), 43–44, points out that we do not have dimensions for the earlier manuscripts in the Villa collection, only for those of Philodemus.

86. Basing his conclusions on the evidence available when he was writing, Cavallo suggested that the Villa papyrus rolls were for the most part close to 10 m in length and suggested that that was the "standard" length. Both the specific length and the concept of a standard length have entered the literature. Work since Cavallo, however, has revealed that there is considerable variation in the length of rolls, and it now seems misleading to speak of a "standard" length. Some examples: *P.Herc.* 1424 was 6.5 m long (Delattre [2006], 47); *P.Herc.* 1414 9 m long (Delattre [2006], 49, citing Cavallo); *P.Herc.* 1050 10 m long (Cavallo [1983], 15); *P.Herc.* 1497 + other fragments probably about 11 m long (Janko [2000], 119); *P.Herc.* 1471 about 12 m long (L. M. White [2009], 38 and 61); *P.Herc.* 1426 12.2 m long (Janko [2000], 119); *P.Herc.* 1427 was 15 to 16 m long (Puglia [1997b], 123–25; cf. Janko [2000], 119); and *P.Herc.* 1783 + 1691 + 1010 (Epicurus, *On Nature*, Book 2) may have been 20 m long (Leone [2012], 353–54). The roll containing *On Piety* seems to have been over 23 m in length (Janko [2000], 114).

87. Delattre (2006), 51–52, gives 6 to 8 cm as the normal diameter; Capasso (2007), 77, some 4 to 6 cm. Allowing for shrinkage due to the volcanic material, we might take the diameters of rolls as varying from about 4 to about 9 cm. The longer the roll, of course, the greater its diameter when it is rolled up.

88. *P.Herc.* 1061, 1642, and 1822, all of them texts by Demetrius Laco. The first two date to the second century BC, the last from the first century BC or the first century AD. See Horak (1992), 244, for *P.Herc.* 1061 and Tepedino Guerra (1991), 95–96, for *P.Herc.* 1642 and 1822.

nides as self-identifying signatures; so far as we can tell, such marks served only to mark ends of passages with decorative signs.[89]

Some manuscripts were copied with particular care or appear to be unusually elegant. Thus *P.Herc.* 1027, a copy of Carneiscus's *Philistas*, Book 2, probably dating to the second century BC, contains few or no corrections, is written in an elegant script with generous margins, and includes stichometric counts in both the margins and the *subscriptio*.[90] A copy of Demetrius Laco's *On Some Topics for Discussion* (*P.Herc.* 1006, first century BC) has wide margins and large letters, and even though the letters vary in form, ranging from formal to a near-cursive, its editor takes it as a high-value manuscript.[91] *P.Herc.* 1113a, a treatise probably on sensation and perhaps part of Epicurus's *On Nature*, is written in large letters by an expert hand.[92] Several other manuscripts, including some texts of Epicurus and Philodemus, are classed by their modern editors as high-quality copies.[93] At least one such high-quality manuscript is known from every century from the third BC through the first AD.

On the other hand, some of the Villa's manuscripts were carelessly copied.[94] A late first-century BC copy of Polystratus's *Against Irrational Doubters* (*P.Herc.* 336 + 1150) contains numerous omissions, repetitions, and errors, often but not always corrected by the original scribe.[95] *P.Herc.* 1418 (Philodemus, *Sketches of Epicureans*) and *P.Herc.* 346 (a work on Epicurean ethics by an unknown author), both of the first century BC, were copied by particularly careless scribes, and *P.Herc.* 1065 (Philodemus's *On Methods of Inference*) is "a poor copy. It contains many scribal errors, some of which were corrected through deletions and superscriptions."[96]

---

89. This is unfortunate for us because if each scribe had developed his own *coronis* as a kind of signature, the *coronides* could have helped us identify scribes and perhaps the place and date of copying.

90. Capasso (1988), 140–44, 147–50.

91. Assante (2008), 112–13, 156.

92. Janko (2008), 82–85. Janko calls it an "elegant edition" and dates it in the second or first century BC. It may come not from Epicurus, but from a work by Philodemus on poetry: Janko (2008), 84.

93. Epicurus: *P.Herc.* 1149 + 993, third or second century BC (see Leone [2005], 25); *P.Herc.* 1413, first half of the third century BC (see Crisci [1999], 54–56, and Janko [2008], 89); Demetrius: *P.Herc.* 1055, first century AD; Philodemus's *On Poems*, Book 1 or 2, for which see Janko (2000), 76. The last included stichometric counts.

94. Editors often comment on this. Capasso (1982b), 24, n. 21, for example, remarked that inattentive transcription is quite frequent ("la trascrizione disattenta . . . è abbastanza frequente nei rotoli ercolanesi").

95. Indelli (1978), 87–93.

96. *P.Herc.* 1418: Militello (1997), 101–3. *P.Herc.* 346: Capasso (1982b), 24. *P.Herc.* 1065: De Lacy and De Lacy (1978), 11. Janko (2000), 81–83, noted that the manuscript of Philodemus's *On Poems*,

The mistakes in these manuscripts are instructive in at least two ways. First, the majority of them seem to be due to faulty readings, rather than to the scribe mishearing a dictated text. The scribes, we may infer, were for the most part writing not from dictation, but by copying out written texts one at a time.[97] Second, mistakes in the texts that survive often seem to have arisen from corrections in the exemplars from which they were copied; the scribe of the copy that survives in the Villa did not understand or correctly interpret a correction in his exemplar, and that led to the error we see. We may probably conclude that, even in the case of manuscripts containing works by Philodemus, we are dealing not with the original archetype, but with copies, and perhaps with copies of copies.[98]

A number of manuscripts were damaged but still—whether repaired or not—retained in the collection. *P.Herc.* 1420 + 1056 (Epicurus's *On Nature*, Book 25) was copied in the second century BC, torn into two parts not long thereafter, and then repaired, the second section (*P.Herc.* 1056) being attached to the first. It is not known why the roll was torn in two. It may have been an accident, but the original roll (now represented by *P.Herc.* 1420) was carelessly copied, and it is possible that the second half of the roll was removed on purpose and replaced with a more accurate copy.[99] *P.Herc.* 176 (*Sketches of Epicureans*, by an unknown author, copied in the second century BC) changes scribal hands after about 1.7 m of text. The first part of the text (A) was copied later than the second part (B), and in the last four columns before the change from A to B the letters are crowded together. It may be that the original of part A was damaged during use and therefore recopied, and that the scribe who did the recopying wanted to end his new copy at the bottom of a column, so that it would join neatly with what followed (B). The scribe could then have found himself compelled, as he approached the end of part A, to crowd his text in, in order to avoid starting another column.[100] In *P.Herc.* 1050 (Philodemus's *On Death*, Book 4, copied

---

Book 1, had many errors and that most were left uncorrected. The list of low-quality manuscripts could easily be extended.

97. I give here a simple statement of a complex matter. For a careful consideration of the question (scribes working from a text, or from dictation?), see Yuen-Collingridge and Choat (2012), especially 827–30. They are concerned with documents rather than literary texts, but the same considerations will apply to both.

98. Rispoli (1988). She notes also that, for many of the texts she studied, more than one exemplar seems to have been available to the scribe.

99. Puglia (1997b), 40–42, provides a detailed analysis of this repair. See also Del Mastro (2010a), 40–47.

100. Puglia (1997b), 42–43 and 96. Perhaps, though, it was simply that the end of the roll was damaged in use and replaced. So Henry (2010), xxvi, with n. 49.

in the third quarter of the first century BC), there is a change of hands, column heights, column widths, and even of the width of the papyrus, so that the most likely explanation is that the end of the roll was damaged and subsequently replaced.[101]

In some cases it is difficult to tell if a manuscript was damaged and repaired, or if in the process of copying one scribe simply replaced another for a certain period of time.[102] In a copy of Philodemus's *On Poems*, Book 2 or Book 3 (*P.Herc.* 1074b + 1677a + 1081b et al.), hand B substituted for hand A for perhaps seven to ten columns.[103] In this instance, it is likely that one scribe replaced another. Similarly, in an uncertain book of Philodemus's *On Rhetoric* (*P.Herc.* 1669 plus other fragments), a second scribe took over the copying at a certain point, but the first hand returned and copied the last column.[104] In a number of cases, it is unclear if the presence of two scribal hands is due to a repair or to having two scribes work on separate parts of the manuscript.[105]

The Latin manuscripts are generally less well preserved, so that judging their original quality is difficult, but both formal and informal scribal hands are represented.[106] *P.Herc.* 817 (the so-called *Carmen de bello Actiaco*) has columns that average 19.5 cm in width, or about 50 percent wider than the norm for columns of hexameter verse in papyri from Oxyrhynchus, but this simply reflects the fact that it is written in an unusually large script.[107]

There does not appear to be evidence of damage caused by insect larvae or mice in the Villa papyri. Damage from mice would be difficult to detect in rolls so disastrously damaged, but worm holes, if they existed, could be expected to show up in the form of a series of small holes recurring at regular intervals. I have found no evidence of such in the plates in Cavallo (1983) and conclude that the Villa volumes were adequately protected against insect larvae.[108]

101. Henry (2009), 90–91. The two hands belong to different groups (I and K) in Cavallo's classification.

102. Robert Babcock tells me that it is common to find places in medieval manuscripts where one scribe has replaced another for a number of lines. If a scribe was called away from his copying, another one would replace him so that the ink, which dried quickly, would not be wasted.

103. Del Mastro (2009), 285; Del Mastro (2010a), 6–9. The change of hand takes place in the middle of a column. A third hand added some annotations in the bottom margin.

104. Del Mastro (2010a), 9–20, with a summary at 19.

105. Del Mastro (2010a), 20–40, discusses several examples (*P.Herc.* 807, 1050, 1670, and 1738).

106. Variations in Latin hands: Radiciotti (1998), 356–59.

107. Width of columns in *P.Herc.* 817: Lowe (1938), no. 385. Hexameter verse at Oxyrhynchus: Johnson (2004), 116.

108. Cavallo (1983), plates 1–60. Worm holes are known from papyri found in Egypt: Cockle (1983), 152; Puglia (1991), 30–32, with an excellent photograph of a papyrus that exhibits such holes. Insect

A few of the manuscripts contain writing, or traces of writing, on both sides of the papyrus and thus might be opisthographs.[109] Mario Capasso studied the known examples and concluded that in most cases the texts on the verso were short and probably intended to add something to or modify the text on the recto; that we have no example of a book roll from the Villa in which both sides were completely covered with text, or in which the verso of a roll was reused to copy an extended text distinct from the one on the recto; and that only two rolls are known in which the text on the recto may have been continued on the verso.[110] These are *P.Herc.* 972 and *P.Herc.* 1670. The first has not been unrolled and its contents are unknown, but traces of Greek text can be seen on exposed sections of both the recto and the verso. *P.Herc.* 1670 is more interesting: parts of thirty-six columns survive on the recto, and parts of seven are known to have survived on the verso. Author and title are unknown, but the texts on both recto and verso seem to be responses by an Epicurean to a Stoic or to Stoic arguments, and both responses could thus come from the same text.[111]

More interesting yet is *P.Herc.* 1021, a famous fragment that clearly has writing on both the recto and the verso. The text on the recto contains notes, revisions, additions, and deletions. A few columns are out of order. At one point a note, ὀπίσω ("over"), appears, and several lines of text, evidently an addition, are entered on the verso at this point in the roll. Guglielmo Cavallo, who first drew attention to the nature of this roll, pointed out that it is clearly not a final draft, nor even a continuous text, but rather notes, drafts of passages arranged in a roughly logical order, and revisions toward a text.[112]

In short, there is no clear evidence at present to suggest that in the Villa the backs of papyrus rolls were reused to copy new texts, or that texts continued from one side of a roll to another. If someone compiled a book list of these manuscripts like the lists in chapter 2, he probably would not have

---

larvae and the damage they could cause were well known to ancient book owners: Vitr. *De arch.* 6.4.1, 5.12.7; Lucian *Ind.* 17; and in general Puglia (1991), 35–42.

109. The Villa manuscripts that have been unrolled are glued to a backing to give them stability. As a result, the writing on the verso, if there is any, cannot ordinarily be seen, and we depend upon old reports, mostly from the time of the unrolling, for our knowledge of opisthographic material. Any account of opisthographic material is therefore tentative.

110. Capasso (2000), 24. A total of eight manuscripts from the Villa are now known to have had at least some writing on both the recto and the verso: Capasso (2007), 75.

111. Capasso (2000), 8–9 and 13–20, for these two papyri.

112. Cavallo (1984), 14–17; cf. Capasso (2000), 21–24. The work is probably Philodemus's history of the Academy and, if that is the case, a revised version of the text may well survive in *P.Herc.* 164.

entered the annotation "opisthograph" beside any of the entries. In this collection, evidently, such economies were unnecessary.

Very few of the manuscripts in the Villa collection contain writing in the margins, and, where such writing does appear, it consists for the most part of corrections or revisions to the text. In some cases, there are entries of several lines but uncertain content, written in the hand of the original scribe.[113] In a few instances, a second hand has entered what might be explanatory text or some sort of commentary. A fragment of Philodemus's *On Poems* (*P.Herc.* 994) contains such a note, in a second hand, at the bottom of one column. In *P.Herc.* 243, fragment 3 (Philodemus, *On Piety*, second part) a second hand entered lines that pertain to passages from the *Iliad* quoted in the text above; and Dirk Obbink noted that some passages in Philodemus's *On Rhetoric* contain what may be scholia.[114] I have not found any clear example of a comment added by a reader of the text.[115] In this respect, the Villa texts are similar to the papyri from Egypt, where about 5 percent of all texts contain marginalia, most of the marginalia consist of scholarly notes copied by the scribe along with the rest of the text, and very few marginalia appear to be readers' interventions or personal thoughts. Ordinarily, it seems, readers did not write in their book rolls.[116]

3.8. PARATEXTUAL MATERIAL IN THE VILLA PAPYRI

Many of the papyri from the Villa include paratextual material, or brief annotations that stand outside the text proper and provide information about the content of the roll. Most often, this consists of an end title writ-

---

113. At the bottom of at least five columns in *P.Herc.* 152 (Philodemus's *On the Gods*) there are notes of three or four lines each, in the same hand as the main text, but much smaller: Diels (1916), 20, column f, 4; 22, column g, 5; 24, column 6; 50, fragment 28a; and 51, fragment 31. Diels noted that these might be the comments of someone on the text of Philodemus, or material omitted by the scribe, or additions by Philodemus that were written in by the scribe either from dictation or from a written note. Diels was inclined to think they were additions by Philodemus.

114. *P.Herc.* 994: Sbordone (1976), 6, fragment 5; *P.Herc.* 243: Obbink (1996), 78; *On Rhetoric*: Obbink (1996), 78.

115. I have searched for signs of marginal comments in the texts published in the series *La scuola di Epicuro* (Naples) and in a few other extensive texts. The *P.Herc.* entries I have searched are *P.Herc.* 26, 152, 157, 182, 310, 460 + 1073, 994, 1005, 1018, 1065, 1074 + 1081 + 1676, 1418, 1425 (all texts of Philodemus); and *P.Herc.* 188, 1014, 1027, and 1055 (by authors other than Philodemus).

116. There are a few striking exceptions. Among the Villa papyri, someone reading *On Poems*, Book 1 (or 2), seems to have added accents as a test of statements made in the text: Janko (2000), 84–85. In Egypt, one of the papyri from Oxyrhynchus is a text of Plato's *Republic* that was extensively annotated by a reader, perhaps as he listened to a lecture on or discussion of the text: McNamee and Jacovides (2003).

ten by the scribe who copied the text and providing the name of the author, the title of the work, and, where appropriate, the number of the book:
Ἐπικούρου περὶ φύσεως Β΄ ("Epicurus's *On Nature*, Book 2"; *P.Herc.* 993), for
example.[117] Typically, the *subscriptio* was written in two or three lines that
were centered on a single axis, and it was placed to the right of the last column of text. Occasionally, the scribe placed the *subscriptio* below the final
column, and in at least two cases there are two *subscriptiones*, the second
entered to the right of the first and containing the same information, but
written in calligraphic script. The purpose of these second *subscriptiones* is
not obvious, but since they give no additional information, they may have
been purely decorative. It appears that the same information—author, title,
book number—was often and perhaps regularly included in an initial title
at the beginning of the roll, and that would obviously make it much easier
to locate a given title or a particular roll within the collection.[118]

About 30 percent of the known *subscriptiones* contain information that
goes beyond the basics of author, title, and book number. So far as we can
tell at present—and the evidence is very limited—there is no discernible
standardization of either content or form in such extended *subscriptiones*.
In the case of a multivolume work such as Philodemus's *On Vices*, where the
individual books or sections may have had their own distinct subtitles, we
sometimes find the title of the whole work written out in full, followed by
a book number, and then, after ὅ ἐστι ("that is"), the title of the individual
book or section.[119] In at least two cases, the book number is provided but
the subtitle, if there was one, is omitted. Thus *P.Herc.* 1424 provides an extended version of the title of the large work, *On Vices*, of which it forms a
part, and its own book number (9), but it gives no subtitle for Book 9, and
in *P.Herc.* 1008 the *subscriptio* reads in its entirety Φιλοδήμου Περὶ κακιῶν Ι΄
("Philodemus's *On Vices* [Book] 10"). These last two are of interest from the
librarian's point of view. If the physical volumes were stored in alphabetical

117. Note the list of *subscriptiones* given by Gigante (1979), 45–48: fifty-one of the seventy-two
subscriptiones, or 70 percent, certainly or probably provided author and title, book number in those
cases where a work consisted of more than one book, and no other description of the text. Some, as we
will see shortly, added counts of lines, columns, or papyrus sheets. Papyrologists generally regard such
counts as separate from the *subscriptio* proper, and I follow that convention here.

118. Few initial titles survive in the Villa manuscripts because the outer layers of most rolls were
destroyed in the eruption of Vesuvius. Where they do survive, they usually provide the same information about the roll as one finds in the *subscriptio*. An exception is *P.Herc.* 1457 (Philodemus, *On
Vices*), where the initial title provides the title of that particular roll, while the end title gives only the
book number.

119. Thus *P.Herc.* 222, an initial title of *On Flattery*, Book 1 of *On Vices*. See on this Capasso
(2001b), 194. The formula ὅ ἐστι appears also in works not by Philodemus, for example in *P.Herc.* 1786
by Demetrius Laco (title unknown).

order as in lists 5 and perhaps 4 in chapter 2—that is, first by author, then by title—then these works must have been filed by the title of the general work, *On Vices*, rather than by the title of the individual volumes, because the individual titles were not supplied in the manuscripts.[120] Such an arrangement—by book number, not title of book—is also suggested by the probable extension of a given subject, flattery and related topics, over the first two books of Philodemus's *On Vices*: the easiest method of identifying a specific book would be by book number.[121]

At least four manuscripts identify themselves in their *subscriptiones* as *hypomnematica*: *P.Herc.* 168 (title unknown); and *P.Herc.* 1427, *P.Herc.* 1674, and *P.Herc.* 1506, copies of Philodemus's *On Rhetoric*, Books 1, 2, and 3, respectively.[122] There has been much discussion about the exact meaning of the term *hypomnematicon*, with Tiziano Dorandi arguing that it indicates an early draft of a manuscript intended for circulation among friends, as opposed to a final copy for general distribution.[123] If this is correct, these manuscripts include an unusual type of information in their end titles: not the *identification* of the roll by author, title, and book number, but the *function* or *status* of the roll. Such bibliographical information is rare in other *subscriptiones*, although we will consider a few other examples in the next paragraph, and we may well consider this thesis uncertain; the term *hypomnematicon* might simply be a part of the title of these works, more or less the same in meaning as *hypomnema* ("notes," "commentary," or "summary") and omitted or included at the discretion of the scribe.[124]

Several other types of information occur, although rarely, in the *subscriptiones* of manuscripts in the Villa collection. The questions to be asked about them are these: Does this information appear to have been included in order to help identify specific texts and distinguish them from others?

120. There are uncertainties. Initial titles or *sillyba* in these manuscripts may have included the titles of the individual books.

121. Book 1: *P.Herc.* 222, Περὶ κολακείας. Book 2: *P.Herc.* 1457, [Περὶ τῶν] κολ[ακείαι ὁμοειδῶν]. The title of Book 2 is largely a modern reconstruction, but it accords with the content of the book and has generally been accepted. See, e.g., Monet (2001), 200.

122. For *P.Herc.* 168, see Del Mastro (2010b). Dorandi (2007), 70–71, sets out the evidence for the other three manuscripts. *P.Herc.* 89 and 1001, sometimes taken as *hypomnematica*, are too fragmentary to permit any conclusion, according to Del Mastro (2010b).

123. Dorandi (2007), 70–77. In two cases, we have what may be more polished and professional versions of the same texts: *P.Herc.* 1672 (*On Rhetoric*, Book 2) and *P.Herc.* 1426 (*On Rhetoric*, Book 3). It is not entirely clear, however, that the changes from one version to another represent purposeful revisions. It is possible that some or all are simply scribal errors or variants: Blank (1998), esp. 133. I am grateful to Professor Blank for an email discussion of this matter.

124. So Blank (1998). We have seen variations in titles above in, for example, Philodemus's work *On Vices*, the title of which appears in at least three different forms.

Using this information as our evidence, can we argue for some sort of systematic classification of manuscripts? Do we find signs of persons working on, sorting, or arranging the manuscripts? The items in question are as follows.

In *P.Herc.* 336 + 1150 (Polystratus, *Against Irrational Doubters*), the *subscriptio* provides a title, then adds οἱ δὲ, or "but some give it the title . . ." This can hardly be part of the title Polystratus himself assigned the work, and is more likely a note by a scribe, added to avoid confusion and to help those searching for the work by its alternate title.

In three manuscripts the *subscriptio* supplies the information that the particular work stretches over two book rolls, and that this is the first (or second, as the case may be) of the two rolls.[125] This, too, is unlikely to have been the author's concern, and we might see in these notes an attempt to provide bibliographical information that would assist both the library worker, who would want to know where to file the roll, and the reader, who would want to know where to find it.

In *P.Herc.* 163 (Philodemus, *On Wealth*), the number of columns (*selides*) is given in tiny letters between the last column and the *subscriptio*.[126]

In at least two manuscripts, a scribe entered Greek numerals above and to the right of the *subscriptio*, probably to indicate the number of books in the entire work. Thus in *P.Herc.* 1005 (title uncertain) the Greek numerals [A], B, Γ, Δ, and E appear, one below the other, and in *P.Herc.* 1497 (Philodemus, *On Music*, which was in four books), the scribe wrote A, B, Γ, and Δ, again in a vertical column. In both cases, the numerals may have been intended to help users organize and keep track of the rolls in multivolume works.[127] This could certainly have helped the reader or collector tell if he had the entire work, and it could assist anyone who was assembling a list of the book rolls in a collection.

In *P.Herc.* 1426 (Philodemus's *On Rhetoric*, Book 3) there is written, below the end of the final column of text, "Of Poseidonax, son of Biton." Poseidonax might be the scribe of this (or an earlier) copy, identifying himself; or it might be the name of a bookseller. Most probably, however, this is the name of neither a scribe nor a bookseller, but of a former owner of the manuscript.[128]

---

125. *P.Herc.* 1423: "*On Rhetoric*, Book 4, in two parts of which this is the first"; *P.Herc.* 1007 + 1673: "*On Rhetoric*, Book 4, in two parts of which this is the second"; *P.Herc.* 1538: "*On Poems*, Book 5, the second of the two parts."

126. Del Mastro (2003), 326. The number given is 110 or perhaps more.

127. Del Mastro (2002), 247 and 253–54.

128. Bookseller or scribe (the same person might be both, of course): Bassi (1909), 484. See also

Similarly, in *P.Herc.* 1032 (Colotes, *Against Plato's Euthydemus*), the name Χαρισίου appears below the last line of the last column, a bit to the right of and above the *subscriptio* that gives the author and title. As in *P.Herc.* 1426, this might be the name of a copyist, but it was taken by Crönert as the name of a former owner, and that is probably the correct interpretation.[129]

Three manuscripts containing books of Epicurus's *On Nature* contain archontal dates, and in one of them (*P.Herc.* 1479 + 1417, dated on paleographical grounds to the second century BC) there is a brief note below the usual *subscriptio*: [. . ? . .] τῶν ἀρχαίων [. . ? . .] / [one line seems to be missing] / ἐγ[ρ]άφη ἐπὶ Νικίου τοῦ μ[ετ]ὰ Ἀν[τι]φάτην: "of (or from or about?) the old ones . . . written in the archonship of Nicias who succeeded Antiphates [= 296–295 BC]." This is all in the hand of the scribe who wrote the text. The meaning of τῶν ἀρχαίων, and the reason for the inclusion of the dates in the three manuscripts, has been much discussed.[130] To omit the details, it is very likely that the dates represent the dates of composition of the three works, because the manuscripts concerned—*P.Herc.* 1148, 1151, and 1479 + 1417—contain Epicurus's *On Nature*, Books 14, 15, and 28, and the archontal dates 301/300, 300/299, and 296/295, respectively.[131] The archontal dates, then, provided the owner or collector with no useful information about the date, place, or quality of the earlier copy. On the other hand, the phrase [ἐκ] τῶν ἀρχαίων—if that is how the phrase is to be restored—may have been added by the scribe who copied the text to indicate that he had used as his exemplar a reliable old manuscript.[132] If this is correct, then

---

Ohly (1924), 202 (Poseidonax as owner); Cavallo (1983), 46 (scribe, because, Cavallo argues, text and name are in the same hand); Delattre (2006), 67 (scribe, agreeing with Cavallo). Hammerstaedt (1992), 13, disagreed with Cavallo, noting that the hand that wrote "Poseidonax" is not that of the main text. In that case, Poseidonax might be the name of a *diorthotes*, or professional corrector. I would note three things: the hand that wrote Poseidonax appears in Cavallo's plate—Cavallo (1983), plate 43—to be quite different from the hand that wrote the text; second, the inclusion of the filiation, "son of Biton," ought to mean that Poseidonax was not a slave copyist, since only a freeborn man would ordinarily carry a filiation; and third, we appear to have the name of a book owner, Marcus Octavius, written in two other manuscripts from the Villa collection. While certainty is impossible, the evidence available at present points to Poseidonax being an owner of the manuscript at some point.

129. Crönert (1906), 162; text on 170. Cavallo (1983), 57, assigned this manuscript to the late first century BC or early in the first century AD. If that is correct, the manuscript may have entered the Villa collection at quite a late date: it was copied, then owned for some unknown period of time by a man named Charisius, and then found its way to the Villa.

130. For the archontal dates, see Leone (1984), 37–38, and Millot (1977), 26. Earlier bibliography and theories: Puglia (1997d), 103–5.

131. I owe this observation to a reader for the University of North Carolina Press.

132. For the preposition [ἐκ], see Puglia (1997d), 105–6. Puglia suggests that the archontal date is the date at which this "old one" was copied, and that the second line, now lost, may have added more information.

we have an instance of a scribe specifying the nature (and implicitly the quality) of his archetype.

Three manuscripts are identified as "from the lectures of Zeno."[133] This might have been an annotation added by someone organizing the collection or sorting rolls in it, but it is much more likely part of the title as conceived by the author Philodemus.

In the aggregate, these bits of evidence provide welcome indications of scribal initiatives, but they do not suggest large-scale or systematic professional work on the collection. None of the types of information appears in more than three manuscripts; the notes are short and often cryptic; there is no unambiguous example of a person working with the collection and adding information that would help in the identification, organization, or storage of the manuscripts. On the contrary, the very rarity of such bits of information calls attention to the fact that there was not, in the manuscripts from the Villa of the Papyri, any systematic effort to provide bibliographical information beyond the basics of author, title, and book number. Scribes (with the possible exception of Poseidonax) do not identify themselves; place and date of the copies are not included; identity or source of the archetype from which a copy was made is seldom or never included.[134]

Calligraphic *Subscriptiones*

Most end titles were written by the scribe who copied the main text, using the same script in both text and title.[135] Cavallo, however, noted that a few manuscripts include *subscriptiones* written in particularly handsome calligraphic scripts.[136] Since Cavallo wrote, scholars have both refined and expanded his list, and at present it appears that at least two different scribes wrote out calligraphic titles (some initial, some final) in at least eleven different manuscripts, all of them containing texts by Philodemus.[137] The texts, as opposed to the titles, of these manuscripts were written by at least

---

133. *P.Herc.* 1003, *P.Herc.* 1385, and *P.Herc.* 1471. The Greek is ἐκ τῶν Ζήνωνος σχολῶν.

134. From Egypt, we have one or two possible exceptions to this general rule. See above in the introduction on initial titles and end titles.

135. Delattre (2006), 55–56; cf. Cavallo (1983), 23.

136. Cavallo (1983), 23, discussing *P.Herc.* 873, 1005, 1275, 1424, and 1497.

137. The basic discussion is Del Mastro (2002). One scribe, it seems, wrote the calligraphic titles in *P.Herc.* 222, 253, 873, 896, 1275, 1424, 1457, 1583, and 1675, another those in *P.Herc.* 1005 and 1497. Del Mastro assigned *P.Herc.* 1583 to the second group, but it probably belongs to the first: Delattre (2006), 58–60. In *P.Herc.* 1675 there are two *subscriptiones*, the first an ordinary one and the second calligraphic.

five different scribes.[138] Thus it would appear that one or more scribes were working on texts that had been copied at some earlier time, and that in the course of their work they added calligraphic titles. It is, however, difficult to see what the purpose of such decorative titles might have been. In only two cases—the *subscriptio* of *P.Herc.* 1424 and the initial title of *P.Herc.* 222—do they provide any information other than author, title, and book number, so they apparently were not intended to provide special or additional bibliographic information.[139]

In several cases, the calligraphic titles could well have been added in connection with repairs to the volumes. Noting that at least three of the eleven manuscripts show clear signs of repair, and that several others may have been repaired, Gianluca Del Mastro suggested that the calligraphic titles could have been added in the course of work on the collection late in the first century BC.[140] In *P.Herc.* 1424, for example, the original papyrus sheet at the end of the text was trimmed off, and new sheets were glued to it, suggesting that the end of the roll had been damaged or badly worn and so was cut off and replaced, with a new decorative *subscriptio* then being added. In two other manuscripts, *P.Herc.* 1005 (Philodemus; title unknown) and *P.Herc.* 1497 (Philodemus's *On Music*, Book 4), a scribe entered Greek numerals above and to the right of the calligraphic *subscriptiones*, and Del Mastro suggested that this work, too, might have been carried out as part of an effort to restore and upgrade the collection.[141] If Del Mastro is correct, that would help identify the occasion for the addition of such decorative titles, but it would not necessarily explain why calligraphic titles, as opposed to ordinary *subscriptiones*, were added.

138. Cavallo (1983), 45–46, assigned *P.Herc.* 873 to his scribe 18, *P.Herc.* 1275 to scribe 28, *P.Herc.* 1005 to scribe 10, *P.Herc.* 1497 to scribe 26, and all of the others, except *P.Herc.* 1583, which he left unassigned, to scribe 25.

139. One manuscript not in this group shows that a second hand could add such information. In *P.Herc.* 1414, the original scribe wrote a standard three-line *subscriptio*, with author, title, and stichometric count. A second hand added three more lines: δι(ώρθωται?) (= "corrected"?), then the number of papyrus sheets and columns in the roll. Delattre (2006), 48, suggested that in this case part of the roll might have been damaged, and that, after it had been repaired, the corrector checked the repairs by counting and confirming the number of columns and papyrus sheets.

140. Del Mastro (2002), 251–54. The manuscripts that show clear signs of repair are *P.Herc.* 1424, 1497, and 1675; less certain are *P.Herc.* 873 and 1005, and the beginnings of *P.Herc.* 222 and 1457. The calligraphic titles known at present suggest that there was particular interest in the book rolls of the *On Vices*. Six of the manuscripts (*P.Herc.* 222, 253 + 1090, 896, 1424, 1457, and 1675) contain books of that work.

141. Del Mastro (2002), 247 and 253–54.

Stichometric and Other Counts

Many of the manuscripts in the Villa collection, both those containing texts by Philodemus and those containing texts by other authors, include some form of line or other count. There has been considerable discussion of the purposes of such counts, as we noted above in the introduction. Here I will simply assume that their basic purpose was to determine the scribe's fee, but that they may well have served a number of other purposes as well. My principal aim here is to set out the evidence for line and other counts in the Villa manuscripts.

In the Villa manuscripts, stichometric and similar counts take various forms, and the information they provide varies from one manuscript to the next. Taking into account just the manuscripts of works by Philodemus (which might be expected to show some uniformity), we find that counts may appear as summary counts immediately below the *subscriptio* (*P.Herc.* 182, 1389), as running counts in the margins (*P.Herc.* 1424, 1471), or both (*P.Herc.* 1507). Stichometric counts often appear by themselves, but sometimes they are combined with counts of columns (*P.Herc.* 1050, 1675), and one manuscript provides a count of *stichoi*, columns, and papyrus sheets (*P.Herc.* 1414). When we find counts in the margins, they consist sometimes of Greek numerals (*P.Herc.* 1423), sometimes of a combination of points and numerals (*P.Herc.* 1428: a point marks every twentieth *stichos*, a numeral every two hundred *stichoi*), and they may be written in the top margin (*P.Herc.* 1497, in which every tenth column is numbered) or the bottom (*P.Herc.* 1423).[142] A given scribe may vary his practice from one roll to another. Thus Cavallo's scribe 25 recorded the stichometric and column counts in the *subscriptio* of *P.Herc.* 1675, but in *P.Herc.* 1424 he provided only stichometric counts and put them in the margins rather than in the *subscriptio*. There does not, in short, appear to have been any standardization, either in the placement or in the type of counts, in the manuscripts of Philodemus.

Even if they were not standardized, counts were commonly included in the manuscripts of Philodemus and regularly, if somewhat less commonly, in the works of other authors.[143] We have at least forty-nine manuscripts of

142. These manuscripts—just examples, not a complete catalog of book rolls with counts—are all of works by Philodemus and date ca. 70 BC or later. Evidence for the counts is in Bassi (1909); I avoid uncertain cases.

143. It is probable that more manuscripts than we know contained stichometric counts, because the *subscriptiones* and accompanying material are often preserved only in a fragmentary state or not at all.

Philodemus in which the *subscriptio,* initial title, or both survive; of these, at least twenty-two, or 44.9 percent, contain counts of some sort. The counts are usually line counts, or counts of lines, columns, and papyrus sheets, but in three cases we find just counts of columns.[144] Similarly, we have fifteen rolls of Epicurus's *On Nature* that have *subscriptiones* or initial titles or both, and of those, four, or 26.7 percent, have stichometric counts.[145] The comparable figures for manuscripts of all authors other than Epicurus and Philodemus are seventeen rolls that contain a *subscriptio* or initial title or both; of those, six, or 35.3 percent, have stichometric or other counts, or both, in their *subscriptiones* or initial titles.[146]

How are we to interpret these figures? If we assume that the presence of stichometric counts is a strong indication that a scribe had been commissioned or paid to copy the text, then are these texts a sign that some of the works of Philodemus were prepared by professional scribes who were not working in-house? We might well imagine the owner of the collection commissioning copies of certain works, and the scribes therefore including stichometric counts in order to establish what they should be paid. In this connection, it is worth recalling what we noted above in section 3.7: the patterns of errors found in the Villa manuscripts indicate that they were not originals or archetypes, but copies made by scribes reading an archetype and then reproducing it. Even in the case of manuscripts containing works by Philodemus, it seems, we are dealing not with the archetype, but with copies; and they may have been made, on commission, by professional scribes.[147]

---

144. The basic database—that is, the list of manuscripts with titles—consists of the forty-seven items listed as having surviving titles in Gigante (1979), 45–48. To this we can now add three manuscripts. These are *P.Herc.* 209 (Del Mastro [2003], 328–29), *P.Herc.* 310 (Militello [1997], 81), and *P.Herc.* 1583 (Delattre [2006], 58–59). But we must subtract *P.Herc.* 1425, which seems to belong to the same roll as *P.Herc.* 1581: Janko (2000), 13. The three manuscripts that contain column but not (so far as is known) line counts are *P.Herc.* 163 (Del Mastro [2003], 327), *P.Herc.* 1423 (Bassi [1909], 333), and *P.Herc.* 1497 (Bassi [1909], 329–31).

145. The database is again the list in Gigante (1979), 45–48. To that we may add *P.Herc.* 1191 (Laursen [1987]). The four manuscripts with stichometric counts are *P.Herc.* 1042, 1148a, 1151, and 1385. *P.Herc.* 154 may be a fifth example. Houston (2013), 201–2, gives the bibliography.

146. Gigante (1979), 45–48, lists fifteen. To those we may add *P.Herc.* 1380 (Del Mastro [2005a]) and *P.Herc.* 1533 (Kleve and Del Mastro [2000]). *P.Herc.* 1384 includes a line count in the margins, but its end title is lost, so it is not in Gigante's or my list. The six manuscripts with stichometric counts are *P.Herc.* 1027 (Carneiscus), 1032 (Colotes), 1038 (Chrysippus), 1041 (incertus), 1533 (Zeno), and 1786 (Demetrius Laco). Note also *P.Herc.* 1384 (count in margins) and 1158 (column count above every tenth column).

147. I am concerned here with those manuscripts that could reasonably be considered finished copies. Early drafts, in particular the unique manuscript *P.Herc.* 1021, may well be the original or archetypal texts.

Alternatively, it is at least theoretically possible that copies were pre-pared in-house for sale elsewhere and that counts were included in them in order to establish a basis for pricing them on the market. It should be noted, however, that *P.Herc.* 1674, a copy of Philodemus's *On Rhetoric*, Book 2, probably included counts of both lines and columns in its *subscriptio* but is a relatively unfinished copy, with variable script and irregular features.[148] This, in short, should be a manuscript that was by its very nature *not* des-tined to be sold and so not needing to be priced, and yet it seems to include stichometric counts. It is also worth looking at some of the later manu-scripts in the collection. *P.Herc.* 1038, for example, is a copy of Chrysippus's *On Foresight*, Book 2. It was copied late in the first century BC or early in the first century AD, and it includes a stichometric count in the *subscriptio*.[149] Chrysippus was a Stoic, not an Epicurean, and it seems unlikely that the owner(s) of the Villa collection would be producing texts of Stoics for sale; it is far more likely that they purchased this roll either on commission or on the market, and that in either case it had been prepared by a professional scribe. The evidence from within the collection is slim but seems to indicate that a significant proportion of the rolls from the Villa collection that have stichometric counts were produced not in-house but outside the collection; we might well believe that they were commissioned, rather than purchased ready-made, but that cannot be demonstrated.[150]

3.9. THE USEFUL LIFETIMES OF THE PAPYRI

Most of the papyrus rolls that survive in the Villa collection are texts writ-ten by Philodemus, and most of them seem, on paleographical grounds, to have been copied during Philodemus's lifetime. Thus most of the rolls in the Villa collection were some 120 to 160 years old when Vesuvius erupted.

---

148. Cavallo (1983), 63–64; Dorandi (2007), 71–72. It is one of the manuscripts that calls itself, in its *subscriptio*, "hypomnematicon." If we accept the thesis of Dorandi, that *hypomnemmatica* were drafts for discussion, we would have a manuscript that by definition was not intended for circulation, and yet was provided with stichometric and column counts.

149. For the count, see Bassi (1909), 356–57. Note also *P.Herc.* 1384, perhaps another work by Chrysippus, which includes a running stichometric count in the margins: Antoni and Dorival (2007) for the author; Antoni (2007) for the count.

150. Such an assumption—that at least some of the Villa's manuscripts of works by Philodemus were produced by professional scribes working outside the collector's house, as opposed to in-house copyists—might help to explain the large number of different scribes whom Cavallo identified as work-ing on various texts. He identified twenty-one different hands among the manuscripts of Philodemus (his scribes 8 to 28): Cavallo (1983), 45–46. There must be numerous other scribes as well, because there are many manuscripts of works by Philodemus that have not been assigned to any particular scribe.

Manuscripts copied earlier or later than Philodemus's lifetime can be tabulated as follows:

Copied in the third century BC: three manuscripts.[151]
Copied in the third or second century BC: six manuscripts.[152]
Copied in the second century BC: twenty-three manuscripts.[153]
Copied after about 50 BC: fifteen manuscripts.[154]

Thus a majority of the Villa's manuscripts were roughly 120 to 160 years old in AD 79, a small but significant number were from 180 to 280 years old, and a very few were between 300 and 350 years old. It is likely that all or most would have remained usable for some additional period—a generation at least, and perhaps a century—had they not been caught in the eruption of Vesuvius. The useful life of these manuscripts, then, will have been around 200 years on average, with some lasting significantly longer than that. This is comparable to, but slightly longer than, the average age of manuscripts found in concentrations from Oxyrhynchus in Egypt (4.13 below).

3.10. POSSIBLE HISTORIES

Working primarily on the basis of his paleographical analysis and dating of the Herculaneum fragments, Cavallo posited three major stages in the evolution of the Villa collection, as follows.

Stage One. The early manuscripts—those copied in the third, second, and early first centuries BC—formed a core collection of basic Epicurean works. These included most of the manuscripts of Epicurus and Demetrius Laco, the *Philistas* of Carneiscus, Polystratus's *On Philosophy*, and at least one of the works of Metrodorus. These manuscripts had been copied, Cavallo thought, not in Italy or Egypt, but in Greece or the eastern Mediterranean. Philodemus acquired the collection, possibly as a gift or bequest from one of his teachers, and brought them to Italy.[155] If we assume that Philodemus

---

151. *P.Herc.* 1413 (Epicurus); *P.Herc.* 255 + 418 + 1084 + 1091 + 1113 (Metrodorus); *P.Herc.* 439 (incertus).

152. *P.Herc.* 335, 989, 1149 + 993, 1191, 1431, 1479 + 1417. All are texts of Epicurus.

153. *P.Herc.* 1027 (Carneiscus), 1429, 1083, 1647, 1642, 1061, 233 + 860, 188, 1012, 128, 1013 (all Demetrius; some of these fragments may come from the same roll), 1010, 154, 1042, 1148, 1151, 1420 + 1056, 908 + 1390, 1039, 996 (all Epicurus), 1520 (Polystratus), 176, and 1158 (both incerti).

154. *P.Herc.* 1020, 1038, 1380, 1421 (all certainly or possibly by Chrysippus), *P.Herc.* 208, 1032 (Colotes), *P.Herc.* 1055 (Demetrius Laco), *P.Herc.* 362, 1199, 1398 (possibly Epicurus), *P.Herc.* 566 (Epicurus's *Echelaus*), *P.Herc.* 200 (Metrodorus), *P.Herc.* 360 + 1150 (Polystratus), *P.Herc.* 831, 1044 (incerti). For dates and further notes, see Houston (2013), 194, table 11.2.

155. Cavallo (1983), 58–60; Cavallo (1984), 5–12. Cf. Gigante (1995), 18–19. When Cavallo was writ-

had assembled a complete set of Epicurus's *On Nature* in thirty-seven rolls, plus some duplicates, as well as copies of most or all of Demetrius's works and other important Epicurean texts, we can without difficulty imagine a core collection of many dozens and perhaps one or two hundred rolls. It is also possible, of course, that Philodemus brought with him non-Epicurean rolls such as the *Iliad*, but no trace of any such has been identified yet.

Stage Two. This stage consists of copies of various works that were made in the first century BC, more or less during the lifetime of Philodemus.[156] In numbers, this is by far the largest of the three groups. We have forty or more works by Philodemus, several were in more than one book, duplicates of a number have been found, and a few manuscripts by authors other than Philodemus date to this period as well.[157] Cavallo believed that the copies of Philodemus's works, and perhaps some of the others, were produced by slave scribes within the Villa. He noted that in at least one case— Philodemus's *On Rhetoric*—many of the rolls were written in similar hands but over an extended period of time, and from this he concluded that there was an attempt to provide multivolume works with a certain homogeneity in appearance. That might, he thought, be most easily accomplished by in-house slaves trained to certain standards.[158]

Stage Three. Cavallo thought that a number of manuscripts, some of them works of Philodemus, some by other authors, were certainly or probably copied after Philodemus's death.[159] In this group he placed some of the manuscripts of Epicurus as well as copies of works by Polystratus, Metro-

---

ing, the author of *P.Herc.* 255, which he assigned to this early group, had not been identified. We now know it was Metrodorus: Spinelli (1986); Tepedino Guerra (1992); cf. Janko (2008), 56. We may probably add *P.Herc.* 1533, now known to be a work by Zeno of Sidon, and dated in the early first century BC by Kleve and Del Mastro (2000).

156. The exact dates of Philodemus's life are not known, but he seems to have been born around 110 BC and died in the early 30s BC. See Janko (2000), 4–7. It is possible that he died later than is usually thought.

157. These include a copy of Book 1 of Demetrius Laco's *On the Aporiae of Polyaenus* (*P.Herc.* 1258), Demetrius's *On Some Topics for Discussion Concerning the Manner of Life* (*P.Herc.* 1006, an expensively produced roll), one of the copies of Book 25 of Epicurus's *On Nature* (*P.Herc.* 459), and Zeno's *Response to the "On Geometric Proofs" of Craterus* (*P.Herc.* 1533).

158. *On Rhetoric*: Cavallo (1983), 64; cf. Gigante (1995), 29. In-house scribes: Cavallo (1984), 20–21. Cavallo took the creation of copies in-house to be motivated primarily by a desire to increase the number of volumes in the Villa's collection. Any desire to create copies for distribution outside the Villa was, he thought, of secondary importance. Other scenarios have been imagined. Grafton and Williams (2006), 50–51, take Philodemus's volumes as possibly representing "the material remains of a scriptorium devoted to the dissemination of Philodemus's writings."

159. Cavallo (1983), 65. Late manuscripts of Philodemus's own work include *P.Herc.* 1232 (*On Epicurus*), 310 (*Sketches of Epicureans*), 164 (*On Plato and the Academy*) and 1018 (*On the Stoics*). On *P.Herc.* 1018, see Cavalieri (2010), 126, n. 33, supporting Cavallo's late date.

dorus, Colotes, and Demetrius Laco; to his list we may add some and probably most of the Latin manuscripts and most or all of the copies of works by the Stoic Chrysippus.[160] Cavallo noted that no manuscript in the Villa collection can be certainly dated after the earliest decades of the first century A D, and accordingly he suggested that, by the time of the eruption of Vesuvius in A D 79, interest in Epicureanism had fallen off in Campania, and Philodemus had been forgotten. Others have taken the absence of first-century A D manuscripts simply as an indication that the Villa itself had changed hands, with the new owner(s) being less interested in Epicureanism.[161]

If we consider simply the collection of books from the Villa, Cavallo's thesis of three major periods is reasonable. It corresponds to what we might expect, and the rhythm of the collection's development, if we accept this scenario, would be broadly similar to what emerges from a study of a collection known from Oxyrhynchus, Grenfell and Hunt's second find (section 4.10 below). This seems to have included a first group of older manuscripts; a second and substantially larger group, all datable to a period of some fifty years and probably assembled by one or a small number of persons; and a third group that indicates continued but waning interest in the materials in the collection.[162]

What is reasonable, however, is by no means certain, and a number of problems remain. Dates based upon paleographical grounds are necessarily approximate, and they are subject to change as papyrologists continue to study the papyri. Even if the date at which a manuscript was copied can be established, it is not necessarily the date at which that manuscript entered the collection, because any given volume or group of volumes might have been added at any time after it was copied.[163] Also, we have no way of knowing how many rolls, if any, were removed from the collection as time went by. Texts might have been damaged and discarded, given away as presents, lent and not returned, or sold.[164] One of the manuscripts of works by Demetrius Laco that was copied around the end of the second century B C (*P.Herc.*

---

160. See above, n. 154, or Houston (2013), 193–95, for a list and discussion of the late Greek manuscripts. The fifteen Greek rolls were copied by thirteen different scribes. For the dates of the Chrysippus manuscripts, see Del Mastro (2005a), on *P.Herc.* 1380; Delattre (2006), 74, n. 155 (*P.Herc.* 307); and Obbink (1996), 76, n. 1 (*P.Herc.* 1020). To the late manuscripts we may now add *P.Herc.* 566 (Epicurus's *Echelaus*), but almost nothing is known of that work.

161. So, for example, Capasso (1991), 198.

162. Houston (2009), 259–61.

163. There is good reason to believe that one of the copies of Epicurus's *On Nature*, Book 2 (*P.Herc.* 1149 + 993), which was copied in the third or second century B C, did not enter the Villa collection until well along in the first century B C, long after it was created. See Houston (2013), 192–93.

164. This point was made by Sider (1997), 14.

1014) was probably dedicated to a Roman, suggesting a connection between Roman readers and volumes in this collection at least a generation earlier than Philodemus.[165] In sum, a number of the early book rolls might have come to Italy separately from, and well before, Philodemus.

Cavallo's scenario is to some extent dependent upon the assumption that the Villa belonged to L. Calpurnius Piso Caesoninus, the consul of 58 BC and Philodemus's patron, and that Philodemus lived and worked in the Villa. That thesis, which occurred to the scholars working on the Villa papyri very early on, has been either accepted or regarded as likely by many scholars, although there have been some who have had doubts.[166] Recently, however, art historians and archaeologists have reexamined the Villa and its contents, and it has been suggested that the Villa and the sculpture within it were not created until the third quarter of the first century BC, or some twenty-five to thirty years after Philodemus's probable arrival in Italy. In their analysis of the Villa's structure following investigations carried out in 2007 and 2008, Maria Paola Guidobaldi and Domenico Esposito noted that it seems to have been built not in stages, but all at once, and not before the third quarter of the first century.[167] Nothing in the archaeological record as known so far shows that Piso built, owned, or had any connection with the Villa. Pending further investigation, it is best to be cautious. We cannot assume that the Villa belonged to Piso or that Philodemus lived and worked there; both assumptions may well prove to be true, but neither can be established beyond doubt at present.[168]

---

165. Book 2 of Demetrius's *On Poems*, and perhaps Book 1 as well, seems to have been dedicated to a Nero, probably early in the first century BC: Romeo (1988), 66–67. We do not know where Nero would have met Demetrius. Demetrius is, however, known to have lived for some time in Miletus, and Romans might have come to know him there and brought his books and those of other Greek writers back to Italy with them. See Romeo (1988), 66.

166. Delattre (2006), 18–19, and Capasso (2010b) set out the thesis and evidence. For a history of the debate and a clear statement of the arguments on both sides, see Sider (2005), 5–8. For doubts: Mommsen (1880), 32–36; Costabile (1984), 599; and Porter (2007), 99. Variations on Cavallo's thesis have been suggested. Philodemus, for example, might have brought the volumes to Italy, but to Rome rather than Herculaneum, and it is possible that he worked, at least part of the time, in Rome. Gigante (1988), 61, notes that he had a modest home in the city.

167. Guidobaldi and Esposito (2009). They note an essential unity of plan, a similarity of constructional techniques through all the known parts of the Villa, and stucco and mosaic decorative elements that are consistent with a date in the third quarter of the first century. In addition, they note that C. Moesch has recently dated the nucleus of the Villa's sculptural collection to the third quarter of the century: Guidobaldi and Esposito (2009), 368. See also Guidobaldi (2010), 69, dating the Villa itself to the period 40–20 BC, and its furniture to the late Augustan or early Julio-Claudian period. The date of the Villa is, however, far from settled. De Simone (2010), 11, for example, noted that the Villa fits comfortably within the context of luxury residences built between about 60 and 40 BC.

168. Piso was active politically until early in 43 BC, but he then disappears from the historical

Alternative scenarios may be suggested. Plutarch tells us that the collection of texts brought to Italy by Lucullus attracted Greek scholars.[169] Perhaps, then, a wealthy Roman bought a collection of book rolls in Greece that contained a number of Epicurean texts and brought it to Italy. Lodged in his house in Rome or in a country villa, such a collection would have attracted Greek and Roman scholars, and Philodemus could have been one of them.[170] Or perhaps a Roman of the early Empire became interested in Epicureanism, bought Philodemus's works en bloc from Philodemus's heir or heirs, added any other volumes he could find or have copied, and eventually housed them in the Villa. It is useful to recall that many of the Villa's volumes contained stichometric counts, suggesting if not proving that they were commercially produced. It is therefore possible that the copies of Philodemus's works found in the Villa were commissioned and made in Rome and only later transferred to the elegant villa on the Bay of Naples. Finally, we may note that the Villa collection included copies of various books of Epicurus's *On Nature* that were produced over many generations, and that one or more of the Villa's manuscripts of *On Nature* was produced in almost every period from about 250 BC to the early first century AD.[171] We cannot know precisely what this means in the context of collection building. It might indicate that the collection grew gradually through copying or commissions, but it might also suggest retrospective purchases in a used-book market.

3.11. CONCLUSION

The collection of book rolls known to us from the Villa of the Papyri existed, in the form we know it, in AD 79 and consisted, in all probability, of some 600 to 1,000 rolls, most of them about 150 years old at the time Vesuvius

---

record, and he may have died in that year: *RE* 3.1389–90, s.v. Calpurnius, no. 90 (F. Münzer). It is not impossible, then, that Piso died before the Villa was built. An inscription from Pola, on the other hand, may provide evidence that he was still alive in the late 30s BC. See Frischer (1991), 115–25; but note also the doubts of Muecke (1993), 214. At present, we do not know when Piso died.

169. Plut. *Luc.* 42.1–2.

170. Lucullus's collection contained a significant number of Stoic texts: Cic. *Fin.* 3.7. Like the Villa collection, it was strong in at least one philosophical school.

171. Early third century BC: *P.Herc.* 1413. Third or second century BC: *P.Herc.* 1149 + 993 (Book 2), 1191 (Book 25). Second century BC: *P.Herc.* 1148 (Book 14), 1151 (Book 15), 1420 + 1056 (Book 25; repairs in second century BC). Late second century BC: *P.Herc.* 154 and 1042 (both Book 11). Second or first century BC: *P.Herc.* 697 and 1634 (both Book 25). Late first century BC: *P.Herc.* 362 (Book 21). Late first century BC or early first century AD: *P.Herc.* 1199 and *P.Herc.* 1398, both of which are probably but not certainly from *On Nature*. No manuscript containing Epicurus's *On Nature* was dated by Cavallo to the middle of the first century BC. Otherwise, every broad period is represented.

erupted, but some younger than that and a few as much as 300 years old. In several respects, this collection resembles, either in general or in some details, one or more of the collections known from the book lists in chapter 2. In general content, it is not unlike the collection recorded in *P.Ross. Georg.* 1.22 (list 2). Both collections are to a considerable degree focused on philosophical topics and include other materials consistent with such a focus. In the list from Egypt, we found treatises, dialogues, and letters—all genres that were common in ancient philosophical discourse—covering a wide range of topics, including ethics, discussion of abstract concepts, and political science (two of Aristotle's *Constitutions*). Beyond the philosophical works, there may have been a novel. Similarly, the Villa collection includes a broad range of formal genres and subjects, as we have seen. Duplicate copies of some works appear in the Villa collection, just as they do in some of our lists, as for example list 7 (*PSI Laur.* inv. 19662 verso) and list 5 (*P.Oxy.* 33.2659). Works of reference appear both in the Villa collection and in the Egyptian lists, though no lexicons have yet been discovered among the Villa's manuscripts. In size, the Villa collection is of the same order of magnitude as, for example, the collection represented by list 4 (*P.Vars.* 5 verso): both are very substantial but not enormous, containing hundreds but not, it seems, thousands of book rolls.[172] In a pre-Gutenberg context, of course, this is an impressive collection, and it is larger than the likely size of all but one of the collections known from our Egyptian lists. In general, then, the Villa collection resembles, within predictable limits, the collections that we can reconstruct from the book lists found in Roman-era Egypt.

The Villa collection tells us much more about the individual manuscripts than the Egyptian lists do. Its manuscripts tend on the whole to be serviceable texts with numerous mistakes that were usually corrected by the original scribe. There are, however, a significant number of manuscripts that are either more elegant or considerably less elegant than the norm. Some, like *P.Herc.* 1027 (Carneiscus) are unusually accurate; some have wide margins and letters that are large or well formed or both (for example, *P.Herc.* 310, 1006, 1113a, 1787); others are simply judged by their modern editors to be particularly high-quality copies (section 3.7 above). Cavallo suggested that the various manuscripts of the *Rhetoric* were copied by scribes trained to write more or less in the same hand, even though they were copied over a period of many years, and that the intent was to give the whole work a con-

---

172. As we have noted, it is possible that more volumes will be found in the course of future excavations in the Villa. In that case, we might compare the collection implied by *P.Oxy.* 33.2659 (list 5), another collection that may have contained thousands, but probably not tens of thousands, of volumes.

sistent and elegant appearance.[173] A few manuscripts were provided with highly decorative titles. As seems to be usual in ancient book rolls, there are very few marginal annotations that contain a reader's personal reactions.

A considerable number of the Villa's manuscripts were carelessly copied, and in some cases we can see that the exemplars from which the copyists were working were faulty.[174] Cicero's complaint, that it is difficult to find high-quality copies of texts, is here made manifest. In the manuscripts we have, column widths in any given manuscript may vary widely from the norm, and letter sizes, especially in the Latin manuscripts, can vary as well. Particularly interesting, given the wealth evident in the Villa, is the fact that a number of manuscripts were apparently damaged but then repaired and preserved, as opposed to being replaced with sound new copies; thus *P.Herc.* 1420 + 1056 (Epicurus) and *P.Herc.* 1050, both discussed above. (Of course, they may have been damaged even before they entered the collection.) There are also instances of manuscripts copied by more than one scribe. Very few if any of the Villa manuscripts seem to have been conceived or produced as ostentatious and expensive pieces. As far as we can tell at present, the collection does not contain as high a percentage of high-quality or expensively produced manuscripts as one of the concentrations known from Oxyrhynchus in Egypt. The latter is the collection represented by the papyri found by Breccia in 1932 and by Grenfell and Hunt in their third find; I will describe this in detail in the next chapter, and here we need remark only that it is of some interest that a collection from a city of moderate importance in Egypt could, so far as we can tell, surpass in terms of quality and elegance the collection from the Villa of the Papyri.

The manuscripts in the Villa collection were copied by many different scribes. Cavallo identified thirty-four different hands, and there are hundreds of rolls or fragments that have not yet been assigned to any individual scribe, so the total number of scribes could well be many dozens. Combined with the fact that close to half of the surviving manuscripts include stichometric counts (section 3.8 above), this may indicate that a significant percentage of the Villa's collection was produced commercially, rather than by slaves within the household. It is important to note what this means. First, commercial production need not mean that booksellers produced copies of the works found in the Villa on speculation, hoping to sell them. It more

---

173. Cavallo (1983), 64: "omogeneità grafica." He also suggested that the various parts of the *History (Syntaxis) of the Philosophers* were copied by scribes who were trained to write in a similar fashion: Cavallo (1983), 62.

174. Above, section 3.7, for examples.

likely means that professional scribes were commissioned to produce useful copies of the works. The absence of a second hand as corrector in many or most of the first-century BC manuscripts (which tend to contain numerous small errors) may indicate that the person commissioning the work was not overly concerned with accuracy, and just wanted a readable text. We must also note that, in the light of the recent archaeological work indicating that the Villa itself was not built before the third quarter of the first century BC, while many of the manuscripts seem to have been copied rather earlier, the locus of commissioning and copying may have been not the Villa, but elsewhere, perhaps in Rome, where it would have been possible to find large numbers of scribes.[175]

The Villa collection was, as might be expected given the context, reasonably well cared for and managed. There are a few duplicates, but not many, and that may imply careful management and oversight: why, the collection's owner may have thought, spend money on unnecessary volumes?[176] We will consider the Villa's storage facilities in chapter 5, but we may note here several indications of careful maintenance: the absence of worm holes, the repairs to manuscripts that had been damaged, and the occasional signs that workers provided assistance, in the form of paratextual materials, to potential readers.[177] We may also note that such assistance is relatively rare, and that the Villa collection, like the Egyptian lists, gives no indication that there was systematic cataloguing or comprehensive organization of the collection that was designed to help readers find specific volumes. We may assume that there was a book list somewhere in the Villa, and that, like the Egyptian lists described in chapter 2, it provided the names of authors and the titles of their works, probably in alphabetical order, and it may have given the number of rolls of each work present in the collection.

By analyzing and reorganizing the information so painstakingly acquired

---

175. Del Mastro (2000), 251–54, noted that repairs to some manuscripts and additions of calligraphic *subscriptiones* may have been carried out in the course of a general restoration of the collection late in the first century BC. It might be useful to place that observation within the context of the newly proposed date of construction of the Villa. If the collection was originally housed in Rome, it might have been transferred to the Villa late in the first century BC, once the Villa had been built, and that transfer might have been the occasion for repairs and improvements to the collection.

176. In some cases, the volumes that were present in duplicate may have been of special interest. Examples might be Books 2, 11, and 25 of Epicurus's *On Nature* and Books 2, 3, and 4 of Philodemus's *Rhetoric*. But there were also two copies of a work on various Epicureans (*P.Herc.* 1418, 310, and 239a + 1787) and perhaps three copies of Philodemus's *On the Stoics* (*P.Herc.* 339, 155, and 1018), neither of which is likely to have been considered a seminal or historically essential work.

177. It should be noted, however, that we usually cannot know when a repair was carried out, and that some manuscripts may have been damaged and repaired before they entered the collection. This was certainly the case with *P.Herc.* 1420 + 1056, which was repaired in the second century BC.

by the papyrologists, we have been able to suggest answers, some tentative and some quite secure, to many of the questions that our examination of the Egyptian book lists in chapter 2 left open, especially those concerned with the physical properties of an ancient collection. Still, we are not yet in a position to understand the Villa collection fully nor to assess every aspect of it. We will need to consider the physical space and the storage containers in addition to the book rolls themselves, and that will take up a part of chapter 5. More immediately, we need to look at other collections of book rolls so that we can put the Villa collection within a useful context. How typical is the Villa collection? In what ways, if any, do other collections differ from it? How wide a range of variations is there? To provide such contextual material, we will turn, in chapter 4, to the archaeological remains of book collections found in the Egyptian city of Oxyrhynchus.

4

The Book Collections of Oxyrhynchus

4.1. INTRODUCTION

Situated on a western branch of the Nile about two hundred kilometers south of Cairo, the ancient Oxyrhynchus (modern el-Behnesa) was a city of considerable size and importance. Its population probably numbered, at its height, between fifteen and thirty thousand, making it roughly the size of, or somewhat larger than, Pompeii, and it was the administrative center of the Oxyrhynchite nome.[1] Over the course of time, the people of the town discarded huge amounts of material, creating vast trash heaps; and fortunately for us, they occasionally discarded rolls and sheets of papyrus that contained works of literature, reference works, and documents of all sorts. Thanks to the dry climate, some of those sheets and rolls survived, generally as small fragments, to modern times, and in the period from 1896 to 1907 the British papyrologists Bernard Grenfell and Arthur Hunt explored the trash heaps of Oxyrhynchus and salvaged as many such fragments as they could.

From very early in their explorations, Grenfell and Hunt noticed that the ancient residents of the town had occasionally thrown out not just random materials, but substantial collections of interconnected written materials. These concentrations, coherent in date and content, usually consisted of official documents or of some individual's letters and accounts, but in the winter of 1905–6 Grenfell and Hunt discovered three concentrations each of which contained numerous literary papyri.[2] The first of these finds, consisting of fragments found so close together that Grenfell and Hunt were confident they had all been discarded at one time and all came from a single library, was made on January 13 and 14 of 1906. The second find came to

---

1. Estimates of the ancient population: Bowman, Coles, et al. (2007), 171, n. 3.

2. Bowman, Coles, et al. (2007), 360–61, reprinting the annual accounts provided by Grenfell and Hunt in the *Egypt Exploration Fund Archaeological Reports*.

light at some point between January 17 and January 22, 1906, and took many weeks to recover, while the third concentration was excavated and recovered in the period from January 27 to January 29 of the same year. A generation later, in 1932, the Italian papyrologist Evaristo Breccia discovered an important concentration of fragments that almost certainly derives from the same collection as Grenfell and Hunt's third find.[3]

In this chapter, I will describe and analyze these three concentrations and, more briefly, two other identifiable collections from Oxyrhynchus: a number of astronomical papyri that seem to have been recovered together and that have now been identified by Alexander Jones as apparently deriving from a single ancient collection;[4] and finally a small group of manuscripts that Roger Bagnall has shown belonged to a woman, Aurelia Ptolemais, or to her family. These five groups of papyri provide evidence of several different types of collection; study of them illustrates a variety of methodologies that can be employed to assess such materials; and their shared provenance (Oxyrhynchus) and dates of deposition (all within a period of about 150 years) provide some assurance that they can reasonably and usefully be considered together.

Grenfell, Hunt, and Breccia all believed, and it is the essential assumption of this chapter, that the fragments in each of these concentrations of papyri came from a single ancient book collection and were thrown out together when the owner(s) no longer wanted them. Each such concentration thus represents all that survives of some one book collection or library.[5] It must be acknowledged at once that it is impossible to prove that the literary papyri in each of these concentrations were thrown out together and originated in a single and distinct collection or library.[6] There are, however, good reasons to believe that this is in fact the case.

First, we have concentrations of documentary papyri that were excavated together and can be shown, thanks to the names and dates on them, to have

3. It is just possible that Breccia's find represents a separate concentration and thus a fourth ancient collection. See section 4.4 below.

4. As we will see, these are not literary papyri, but the collection is of interest in the context of our study for a number of reasons.

5. Similarly, a concentration of literary texts from Kôm M (one of the trash heaps) at Antinoe was taken by the papyrologist John de M. Johnson as "the tattered fragments of what must once have been a small Byzantine library": Johnson (1914), 175. The collection associated with Aurelia Ptolemais is somewhat different in nature, as we will see.

6. It should also be noted that trash heaps are problematic as archaeological sites. Items thrown out together may be caught up by the wind and dispersed; they may slide about or be disturbed by humans or animals; and so on. This probably means that we have been deprived of some groups of papyri that were thrown out together; it is much less likely that concentrations of papyri were created by such movements and disturbances.

come from single and distinct archival collections. Thus we have clear evidence of what we might have assumed in any case, that groups of closely related papyri were sometimes thrown out together.[7] Second, the fragments found in each of the concentrations from Oxyrhynchus, when considered together, suggest a more or less distinct personality. They do not appear to be random batches of texts thrown on the dump by many different persons, but rather collections shaped, in large part, by a single intelligence and in response to specific interests. Third, if we do not believe that the papyri in each concentration were discarded by one person at one time, then we must assume that a number of individuals each brought one or more literary texts to the same spot in the dump—and at the same time—to discard them. Given the rarity of such papyri and the size of the Oxyrhynchus dumps, this would be an extraordinary coincidence. Finally, the circumstances of their discovery left Grenfell, Hunt, and Breccia in little doubt that the fragments in each of their finds had been discarded together and probably came from the same library. Subsequent scholars have tended to accept this, but the important implications for book collections and library history were not recognized until the 1990s, when Maria Serena Funghi and Gabriella Messeri Savorelli first began to analyze and comment on such concentrations.[8] What follows builds upon and is much indebted to the pioneering work of Funghi and Messeri Savorelli.[9]

There is, of course, another problem when we employ such concentrations in an attempt to explore specific ancient manuscript collections: these manuscripts were thrown out. They may, of course, represent virtually all of a collection of rolls that was thrown out because it was worn out, no longer of interest, or being replaced by codices. In that case, we would be dealing with actual whole collections. But there is also the possibility that the concentrations we have are manuscripts that someone decided to eliminate from a collection while keeping others—perhaps many others—and in that

---

7. More than 460 archives—concentrations of documents that are related to one another—are listed online at www.trismegistos.org/arch/index.php (accessed April 2013). Some are very small, but many consist of dozens or hundreds of documents. For a sample of the more substantial ones, see Montevecchi (1973), 248–61. Not all archives, however, consist of papyri that were found together in a single spot. Some come from mummy cartonnage and thus do not support the assumption made here concerning concentrations of papyri found together.

8. Funghi and Messeri Savorelli (1992a) and (1992b).

9. Several collections of texts, such as those found at Qumran in Israel and Nag Hammadi in Egypt, are known from sites other than Oxyrhynchus. They are certainly worthy of study, but the problems involved in describing and analyzing them are complex and would take us far beyond the scope of this book. (See further on them in the introduction, above.) I concentrate on the materials from Oxyrhynchus, where the collections derive from a single cultural context, are relatively close in date, and are sufficiently extensive to provide a useful sample.

case the ones that have survived may represent either a large or a small part of the whole. We cannot tell which of these two scenarios pertains in any given case. I see no way to avoid this problem, but we can be aware of it and of the limitations it imposes upon our conclusions. We cannot, for example, worry about texts that are not found in a given concentration. There may be no Homer, but that does not necessarily mean that the original book collection included no copy of the *Iliad* or *Odyssey*: it could be that the owner decided to keep his Homer and discard other items. When we find a particular interest manifested—in, say, lyric poetry, or a particular historical period, or annotated texts—we must be aware that whoever discarded the texts may have thrown them out specifically because he was *not* interested in such things. But the important point is that, at some point, someone *was* interested in them and brought them together within or as a collection. That, ultimately, is why we find them together. If we draw conclusions that are closely defined and carefully delimited, if we concentrate on what is here, and not on what is missing, we will find useful and interesting information about ancient book collections.

I will describe and analyze the five collections, arranging them roughly in the order in which they were discarded, and I will then draw some general conclusions that emerge from the detailed analyses.

4.2. GRENFELL AND HUNT'S FIRST FIND (DISCARDED LATE THIRD CENTURY AD)

Grenfell and Hunt came upon the papyri that they subsequently called their first find late in the afternoon of January 13, 1906, and recovered almost all of the fragments either that evening or the next morning.[10] They clearly regarded all of the papyri in this concentration as coming from a single source, for they described the find as "a place where in the third century AD a basketful of broken literary papyrus rolls had been thrown away."[11] They did not publish them as a group, and they nowhere gave a complete inventory of them, so the contents of this concentration must be reconstructed from what Grenfell and Hunt tell us in the prefaces of the relevant volumes, in the introductory comments to individual papyri, or elsewhere.[12] I begin

---

10. Bowman, Coles, et al. (2007), 361. Note, however, that fragments 8 to 18 of *P.Oxy.* 13.1606 were found "separately in a different part of the same mound": Grenfell in *P.Oxy.* 13, p. 48.

11. Bowman, Coles, et al. (2007), 361.

12. Cockle was the first to note that one could generate a catalog of the items in this find from the scattered comments of Grenfell and Hunt: Cockle (1987), 22, n. 14. He listed twelve manuscripts, and four more may be added to his list (nos. 1, 3, 14, and 15 in the catalog below). The manuscripts in the

with a descriptive catalog of the sixteen literary pieces in the first find, arranged in alphabetical order by author, with *adespota* coming at the end.[13] I give each manuscript a catalog number for ease of reference in the discussion that follows.

1. Aeschines Socraticus, *Alcibiades. P.Oxy.* 13.1608 (= MP^3 19). On the recto, it seems. About seventy-five lines survive. Hand a "good-sized elegant uncial" of the second half of the second century AD. A corrector altered mistakes in three lines and added one accent and one breathing. No sign of stichometric counts.[14]

2. Antiphon Sophistes, *On Truth*.[15] *P.Oxy.* 11.1364 + 52.3647 (= MP^3 92). On the recto; verso left blank. Copied probably in the early third century AD on "rather coarse papyrus" by scribe A24.[16] A second hand made alterations to the text and is probably the scribe responsible for the occasional accents, breathings, and other such marks. No marginal annotations appear. One stichometric count (δ = 400) survives.

3. Antiphon Sophistes (?), *On Truth*, perhaps Book 1. *P.Oxy.* 15.1797 (= MP^3 93).[17] On the recto. Copied early in the third century AD by a hand similar to the hand of number 2. A second hand added breathings, accents, and quantities, and seems to be identical to that of the corrector of number 2. In his introduction to 15.1797, Hunt suggested that it and 11.1364 (our number 2) may have come from the same roll. If this is correct, the two fragments may provide an example of one scribe replacing another for a certain number of lines.[18]

---

first find were published gradually in volumes 5, 6, 7, 11, 13, and 15 of the *Oxyrhynchus Papyri*. The last item published was *P.Oxy.* 15.1797, which, as Hunt states in his introductory comment, "belonged to the same find as 1364."

13. All information and dates are those provided in *The Oxyrhynchus Papyri* unless otherwise indicated.

14. A mark in the margin at line 138 was taken by Grenfell and Hunt as perhaps referring to a now lost marginal annotation.

15. Probably Book 1 (of 2). It is not certain that this papyrus preserves a part of Antiphon's *On Truth*, and Bilik (1998) argued that these fragments should be considered *adespota*. See, however, Bastianini and Caizzi in *CPF* I.1*, p. 182.

16. Johnson (2004), 24–25, for the scribe and "coarse papyrus." Grenfell and Hunt suggested a date of late second or early third century, but see Del Corso (2006), 84. Johnson provides tables with the scribes whose hands have been identified by papyrologists, together with the papyri assigned to them so far: Johnson (2004), 61–65. I follow his identifications of the scribes and the numbers assigned them.

17. Bilik (1998) argued that this fragment should not be assigned to Antiphon Sophistes, but see Pendrick (2002), 33.

18. It is also possible that the two sets of fragments derive from the same work (*On Truth*), but from different books in that work. See Bastianini and Caizzi in *CPF* I.1*, pp. 182–83. Or perhaps the owner of this collection possessed duplicate copies of Antiphon, given that he seems to have had two copies of at least the proemium of Plato's *Phaedrus* (below, nos. 8 and 9).

4. Euripides, *Hypsipyle. P.Oxy.* 6.852 (= *MP*[3] 438), republished by Cockle (1987). Copied in the period from AD 175 to 225 on the verso of a financial document (*P.Oxy.* 6.985) that dates from late in the first or early in the second century AD.[19] Stichometric counts appear in the margin, apparently at one-hundred-line intervals. The copyist added accents, breathings, and marks of elision, and occasionally supplied names of the *dramatis personae* in the margins. The first hand was careless, and both the first and a second hand made numerous corrections. Two short marginal annotations by the second hand survive.[20]

5. Isocrates, *Panegyricus. P.Oxy.* 5.844 (= *MP*[3] 1263). On recto. Chapters 19 to 116 survive, though with lacunae. Copied in the early second century AD by scribe A1.[21] A handsome manuscript "written in a rather large calligraphic uncial hand," with corrections, alterations, and some lectional signs added by a second hand. No marginal annotations or stichometric counts survive. The archetype from which the scribe made this copy appears to have been defective at lines 33–35, 291, and 605, for the scribe simply left blank spaces there, but a corrector provided text to fill in the blanks in the first two instances and so probably had access to a second exemplar. Substantial corrections were entered by the second hand, sometimes at the foot of the column (correcting lines 106–7), sometimes in the margins (lines 410 and 595).

6. Lysias, *Against Hippotherses, Against Theomnestus,* and other speeches. *P.Oxy.* 13.1606 (= *MP*[3] 1293), republished by Medda (2003).[22] Portions of at least six and perhaps more speeches, copied on the recto in the late second or early third century AD. The copy was carefully made with generous spacing. No marginal annotations or stichometric counts survive. The copyist, scribe A8, entered some corrections but also left some mistakes, and there is no evidence of a second corrector.[23] A *subscriptio* follows the *Against Hippotherses,* and it would seem that end titles followed each of the speeches but that there were no initial titles.[24]

19. Date of the copy of *Hypsipyle*: Turner and Parsons (1987), 62. Date of the document on the recto: Cockle (1987), 209–10, suggested AD 90. Papyri.info supplies "ca. 106 (?)": http://papyri.info /ddbdp/sb 20 14409.

20. The notes are definitions of proper nouns: McNamee (2007), 257, number 438. See Turner and Parsons (1987), 62, for the hand of the scribe who added the marginal notes.

21. Johnson (2004), 17 and 61. Only one other manuscript has been assigned to this scribe: *P.Oxy.* 10.1246, a copy of Thucydides, Book 7.

22. According to Grenfell and Hunt, fragments 8 to 18 were found "separately in a different part of the same mound, but no doubt belong to the same roll."

23. Number of speeches in the manuscript: Medda (2003), 27. Quality of the copy: Medda (2003), 11, 14–15. Scribe A8: Johnson (2004), 62.

24. Medda (2003), 22.

7. Pindar, *Paeans*. *P.Oxy.* 5.841 (= *MP*³ 1361). Copied in the second century AD on the verso of two or more rolls. The recto contained a census list and, in a different hand, a few lines of a land survey.[25] The bottom edge of the papyrus that contained the census list was trimmed off before the roll was reused for the *Paeans*, so that the column heights of the Pindar text are unusually short, each column containing only some fifteen to seventeen lines. Two hands or scripts appear in the fragments: it is possible that the *Paeans* required more than one papyrus roll, with a different scribe working on each roll.[26] Grenfell and Hunt described the first hand as a good-sized uncial; the second hand, which appears on fewer fragments, is, according to Rutherford, "more elaborate and hooked."[27] Both are formal, not cursive. There are stichometric counts in the margins, continuing from one poem to the next.

The scribe or scribes left extraordinarily wide margins—some 14 or 15 cm between columns—apparently for the insertion of scholia, notes, and commentary, and the resulting space was fully utilized. More than 160 separate notes can be identified, with those that can be read containing factual information (historical, geographical, or mythological, for example), paraphrases, explanations, and interpretations. Some of the notes are by the same hand(s) as the main text, but at least four other hands added notes as well. All of the notes seem to be derived from earlier commentaries; none gives the personal reaction of a reader.[28]

8. Plato, *Phaedrus*. *P.Oxy.* 7.1017 (= *MP*³ 1401). On the recto. Dated by Grenfell and Hunt in the late second or early third century AD and characterized by them as a "fine copy" in a "regular and graceful" hand on papyrus of superior texture. A second hand added corrections and variant readings and was probably responsible for most of the accents, breathings, and marks of elision that occur.[29] The numerous variants seem to be due to collation of the manuscript with a second exemplar.[30] No marginal annotations (other than the variants) and no stichometric counts survive.

9. Plato, *Phaedrus*. *P.Oxy.* 7.1016 (= *MP*³ 1400). This second (partial?) copy of the *Phaedrus*, less elegant than number 8, was made in the middle

25. The census list was published by Bagnall, Frier, and Rutherford (1997). They date it (pp. 20–22) to the Flavian period, most likely AD 91–92. The land survey remains unpublished and undated.

26. Rutherford (2001), 142. It may be, however, that a single scribe was responsible for both scripts.

27. Rutherford (2001), 140.

28. Annotations: McNamee (2007), 315–43. Grenfell and Hunt took all of the annotations as roughly contemporary with the main text.

29. A third hand entered a single letter at one point (column 35, line 5).

30. Haslam in *CPF* I.1***, pp. 257–58: the variants were not entered as corrections or conjectures, but added to the main text as possible alternative readings.

or second half of the third century AD on the verso of a roll that contains, on the recto, a register of landowners and their properties, which is probably to be dated to AD 235.[31] The surviving fragments all come from the proemium of the *Phaedrus* and are followed by a long blank section of papyrus, so this roll may have included only the proemium.[32] At two points (lines 160 and 229) the copyist, scribe A35, had difficulty reading the archetype, and that led to errors.[33] A second hand made at least some alterations.[34] No signs of marginal annotations or stichometric counts appear.

10. Plato, *Symposium. P.Oxy.* 5.843 (= *MP*³ 1399). Long sections of the second half of the roll survive. Text on recto; verso left blank. Grenfell and Hunt estimated that the full roll would have been some 23 to 24 feet (7 to 7.3 m) in length. The *subscriptio*—ΠΛΑΤΩΝΟΣ / ΣΥΜΠΟΣΙΟΝ—survives intact, with ornamental dashes, to the right of the final column. The copy, dated to about AD 200, was made by a careless scribe who wrote in a small, well formed, but heavy hand.[35] A second hand, roughly coeval with the first, corrected almost all of the mistakes and added a few lectional signs.[36] A single brief but incomplete annotation explicates a phrase of either Socrates or Diotima.[37] No signs of stichometric counts.

11. Thucydides, Book 7. *P.Oxy.* 11.1376 (= *MP*³ 1531). On the recto. Written in an "elegant medium-sized uncial" and dated to the early third or late second century AD. The lines vary in length from fifteen to twenty-three letters. No breathings or accent marks. The first hand made some corrections, but there are also corrections and variant readings by a second and a third hand. No marginal annotations or stichometric counts survive.

12. Incertus, *Commentary on Thucydides*, Book 2. *P.Oxy.* 6.853 (= *MP*³ 1536). Some 600 lines survive. Copied by a scribe who was "not . . . very careful" on the verso of a roll that was created by gluing together three documents, one of which is dated AD 131–32.[38] The few corrections are in the

---

31. For the date of the document (*P.Oxy.* 7.1044), see Youtie (1976), arguing for 235, and Rowlandson (1987), 290, pointing out that the date is not quite certain. The upper and lower margins of the documentary text were cut down, it seems, before the roll was reused for the copying of the *Phaedrus*.

32. Haslam in *CPF* I.1***, p. 232. Puglia (1997b), 46, takes it as a given that it contained only the proemium.

33. Scribe A35: Johnson (2004), 64. Johnson (2004), 44, analyzes one of the mistakes made by the scribe and notes that it may be explained on the assumption that the scribe was copying his text from an exemplar that had lines different in length from those in his own text.

34. Turner and Parsons (1987), 142.

35. Cf. the comments of F. Vendruscolo in *CPF* I.1***, pp. 378–79.

36. The corrector seems to have had a second exemplar that he used for a few of the corrections: Vendruscolo in *CPF* I.1***, pp. 383–84.

37. For this annotation, see Vendruscolo in *CPF* I.1***, pp. 414–15.

38. The documents on the recto were published in summary form as *P.Oxy.* 6.986.

first hand. No marginal annotations or stichometric counts survive. Internal evidence indicates that the commentary was composed at some point after about 10 BC; this copy of it, Grenfell and Hunt thought, was not likely to have been made later than AD 200.[39] The comments most often deal with the meanings of words or phrases, but the work begins with a discussion of Dionysius of Halicarnassus's criticism of Thucydides's historical methods.

13. Incertus, *Hellenica Oxyrhynchia*. *P.Oxy.* 5.842 (= *MP*³ 2189). Fragments of a history of events in Greece in the early fourth century BC, written on the verso of a roll.[40] The papyrus was strengthened before being reused.[41] The recto (*P.Oxy.* 6.918) contains a land survey that dates to the middle of the second century AD, and the copy of the history was probably made late in the second or early in the third century AD. Grenfell and Hunt identified two hands in the surviving fragments of the history. The first hand, a small neat uncial, was responsible for all but a small section of what survives; the second hand, smaller and rougher, copied column 5; column 6, lines 1–26; and perhaps two other small fragments. There is no indication of a repair at this point, so presumably the second scribe simply replaced the first one for a certain period of time. Possible stichometric count (δ = 400) in the margin opposite column 5, line 45, a line copied by the second hand. Hand 1 omitted many words but generally made corrections himself. No annotations survive.

14. Incertus, *Speech for Lycophron*. *P.Oxy.* 13.1607 (= *MP*³ 2500).[42] On the recto. Grenfell and Hunt suggested Hyperides as a possible author, but that was refuted by Körte.[43] The copy was made in the late second or early third century AD in an "upright, rather irregular uncial," and the scribe added some lectional signs. A second hand may have made a few corrections. No signs of marginal annotations or stichometric counts survive.

15. Incertus, *Speech on the Cult of Caesar or an Emperor, or on the Imperial Cult*. *P.Oxy.* 13.1612 (= *MP*³ 2517).[44] One column and fragments of a second from a copy of a speech, in Greek, made in a "not very elegant" hand; the copy, on the recto, is dated on paleographical grounds to the third century AD. The verso was left blank. The first scribe added some lectional

---

39. Puglia (1997b), 56, n. 113, also dated the copy of the commentary to the late second century AD.

40. The author is unknown. Cratippus, Theopompus, and others have been suggested as possibilities. For a summary of the literature on the question, see McKechnie and Kern (1988), 7–14.

41. Puglia (1997b), 44–45.

42. Evidence that this manuscript belonged to Grenfell and Hunt's first find is in the introduction to *P.Oxy.* 13.1606.

43. Körte (1923). No consensus on the author has been reached since Körte wrote.

44. Evidence that this manuscript belonged to Grenfell and Hunt's first find is in the introductions to *P.Oxy.* 13.1606 and 13.1612.

signs and punctuation, and a second hand made at least one correction. The emperor concerned has not been identified, and the date of composition of the speech cannot be determined: it could date anywhere from the time of Augustus to the third century.[45] No stichometric counts or annotations survive.

16. Incertus, *Treatise on Literary Composition. P.Oxy.* 7.1012 (= *MP³* 2289). A treatise or series of essays on a variety of topics—comments on Lysias, systems of ethics, the omission of names in various prose writers, a critique of Xenophon, a list of words having double meanings, and others— copied on the verso of an official account that is dated ca. AD 204–5.[46] Grenfell and Hunt puzzled over the focus of the work (if there is any), but suggested that "the most natural conclusion is that [the author] was a literary critic, and that his treatise related in a general way to composition or style." The unknown author refers to writers of the first century AD, so the composition must be later than that; this copy must be later than 204–5 (the date of the document on the recto) and was probably made in the middle of the third century AD. The scribe's occasional errors are left uncorrected. Lectional marks are rare. No marginal comments or stichometric counts survive.

4.3. ANALYSIS OF THE MANUSCRIPT COLLECTION REPRESENTED BY GRENFELL AND HUNT'S FIRST FIND

This concentration included some sixteen manuscripts, all but two of them—Euripides's *Hypsipyle* and Pindar's *Paeans*—prose works. In terms of genre, there are speeches (numbers 5, 6, 14, and 15), historical works (11 and 13), a commentary (12), a biography (1), one or two philosophical treatises (2 and 3), philosophical dialogues (8, 9, and 10), and what appears to be a literary miscellany (16). At this level, then, the collection appears both eclectic and to some extent unfocused, although there is a clear enough emphasis on oratory and history. If we consider the subjects of the various manuscripts, however, we might well conclude that the collector was particularly interested in the events of the end of the fifth century BC and the early decades of the fourth century. He owned at least some part of Thucydides and of a commentary on Thucydides, as well as a life of Alcibiades. The *Hellenica Oxyrhynchia* deals with events of the 390s BC, and the

---

45. Dognini (2000) argues that the cult is that of Julius Caesar. It is possible that the speech dealt with the imperial cult in general, rather than the cult of a single emperor.

46. Part of the document on the recto was published as *P.Oxy.* 7.1045.

Panegyricus of Isocrates (5) and at least two of the speeches of Lysias (6), delivered in the early decades of the fourth century, are concerned in part with political events of the time. Parts of the literary miscellany (16), too, deal with this period: there are comments on Lysias and Xenophon. With the exception of 15 (the oration on the imperial cult), every one of the prose works either deals with events in the period 430–340 BC or was originally written in that period or both.

The manuscripts were copied by at least five and perhaps as many as fifteen different scribes. Known scribes include A1, who copied Isocrates's *Panegyricus* (5), A8 (the speeches of Lysias in 6), A24 (Antiphon, *On Truth*, 2), and A35 (the less handsome copy of Plato's *Phaedrus*, 9).[47] Since none of the other manuscripts seems to have been copied by any of these scribes, and no two of them by the same scribe, it would appear that most of the manuscripts were written by different scribes.[48] It is possible, of course, that the collector himself copied at least one of the manuscripts; he was, to judge from his tendency to reuse papyrus rolls, keen to save money, and doing his own copying might have appealed to him.[49]

At least three, probably four, and perhaps more of the manuscripts included stichometric counts.[50] Two of those (4 and 7), as well as four others (9, 12, 13, and 16), were written on the verso of documents. The texts written on the verso include both of the works of poetry—the play by Euripides and the *Paeans* of Pindar—as well as the secondary copy of Plato's *Phaedrus*, the commentary on Thucydides, Book 2, the literary miscellany, and the *Hellenica Oxyrhynchia*. It would be tempting to argue that the verso of documents was used for texts considered less formal or important, but the presence in this group of both the *Hellenica Oxyrhynchia*, evidently an historical work of some significance, and the poems of Pindar makes that a difficult position to sustain.

Eric Turner argued that "the presence of stichometrical letters in texts copied on the versos of a documentary roll may be taken as an indication that we have a professional copy, privately commissioned and written on

47. Scribes: Johnson (2004), 16–17, 60–65.
48. Scribal hands can be very difficult to identify, especially in small fragments. See, for example, the discussion by Parsons (2007), 265. Further work may lead to assigning some of the manuscripts in this collection (and others) to known scribes, which would reduce the theoretical number of scribes who produced the rolls in it.
49. We know of individuals copying works for their own use, although our evidence is very thin. See above, section 1.2.
50. These are 2, 4, 7, and probably 13; in most cases the fragmentary nature of the texts makes it impossible to know if stichometric counts were included or not.

paper supplied to the scribe by the person giving the commission."[51] While that cannot be proved, it remains a reasonable hypothesis, and in this concentration it is consistent with the fact that all of the manuscripts were, so far as can be determined, copied by different scribes. What we seem to have here, in short, is not a collection of texts created in-house by a single scholar or a limited number of (slave) copyists, but a collection of texts produced by professional scribes, whether on commission or on speculation.[52] The rolls produced by this variety of copyists are predictably mixed in quality. Some of the manuscripts are handsome but have many mistakes (5, Isocrates), some were copied very carefully (6, Lysias), at least one shows no signs of checking or correction (12, the commentary on Thucydides), at least two seem to have been checked against second exemplars (8 and 10, Plato's *Phaedrus* and *Symposium*), in two cases more than one scribe may have been involved in copying the text (7, Pindar; and 13, the *Hellenica Oxyrhynchia*; cf. 2 and 3, Antiphon), and in the manuscript of Pindar the scribe left extraordinarily wide margins, which were filled with annotations entered by at least five different hands; both size of margins and number of annotations are unparalleled elsewhere in this collection and highly unusual anywhere.[53] These manuscripts were not produced to a set of standard specifications.

The physical nature of the manuscripts occasionally gives us a glimpse of the scribes dealing with their materials. In a couple of cases, they had faulty exemplars to work from, and we find them having to leave blank spaces (5, Isocrates; and 9, the *Phaedrus*). In two of the texts written on the verso of documents, the scribes had to go to considerable trouble to assemble a roll of sufficient length. Thus the scribe trimmed down, pieced together, and strengthened papyrus from at least two different documentary rolls in order to copy Pindar's *Paeans* (7), and the commentary on Thucydides (12) was copied on the verso of a roll that was pieced together from at least three earlier documents.

The copies in this concentration appear to have been made over a relatively short period of time, and none was particularly old when, toward the

51. Turner (1980), 95. It is not impossible, however, that the scribe, not the person commissioning the work, supplied the old papyrus rolls.

52. It is not likely that any single household would include fifteen different scribes, or that a master would give each new copying project to a different slave. It is, of course, possible that some of the manuscripts were produced in-house.

53. Aside from this case, annotations are rare in these manuscripts. There may have been one in the *Alcibiades* (1), there are two short definitions in the margins of the *Hypsipyle* (4), and there may be a marginal note in the *Symposium* (10).

end of the third century, the collection was discarded.[54] Nine of the sixteen texts are dated, primarily on paleographical grounds, to the period from AD 175 to 225, two (1 and 12) are dated in the second half of the second century, and three others (9, 15, and 16) in the third century.[55] We may reasonably infer that the core of the collection was assembled sometime in the half century from AD 175 to 225, perhaps within the period of a single person's lifetime or even the course of a single decade. The three items not produced in this period are number 5 (Isocrates's *Panegyricus*), which seems to have been copied early in the second century AD, number 7 (Pindar's *Paeans*), which could date from late in the second century but is probably a bit earlier, and perhaps number 9, the less handsome copy of Plato's *Phaedrus*, which was copied on the verso of documents one of which may be as late as AD 235.

The collector of these texts emerges as a serious reader, concerned to obtain correct texts but not necessarily elegant or impressive ones. Most of the manuscripts he obtained were corrected by a second reader, and at least two were collated against second exemplars. An unusually high percentage of the manuscripts — six of about sixteen, or some 37 percent — were copied on the verso of documents, probably as a money-saving strategy. The wide variety of scribal hands attested may imply an extended search, on the part of the collector, for manuscripts of interest to him that were reasonably accurate and affordable; he seems to have had a particular interest in the history and literature of the late 400s and early 300s BC. Several of the authors he chose to collect are popular at Oxyrhynchus and might be expected to show up in any collection of book rolls, but others — Aeschines Socraticus, Antiphon Sophistes, Lysias, the *Hellenica Oxyrhynchia* — are seldom or rarely found there.[56] There are some reference works: the commentary on Thucydides, the literary miscellany, and perhaps the Pindar with its vast assortment of annotations drawn from earlier commentaries. This concentration, then, does not seem to represent a broadly based collection of the most popular Greek literary works, but rather a focused and intelligent collection of works chosen for their relevance to the collector's interests.

---

54. Grenfell and Hunt state in their archaeological report that the first find had been deposited on the Oxyrhynchus dump in the third century: Bowman, Coles, et al. (2007), 361. They do not give the evidence for this, but presumably they found the materials within a stratum of third-century documents. If they are correct, then most of the manuscripts in this collection were some seventy-five to one hundred years old when they were discarded, only no. 5 (*P.Oxy.* 5.844, Isocrates) being clearly older.

55. The texts dated specifically in the period 175–225 are 2, 3, 4, 6, 8, 10, 11, 13, and 14.

56. In his list of authors attested in papyri found at Oxyrhynchus, Krüger lists Plato, Euripides, Thucydides, Pindar, and Isocrates among the fifteen most frequently attested authors. Aeschines and Antiphon are known from just three fragments each, Lysias from two, and the *Hellenica Oxyrhynchia* only from this one copy. See Krüger (1990), 214–17.

4.4. BRECCIA + GRENFELL AND HUNT'S
THIRD FIND (DISCARDED CA. AD 300)

Soon after their discovery of the first two major concentrations at Oxyrhynchus, Grenfell and Hunt made a third find, "which," Grenfell wrote, "though it cannot be compared in importance to its predecessors, was quite exceptionally good."[57] The papyri in this find included a number of Homer texts, several columns of prose that Grenfell took to be by Plato, and numerous documents of the first three centuries AD.[58] Unfortunately, Grenfell and Hunt seem never to have compiled, and they certainly never published, a list of the papyri in this find, and they did not begin systematic work on the texts themselves for some eighteen years. In the preface to *P.Oxy.* 17, which was published in 1927, Hunt remarked that "many of the [literary texts published in *P.Oxy.* 17] come from the third of the large groups found in 1906," but no further indication as to which of the texts in *P.Oxy.* 17 came from the third find, and which were found in other contexts, was provided, then or later. The precise contents of the third find, in short, remain uncertain. I will return to this matter below.

Grenfell and Hunt were not able to complete the excavation of the mound they were working on in January of 1906, when they made the second and third finds, because the top of the mound was occupied by the tomb of a revered sheikh.[59] Years later, however, in 1932, an Italian team under the direction of Breccia, wanting to dig in a mound known as the Kôm Ali el Gamman after the sheikh whose tomb sat atop it, arranged to have the tomb moved and excavated the mound. It is now all but certain that the mound Breccia excavated in 1932 was the very one that Grenfell and Hunt had been working on in 1906, namely the Kôm Ali el Gamman, and that the concentration of papyri Breccia found was a continuation of the concentration Grenfell and Hunt called their third find.[60]

---

57. Letter from Grenfell to H. A. Grueber, dated February 18, 1906. Grenfell dated the find to January 27–29. For the text of the letter, see Houston (2007), 332–33.

58. On the dating of the documents, see Houston (2007), 333, with n. 10. The Plato text mentioned by Grenfell in his letter to Grueber may well be the long section of the *Phaedrus* contained in *P.Oxy.* 17.2102, which joins with a fragment found by Breccia that has been published as *P.Turner* 7 (cf. *MP³* 1400.1).

59. Grenfell and Hunt did not identify the specific mound in which they were digging, and they did not name the sheikh, probably because they did not want others to dig there, as Ciampi (2009), 137, cf. 130, acutely observed.

60. For the identification of the mound as the Kôm Ali el Gamman, see Turner (1952b), 80–81, with n. 8; and Ciampi (2009), 130–32. The connection between the two finds has been worked out gradually by several scholars, developing what Turner was the first to observe. See Funghi and Messeri Savorelli

It will be useful, then, to combine the papyri found by Breccia in 1932 with those in Grenfell and Hunt's third find, and to treat them as a single concentration, thrown out together and deriving from a single original collection. How, though, are we to know which papyri belong to the third find, given that Grenfell and Hunt published no inventory of them? Our only evidence is Hunt's statement in the preface to *P.Oxy.* 17 that "many" of the literary texts in that volume come from the third find. For the purposes of this study, I will take Hunt at his word and assume that a literary papyrus published in *P.Oxy.* 17 comes from the third find unless there is reason to believe that it did not. Some of the papyri can be ruled out because they were not copied until the fourth or fifth century and so cannot have been discarded ca. 300 (the approximate date of deposition of the third find), while others have inventory numbers that show they were found in some year earlier than 1906.

In all, there are thirty literary fragments in *P.Oxy.* 17.[61] Of these, ten certainly or probably do not come from the third find, leaving us with twenty.[62] The roughly fifty manuscripts found by Breccia in 1932, plus the twenty from *P.Oxy.* 17, give us a total of about seventy manuscripts in this concentration.[63] In describing and analyzing this collection, I will refer to it, for brevity's sake, as "Breccia + GH3."

(1992a), 55–59; Houston (2007), 336–38; and Ciampi (2009), 142–51. Some perplexities remain. For example, where we can trace direct links between papyri found by Breccia and papyri found by Grenfell and Hunt, they are usually between items published in *PSI* volume 11 and *P.Oxy.* 18 (or even later volumes), rather than between *PSI* volume 11 and *P.Oxy.* 17. This is disconcerting, since *P.Oxy.* 17 is the only volume in which Hunt specified that texts from the third find were published. Perhaps we may infer that Hunt began publishing fragments from the third find in *P.Oxy.* 17 and simply continued in *P.Oxy.* 18 without remarking on that fact.

61. *P.Oxy.* 17.2075 to 17.2103 inclusive; 17.2086 has texts on both sides.

62. The ten that can be excluded are *P.Oxy.* 17.2083 and 17.2089 (copied too late to have been discarded ca. 300); 17.2075 (comes from the same roll as *PSI* 14.1384, which seems to have been found in a different kôm; see Ciampi [2009], 129); 17.2078 (seems to come from the same roll as *P.Oxy.* 50.3531, which has an inventory number indicating that it was found a year earlier); 17.2081 (consists of small fragments of texts belonging to the second find); 17.2084 (found with *P.Oxy.* 7.1015 and so in the second find); 17.2094 (from the same roll as *P.Oxy.* 49.3445, which has an inventory number indicating that it was found a year earlier); 17.2096 (from the same roll as *P.Oxy.* 48.3374, which has an inventory number indicating that it was found a year earlier); 17.2098 (its inventory number indicates that it was found a year earlier); and 17.2100 (inventory number indicates it was found in the third season). On the importance of inventory numbers and their relevance here, see Ciampi (2009), 148–50. I am most grateful to Professor Ciampi for sending me the few inventory numbers that survive, and to Professor Nikolaos Gonis, who supplied them to Professor Ciampi.

63. Other fragments, published later in subsequent volumes of the *Oxyrhynchus Papyri*, may derive from the third find. We know from their inventory numbers, for example, that *P.Oxy.* 67.4560, 67.4637, 69.4722, 69.4737, and various others were found in the course of the fifth season (1905–6) at Oxyrhynchus; they may belong to the second find or the third find, or they may be individual scraps not part of any significant concentration.

4.5. SARAPION ALIAS APOLLONIANUS

Before we turn to the content and nature of the book collection, it is important to note that the literary texts recovered by Breccia and his team were found commingled with documentary papyri, many of which derived from a family prominent at Oxyrhynchus for well over a century, from at least the 130s to the 260s AD.[64] Several of the men in this family were named Sarapion, and the family is identified by papyrologists by reference to one of its principal members, a certain Sarapion who was also called Apollonianus and who was strategos of the Arsinoite nome in 207–10 and of the Hermopolite nome in 219–21. At least eight of the documents found by Breccia, dating from AD 186 to 265, pertain to members of this family.[65] The documents are important for several reasons.

First, they help us determine when the literary papyri that were found so closely intermingled with them were discarded. If we assume that the documents were retained for a generation or two after the latest dated ones—that is, after AD 265—we can reasonably assume that they were thrown out at some point in the period from AD 300 to 320. That means that the literary papyri were thrown out then, too, and that will help us estimate how old the manuscripts were when they were discarded.

Second, Grenfell and Hunt found documents pertaining to this same family. They did not discuss them or specify which mound they came from, but the fact that Hunt published many of them in *P.Oxy.* 17, the volume in which he published "many" of the literary finds from the Kôm Ali el Gamman, suggests that the documents too were found in that kôm.[66] I agree with Ciampi that this can hardly be coincidence, that it helps to confirm that the Breccia 1932 find was a continuation of Grenfell and Hunt's third find, and that the literary texts in the two finds should be taken as what survives of a single ancient collection of manuscripts.[67]

---

64. Several scholars have worked on this material. See Moioli (1987) for earlier bibliography, a stemma of the family, and a list of the papyri published before 1987 that come from the family's archive.

65. They are listed by Moioli (1987), 135–36: *PSI* 12.1243, 12.1244, 12.1248–50, 12.1253, *PSI Congr. XVII* 25, and *PSI* inv. 429. The earliest of these is *PSI* 12.1253 of AD 186. The latest are *PSI* 12.1249 and 12.1250, both of AD 265.

66. Moioli (1987), 135–36, lists twenty-three documents pertaining to the family of Sarapion and published in the *Oxyrhynchus Papyri*. Of those twenty-three, twelve were published in *P.Oxy.* 17, two more in *P.Oxy.* 18, and the rest in later volumes. Of the ones published later, Ciampi (2009), 151, notes that at least two (*P.Oxy.* 46.3290 and 46.3291) have inventory numbers consistent with their having been discovered along with the third literary find.

67. Ciampi (2009), 150–51.

Third, the documents may provide evidence on the owner(s) of the manuscripts. Papyrologists have in general been appropriately cautious about concluding that the literary manuscripts belonged to the family of Sarapion. There is, of course, no proof that they did: none of the literary manuscripts contains any mark that might identify its owner.[68] Yet there is also no good reason to doubt that the literary collection was the property of one or more members of the family of Sarapion. This was a wealthy family, and its wealth is attested over a long period in various ways, including loans made to others, the assumption of local offices that imposed financial burdens, and a very substantial dowry. In her study of the family, Moioli took the names given members of the family as an indication that the family was Greek in origin; even if that is not the case, the onomastics certainly indicate a family that was culturally Greek.[69] This is, in short, a family that might well be interested in Greek literature and that would have the money to accumulate a collection of manuscripts. We cannot, of course, know which member or members of the family might have first begun to acquire manuscripts, nor which members might have developed the collection further or actually read the texts, but it is very likely that it was this family that owned, and that ca. 300 discarded, the literary manuscripts in Breccia + GH3.

4.6. BRECCIA + GH3: CONTENTS OF THE COLLECTION

I begin with a summary of the contents of the concentration: a list of the authors and works attested in the fragments. I arrange them by genre, as an ancient list maker might, and within each genre I list the authors chronologically. A complete inventory of the concentration, with information on the physical state of the rolls and bibliography, is provided in appendix 3.

Epic

Homer	*Iliad*, Books 6 (two copies), 9 (two copies), 10, 23, 24
	Odyssey, Books 5, 16
Hesiod	*Works and Days*

---

68. For a book roll bearing a name that is fragmentary but certainly includes Σαραπίωνος, and that may therefore indicate a Sarapion as owner of the roll, see Canfora and Pintaudi (2004–5); but we do not know the exact provenance of this papyrus. It was found at Oxyrhynchus at some point before 1923, when it was known to Medea Norsa (Pintaudi, in Canfora and Pintaudi [2004–5], 15, n. 11), so that it cannot have been found by Breccia; and it was not found by Grenfell and Hunt either. It is now in Florence.

69. Moioli (1987), 133–34, gives the details. The documents date through all of the second century and the early years of the third century.

	Theogony (probably two copies)
	Catalog of Women
Lyric	
Sappho	Book 2
Pindar	*Olympian* 2
Incertus	A commentary on choral lyric, probably Pindar
Tragedy	
Aeschylus	*Dictyulci, Glaucus Potnieus, Myrmidons* (probably two copies), *Niobe*
Sophocles	*Ajax, Oedipus Rex, Scyrii* (? or *Nauplius*?)
Euripides	*Phoenissae, Alcmaeon*
Comedy	
Cratinus	*Ploutoi*
Eupolis	*Prospaltioi* (?)
Aristophanes	*Thesmophoriazusae*
Incertus	Two comedies by unknown authors
Incertus	A commentary on a comedy (probably of the Old Comedy)
Elegiac	
Callimachus	*Aetia*, Books 1 (two copies), 2, 3 (perhaps two copies), 4
Incertus	Commentary on Callimachus, *Aetia*, Book 1
Other Poetry	
Callimachus	Selection (*Iambi*?)
Euphorion	*Thrax, Hippomedon*
Incertus	Commentary perhaps on Euphorion's *Chiliades*
History and historical matters	
Herodotus	Books 1 (two copies), 8
Thucydides	Book 1
Xenophon	*Anabasis*, Book 6; *Cyropaedia*, Book 1; *Hellenica*, Books 5 and 6
Incertus	A work on Hellenistic history, probably written in the second century AD and perhaps by Arrian
Phlegon (?)	*Chronica* (?)
Incertus	A work in Latin that included information on Servius Tullius
Rhetoric and Oratory	
Lysias	*Epitaphius*
Demosthenes	*Olynthiac 3, Against Leptines, Against Androtion, Against Aphobus*

Isocrates	*On the Peace, To Nicocles*
Incertus	A speech delivered before an emperor
Philosophy	
Plato	*Phaedrus, Gorgias, Timaeus*
Incertus	A Socratic-style dialogue
Prose Fiction	
Sophron	One or more mimes
Incertus	Novel with Ninus as protagonist
Incertus	Fragments from what may be a novel with Panionis as protagonist

Other Prose (note also the commentaries on Callimachus, Euphorion, choral lyric, and comedy, cited above)

Incertus	A glossary
Incertus	A work on stories or proverbs
Incertus	A list of words with their tachygraphic symbols (on the verso of the work on Hellenistic history)
Gaius	*Institutiones* (in Latin)

This is a remarkable collection. The authors it includes, so far as can be established, are almost all first-rate, and most of them were highly popular. The reverse is true, too: almost all of the most frequently attested authors in Roman-era Oxyrhynchus are represented in the collection. Every major genre is represented, and it is generally the most famous or widely read authors in the genre that are the ones present here. This is obvious even at a first glance at the list of authors, and that general impression can be made more precise by comparisons with Julian Krüger's frequency lists: of the ten authors most frequently attested in papyri from Oxyrhynchus, only Menander is not represented among the fragments in this concentration.[70] Most of the authors in the concentration are among the thirty most frequently attested at Oxyrhynchus (out of a total of 119 found there so far), and about two-thirds of the book rolls in the concentration are by authors who rank among the top twenty in Krüger's list.[71]

At least four, and perhaps as many as seven, of the titles in the Breccia + GH3 concentration are present in more than one copy. The four cer-

---

70. Krüger (1990), 214–15.

71. The only authors attested in this collection who are not in Krüger's top thirty are Lysias, Phlegon, Sophron, and Gaius (who wrote in Latin). All four of these are prose authors. There are about seventy book rolls in the collection, and at least forty-seven, or 67 percent, of them have been attributed to an author who is among the twenty most commonly attested authors at Oxyrhynchus, according to the frequency list in Krüger (1990), 214. To these forty-seven we might add the commentaries on Callimachus and Euphorion, both top-thirty writers.

tain examples of duplicates are *Iliad*, Book 6; *Iliad*, Book 9; Callimachus, *Aetia*, Book 1; and Herodotus, Book 1. Two others are probable—Hesiod, *Theogony*; and Aeschylus, *Myrmidons*—and one, Callimachus, Book 3, is possible. Duplicates are common in ancient book collections. We have seen them in the book lists in chapter 2, and there are examples in the collections from Herculaneum and the two other large concentrations from Oxyrhynchus. Ordinarily, we cannot know how a collection came to have more than one copy of a work, but in this case we can suggest a reasonable possibility. The collection, as we saw above, seems to have been connected with the Sarapion family. That family included several different branches (see the stemma in Moioli [1987]), both contemporaneous and in successive generations. It is thus possible that various members of the family acquired book collections for their own use, and over time those separate collections were passed down and combined, at least in part. What began as two copies of, for example, the *Iliad*, in separate households of the Sarapion family, might have ended up in one single collection. Such a scenario would be consistent with the authors represented in the list of duplicates here: all five authors are among the ten most frequently attested at Oxyrhynchus, and any collector is likely to have wanted copies of Homer, Hesiod, and Callimachus for himself.

In contrast to the collections represented by Grenfell and Hunt's first find and by the materials from the Villa of the Papyri at Herculaneum, the genres and types of work represented in this collection do not imply any special interests or professional specialization on the part of the collector. There are roughly equal amounts of poetry and prose. No genre, let alone any author, dominates to the exclusion of others. Certainly there is an emphasis on preclassical and classical Greek literature, but that is to be expected, and there are also authors of the Hellenistic period (Callimachus, Euphorion) and later (the novel about Ninus, Phlegon, the fragment on Hellenistic history, and Gaius).

Perhaps, then, we should look at the other works in the collection, the *adespota* and the less famous authors: here we might hope to obtain some insight into the particular (or peculiar) interests of the collector. There are four commentaries, but all of them certainly or probably pertain to authors or genres represented in the collection: Callimachus, perhaps Euphorion, choral lyric (perhaps Pindar), and a comic drama. Three historical works are by less popular or unidentified writers: the work arranged by Olympiads and perhaps by Phlegon (attested only here at Oxyrhynchus); the work on Hellenistic history perhaps by Arrian (who is attested only twice at Oxyrhynchus); and the work in Latin, probably antiquarian rather than narrative history, that deals with Servius Tullius. No particular field of specialization is suggested by these fragments, only a rather vague interest in matters historical.

We have in addition a speech delivered before an emperor, probably but not certainly a real speech as opposed to a rhetorical exercise; fragments of one and probably two novels; a fragment that may be part of a rhetorical work and that deals with proverbs or stories; a section of Gaius's *Institutiones*; a Socratic-style dialogue; a glossary of words that has no identifiable focus; a list of words with their tachygraphic equivalents (written on the verso of an historical work, and probably quite late in date); and, finally, fragments of two comedies.[72] One might perhaps infer from this miscellany an interest in rhetoric (to which Roman law could well be relevant), but the evidence is hardly overwhelming. Rather, the *adespota* and lesser works, like the fragments of the identifiable and more famous authors, seem to be spread across genres and fields. I cannot identify any single area of concentration, nor any subset of the works, that suggests a professional interest.

In terms of content, then, the papyrus fragments in the Breccia + GH3 concentration appear to represent a broadly based collection of the greatest poets and prose writers, with an admixture of mostly similar but less well-known materials, including commentaries that seem to have been chosen specifically to assist the collector in reading works contained in the collection. Let us then turn to the physical characteristics of the surviving papyri. Do they corroborate what we infer from the selection of authors and works in the collection, or do they lead us in a different direction?

4.7. BRECCIA + GH3: THE PHYSICAL CHARACTERISTICS OF THE BOOK ROLLS

A majority, and probably the vast majority, of the literary texts in Breccia + GH3 display one or more of the characteristics associated with book rolls produced by scribes trained to professional standards: a clear and practiced script (often calligraphic); generous top and bottom margins; columns that lean slightly to the right (that is, follow Maas's Law);[73] columns with even

---

72. On the novel about Ninus, see Del Corso (2010), 247 and 252–54. He suggests that this and a number of other similar texts, clearly written but inexpensively produced, were copied by professional scribes and intended for "ordinary readers" ("lettori comuni," a term he adopts from Cavallo); such readers, Del Corso argues, would be neither scholarly nor particularly wealthy. For the second novel (Panionis?), see Del Corso (2010), 257–58, and Parsons (2010).

73. The presence or absence of columns that follow Maas's Law is never mentioned in the introductions to the papyri in *PSI* volumes 11–14, but it can occasionally be observed in the plates of these

right edges. The editors of the texts in *PSI* regarded these texts as luxury products, and as one reads through the introductions to the papyri in *PSI* volumes 11 and 12 one is struck by the number of papyri that they described as having "scrittura calligrafica" or as being "di lusso" or "di gran lusso."[74] William Johnson, however, has shown that such characteristics were standard for good-quality literary texts, as opposed to less formal texts and paraliterary items such as glossaries and commentaries, and that they are characteristic not of "luxury" items, but simply of professionally prepared manuscripts.[75]

Almost all of the literary texts in the Breccia + GH3 concentration fit comfortably within Johnson's definitions of professionally prepared copies. They are written in handsome, clear scripts, and the upper and lower margins may be as much as 7 cm. The paraliterary texts, for their part, are written in clear hands that imply professional copyists, even if they were not characterized by their editors as *di lusso* or sumptuous.[76] As a whole, in short, Breccia + GH3 consists of manuscripts—both formal literary rolls and less formal texts or paraliterary works—that seem to have been prepared by copyists who were trained to, and followed, professional standards. Such copyists might be either in-house or associated with independent, commercial enterprises. We can reasonably assume, at this point, that there were no serious financial constraints upon the collection. The collector was able to buy or commission clear and often handsome copies of the literary texts he wanted, and competent copies of reference materials.

Four of the book rolls in this concentration are opisthographs. Ordinarily, that would imply a desire for economy, but that does not seem to be the case in this collection. In two cases, rolls of administrative documents were turned over and used to copy part of the *Iliad*. *PSI* 11.1185 (= *MP*³ 795) is a copy of *Iliad*, Book 6, but even though it was copied onto reused

---

volumes, as for example *PSI* 11.1212 (plate 7 in vol. 11) and, probably, *PSI* 11.1214 (plate 8). Hunt notes the presence of columns leaning to the right in *P.Oxy.* 17.2101 and 17.2102, and in the introduction to the latter he notes that, in papyri, columns of text are "often . . . slightly inclined to the right." The novel of Ninus (*PSI* 13.1305) follows Maas's Law: Bastianini (2010), 280.

74. Thus, for example, *PSI* 11.1188, 11.1191–94, 11.1196, 11.1197, 11.1200–1201, 11.1203–4, and many others. In *P.Oxy.* 17, Hunt was less likely to categorize texts in this way, but he does call *P.Oxy.* 17.2075 "unusually sumptuous" and *P.Oxy.* 17.2098 a "handsome roll," and he comments on the clarity of the scribal hands in *P.Oxy.* 17.2077, 17.2080, 17.2086, 17.2095, and others.

75. Johnson (2004), 160.

76. Thus *PSI* 11.1219 (a commentary) has "scrittura non calligrafica" and many abbreviations. *P.Oxy.* 17.2087 (a glossary) is written in a "small upright semicursive" with many abbreviations, *P.Oxy.* 17.2086 (a commentary) in a "small neat" hand, and *P.Oxy.* 17.2085 (a commentary) in a "medium-sized, upright" hand.

papyrus, it was a high-quality copy, with wide margins, handsome script, and an elaborate *coronis* marking the end of Book 6. Similarly, *PSI* 11.1188 (= *MP*³ 852.02) is a copy of *Iliad*, Book 10, done on the back of administrative documents, but it too has ample margins and large elegant letters, and it was characterized by its editor as an "edizione di gran lusso."[77] Cost does not seem to have been the overriding concern here, for the copying itself, done with care by a well-trained scribe, would have been the major expense. It is quite possible that the papyrus containing the administrative records was still in particularly good condition and that it was used primarily for that reason rather than to keep the cost down.[78]

The other two opisthographs in this concentration are both instances of the reuse of papyrus rolls for what may have been pedagogical purposes, and the text on the verso in each case was not a work of literature. Thus *MP*³ 2860, which may contain comments on a comedy, was turned over and reused at some point in the third century, its verso (*MP*³ 2300) being used for what seems to be a series of informal notes on rhetoric, perhaps taken during a lecture or discussion. In the other case, an historical work composed in the second century AD (*MP*³ 168.01) was reused, about a century later, for a list of words with their tachygraphic equivalents (*MP*³ 2776.5). The tachygraphic text may have filled the verso of the entire roll, so it was not a trivial work, and it probably reflects a change in interests rather than a need to save money.

The small number of opisthographs—four out of some sixty-eight rolls, or about 6 percent—is comparable to the percentage in the collection represented by Grenfell and Hunt's second find (two opisthographs out of thirty-five texts, or 5.7 percent), but far fewer, in terms of percentages, than those in Grenfell and Hunt's first find (37 percent). The figures in Breccia + GH3 thus emphasize the exceptional nature of the collection in Grenfell and Hunt's first find in this regard.

Nine of the seventy texts in Breccia + GH3, or about 13 percent, contain annotations of some sort. Three of the nine have notes, all certainly or probably added by a second hand, that are simple paraphrases of words in the

77. Literary texts copied on the verso of documents are not rare, but particularly handsome copies such as these are certainly unusual. Lama (1991) gathered a group of 182 literary texts copied on the verso of documents and analyzed, among other things, the scripts and format of the literary texts. She would characterize 5 of the 182 as having true calligraphic scripts: Lama (1991), 94–99. Two of those 5 are the Homer texts in this concentration, *PSI* 11.1185 and 11.1188, meaning that only 3 others appear in her sample. She goes on to list (99–100) seven more literary texts that are written on the verso of documents and are clear, if not particularly elegant.

78. *PSI* 11.1188 (*Iliad*, Book 10) was copied on the verso of documents that may have been only a few decades old when they were reused for the Homer.

text, but the other six are more interesting.[79] A copy of Callimachus's *Aetia*, Book 2 (*MP³* 206), the only manuscript in this collection that has annotations certainly in the hand of the original copyist, includes numerous notes, among them etymologies, explanations, and paraphrases. Callimachus emerges as a particular interest of the collector. There are six manuscripts of his works, including two copies each of *Aetia*, Books 1 and 3; there is a commentary on *Aetia*, Book 1; three of the nine manuscripts that contain annotations are texts of Callimachus; and the single most thoroughly annotated manuscript in the entire collection is *MP³* 206, the copy of *Aetia*, Book 2.

The other manuscripts with annotations are *MP³* 371 (Euphorion), with notes in two different hands, both of them distinct from that of the original scribe; *MP³* 431 (Euripides, *Alcmaeon*), in which one of the notes may be a stage direction, implying that the manuscript was used for oral presentation; *MP³* 1414 (Plato, *Gorgias*), in which one of the notes appears at the top of a column and may be intended as a summary of the contents of the column below it; *MP³* 1466 (Sophocles, *Oedipus Rex*), which seems to have been heavily annotated by a second hand; and *MP³* 1448 (Sappho, Book 2), in which the annotations are numerous—parts of five or six survive—even if their precise content cannot be determined.[80] The number of annotated manuscripts thus is not particularly high, but when combined with the presence of four commentaries—on Callimachus, on a work probably by Euphorion, on choral lyric, and on a comedy—it indicates a collector who was willing to and did seek help in reading and understanding difficult authors.

The book rolls in Breccia + GH3 were copied by at least eight different scribes whose hands have been recognized in more than one papyrus, and probably by a large number of different scribes, since more than fifty of the texts are in hands that all seem to be different from one another.[81] Arranged in roughly chronological order, the identifiable scribes and the works they copied that were found in this concentration are as follows.[82]

Scribe A6: *MP³* 1448, Sappho; late first or early second century AD
Scribe A3: *MP³* 26, 28, 33, 36, all of them Aeschylus;[83] second century

---

79. The three with paraphrases only (so far as is known) are *MP³* 34 (probably Aeschylus's *Myrmidons*), 195 (Callimachus, *Aetia* 1), and 222 (Callimachus).

80. The evidence on the content and nature of the annotations is given in appendix 3.

81. At least, papyrologists have not yet isolated hands that copied one of these fifty texts and some other manuscript. That is likely to change as work continues on the Oxyrhynchus texts, but it is clear that many different scribes worked on the manuscripts in this collection.

82. Numbering of scribes: Johnson (2004), 61–65.

83. This scribe has been identified as the copyist of twenty plays of Aeschylus and one manuscript of Babrius: Johnson (2004), 61.

Scribe A5: MP^3 371, Euphorion, and 1949, commentary on choral lyric;
  second century
Scribe A10: MP^3 34, Aeschylus; second century
Scribe A24: MP^3 431, Euripides, and 1478, Sophocles; second century
Scribe A8: MP^3 326, Demosthenes, and 1291, Lysias; late second or
  early third century
Scribe A33: MP^3 1509, Thucydides; second or third century
Scribe B3: MP^3 493.2, Hesiod; second or third century

We may make a number of observations. Two of the scribes whose work is present in this concentration, A8 and A24, are present also among the papyri in Grenfell and Hunt's first find.[84] One scribe, A5, appears in both Breccia + GH3 and in Grenfell and Hunt's second find (MP^3 65, Alcaeus; and MP^3 473, Herodotus). In addition, one of the copyists listed above, B3, is known from a manuscript found outside Oxyrhynchus. These copyists are most likely to have been scribes by profession, producing texts that others bought. They are less likely—given that in each case their work appears in the collections of at least two different households—to have been in-house slave copyists.[85] The very number of different hands—perhaps twenty-eight in Grenfell and Hunt's second find, and as many as fifty in Breccia + GH3— points in the same direction: no household is likely to have had twenty or thirty individuals trained to professional standards in copying, even over the course of two or three generations.[86] These manuscripts thus suggest that collectors, when they wanted a given text, regularly employed scribes outside their household who made a living doing copies, whether or not they used slaves or others in their own *familia* or staff to make copies. It is possible that some of those professional copyists may have resided elsewhere than at Oxyrhynchus.[87]

While these considerations—the consistently high quality of the manuscripts and the number of distinct scribal hands—point to independent, professional scribes as the men who produced the texts in Breccia + GH3,

---

84. Scribe A8 copied *P.Oxy.* 13.1606, containing several speeches of Lysias, and scribe A24 copied *P.Oxy.* 11.1364 + 52.3647, Antiphon's *On Truth*. The collection represented by the first find appears to have been discarded late in the third century, or not long before Breccia + GH3.

85. It is possible, of course, that the work of an in-house copyist might be given away as a present, lent to a friend, or sold. But the odds here favor the thesis that the collectors commissioned or bought these works from independent scribes.

86. Compare Cicero: a wealthy man and obviously committed to books, he appears to have had few men in his *familia*, and at times none at all, who could produce copies at a professional level.

87. Turner and Parsons (1987), 18, suggested that particularly fine copies, such as the texts of Aeschylus copied by scribe A3, far from having been made in-house, were perhaps copied in Alexandria or even outside of Egypt.

there are few other indications of professional activity in the manuscripts. Only two contain stichometric counts. One of the plays of Aeschylus that was copied by scribe A3, *MP³* 26, had a running stichometric count in the margin, and the copy of Aristophanes's *Thesmophoriazusae* (*MP³* 154) almost certainly includes a final line count just below the *subscriptio*.[88] Many of the manuscripts were proofread, though with varying degrees of care, and at least two (*MP³* 1400.1, Plato; and 1509, Thucydides) were carefully checked not only for copyists' errors, but, it seems, against a second exemplar. That would indicate a concern to obtain the best possible text. Two manuscripts (*MP³* 431, Euripides; and 1482, Sophron, *Mimes*) were provided with annotations or marks that suggest they were or could be used for oral presentations.

Most of the manuscripts in Breccia + GH3 seem to have been between one hundred and two hundred years old when they were discarded, if we are correct in thinking that the literary texts were thrown out, along with the documents from the family of Sarapion, at some point in the years from roughly AD 300 to 320. Two (*MP³* 1482, Sophron, *Mimes*; and 2617, the Ninus novel) have been dated on paleographical grounds to the first century AD and so were older, probably something over two hundred years old. Seven rolls seem to have been copied in the third century and may have been less, and perhaps a good deal less, than a century old when they were discarded. These include one of the copies of Herodotus, Book 1; Hesiod's *Works and Days*; and Xenophon's *Cyropaedia*, as well as the four texts written on the verso of rolls. The four written on the verso include one of the two copies of *Iliad*, Book 6, and the copy of *Iliad*, Book 10 (both of which are on the back of administrative documents), and the list of tachygraphic symbols and the notes on rhetoric (each of which is on the verso of a text that dates on paleographical grounds to the second century).[89]

Papyrologists have assigned most of the other texts to the second century, although seven are dated in the "first or second" century, and nine in the "second or third" century. In short, there are no strikingly ancient manuscripts, in contrast to Grenfell and Hunt's second find or to the book rolls from the Villa of the Papyri. Given this, it is worth noting that only one manuscript in Breccia + GH3 shows any sign of repair: *MP³* 462, one of the collection's two copies of Herodotus, Book 1, was strengthened by the addition of strips

---

88. We may contrast Grenfell and Hunt's first find, in which four of the sixteen manuscripts contain stichometric counts. The rarity of such counts in Breccia + GH3 may be due to accident: the fragments that have survived seldom come from the ends of rolls, where counts were regularly placed.

89. These are, respectively, *MP³* 464, 490, and 1545; the opisthographic texts are *MP³* 795, 852.02, 2776.5, and 2300.

of papyrus that were glued to the verso. Repairs may have been needed only rarely because most of the manuscripts were not particularly old when they were discarded, or because they were of high quality to begin with, or both.

We cannot know in detail how this collection came together, but we may make some tentative observations. It is conceivable that some one person, early in the third century, purchased most of the collection on the used-book market and commissioned or bought a few other rolls, namely those that were copied in the third century. It is also conceivable, at the other end of the spectrum, that all of the texts were commissioned or bought at the time they were copied. A scenario somewhere between these two extremes is surely more likely. One could imagine a person or persons beginning with a small group of first-century texts, either inherited or assembled through purchase or both, and over the course of a few decades (roughly AD 150 to 200) commissioning or buying new copies of many of the major works of Greek literature. Once assembled, such a collection might well pass from one member or branch of a family to another, with each successive generation discarding some items and adding others. In this scenario, the main part of the collection could have been assembled in the second half of the second century (the years in which a majority of the manuscripts were copied), and the last major set of acquisitions would have been early in the third century. By late in that century, the collection, or parts of it, may have been of decreasing interest to its owners, so that some manuscripts could be and were reused for educational purposes; hence the list of tachygraphic symbols and the notes on law. A generation or two later, we might surmise, the collection, or the part of it we have, no longer seemed of use or interest, or perhaps had been replaced by codices. Its owners threw it out.

4.8. THE COLLECTION OF THE FAMILY OF AURELIA PTOLEMAIS (DISCARDED PROBABLY IN THE PERIOD AD 300–320)

In a short but very useful article published in 1992, Roger Bagnall argued convincingly that a woman named Aurelia Ptolemais, a resident of Oxyrhynchus who is known to us from a lease agreement of AD 287, was the owner of at least three literary manuscripts, namely Books 4 and 15 of the *Iliad* and an anonymous prose work dealing with Greek history.[90] Not

---

90. Bagnall (1992). The papyri are *P.Oxy.* 11.1386, 11.1392, and 11.1365, respectively. According to the editors, Grenfell and Hunt, these three literary papyri were found together with the lease agreement (*P.Oxy.* 14.1690).

only that: she is very probably to be identified, Bagnall suggested, with the
Aurelia Ptolemais who is known to us from a copy of the will of Aurelius
Hermogenes, who died in AD 276. The copy of the will (*P.Oxy.* 6.907) is on
the verso of part of Book 18 of Iulius Africanus's *Cestoi* (*P.Oxy.* 3.412), so if
Bagnall's inferences are correct, the Aurelius family—and possibly Aurelia
Ptolemais herself—probably also owned at least part of the *Cestoi*. Aurelia
or another member of the family turned the copy of the *Cestoi* over, cut off
a piece, and used it to make a copy of the will at some point after the death
of Hermogenes.[91] Thus we have four manuscripts associated with Aurelia
or her family and can compile a short catalog.

1. A work dealing with early Greek history by an unknown author.
   P.Oxy. 11.1365 (= *MP³* 2181). A third-century copy. The surviving
   fragment has to do with the city of Sicyon in the Peloponnese.[92] The
   manuscript is of good quality: letters are large and clear, and there
   are thirty-five lines per column.
2. Homer, *Iliad*, Book 4. *P.Oxy.* 11.1386 (= *MP³* 718). A third-century
   copy "in an upright informal hand," on the verso.
3. Homer, *Iliad*, Book 15. *P.Oxy.* 11.1392 (= *MP³* 921). A third-century
   copy "in upright calligraphic uncials," on the recto. On the reverse is
   third-century cursive, and the back is strengthened by the addition
   of strips of papyrus glued to it.
4. Iulius Africanus, *Cestoi*. *P.Oxy.* 3.412 (= *MP³* 53). Two columns
   from the end of Book 18 of the *Cestoi*. The top and bottom margins
   are narrow, but there is ample space between columns, the letters
   are "well-formed round uncials of medium size," and there is a
   subscriptio below the final column. This was a manuscript of good,
   but not the highest, quality. Africanus's text is on the recto; the
   verso of this part of the manuscript was reused for the copy of
   Aurelius Hermogenes's will. Africanus seems to have composed
   the *Cestoi* in the 220s or 230s, so this copy cannot have been made
   before about 220, and when it was reused in 276 to make a copy of
   Hermogenes's will it cannot have been much more than fifty years
   old, if that.

91. It is conceivable, as Bagnall noted, that the roll containing the *Cestoi* had been sold by someone outside the Aurelius family as scrap paper. In that case, the Aurelius family would not have owned
the *Cestoi*. This is unlikely, however, because we do not know of a trade in discarded literary papyri (as
opposed to out-of-date documents) as scrap.

92. The work seems to have been composed in the fourth or third century BC. Ephorus and Aristotle have been suggested as authors.

The titles in this small collection reflect the variety that often appears in both the book lists in chapter 2 and the larger concentrations of texts described in this chapter: we find prose and poetry, three different genres (epic, history, and literary criticism), classics and less well-known works, ancient and recent authors. All four manuscripts seem to be good readable copies, but not elegant ones. The copy of Africanus's *Cestoi* was scrapped and reused not long after it was copied, and the other three may well have been discarded early in the fourth century along with the lease agreement, originally signed in 287, with which they were found; in that case, they too would have been less than a century old when they were discarded.[93] The collection is also remarkable for two reasons. First, we know with reasonable certainty the name of one of its owners, a rare occurrence.[94] Second, this is one of the very few instances of a woman attested in connection with a Roman library or book collection in any way, whether as owner, scribe, scholar, or member of a library staff. [95]

4.9. GRENFELL AND HUNT'S SECOND FIND (DISCARDED CA. AD 400)

Grenfell and Hunt's second find comes from the same mound—almost certainly the Kôm Ali el Gamman—as their third find and the manuscripts recovered by Breccia in 1932.[96] The second find, however, was discovered at a much higher level in the mound than the third find, so it must have been discarded later; Grenfell and Hunt reckoned that the manuscripts in it were discarded in the fifth century.[97] The second find consisted of thousands of fragments, many of them quite small, and papyri belonging to it continued to appear for many weeks after its first appearance in late January of 1906, and even into the next year's campaign.[98] The fragments come from what appears to have been a collection of at least thirty-five book rolls.[99] I list the

93. Given the relatively young age of the manuscripts, it is of interest that at least one of them, no. 3 (*Iliad*, Book 15), had been strengthened at some point.

94. The collection of books in the Breccia + GH3 collection probably belonged to the Sarapion family, but we cannot name any one member of the family who certainly owned it. We also know the name of Dioscorus, the owner of a large collection of documents and literary texts found in Aphrodito, but his collection is very late, Byzantine rather than Roman.

95. As Bagnall (1992), 140, with n. 18, pointed out, Aurelia Ptolemais could certainly read and write, for her signature—a lengthy one—is written in a fairly practiced hand.

96. For the Kôm Ali el Gamman, see above, n. 60.

97. On the archaeology of this mound and the second and third finds, see Houston (2007), 327–33.

98. Houston (2007), 335 (size of fragments), 339 (date of first discoveries); Bowman, Coles, et al. (2007), 365 (continuing discoveries in 1906–7); cf. Hunt's introduction to *P.Oxy.* 9.1174.

99. The basis for assigning each of these papyri to Grenfell and Hunt's second find is set out in

rolls below, giving each one a reference number to be used in the discussion that follows, and I arrange them chronologically (that is, in the order in which they were copied, not the order in which they were originally composed) within periods of roughly a half century.

Date of the Copy	Reference Number	Author and Title	MP³ Number[100]
Ca. 130 BC			
	1	Ibycus, *Ode to Polycrates*[101]	1237
First century AD			
	2	Bacchylides, *Encomia* (?)[102]	179
	3	Callimachus, *Aetia*	216
	4	Theocritus, *Idyll* 22	1495
Late first or early second century AD			
	5	Herodotus, Book 3	474
	6	Alcaeus[103]	55
	7	Demosthenes, five or more speeches	256
Early second century AD			
	8	Pindar, *Prosodia* (?)[104]	1363

Houston (2009), 262–64. To that list should be added *P.Oxy.* 2064, published in Hunt and Johnson (1930); see p. 3 of their edition for *P.Oxy.* 2064 as part of the second find.

100. I provide the *MP³* number rather than *P.Oxy.* numbers because in many cases fragments of a given manuscript have been published at different times under two or more *P.Oxy.* numbers. Thus, for example, fragments of Alcaeus that all seem to come from one and the same book roll were published as *P.Oxy.* 10.1234; 11.1360; 18.2166, fragment C; volume 18, addenda 182; and volume 21, addenda 130–34. All of these are reported in the Mertens-Pack database as *MP³* 59 (no. 17 in this list).

101. The identity of the author is not quite certain. See Page (1951), 168; Barron (1969), 132–33; Gianotti (1973), 401, n. 1. On the date, now taken as ca. 130 BC, see Turner, cited by Barron (1969), 119, n. 3.

102. Title and genre of these fragments are uncertain. Fearn (2007), 27–28, n. 2, suggests that the roll as a whole contained Bacchylides's *Encomia*, and that there were probably then subsections, one of which may have been *scolia*. Some or many of the fragments in *P.Oxy.* 11.1361 may thus have been known as *scolia*, as they are labeled in *P.Oxy.* vol. 11.

103. Dated in the first century AD when published as *P.Oxy.* 15.1789. For the possibility of a date early in the second century, see Porro in *CLGP* 1.1.1 (2004), 114.

104. The exact title and genre of the poems in this papyrus are not certain. See D'Alessio (1997), 25–30, noting that paeans and prosodia (sung in processions) will have been similar in content, because in both cases the poet was praising the god.

Date of the Copy	Reference Number	Author and Title	MP³ Number
Second century AD			
	9	Alcaeus	56
	10	Bacchylides, *Dithyrambs*	177
	11	Cercidas, *Meliambi*	237
	12	Sappho, Book 1	1445 (parts)
	13	Lyric (Sappho? Or another poet?)[105]	1445 (parts)
	14	Satyrus, Book 6 of his *Lives*: Lives of Aeschylus, Sophocles, and Euripides	1456
	15	Satyr plays, or an anthology of excerpts from satyr plays	1739[106]
	16	Reader's guide to plays of Menander[107]	1321
Second half of the second century AD			
	17	Alcaeus	59
	18	Alcaeus	65
	19	Alcaeus (?)[108]	61
	20	Herodotus, Book 2	473
	21	Pindar, *Dithyrambs*	1367
	22	Pindar, *Dithyrambs*? and perhaps other works[109]	1368

105. A number of fragments originally published as part of *P.Oxy.* 10.1231 are now taken as coming from another manuscript. They may, like others in *P.Oxy.* 10.1231, be by Sappho, or they may be by another author. For the fragments in question, see Lobel and Page (1955), 25, on no. 29. Thus we seem to have at least two separate manuscripts in *P.Oxy.* 10.1231 (= *MP*³ 1445).

106. These fragments were published in two groups, *P.Oxy.* 8.1083 and *P.Oxy.* 27.2453. The latter group showed that more than one play was represented, and it seems likely that at least one of the plays was by Sophocles. We do not know if these fragments represent two or more rolls each containing a complete play (cf. Turner, ad *P.Oxy.* 27.2453) or one roll containing an anthology of excerpts from several plays (so Pechstein and Krumeich in Krumeich, Pechstein, and Seidensticker [1999], 369).

107. This manuscript contains plot summaries (or "arguments") of the plays, plus additional information. At the end of each summary, there is a judgment on the quality of the play, and the first two lines are quoted in full. More importantly, information on the production of each play—when it was performed, and by whom, for example—is also provided. Parts of the entries on three plays survive; each occupies about two columns of text.

108. Some scholars have assigned these fragments to Sappho. Alcaeus: Lentini (2007).

109. Date: Lobel in the "Table of Papyri," *P.Oxy.* vol. 26, p. viii. The fragments published as *P.Oxy.* 16.2445 may come from more than one roll and more than one author: Lobel, in the introduction to *P.Oxy.* 16.2445.

Date of the Copy	Reference Number	Author and Title	MP³ Number
	23	Plato, *Republic*, Book 8	1421
	24	Sappho, perhaps from Book 4[110]	1449
	25	Sophocles, *Eurypylus*	1472
	26	Sophocles, *Ichneutae*	1473
	27	Theocritus, *Idylls* 1, 3–9, 11[111]	1489
	28	Incertus, on Alexander the Great[112]	2195
	29	Lexicon of rare words, mostly from non-Greek languages[113]	2127

Late second or early third century AD

	30	Callimachus, *Iambi*	218
	31	Ephorus, *Universal History*, Book 12 (or 11)	357
	32	Hesiod, *Catalog of Women* (?)	525
	33	Sophocles, *Trachiniae*[114]	1471
	34	Passages on literary topics[115]	2290
	35	Series of short biographies[116]	2070

110. Dated in the last quarter of the second century by Funghi and Messeri Savorelli (1992a), 52.

111. For the assignment of these fragments to the second find, see Hunt and Johnson (1930), 3.

112. A complete new edition of the fragments of this work: Prandi in *CPS* A.2.9F (2010). We do not know if this was a biography or an historical work.

113. The lexicon was copied on the verso of *MP³* 2195, the work on Alexander the Great, and it seems to be not much later than that text. For the date of the lexicon, see Schironi (2009), 5. The lexicon cites no authorities who lived after the first century BC, and so could have been composed at any point between, say, 150 BC and 50 BC.

114. Date: Helen Cockle, ad *P.Oxy.* 52.3687.

115. The subjects treated include Old Comedy, the myth of Caeneus, the various persons named Thucydides, the authorship of an ode to Pallas, and others.

116. Each biography is two or three columns in length. Those that survive treat literary figures, such as Sappho and Aesop; orators, including Demosthenes and Aeschines; men involved in politics (Thrasybulus); and two fictional/mythical figures, Leucocomas (the protagonist of a novel) and Abderus. Incorporating both scholarly material (e.g., the story of the death of Aesop) and romanticizing anec-

Date of the Copy	Reference Number	Author and Title	MP^3 Number
Third century AD			
	36	Pindar, various works[117]	1360

In addition to the manuscripts listed above, two short speeches written on single sheets of papyrus belong in the second find. One of these is *P.Oxy.* 7.1015 (= MP^3 1847), a verse panegyric on a certain Theon, datable on paleographical grounds to the middle or second half of the third century AD. Turner, in Turner and Parsons (1987), 90, noted that the text contains a number of revisions and suggested that this is the author's own copy "of what may be a prize poem." The other composition, *P.Oxy.* 17.2084 (= MP^3 2527), is a brief encomium on the fig, written to be delivered, it seems, at a real or imagined festival of Apollo. It may be the practice composition of a student.

4.10. PHYSICAL CONDITION OF THE MANUSCRIPTS IN THE SECOND FIND

The literary fragments that constitute the second find were discovered within a broad stratum of documents that dated to the fourth and fifth centuries AD. As Grenfell and Hunt noted, this means that the manuscripts of the second find must have been thrown out at some point in the fourth or fifth century.[118] As a reasonable and conservative guess, I will assume that they were thrown out in about AD 400. This gives us information on the durability of ancient papyrus rolls. In this collection, one manuscript (the text of Ibycus, number 1) was some 500 years old when it was discarded, and at least three others (numbers 2–4) were some 300 years old. Clearly some papyri could and did remain usable for three centuries or more.[119] On the other hand, the vast majority of the manuscripts in the second find date certainly (numbers 17–35) or possibly (numbers 9–16) to after about AD 150, and they were therefore some 150 to 250 years old when they were

---

dotes, they are probably condensed from, or extracts from, more complete lives. See further Calderini (1922), 263; Lamedica (1985); and Bollansée (1999), 245–49.

117. Date: Lobel in the "Table of Papyri," *P.Oxy.* vol. 26, p. viii. As Lobel noted, these fragments, copied by the same scribe and found together, may come from five or more book rolls.

118. Bowman, Coles, et al. (2007), 362.

119. As we have seen, this is true of the materials from Herculaneum as well, where a small number of texts were copied in the third century BC and so were some three hundred years old when Vesuvius erupted. See further above, section 3.9.

discarded. That may be taken as the norm for the manuscripts in this collection.

Only three of the manuscripts in the second find are known to have been repaired or treated with special care. Two of these are among the oldest in the collection. The second-century BC manuscript of Ibycus (number 1) was strengthened by the addition of strips of papyrus, which were pasted onto the top and bottom margins of the recto, and the whole manuscript seems to have been treated with oil of cedar, an insecticide and preservative.[120] A manuscript of Theocritus copied in the first century AD (number 4) was also, it seems, treated with oil of cedar, which was applied to the upper and lower margins of the recto.[121] One of the later manuscripts, the guide to the plays of Menander (number 16, second century AD), was strengthened through the addition of a strip of papyrus to the verso of the roll. Since only fragments remain of most of the manuscripts in this collection, we cannot be sure how many were at some point repaired, but it is reasonable to conclude that papyrus book rolls, with or without repairs, could and often did remain in use for two centuries or so.

In general, the manuscripts in Grenfell and Hunt's second find are of high quality. By this I mean not that they were deluxe editions, or lavishly produced (although some perhaps were), but rather that one can infer, from the care with which they were corrected, and from the frequent inclusion of variant readings, a concern for full and accurate texts. Four of them contain stichometric counts and were probably copied by professional scribes.[122] A few, such as number 31 (Ephorus), are remarkably free of errors. Most of the manuscripts were corrected by the original scribe, a professional corrector (*diorthotes*), or both. Many others were treated with particular care. In numbers 11 (Cercidas) and 12 (Sappho), for example, a second hand added not only corrections, but also variant readings in both the margins and the interlinear spaces. In number 20 (Herodotus), a second hand added an alternate version of at least five lines at the top of fragment 9 and the comment, "so in certain other [manuscripts]."[123] Our number 6 (Alcaeus) was

120. Barron (1969), 121, suggests that the work on the papyrus should date in the first century AD or later.

121. Hunt, ad *P.Oxy.* 15.1806.

122. These are no. 6, Alcaeus; for the stichometric count, probably α = 100 or δ = 400 in Alcaeus 6, see Lobel and Page (1955), 117, ad line 28, and Porro in *CLGP* 1.1.1 (2004), 114; no. 12, Sappho; a line total is given just after the *subscriptio* in *P.Oxy.* 10.1231, fragment 56; no. 26, Sophocles; marginal line count by first hand, every 100 lines; and no. 28, on Alexander the Great; line count—2,300—in the intercolumnar space in fragment 5–6. No doubt others were copied by professionals as well; the manuscripts are in such a fragmentary state that few stichometric counts have survived.

123. McNamee (2007), 258. Similarly, a second hand inserted at least twenty-seven variant read-

extensively edited. Two hands, not much later than the hand of the original scribe, added corrections and variant readings in the interlinear spaces. Two hands also annotated the text with paraphrases and explanatory comments; at least one of the latter two hands is distinct from the first two.[124] As Antonietta Porro notes, the extensive editorial work shows that this manuscript was an object of careful study.[125]

There are a number of exceptions, manuscripts that were not prepared or treated with any particular care. Number 14 (Satyrus's *Lives*) does not seem to have been corrected at all, despite the presence of many mistakes, including the omission of a letter in the end title. In addition, the copyist left blank spaces at two points in the text, so perhaps the exemplar was faulty.[126] A second interesting case is number 29, the lexicon of rare words. This was written on the verso of the work on Alexander and left incomplete, so it might be considered an informal work. It includes no corrections, accents, or punctuation, and there are some uncorrected mistakes. On the other hand, the words in the lexicon are arranged in rigorously alphabetical order (to at least four letters), implying careful arrangement of the material; and the nature of the subject—odd words from other languages—implies a learned reader.

Only two of the manuscripts in this collection are opisthographs, so far as can be determined: number 30 (Callimachus's *Iambi*) and number 29 (the lexicon of rare words). Both seem to have been copied late in the second or early in the third century AD, and thus relatively late in the life of the collection.

Despite the highly fragmentary state of the manuscripts, one of them was found with a parchment *sillybon* still attached, and the *subscriptiones* of three others survive. The *sillybon*, on a text of Bacchylides's *Dithyrambs* (number 10), was written and glued to the edge of the papyrus a generation or more after the text was copied. It was large, 2.1 by 10.1 cm, and enough of it was left extending beyond the edge of the manuscript so that the content of the book roll would be clear.[127] Its presence raises questions. Were all of the manuscripts provided with *sillyba*, either as a regular practice or

---

ings in the text of Sophocles's *Ichneutae* (no. 26), often citing one of his three or four sources ("Thus it was in Theon's version," for example). Clearly the concern was to obtain an accurate text.

124. McNamee (2007), 137–38. The one surviving comment is on a dialectal form.

125. Porro in *CLGP* 1.1.1 (2004), 115.

126. This text was written with very small spaces between columns and lines, so entering corrections would have been difficult. Not impossible, however.

127. The *sillybon* says simply "Bacchylides's dithyrambs." It is a palimpsest: at first, the scribe wrote on it the title of just one of Bacchylides's poems, but later that was partially erased and the present text written in its place. See Fearn (2007), 210, n. 130.

as part of some systematic restoration and preservation of the collection? Or were just a few—perhaps particularly valuable manuscripts, or ones the collector wanted to be able to find easily—given *sillyba*? At present, we cannot answer these questions.

In the manuscript of Cercidas (number 11), there is a blank space of two or three lines at the foot of the last column, and then we are given a *subscriptio*: "Cercidas, / Cynic, / [Me]liambi." The *subscriptio* of number 14 is more elaborate. The scribe wrote it in the empty space to the right of the last column, and it includes the author's name, the title of the work, the book number of this book roll, and the three lives contained within this roll: "Satyrus's / Register [*anagraphe*] of Lives / [Book] 6 / Aeschylus / Sophocles / Euripides."[128] One of the rolls containing poems of Sappho (number 12, fragment 56) includes a *subscriptio* that does not provide the name of the author, but does give a stichometric count: ΜΕΛΩΝ / Α / ΧΗΗΗΔΔ ("Poems, Book 1, 1320 [*stichoi*]."[129] In at least two manuscripts, titles of individual poems or works are provided: in number 21 (Pindar, *Dithyrambs*), one of the poems is given its own title in the margin; and in number 7, which contains five or more speeches of Demosthenes, there is an end title at the end of the fourth speech.

The surviving book rolls were copied by at least eight identifiable scribes, by which I mean scribes whose hands are known from more than one manuscript. One of the eight is known from manuscripts found both at Oxyrhynchus and elsewhere. Most of the manuscripts were written by scribes who have not yet been identified, but the number of such copyists, although clearly large, cannot be determined. The known scribes and the works they copied that are found in this collection are as follows (arranged chronologically):[130]

Scribe A28: copied number 4, Theocritus; active in the first century AD
Scribe A7: number 5, Herodotus, Book 3; late first or early second century AD
Scribe A4: number 11, Cercidas; second century AD
Scribe A11: number 15, satyr play(s), or an anthology of excerpts from satyr plays; second century AD

128. For *Bion anagraphe* ("Register of Lives") as the title of the whole work, see Schorn (2004), 15–17.

129. The name Sappho did not appear in the *subscriptio*, which is visible in *P.Oxy.* 10, plate 2, no. 56.

130. In addition to the eight scribes listed here, note that our manuscript no. 9, Alcaeus, was assigned to scribe A32 by Haslam, ad *P.Oxy.* 3891; cf. Johnson (2004), 64.

Scribe A5: number 18, Alcaeus; and number 20, Herodotus, Book 2;
late second century AD

Scribe A20: number 19, Alcaeus (?); and numbers 21 and 22, both
Pindar; late second century AD

Scribe A30: number 24, Sappho; and number 36, Pindar;[131] late second
and third century AD

Scribe B1: numbers 25 and 26, Sophocles, *Eurypylus* and *Ichneutae*;
late second century AD

Note also scribe A32: number 9, Alcaeus; second century AD

Many other scribes must also be represented in the collection. The Ibycus manuscript (number 1), for example, was copied in the second century BC and so could not have been copied by any of these eight scribes. Moreover, the hands of the twenty or so manuscripts that have not been identified may each represent a different scribe, giving us as many as twenty-eight scribes copying the thirty-six texts in this collection. That in turn implies that the owner of the collection did not simply have one or two trained slaves make his copies for him. That this is the case is supported by another, closely related, consideration: some particular authors are represented by manuscripts that were copied at different times and by different scribes. The collection includes two manuscripts of Bacchylides, one (number 2) copied in the first century AD, the other in the second century (number 10). The two surviving books of Sappho (numbers 12 and 24) were copied by different scribes, as were the two books we have of Herodotus's *History* (numbers 5 and 20, by scribes A7 and A5, respectively). Moreover, the collection includes at least five book rolls of Alcaeus, copied by at least four different scribes over a period of close to a century (numbers 6, 9, 17–19). In short, our collector seems often to have assembled the works of a given author not by buying, commissioning, or having a slave copy the author's *opera omnia*, but by acquiring volumes individually and gradually building up a set.[132]

Given that most of the manuscripts in this concentration were copied in the second half of the second century AD, we might reconstruct a sce-

---

131. Funghi and Messeri Savorelli (1992a) assigned these fragments of Sappho and Pindar to scribe A20, but see Johnson (2004), 26–27. The dates assigned these manuscripts on paleographical grounds imply a long career for the scribe.

132. This is not to say that there was no possibility of sets of books of a given author all copied by the same scribe. We have a matched pair in the two plays of Sophocles (nos. 25 and 26) and, in all probability, another set in the many fragments of Pindar that were copied by one scribe and probably come from five or more book rolls (no. 36). The Pindar volumes may once have constituted a complete Pindar done by a single scribe and in a consistent format.

nario for the life of the collection as follows.[133] Over the course of the late second century AD, a collector or collectors with a particular interest in lyric poetry assembled a collection, largely through commissions or purchases of newly made copies. He obtained some others that had been copied much earlier (numbers 1–7), either through inheritance or gift or retrospective purchases; and a few manuscripts (number 36 and perhaps some of numbers 30–35) may have been added subsequently, perhaps by a second-generation owner. The collection ceased to grow about the middle of the third century but was retained or passed down for several generations until it was discarded sometime around AD 400.[134] Whatever the exact process or processes, the certain and significant fact is that we see here an ancient collection consisting of texts copied not by a limited number of slaves in a household, but rather by many scribes and over many generations.

4.11. CONTENT OF THE COLLECTION REPRESENTED BY THE SECOND FIND

Unlike the collection represented by Grenfell and Hunt's first find, which is almost all prose, this concentration contains an exceptionally strong collection of poetry, in particular early lyric. There are at least five manuscripts of Alcaeus (numbers 6, 9, and 17–19), six or seven rolls containing a variety of works by Pindar (numbers 21, 22, and 36), at least two books of Sappho's poetry (numbers 12, 24, and perhaps 13) copied by two or more scribes, an early copy of Ibycus (number 1), and two or more rolls of Bacchylides (numbers 2 and 10). Other poets present in the collection include Callimachus (numbers 3 and 30), Theocritus (numbers 4 and 27), Cercidas (11), Sophocles (two tragedies, numbers 25 and 33), one or more satyr plays (numbers 15 and 26), and probably Hesiod (number 32). Taken as a group, these are not easy poets or poets ordinarily assigned to students.[135]

The collection also includes a number of prose works, among them an unusual array of what we might call works of reference. We find Herodotus, Books 2 and 3 (numbers 20 and 5), one book of Ephorus's *History* (num-

---

133. The manuscripts are dated on paleographical grounds, so some uncertainty remains. Nos. 17–29 have been dated to the second half of the second century AD, and nos. 9–16 and 30–35 could all date from that period too.

134. Quite different scenarios are possible, too, although no one of them is perhaps as likely. We might imagine, for example, a single person purchasing all of the volumes on the used-book market at some point early in the third century.

135. Cribiore (2001), 194–204, discusses the writers regularly read in schools before the most advanced levels of study. Those most often studied included Homer, Hesiod, Euripides, and Menander.

ber 31), a work that treated Alexander the Great (number 28), five or more speeches of Demosthenes (number 7), and Book 8 of Plato's *Republic* (number 23). Works of reference include Book 6 of Satyrus's *Lives*, which, as the *subscriptio* tells us, included the lives of the three great tragedians (number 14), a guide to the plays of Menander (number 16), a collection of short biographies (number 35), a work on miscellaneous literary topics (number 34), and part of a lexicon of rare words (number 29). This last item merits a particular comment: most of the words are transliterations into Greek from other languages, including Persian, Lydian, Chaldean, and Albanian, implying an interest in a wide variety of topics, and they are carefully arranged in absolute alphabetical order to at least four letters.[136]

The most striking single characteristic of this group of manuscripts is the amount of annotation present. The number of marginal notes is remarkable, as are their contents and variety. Of the thirty-six manuscripts or groups of manuscripts into which the collection can be divided, some seventeen, or 47 percent, contain marginal notes that cite other sources for variant readings, explicate matters in the text, or both.[137] This figure is much higher than the average of about 10 percent for all papyri from Oxyrhynchus, not to mention the estimated 5 percent for all published papyri.[138] Annotated copies of particular authors are present in remarkably high numbers. Some twenty-two manuscripts of Alcaeus are listed in the Mertens-Pack online database, and eleven or twelve of them contain marginalia.[139] Of the eleven or twelve, four, or at least a third, are in this one collection. Similarly, only seven annotated texts of plays of Sophocles seem to be known, and three of them, or almost half, are manuscripts that belong to this collection.[140] Only two annotated texts of Herodotus are known. Both were found in this concentration.[141]

But it is not just that annotated texts are unusually frequent: several of the individual manuscripts are much more heavily annotated than most book rolls from Egypt. Number 17 (Alcaeus) includes numerous notes, including paraphrases, explanations, comments on morphology, variant read-

136. Schironi (2009), 43, pointed out that the glossary does not seem to have been concerned with literary works (as we might have expected, given the clear interest of the collector in Alcaeus and Pindar, for example), but rather with words taken from "religion, everyday life, zoology, and ethnography." The collector evidently had many interests.

137. Nos. 1, 2, 5, 6, 11, 15, 17, 18, 19, 21, 22, 23, 25, 26, 27, 33, and 36.

138. McNamee (2007), 2 and 11, gives the percentages, with appropriate caveats.

139. *MP*[3] 55, 59, 60, 61, 62, 63, 65, 67, 69, 71.1, and 72. No. 1901 may also be Alcaeus.

140. McNamee (2007), 362–71. The annotated plays of Sophocles in this collection are nos. 25, 26, and 33. Moreover, one of the satyr plays in no. 15 may be by Sophocles, and it too is annotated.

141. Ibid., 258–59.

ings with sources cited, and comments on customs.[142] Number 19, probably another Alcaeus manuscript, includes at least sixteen notes in a second
hand; there are textual variants, paraphrases, and a comment on a custom.
One of the notes is nine lines long.[143] In number 21 (Pindar, *Dithyrambs*), a
second hand added, in the margin, the title of the second poem and several
marginalia.[144] Number 27 (Theocritus) includes at least eighty-four different notes, most of them by a second hand. In this manuscript, a great majority of the notes provide paraphrases or explain specific words, but there
are also notes on myth, dialectal forms, ethnography, ritual, and other matters.[145] The fragments of Pindar in number 36 include numerous annotations by both the first and a second hand: there are queries about the text
(implying a concern to generate a correct text); explanations of myth, historical events, and geography; and comments on dialect and spelling.[146]

In several instances, the contents of the annotations are unusual and instructive. The most remarkable example is number 23, the text of Plato's
Republic, Book 8. The scribe who added the notes to this manuscript employed abbreviations and tachygraphic symbols, and the use of shorthand
notes has suggested to Kathleen McNamee that the notes were perhaps
added during the course of a lecture on the text.[147] If that is the case, it is
the only known instance of such note taking; certainly no other example
of annotations that employ shorthand symbols is known. Another unusual
type of note occurs at line 40 in number 19 (lyric, probably Alcaeus). This
note is taken by McNamee as a "quasi-personal" note.[148] Since almost all
notes in Roman-era manuscripts consisted of scholarly matter deriving
from commentaries and passed down from one copy to another, personal
reactions, or comments such as this one seems to be, are exceedingly rare
and indicate an unusually active interest in the text. We have one certain
example of a note added long after the original copy was made. This is in
number 1 (Ibycus). The note, which refers to words in the next-to-last column, is certainly later than the text, and may have been added in the first
century A D.[149] If so, it was added when the manuscript was at least 130 years

---

142. Ibid., 138–44, isolates some thirty-one notes in these fragments.

143. Ibid., 145–47.

144. Ibid., 343–44. Grenfell and Hunt took the marginalia as by a third hand.

145. Ibid., 427–41.

146. Ibid., 308–15.

147. Ibid., 352–54. See also McNamee (2001), 111–15, for the suggestion, advanced with all due
caution, that the notes were added during the course of a lecture; and for the notes themselves—text,
supplements, and interpretation—see the brilliant reconstruction by McNamee and Jacovides (2003).

148. McNamee (2007), 146–47.

149. Barron (1969), 121.

old, and probably close to 200 years old. On the other hand, we also have a manuscript in which it is virtually certain that the annotations were copied onto the papyrus right along with the main text, and by the same scribe. This is number 18, one of the five book rolls containing Alcaeus. Here, the first lines of the annotations in fragment 1 extend into the left margin, like hanging indents, and subsequent lines are indented and aligned with one another. Both the regularity of the format and the fact that the same hand wrote both text and notes suggested to McNamee that the notes were commissioned and copied along with the main text.[150] Similarly, the matched set of two plays of Sophocles (numbers 25 and 26), copied by the same scribe and annotated by the same second hand, may well have been annotated as part of the original commission or production.

It would appear, then, that the owners of this collection were keen to acquire texts that included annotation. The collector may have sought out older, used copies and added notes, or had notes copied in; or he may have commissioned copies that would include annotations; or both. Much of the annotation consists, to be sure, of elementary exegesis, but in this collection of manuscripts there are also many notes in which variant readings are recorded, and we may reasonably assume that a concern with obtaining an accurate text was central. Taken together with the contents of the collection in general—at least five book rolls of Alcaeus, somewhere between six and a dozen manuscripts of Pindar, reference works that include biographies, obscure literary questions, and a lexicon of words from non-Greek languages—the annotations point to a scholarly collector, with both a particular interest in early poetry and broad interests in a range of topics including history, oratory, and drama.[151]

In assessing the significance of these aspects of the collection, it is useful to note that none of its characteristics is to be taken for granted, as becomes clear when we compare it to the collection represented by Grenfell and Hunt's first find. The first find consists very largely of prose, this one of poetry. The first implies a particular interest in historical events of the late 400s and early 300s BC, this one an interest in early lyric poetry. The

---

150. McNamee (2007), 152–54. Identity of hands: Lobel in the introduction to *P.Oxy.* 21.2297. This manuscript contains several types of annotation: comment on word usage, many paraphrases, possibly an interpretation.

151. The presence within this collection of the two short speeches—the encomium on the fig (*MP*[3] 2527) and the panegyric on Theon (*MP*[3] 1847)—may also be taken as an indication of a scholarly context for the collection. Both items are most likely compositions by students, rather than epideictic speeches by professional orators, but where there are students there are teachers, with their more advanced scholarly interests.

first includes a high percentage of opisthographs, the second only one. The manuscripts of the first find in general do not include extensive marginalia, whereas such annotation is a common feature of the second collection. The second is more systematically corrected than the first. Each, however, in its own way, seems to imply a collector who was a serious reader and perhaps a scholar.

4.12. COLLECTION OF ASTRONOMICAL
TEXTS PERHAPS OWNED BY AN ASTROLOGER
(DISCARDED FOURTH OR FIFTH CENTURY AD)

Alexander Jones has identified a group of astronomical papyri from Oxyrhynchus that seem to have been found close together and were very likely owned by one person. This is not, properly speaking, a book collection. It is, rather, what survives of the working papers of a person concerned with astrology and, in particular, with casting horoscopes. We will treat it more summarily than we did the earlier concentrations, but it is instructive both because of the methodology employed by Jones and because, with its distinctive character, it provides useful comparative materials for our other collections.

The fragments were found by Grenfell and Hunt in the winter of 1906–7, their sixth and last campaign at Oxyrhynchus, but they did not comment on them as a coherent body of papyri, nor did they ever mention finding a concentration of astronomical texts. To reconstruct the contents of the concentration, therefore, Jones relied upon inventory numbers. Many of the original inventory numbers are now missing, and some of those that survive cannot be interpreted, but Jones was able to assemble a group of fragments deriving from some thirty to sixty ancient manuscripts, all of which seem to have been found close together.[152] Since he was publishing many other astronomical papyri as well, Jones called this particular concentration "group A" and argued that they very probably belonged to a single ancient collection.[153] He suggested that the collection was discarded early in the fourth century, but the date of deposition may have been somewhat later than that.[154]

---

152. Jones (1999), 57–60, gives an excellent explanation of the inventory numbers and of the problems involved in working with them. Using the methodology he developed, it may be possible in future to identify further concentrations of materials.

153. Jones (1999), 59.

154. The latest date mentioned in any of the papyri is AD 306. A few documents, however, were

The papyri contain several types of astronomical material. There are tables of planetary motion, arithmetical tables, almanacs, a disquisition on the prediction of eclipses, and perhaps two horoscopes. Many of these materials are one-page documents. At least twelve, and probably more, of the manuscripts were codices, the standard format for astronomical tables.[155] There were also, however, some rolls. A striking example of this is *P.Oxy.* 61.4167, containing Ptolemy's *Handy Tables*, which was copied on a roll, or more likely, as Jones notes, on several rolls, since it would have required some thirty meters of papyrus if the whole of Ptolemy's work was included. It is possible that the owner of the astronomical papyri possessed at least some literary book rolls as well. A small number of literary papyri were put by Grenfell and Hunt into the boxes that contained the astronomical papyri: *P.Oxy.* 57.3887 (Thucydides, second or third century); 61.4105, fragment B (Thucydides, a papyrus codex of the second or third century); 66.4514 (Aristophanes, *The Peace*, fourth century); 66.4521 (Aristophanes, *Plutus*, second century); and 68.4665 (Hesiod, *Aspis*, late second or early third century). All of these fragments have inventory numbers that imply they were sorted into boxes that also contained astronomical papyri.

Limiting ourselves to the astronomical materials in Jones's group A, we may note two characteristics that this group shares with the other concentrations we have identified. First, the texts were prepared by a considerable number of different scribes. Jones noted only three pairs of manuscripts that were copied by the same scribe: *P.Oxy.* 61.4154 and 61.4155 (which may be from the same manuscript); *P.Oxy.* 61.4217b and 61.4217c (and possibly 61.4155); and *P.Oxy.* 61.4210 and 61.4213 (perhaps from the same manuscript). Since many of the fragments are very small, identifying hands is difficult, and there may well be more instances of multiple texts copied by one scribe, but it is quite possible that these thirty to sixty texts were copied by dozens of different scribes.

Second, there are several manuscripts that appear to have been rolls consisting of reused documents with astronomical materials on the verso

---

found close to the astronomical papyri, if we can trust their inventory numbers. The documents are dated in the period from the late fourth to the early sixth century, suggesting that they, and the astronomical collection, were thrown out in the fifth or sixth century. The documents, stored by Grenfell and Hunt in boxes with sequence numbers close to those of the boxes in which they placed the astronomical papyri, are *P.Oxy.* 63.4386 (dated AD 393), 50.3583 (November 444), 50.3584 (fifth century), 50.3586 (fifth century), and 68.4699 (January 504).

155. Examples of codices: *P.Oxy.* 61.4169, 61.4173a, 61.4194, 61.4196, and 61.4196a.

(*P.Oxy.* 61.4159, 61.4165, 61.4210, 61.4213, 61.4215, and 61.4224), indicating the sort of interest in economy that we saw, for example, in Grenfell and Hunt's first find. *P.Oxy.* 61.4212 contains what may have been professionally useful texts on both sides: the recto has an astrological text and the verso a five-day almanac.[156]

This collection, however, differs from our other collections in significant ways, above all in its professional and practical character. There is no reading matter, unless the texts of Thucydides, Aristophanes, and Hesiod really did form part of the collection. The great majority of the manuscripts consist not of texts in prose or verse, but of tables, the only significant exceptions being the fifteen theoretical and instructional texts (*P.Oxy.* 61.4133 to 61.4147), themselves highly technical and for the most part brief. One text (*P.Oxy.* 61.4215) may be intended either for professional use or as a textbook example to illustrate method. In sum: this collection (or the part of it that survives) was essentially a reference tool, useful to the owner as he cast horoscopes. Although it included a few explanatory or instructional texts, it was not designed for reading. It serves to remind us that collections of works of literature, whether prose or poetry, are not to be taken for granted, even in the households of literate persons.

4.13. CONCLUSION

At the end of chapter 2 we noted that, although we can learn much from the lists of books on papyri, those lists tell us very little about the physical condition of the books in the collections. The remains of actual book rolls in the various collections from Herculaneum and Oxyrhynchus give us a chance to assess the physical qualities of several ancient collections, or at least the parts of those collections that have survived. In these cases we can move beyond the generic references to books and libraries that we find in literary sources, turn over in our hands the remains of actual manuscripts, and draw conclusions about specific ancient book collections and the condition of the manuscripts they contained.

As we would expect, the quality of manuscripts varies both within a given collection and from one collection to another. Within the single small collection represented by Grenfell and Hunt's first find, for example, we find a strikingly wide range of qualities:

---

156. There are also some rolls with text on the recto and the verso left blank. Economy was not, perhaps, a constant concern.

*MP*³ 438 (Euripides, *Hypsipyle*): on the verso; carelessly written but extensively corrected by the original scribe and a second hand.

*MP*³ 1293 (speeches of Lysias): on the recto; handsome format, with generous spacing. Mistakes only partly corrected, and no evidence of a second hand.

*MP*³ 1263 (Isocrates, *Panegyricus*): on the recto; a handsome manuscript in a large calligraphic hand. It seems to have been corrected by collation with a second exemplar.

*MP*³ 1401 (Plato, *Phaedrus*): on the recto; a particularly fine copy, with papyrus of superior texture and a fine graceful hand. Collation with a second exemplar.

Within the Breccia + GH3 collection, even though it is more homogeneous in terms of overall quality than the collection represented by Grenfell and Hunt's first find, we still find manuscripts of various levels of quality, and with a variety of peculiarities. Some examples will suffice. *MP*³ 1353 (Pindar's *Olympian* 2) was written by two different scribes. *MP*³ 1400.1 (Plato, *Phaedrus*) and *MP*³ 1509 (Thucydides, Book 1) include corrections based, it seems, on a second archetype. *MP*³ 462 (Herodotus) was repaired by means of strengthening strips glued to the back. *MP*³ 1482, a mime by Sophron, was marked, presumably by a reader, in a way that suggests it was, or could be, used in oral recitations. *MP*³ 2954 (Gaius, *Institutiones*, Book 4), in Latin, may have been copied not by a professional scribe, but by the individual who wished to use the text. It is safe to conclude that the various manuscripts within a given ancient collection, as we might have predicted but could not tell from the lists in chapter 2 or from references in literature, could and often did vary widely in quality and condition. One is reminded of Cicero's complaints about the poor quality of available texts: even his collection must have had some particularly fine rolls (for example, the ones stolen by his freedman) and some that were full of flaws.

Similarly, the texts in a given collection varied in age. Isolating collections, as we have done in this chapter, allows us to draw some inferences about the useful life of manuscripts as well as the makeup of particular collections. Omitting the astronomical collection—the life of which was probably determined by professional requirements—we can summarize the information about the ages of manuscripts as follows.

Collection	Date of Deposition	Oldest Manuscript	Age of Oldest Manuscript at the Time of Deposition	A Majority of the Copies Were Made in the Period . . .	Age of the Majority of Manuscripts at the Time of Deposition
Grenfell and Hunt's first find	Late third century?	MP³ 1263 (Isocrates, *Panegyricus*), early second century AD	About 175 years old	Ca. AD 175 to 225	75 to 125 years old
Breccia + GH3	Ca. AD 300	MP³ 1482 (Sophron, *Mimes*) and 2617 (the Ninus novel), both of first century AD	200 to 300 years old	Second century	100 to 200 years old
Aurelius family	Ca. AD 300–320	(All from the third century)	Less than 100 years old	Third century	Less than 100 years old
Grenfell and Hunt's second find	Ca. AD 400	MP³ 1237 (Ibycus), copied ca. 130 BC	About 500 years old	Late second or early third century	150 to 250 years old

Some manuscripts clearly could last for half a millennium, but that was exceptional.[157] It was not unusual, though, for a papyrus roll to have a useful life of a century or two, and the evidence of these collections suggests that a roll might well be expected to last for 150 years, and that in some cases book rolls were kept for much longer than that. On the other hand, we also have examples of manuscripts that were discarded or reused when they were not very old. The copy of Iulius Africanus's *Cestoi* that belonged to the Aure-

157. In addition to the manuscript of Ibycus, at least three other manuscripts in Grenfell and Hunt's second find were some 300 years old or more when they were discarded. These are *MP³* 179 (Bacchylides), 216 (Callimachus), and 1495 (Theocritus). As we have seen, a small number of the manuscripts from the Villa of the Papyri were 250 to 300 years old at the time of the eruption of Vesuvius.

lius family cannot have been made before about AD 220, since Africanus did not write the work until then, yet it was reused to make a copy of the will of Aurelius Hermogenes not long, it seems, after Hermogenes's death in 276. Thus this manuscript was deemed disposable when it was at most some fifty years old.[158]

In all of our collections, so far as we can tell, the various manuscripts were copied by many different scribes. The sixteen manuscripts in Grenfell and Hunt's first find were copied by at least five and possibly fifteen different scribes, the seventy or so in Breccia + GH3 by at least eight and perhaps dozens of different scribes, and the thirty-six in Grenfell and Hunt's second find by at least eight and probably many more scribes. Each of the four manuscripts in the Aurelius family collection was copied by a different scribe, and all but half a dozen of the thirty or more tables and texts identified by Jones as coming from a single collection of astronomical texts seem to have been copied by different scribes. There are few examples of a single scribe copying more than two manuscripts in any given collection.

There are, then, several indications that the commissioning of manuscripts from professional scribes, or purchasing ready-made copies from them, was the norm, as opposed to having one's manuscripts copied by in-house slave scribes. I would note the following such indications:

1. The number of different hands, and thus of scribes, attested in the manuscripts of each collection known to us. If even Cicero did not always have a scribe in his household—and we know he did not—it is unlikely that the owners of these book collections had eight or fifteen or twenty such scribes, all trained to professional standards.[159]

2. The variations in quality and in format. If book collectors regularly had their own slaves make copies, we might have expected texts that more closely resemble one another, as opposed to the wide range of qualities and formats that we do in fact find. That texts might be prepared to specific and standardized formats is clear from a few examples, but it is very unlikely that that was the normal practice.[160]

---

158. The very fact that the manuscript was relatively new may have been why it was chosen: the person who commissioned the copy of the will perhaps wanted good sturdy papyrus for her or his copy of the will.

159. The emperor Valens, with all the resources available to him, apparently thought seven copyists (*antiquarii*) a reasonable number when he was setting up a new library in Constantinople: *Cod. Theod.* 14.9.2 of AD 372, on which see further below, section 6.6.

160. An example of multiple copies done in similar format and perhaps forming part of a set of an author's works would be the four plays of Aeschylus, all copied by scribe A3, in Breccia + GH3.

3. The presence in a number of manuscripts of stichometric counts, whether as final counts in a *subscriptio* or as running counts in the margin. The variations in such numeration—from final counts of lines to running counts of lines, columns, or sheets of papyrus— themselves indicate that the texts were not prepared to standardized formats in single households or workshops.

4. The variation, from one manuscript to another within a given collection, in the number of corrections and in the consistency and care with which mistakes are corrected. In some cases, many mistakes are left uncorrected; in others, the corrections are thorough and careful; in some, the corrector seems to have consulted a second exemplar. Such variation, I would suggest, is more likely the result of a collector purchasing copies that were prepared commercially than the result of a master having his slaves make copies. In the latter case, the master could insist on a certain level of consistency, and the copyists involved would be likely to work at a more consistent level.

5. The presence of copies by one scribe in more than one collection at Oxyrhynchus.

6. The presence of copies by one scribe in both Oxyrhynchus and some other city of Egypt.

As for contents, what emerges most strikingly from these collections is how different they are from one another. In each case, the collector has made choices in accordance with his interests or needs or both, and the manuscripts reflect those interests.[161] We have noted the characteristics of each collection as we described them, and here a brief summary will suffice.

Grenfell and Hunt's first find: Almost entirely prose. Several relatively obscure authors; there seems to be a particular interest in one historical period (roughly 430 to 340 BC). The texts contain relatively little annotation.[162] The collector seems to have been concerned to obtain correct texts: most of the rolls had been corrected by a second hand, and two, it seems, were checked against a second exemplar. Elegant copies were of less importance to him than accurate ones. Six of the sixteen manuscripts, or about 37 percent, were copied on

161. As always, I use "the collector" as shorthand for "the collector or collectors," since any given collection may well have reached its final form, part of which is known to us, only after additions and subtractions made over a period of years or decades by a series of owners.

162. In general, prose works are much less frequently and heavily annotated than poetry, so the absence of annotation here is not unexpected.

the verso of documents, a far higher percentage than in our other collections.

Breccia + GH3: This is a broadly based collection of authors who are among the most frequently attested at Oxyrhynchus. I have not been able to identify a particular focus or area of specialization, and the collection would appear to be aimed at general reading.[163] There are a number of commentaries and other supporting works, but they suggest not a scholar but a serious reader who sought help as he read the manuscripts in his collection. The percentage of annotated manuscripts is about average. The texts are mostly high quality and accurate; the percentage of opisthographs is low. The collector seems to have had sufficient funds to assemble a good collection of the classics, and he did just that.

The collection of the Aurelius family: This collection is too small to characterize in any useful way. It is of interest in that it includes Homer, the most basic of authors, but also at least one and probably two very rare works. Perhaps if we had more of the family's collection we would find a wide range of authors both popular and obscure. None of the manuscripts seems to have been kept for more than a century, and at least one, the text of Iulius Africanus's *Cestoi*, may have had a life of only a few decades.

Grenfell and Hunt's second find: Very strong in poetry, especially early lyric, and in this way completely different from Grenfell and Hunt's first find. The collection includes an unusual array of reference works, only a few of which relate clearly to the central interest in poetry. A lexicon of rare words from other languages perhaps indicates that the owner was a scholar, rather than a general reader. There is a very high rate of annotation, and some of the annotations are unusually extensive. In one case, a text of Plato, there are notes in the margins that may have been made during a lecture. All of this seems to point to a scholar or teacher as collector and owner. The presence of two personal compositions — a verse panegyric and a student exercise — are consistent with the hypothesis of a scholar or teacher as collector.

The astronomical collection: Obviously different from our other four, this collection is the virtual opposite of the Breccia + GH3 collection:

---

163. There may be some particular interests represented within the broad collection. Callimachus, for example, is present in several copies. This collection also contains three manuscripts in Latin and in that respect differs from our other four collections.

these were not texts to be read, but one-page reference tables and charts to be used professionally, along with a small number of instructional materials. As in our other collections, a large number of different scribes made the copies that survive, and in some cases the astronomical tables were copied on the verso of documents, perhaps indicating a concern with expense.

Each of these five collections, then, has its own distinct focus and personality. It is reassuring to note that several characteristics that emerged from our analysis of the lists of books in chapter 2 are also attested in these collections. In both cases, we find duplicate copies, occasional opisthographs, Latin texts (though rare) commingled with Greek, and a mix of standard authors (Homer, Hesiod, and Callimachus, for example) with obscure, even unidentifiable, ones. In both bodies of evidence we find collections that reflect distinct personalities. They emerge in the focus of the collections, which can range from general collections to more specialized ones—for example, the relatively obscure philosophical works in *P.Ross.Georg.* 1.22, the works in Epicurean aesthetics and ethics at Herculaneum, and the emphasis on early Greek lyric in Grenfell and Hunt's second find—to highly technical or professional collections, such as the collection of astronomical materials and, among the book lists, the medical and philosophical collection listed on *P.Vars.* 5 verso. The contents thus suggest a wide variation in the collectors' interests and level of training. In our sample we seem to have general readers, readers with particular interests, scholars, and at least one professional with his technical materials.

Having considered in some detail a number of specific ancient Roman book collections, our next task is to consider the physical aspects of their storage and the nonbook materials that were associated with them, whether in personal collections (both small and large), municipal or institutional collections, or the great imperial libraries. This set of interrelated questions will form the subject of chapter 5.

5

Spaces, Storage, Equipment, and Art

5.1. INTRODUCTION

There was more inside a Roman library than a collection of manuscripts. Even small collections required storage facilities of some sort, and if an owner wished to repair old or make new copies, or have his workers do so, scribal equipment would be needed. Book collections could then, as now, be impressive displays of one's taste and intelligence, and the Romans responded to this potential by providing handsome surroundings for their collections, as well as works of art to complement them. In this chapter, we will survey such nonbook materials, treating them in three groups: first, containers and storage facilities for book rolls; second, other equipment and furniture; and finally, decorative elements, in particular statues and other images. Our goal is to be able to reconstruct, in our imaginations, what was inside a Roman library.[1]

5.2. BOXES AND CONTAINERS

Small but coherent groups of manuscripts such as, say, a complete *Iliad* in twelve rolls, or the books one inherited from an uncle, could be kept in a box, either rectangular or cylindrical. The archetypical small collection of this sort is that of Juvenal's hapless Cordus, who kept his entire collection of book rolls in a single container, which Juvenal calls a *cista*.[2] Such containers are well known from references in literature and from depictions in paintings and sculpture. From the written sources, we learn that they were referred to variously as *capsa, cista, scrinium,* or derivatives from those

---

1. Some aspects of the topics I take up in this chapter have been carefully treated in earlier studies. In such cases, I will not attempt to deal with all of the evidence and will be selective in citing references. Full detail is available in the relevant specialist literature. For earlier general treatments, see Birt (1907) or Blanck (2008), esp. 57–103.

2. Juv. 3.206. For the name Cordus rather than Codrus, see Courtney (1980), 182.

terms.[3] No clear distinctions in shape, size, or material can be drawn among them, and all three terms can usually be rendered accurately enough by the English "box" or "container." These words were not technical terms, and they were not library-specific.[4]

A passage in Catullus (68.33–36) illustrates the uses of the boxes. Catullus says that he has taken a single *capsula* full of book rolls with him to Bithynia, but that he had left many more back in Rome; thus such a box could be used either for permanent storage or for transport. *Cistae*, and no doubt *capsae* and *scrinia* too, could be used to carry many different, mostly small, objects. In the case of *cistae*, we find them being used to transport book rolls, coins, turnips, a whole (live) man, and other objects.[5] *Scrinia* could be either small, since we hear of them being used as portable containers for letters (Sallust, *Cat.* 46.6), or large, as when Catullus mentions book dealers keeping their book rolls, presumably fairly numerous, in *scrinia* (Cat. 14.17–20). Book dealers' storage cases are called not *scrinia* but *capsae* by Statius (*Silv.* 4.9.21), indicating the rough equivalence of the terms.

Whatever they were called, book boxes were no doubt ordinarily made of wood; Pliny the Elder (*HN* 16.229) mentions beech as useful for *capsae* and *scrinia*, and small chests made of cypress and chestnut have been found at Pompeii.[6] As for their shape, at least two rectangular boxes containing papyrus rolls were found in the Villa of the Papyri at Herculaneum; one measured 28.6 by 17.6 by 22 cm, the other 52.8 by 26.4 by 26.4 cm.[7] We are told that between them they contained sixty book rolls. Columella (12.56.2) mentions a *quadrata cista*, that is, a rectangular box, in an agricultural context.

---

3. The usual Greek equivalent is κιβωτός or κιβώτιον, but in Greek many other words were used as well: Budde (1940), 5–6.

4. Of the three, *capsa* comes closest to being a technical term, since it is used more often of boxes that contained book rolls than it is of containers for other items, but it is not limited to books or book collections. Martial (11.8.3) and Pliny (*HN* 15.82) both refer to *capsae* that held fruit.

5. References in *TLL*, s.v. The man was Fannius Caepio, concealed in a *cista* to escape after he attempted to assassinate Augustus: Macrob. *Sat.* 1.11.21. This implies a container of some size, a chest rather than a box. On the various contents of *cistae* and the others, see further Small (1997), 50.

6. Budde (1940), 13 and 15. In theory, other materials too were possible. Tin containers, possibly used to store book rolls, are mentioned in our list 3 (*P.Jena* inv. 267, section 2.8 above). Book rolls have been found in ceramic jars at Qumran in Israel and Nag Hammadi in Egypt; cf. Small (1997), 49. These, however, were probably not intended as a standard method of storage, but rather as hiding places in times of trouble.

7. Longo Auricchio and Capasso (1987), 40. It appears that the boxes no longer exist. It is not clear what their exact purpose was: perhaps book rolls were stored in them permanently; perhaps rolls were placed in them during renovations to the Villa; or perhaps rolls were put in them during the eruption of Vesuvius, with a view to moving them to safety.

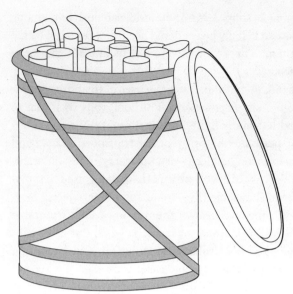

*Figure 7. Cylindrical
book box, used for storage,
transport, or both. The
diagonal straps could
presumably be attached
to loops that would make
the box easier to carry. In
this drawing, the book rolls
are placed vertically in the
box. The small projections
attached to the top of three of
the rolls are probably* sillyba.
*Drawing by Margaret Reid,
based on a wall painting
from Campania (National
Archaeological Museum,
Naples, MN 4675).*

Book boxes of the Roman period could also be cylindrical, and they are attested in this form both in literature and in visual representations. The most
helpful passage in literature is Ovid, *Tr.* 1.1.105–10: Ovid addresses one of
his book rolls and says that it will find its mates at Rome, all neatly ordered
in their cylindrical boxes (*scrinia curva*), with their titles clearly visible, presumably on *sillyba*. This must mean that Ovid thought of the rolls as being
placed vertically in the *scrinia*, with one end—the end to which the *sillybon*
was attached—at the top of the box. This arrangement, which would make
retrieval of specific titles easy, is exactly what appears in a number of visual
representations, including both paintings and sculptures. See Figure 7, a
modern reconstruction, based on a painting from Pompeii, of what such a
cylindrical book box might have looked like. In this case, the box has a lid,
and about a dozen rolls of various sizes stand vertically in it.

Vertical storage of manuscripts has been confirmed recently by observation of the creases in rolls from the Villa of the Papyri, where Richard Janko
noticed that the manuscripts containing Philodemus's *On Poems*, Books 1,
3, and 4, were all bent in a similar way. He suggests that they were stored
upright, that during the eruption of Vesuvius they were soaked with water,
and that they sagged as a result of the soaking, giving them the characteristic crease that we see now.[8] Vertical storage makes sense: if one were storing

8. Janko (2011), 166. He points out that De Jorio, writing in 1825, claimed that many rolls had been
found in this position, that is, upright rather than lying horizontally.

manuscripts in boxes rather than on shelves, it would be helpful to have the end with the *sillybon* readily visible.

In sum, there is considerable evidence for the use of boxes, some cylindrical, others rectangular, for the transport and storage of manuscripts in personal collections. There is no single or specific name in Latin for such containers, nor for containers of a particular shape.[9] Manuscripts in book boxes were probably stored vertically under ordinary circumstances.

5.3. SHELVING

There was another option for the storage of manuscripts: on shelves. In this case, the rolls were stored not vertically, but horizontally, with one of the round ends—the end to which a *sillybon* was attached—facing out, and on each shelf there might be a stack of book rolls two or three (or possibly more) rolls high.[10] Shelves of various sorts are attested in both written and archaeological sources. In setting out the evidence for them, I will arrange them along an imaginary spectrum from simple shelves that held everyday objects to formal, library-specific shelving. The distinction is mine, not the Romans', and it goes without saying that most of the shelves we know about could be used for the temporary or permanent storage of many different household objects.

Single rolls or small groups of rolls could be placed temporarily on any available surface, including a shelf, but shelves were simple household objects, ordinarily not limited to the storage of book collections.[11] One set of shelves that was specifically designed for books was the one that Atticus's men built for Cicero after his return from exile. Cicero wrote to Atticus to express his delight with the new shelves, which he called *pegmata*.[12] Even in the absence of specific evidence, we may reasonably assume that shelves like Cicero's, built expressly for book rolls, were common in the personal

9. Modern scholars occasionally state or imply that the cylindrical containers were always called *capsae*. This would have surprised Ovid, who called them *scrinia curva* (Ov. *Tr.* 1.1.106).

10. Capasso (2007), 76, noted that *P.Herc.* 732 consists of a stack of six papyrus rolls that had been fused together in the eruption of Vesuvius; evidently they had been stacked one upon another. Note also the three layers of rolls in Figure 8, and see further Sève (2010), 26–27 and 29.

11. Mols (1999), 55, with n. 273, and 130, notes holes in walls that imply the use of brackets to support wall shelves.

12. Cic. *Att.* 4.8.2. The word is rare, and exactly what Cicero meant by it is not completely clear; but the *pegmata* were almost certainly shelves of some sort. We can infer that they were open (that is, there were no doors), because Cicero could see the *sillyba* on the rolls. Wendel (1974), 67, suggested that *pegmata* were temporary shelves, and that the book rolls, once sorted, would have been redistributed to Cicero's other properties.

libraries of wealthy families. We know also of shelves that rested on brackets set within niches or recesses in walls; these are attested in Herculaneum and Pompeii, but in no case can we prove they held book rolls.[13] Similar informal shelves set in wall niches appear in houses in Egypt, and in some instances there is evidence to suggest that they were designed specifically for the storage of book rolls.[14]

More helpful is the evidence for wooden cabinets (*armarium* in Latin, κιβωτός in Greek), for here we have clear and specific evidence for the storage of book rolls.[15] In origin, *armaria* were simply items of household furniture that could be used for a great variety of objects, but we know from both depictions in ancient art and references in written sources that they were frequently used for the storage of book rolls.[16] A particularly instructive depiction is found on a sarcophagus of the fourth century AD. (See Figure 8.)[17]

In this relief, a man sits reading a book roll. He is evidently a doctor, to judge from the small folding case of medical instruments in the upper right corner of the relief. Next to him is a cabinet, or *armarium*. The double doors of the cabinet are open, exposing three shelves, the lowest of which is also the bottom of the cabinet. The lowest shelf is empty, and the middle shelf holds a single shallow bowl or basin. On the top shelf are eight small circles representing rolled-up papyrus rolls.[18] The cabinet appears to be mounted on a

13. Mols (1999), 130, with n. 811. Of the eleven sets of shelves Mols lists, three are in private dwellings and could have held household objects, book rolls, or both. The others are in *thermopolia*, or shops.

14. The niches were called θυρίς in Greek and *fenestra* in Latin: Husson (1983), 155–60; cf. Wendel (1974), 78–80. We know of them archaeologically (Husson lists six examples, one with part of a papyrus roll in it) and from a papyrus. In *P.Ross.Georg.* 3.1, an army doctor writes home asking that the book rolls he had left in a θυρίς be removed and shaken out from time to time; this θυρίς was not a windowsill (as previous scholars had taken it) but, as Husson argued, a cabinet built into a recess in a wall.

15. For these terms, see Budde (1940). Following Budde, Richter (1966), 115–16, defined the essential characteristics of an *armarium*: it consisted of a rectangular case, usually mounted on feet; the top was sometimes flat, sometimes gabled; it had doors, and in the interior space were shelves. Croom (2007), 124–32, sets out known variations on the theme; cf. Coqueugniot (2007), 295–97 and 304.

16. Mols (1999), 130–31 and 207–17, describes the *armaria* found in Herculaneum and Pompeii. Their contents included ceramic tableware, drinking glasses, dice, small boxes, and the like. The tallest (Mols's no. 36) is 1.49 m high, while the smallest freestanding one (no. 40) is 52.5 cm high.

17. This relief is the central panel on one side of a sarcophagus that is now in the Metropolitan Museum of Art in New York. Its provenance is unknown but was probably one of the cemeteries of Portus, the town that grew up around Trajan's harbor north of Ostia. The inscription on the sarcophagus (*IG* 14.943), which imposes fines upon anyone who reuses the sarcophagus, cannot date earlier than AD 312: Meiggs (1973), 88; and Dessau, *CIL* 14, p. 6. The sarcophagus is not likely to be much later than that, because the man is reading a book roll, and by AD 400 book rolls had largely been replaced by codices.

18. Petersen (1900), 173–74, first correctly identified the figure as a doctor and showed that the

*Figure 8. Marble relief of a doctor reading. The doctor (identifiable as such from the doctor's kit on top of the cabinet) sits in a high-backed chair holding a book roll. Next to him there is a cabinet (*armarium*). On the top shelf of the cabinet is a small stack of book rolls. Metropolitan Museum of Art, New York, accession no. MMA 48.76.1. Image from Art Resource, New York, © The Metropolitan Museum of Art.*

base or chest that is strengthened by diagonal crossbars, and the base stands on undecorated feet. A decorative cornice runs around the top of the cabinet, and the doctor's instrument case is propped open on top of the *armarium*.

Armaria are mentioned with some frequency in written sources, but it is not always possible to tell whether the *armarium* the author had in mind was freestanding, attached to a wall, or set into a niche. We are told that they could be painted or made of expensive woods and ivory (presumably inlays); that they sometimes had locks (and thus certainly doors); that *armaria* containing books might be very tall; and that they served as storage containers for a variety of objects, including blankets, rugs, clothing, gold, and book rolls.[19] Their interior space could, it seems, be divided not only by horizontal shelves, but also by vertical dividers. This created small compartments, which the Romans called by a variety of not very technical names.[20]

Cabinets of this sort, and containing book rolls, were discovered in the room called room V in Karl Weber's plan of the Villa of the Papyri at Herculaneum.[21] Whatever furniture was in this room seems to have disappeared, but a letter of Carlo Paderni, one of the scholars in charge of the exploration of the Villa, describes (rather imprecisely) what was found: "We have entered into one room, the floor of which is formed of mosaic work, not unelegant. It appears to have been a library, adorned with presses, inlaid with different sorts of wood, disposed in rows; at the top of which were cornices, as in our own times."[22] This description is by and large confirmed, and some further information is added, in a letter Johann Winckelmann wrote after he visited the site: "All around the walls were bookcases like the ones that we have now in archives, as high as a man is tall, and in the middle of the room there was another, similar, bookcase or table, to hold texts, that you

---

round objects in the cabinet were papyrus rolls. The inscription identifies neither the doctor nor his occupation, and, as Petersen pointed out, we must assume that his name appeared on the lid of the sarcophagus, now lost. Jackson (1988), 73–74, discusses the relief and the use of basins by doctors.

19. Painted: Sulp. Sev. *Dial.* 1.21.4. Expensive woods and ivory, and height: Sen. *Tranq.* 9.6 (= *Dial.* 9.9.6). Discussing *armaria* used specifically for book storage, Seneca says that they might be made of expensive materials, and that the shelves might reach as high as the ceiling: *tecto tenus extructa loculamenta.* If we take him literally, we might expect that such tall *armaria* would have been attached to the walls for stability. Locks: *Dig.* 32.52.9. Items stored in them: Budde (1940), 3–4.

20. Thus *forulus* ("little shelf"), *nidus* ("nest") and *loculamentum* ("little compartment"). On these terms, see Johnson (1984), 155–56.

21. A simplified clear plan of the Villa, with find spots of book rolls marked: Longo Auricchio and Capasso (1987), 47. A large-scale reproduction of Weber's plan, with room V clearly marked, is in Mattusch (2005), in the pocket inside the back cover.

22. The letter was written in 1754. I use the text provided by Gallavotti (1940), 60; cf. Longo Auricchio and Capasso (1987), 43. It is not clear to me what Paderni meant by "rows" of bookcases. Winckelmann mentions just one freestanding bookcase; perhaps Paderni meant that and the cases along the two side walls.

could walk around."[23] Some hundreds of rolls were found in this room, stored in the bookcases along the walls or in the central cabinet.[24] What Paderni and Winckelmann described can be visualized if we imagine a series of *armaria* like the one in Figure 8 lined up next to one another, but with each *armarium* somewhat larger than the one in our figure, and more completely filled with papyrus rolls.

Armaria could also be built into the walls and thus made integral parts of rooms. In that case, we have library-specific *armaria* within rooms that were designed expressly to function as storage space for book rolls, as reading areas, or both. Within the masonry of a wall, the builders would fit an *armarium*, with a back, sides, shelves, and one or two doors, all made of wood: in other words, a cabinet like the one in Figure 8, built to fit the dimensions of a niche in the wall. David Petrain has recently pointed out the potential aesthetic appeal of such cabinets when they were built in a row around the walls of a library room, as they clearly were in the imperial libraries of Rome and in larger municipal libraries.[25] Rather than disorderly piles of book rolls, the visitor to such a library would see an impressive display of handsome cases, perhaps inlaid with ivory or decorated in some other way. The cases themselves became an important element in the decorative scheme of the room.

Pliny the Younger, writing to his friend Gallus, tells us about such a cabinet in a private dwelling. He is describing his villa at Laurentum, and in the course of his description he comes to a room that contained a book collection: "Next to this . . . there is a semicircular room. As the sun moves across the sky, it shines in one window after another. A cabinet (*armarium*) like a bookcase (*bibliotheca*) has been set into the wall of this room. In it are books that are not just to be read, but read over and over again."[26] Thus the villa

---

23. Quoted by Gallavotti (1940), 61–62: "Tutto all'intorno del muro v'erano degli scaffali, quali si vedono ordinariamente negli archivj, ad altezza d'uomo, e nel mezzo della stanza v'era un altro scaffale simile o tavola, per tenervi scritture, e tale da potervi girare intorno." The exact nature and function of the piece of furniture in the middle of the room is uncertain. In his German-language "Letter on the Herculanean Discoveries," as translated by Carol Mattusch in Mattusch (2011), 117, Winckelmann described the central piece of furniture as "another shelf, designed to hold texts on either side so that one could walk around it."

24. For the number of rolls, see above, section 3.5. The exact number remains uncertain, but clearly there were hundreds of book rolls in this room.

25. Petrain (2013), 336–38. As he notes, a series of *armaria* could "monumentalize" the collection of books.

26. Plin. *Ep.* 2.17.8 (ca. AD 100): *Adnectitur . . . cubiculum in hapsida curvatum, quod ambitum solis fenestris omnibus sequitur. Parieti eius in bibliothecae speciem armarium insertum est, quod non legendos libros, sed lectitandos capit.* We might also translate: "A cabinet has been set into the wall, in the manner of a library."

had a purpose-built library/reading room, specifically designed to provide good light all day long and outfitted with a bookcase that allowed quick access to rolls that Pliny wanted to consult or read repeatedly.

Wall niches are common in Roman architecture, but they were often filled not with book rolls but with statuary, and it has so far proved impossible to identify a wall niche in a private dwelling that was specifically designed to hold bookcases. There is at least one possibility, but it is only a possibility. At Pompeii, Volker Strocka pointed out that in a room in a private house (Pompeii VI.17.41, room 18) there is a large niche in the north wall, roughly 2.5 m from side to side and varying in depth from 45 to 63 cm.[27] The room also contains wall paintings that include a figure who may well be a lyric poet, and another who is holding a book roll and a staff.[28] On the basis of the niche and these images, Strocka suggested that this room was one in which books were stored.[29] This may be correct, although there is no way to prove that it is, and if it is correct then we may have evidence here for an *armarium*, or at least shelves, designed specifically for the storage of book rolls within a Roman house.

That such built-in *armaria* were fairly common in wealthy homes is clear from the fact that disputes about them arose within the context of bequests, leading to the creation of a body of law that dealt with *armaria* and their contents, as we learn from the *Digest*. We need not be concerned here with the legal issues per se, but the citations from the jurists' opinions make it clear that *armaria* were often firmly attached to the walls, so firmly that they could be considered to be just as much a part of a house as columns, beams, doorways, and water pipes.[30] Even if we have no firmly attested archaeological examples of *armaria*, they were clearly an integral part of many Roman houses, inseparable from the house itself.

---

27. Strocka (1993), 341–51, with a plan on 323; cf. Strocka, Hoffmann, and Hiesel (2012), 170. The height of the niche is unknown, since the wall has not survived above about 3 m. The width, 2.5 m (estimated from the plan), is roughly twice as wide as the niches in the libraries at Ephesus or Timgad, to which we turn in the next section. That is enough of a difference to give one pause.

28. Esposito (2008), 60–61, read the name of the poet as ΦΙΛΟ[Ξ]ΕΝΟΣ, and took this as being Philoxenus of Cythera, author of dithyrambs and a *Cyclops*.

29. Strocka adduced other evidence as well, such as the proximity of this particular room to the *triclinium* (dining room). He suggested that guests might be entertained by readings from books brought from the library, or the host might show his collection to his guests.

30. The legal texts were assembled by Wendel (1974), 65. Disputes about book collections apparently began at least as early as the time of Tiberius, because we find the jurist Cocceius Nerva, who died in AD 33, defining the term *bibliotheca*: *Dig.* 32.52.7. Our earliest evidence for jurists paying attention specifically to *armaria* that held books, however, comes from a *senatus consultum* of AD 122: *Dig.* 30.41.9. See further above, section 1.12, on inheritance of book collections.

5.4. PURPOSE-BUILT STRUCTURES:
THE LIBRARIES AT EPHESUS AND TIMGAD

So far, we have considered storage facilities that consisted, first, of ordinary household objects—boxes, shelves, and cabinets—that could be used to store various items, including book rolls; and secondly, of cabinets and rooms that were specifically planned and built to hold manuscripts. From these purpose-built cabinets and rooms, I turn to whole structures that were designed to hold collections of manuscripts: libraries, in short, whether municipal, imperial, or other.[31] I will consider two examples where an inscription guarantees that the building in question was a library.[32] These are the library of Celsus in Ephesus and the library of Rogatianus in Thamugadi (modern Timgad, in Algeria). In these libraries, we have spaces, storage facilities, and structures all built specifically to house manuscript collections and make it possible to use them.

The library of Celsus in Ephesus (see Figure 9) consists of a single large hall with a highly decorated façade.[33] One approached the building from the east via a set of steps (A) and a shallow covered portico (B). Three doors—the central one is marked C on the plan—provided access to the interior and a source of light. Additional light was provided by windows in the east wall that seem to have been fitted with stone grilles, latticework, or glass.[34] The library hall (D) is 16.72 m wide and 10.92 m deep. Directly across from the central entrance is a podium (G), presumably for a statue,[35] and around

31. I am not concerned with the exterior architecture of such libraries. The plans and design of Roman-era library buildings have been the subject of many studies; see n. 1 in the introduction, above.

32. There are two other reasonably well-preserved buildings where inscriptions guarantee the identification of the buildings as libraries: the library of Pantaenus in Athens, and the library funded by Flavia Melitine in Pergamum. The information they provide on the matter of book storage is not different from that provided by the two libraries I will treat. For further details and bibliography on them, see Blanck 2008, 257–60 (Pantaenus), and 282–85 (Pergamum). A third library identified by an inscription—the second-century AD library at Philippi—is not well preserved, only its plan, not its elevation, being known. It has not been fully published, but for a summary of what remains, see Strocka, in Strocka, Hoffmann, and Hiesel (2012), 169.

33. The library of Celsus was built in the period AD 115–25 by Tiberius Iulius Aquila Polemaeanus in honor of his father, Tiberius Iulius Celsus Polemaeanus. Part of the interior and much of the façade has survived or been rebuilt. My description of the interior of the library depends upon the analysis of the remains by Wilberg (1953), and the dimensions I give derive from his text and plans. For photographs of the restored façade, see Hoepfner (2002b), 123–26. Strocka, in Strocka, Hoffmann, and Hiesel (2012), 167–68, deals with a number of specific problems, such as access to upper floors.

34. Glass is not mentioned in the archaeological reports, but window glass was common by this time. See below, section 5.5.

35. Wilberg (1953), 39, reported, however, that no trace of cuttings to secure a statue survives in the podium.

the south, west, and north sides of the hall runs a continuous platform (E), 94 cm high and 1.025 m deep. On the platform rest the bases for columns (H) that supported an upper gallery, forming a sort of interior portico around the central open space of the great hall. Within the thick exterior walls of the hall are ten niches (F), varying in depth from 57 to 60 cm and in width from about 1.15 m on the north and south walls to about 1.07 m on the west.[36] The niches that survive are 2.55 m high, or roughly two and a third times as high as they are wide. There is a second row of niches on the upper level, but it is not known what purpose they served. Did they hold books? Or statues? Or were they left empty?[37] Some scholars have argued that there was a third level of niches, and that they too held bookcases.[38] We can safely assume that the niches on the ground level were designed to hold books, and that within each of them would have been fitted an *armarium* similar to, but obviously much taller than, the cabinet in Figure 8, and with more shelves. Exactly how many shelves each *armarium* had, and how many rows of book rolls were placed on each shelf, cannot be known, and it is possible that the number of shelves varied from one *armarium* to the next. At the back of the library, below the apse containing the podium (G), is a chamber that contained the tomb of Iulius Celsus (the father of the man who built the library), but it is not connected directly with the great hall and has no bearing on the book collection or storage facilities of the library.[39]

The library of Celsus thus consists essentially of a box-like hall within which were facilities for the storage, use, and perhaps repair of papyrus rolls. Storage facilities included shelves within cabinets that were built into the wall niches, and we might also assume the presence of freestanding *armaria* and perhaps smaller containers, whether rectangular or cylindrical.[40] There was adequate space in the open floor of the hall for such containers, as well as for chairs for those who came to use the library. The obvious question at this point is how many book rolls might have been housed

36. In early publications of the library, it was suggested that the alleyways outside the north, south, and west walls were part of the library structure and designed to protect it from damp, but this was disproved by Hueber (1997), 78–79. The alleys are simply the spaces between the library and other buildings that surrounded it.

37. No trace of stairs to the second level has been found. Strocka, in Strocka, Hoffmann, and Hiesel (2012), 167–68, suggests that narrow ladders provided access to the upper level(s).

38. Most recently, Strocka, in Strocka, Hoffmann, and Hiesel (2012), 167. The walls do not survive to a point high enough to provide evidence on this question one way or the other.

39. The tomb and tomb chamber: Wilberg (1953), 39–41.

40. The existence of *armaria* set into wall niches by no means rules out the presence of smaller movable containers. The latter would be useful for temporary storage (of rolls to be returned to their proper places, for example), transport, and sorting, as well as for the permanent storage of small or specialized collections.

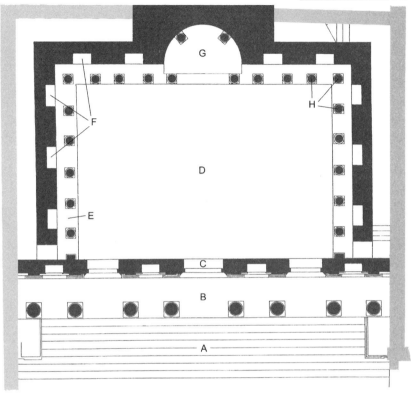

Figure 9. Plan of the library of Celsus in Ephesus, ca. AD 115–120. The steps and entrance are on the east. The darker walls are those of the library itself; the lighter walls are those of neighboring buildings. Plan by Vincas P. Steponaitis, after Wilhelm Wilberg (1908), 120, figure 22.

A. Steps up from street level.
B. Roofed portico, extending across the width of the façade.
C. Main entrance.
D. Main hall (roofed). The open space is 16.72 m wide, 10.92 m deep. There may have
   been chairs, tables, freestanding bookcases, statues, and other objects in this space, or it may
   have been left completely unencumbered.
E. Platform, 94 cm high, 1.025 m deep, running continuously around the south, west, and north
   walls of the hall.
F. Wall niches, about 1.10 m wide and 60 cm deep. In these niches there were presumably
   closable wooden cabinets with shelves for the book rolls. There are ten niches on the ground-
   floor level and probably ten more on an upper level. It is not known if there was a third level.
G. Podium, 4.38 m wide, 2.19 m deep, presumably for a statue. The statue might have
   been a divinity, such as Minerva (= Athena), or a human, perhaps Celsus, the dedicatee, or
   Aquila, the builder of the library.
H. Columns that support an upper balcony. The balcony probably provided access to a
   series of wall niches on the upper floor identical in dimensions to those on the ground floor.

in this hall? No very precise answer can be given to this question, given the number of variables involved, but it will be worth our time to try to estimate the maximum capacity of the *armaria* that were built into the wall niches. To begin, we will need to know or estimate two things: the average size of manuscripts (or the range of commonly occurring sizes); and the number and size of shelves on which the manuscripts were arranged.

The first question has been treated with some care by William Johnson. Working from the lengths of manuscripts, Johnson estimated that, when rolled up to form cylinders, papyrus rolls would have had diameters ranging from about 3.7 to about 12.8 cm. Since very long rolls—those over 20 m—were rare, we may perhaps take 15 m as a more typical maximum length, and such a manuscript, when rolled up, would have had a diameter of about 9 cm.[41] Working from similar evidence and from comparative medieval documents, Michel Sève has recently argued that rolled-up manuscripts were typically some 5 to 8 cm in diameter.[42] This is reassuringly close to Johnson's estimate. In practice, rolls will have varied considerably in diameter depending not only on their length but also on how tightly they were rolled, but we can use these figures—rolls normally some 5 to 9 cm in diameter—as working averages.

Next, we must estimate the number and size of shelves, and the number of rows of papyrus rolls stacked on each shelf. Sève has discussed these matters in detail, and I will set out his assumptions, adding a few qualifications.

1. Assume wall niches 2.5 m high.[43] (Those in the library of Celsus are 2.55 m high.)
2. Assume that the whole height of each niche was used for the inset wooden bookcase.[44]
3. Assume that the vertical space between shelves is 30 cm, so that there will be ample room to move the manuscripts without damaging them.[45]
4. Assume that the rolls are stacked three deep on each shelf, as in our Figure 8.[46]

---

41. Johnson (2004), 143–51, with diameters of rolled-up manuscripts on 149–51. Johnson (2004), 149, emphasizes the fact that there was no standard length of a book roll, and that some known examples reached 30 m in length.

42. Sève (2010), 24–25.

43. Ibid., 28.

44. Ibid., 29. It is possible, however, that the top part of each niche was given over to a decorative element such as a bust or a statue, as Wendel (1974), 66, assumed.

45. Sève (2010), 27.

46. Ibid., 29. A well-known relief from Nijmegen, lost long ago and known only from a drawing,

On these assumptions, Sève estimates that, if the rolls averaged 8 cm in diameter, the library of Celsus might have held a maximum of some 6,500 rolls; if the rolls averaged 5 cm in diameter, the maximum capacity would have been some 10,500 rolls.[47]

There are many variables. Several would decrease the number of volumes in the library. Some shelves, or even whole *armaria*, could have been left empty.[48] We do not know if there were manuscripts in the niches on the second (or third) level of the library, nor if the inset wooden bookcases filled the entire space of the niches. The collection might have contained an atypical number of large book rolls, particularly since it was a library intended in part for display. Stacking manuscripts just two deep, rather than three, would cut the capacity by a third. Other unknowns, however, would tend to increase the library's capacity. Perhaps there were nine or ten shelves per niche, or rolls were stacked not three deep but four deep on some or many of the shelves. Rolls could be wound more tightly, making their diameters smaller. There may have been *armaria* or book boxes that were not set into niches but rather were freestanding and placed out on the floor of the great hall, like the piece of furniture in the middle of room V at the Villa of the Papyri and the *armarium* in Figure 8.[49] Most importantly, it is possible, though by no means certain, that there was a second and even a third level of niches.[50] Despite these uncertainties, Sève's figures are likely to be in the correct order of magnitude: thousands of manuscripts, not just hundreds, but not tens of thousands either. A book collection of several thousand volumes is consistent with the evidence, however problematic, for the sizes of collections—small and large private collections, and perhaps a munici-

---

shows rolls (not quite certainly papyrus rolls) stacked three deep: ibid., 26–27. The drawing has been reproduced many times. See, for example, Blanck (2008), 248, fig. 91. We cannot know how accurate it is as a representation of the ancient relief.

47. Sève (2010), 29. He does not give the math. Briefly for the library of Celsus: eight shelves per niche times ten niches = eighty shelves. Eight of the niches are 1.15 m wide, two slightly smaller; if we allow 4 cm for the wood in the sides of the cabinet, we would have about 1.11 m on each shelf for manuscripts. Assuming rolls with a diameter of 5 cm, we could fit twenty-two rolls on each shelf, and stacking them three deep gives us sixty-six rolls per shelf. Sixty-six rolls times eighty shelves = 5,280 book rolls. Sève, 28, assumes bookcases on two levels, hence his total of 10,500, slightly less than two times 5,280. If we accept Strocka's thesis of bookcases on three levels (Strocka, in Strocka, Hoffmann, and Hiesel [2012], 167), we can increase the maximum (not necessarily the actual) number of volumes that were stored in wall niches to nearly 16,000.

48. This is likely for at least the early years of the library's existence, since Aquila left funds for future purchases and must have expected the collection to grow.

49. Freestanding *armaria* could add considerable capacity. Twenty-five *armaria*, each the area of one of the wall niches, would take up just 10 percent of the floor area but triple the capacity of the library.

50. As argued by Strocka, in Strocka, Hoffmann, and Hiesel (2012), 167.

pal one—that we have seen above at Oxyrhynchus, Herculaneum, and elsewhere.[51]

I turn now to a second municipal library that is known archaeologically, that of Thamugadi (modern Timgad in Algeria). It is of particular interest because, while the main hall with its niches for *armaria* is similar in size to that of the library of Celsus, the overall plan is quite different.[52] (See Figure 10.)

The library at Timgad was probably built at some point in the third century AD, with funding for the actual structure (*opus bibliothecae*) provided by an otherwise unknown citizen of the town, Marcus Iulius Quintianus Flavius Rogatianus.[53] Only the lower part of its walls survives, to a maximum height of somewhat less than 2 m. The building faced west and opened onto the *cardo maximus*, the principal north-south street of the town.[54] One approached it from the street by a short flight of steps (A) leading to a paved but unroofed courtyard (B) some 12 m across. Surrounding the courtyard was a portico (C), the roof of which was supported by twelve columns and, presumably, the walls of the rooms beyond the portico. Opening onto the portico on the north and south sides were four rectangular rooms (D), each about 2.5 m deep by 5.5 m wide. These rooms were entered via broad entrances that seem to have had no doors. We do not know if the rooms had windows. To the east of these rooms were two larger ones (E), roughly 4.5 m wide by 10.3 m long, which, as sockets in the sills show, had doors and so could be closed.

The main hall (G) was a roughly semicircular space about 10 m deep and 12 m wide, and, as in the library of Celsus, there is a podium (J) for a statue directly opposite the main entrance (F). The podium is framed by engaged pilasters, and in front of the pilasters are white marble columns with spiral fluting. Around the room, except in front of the statue niche, there is a low platform (H) some 50 cm high and 60 cm deep.[55] In front of the platform are two low risers. Set into the semicircular wall are eight niches (I) 1.25 m

51. *P.Oxy.* 33.2659 may be part of the book list of a municipal library with an implied size of several thousand book rolls. See section 2.10 above.

52. The open area of the main hall in the library of Celsus is roughly 180 m square, that of the main hall in the Timgad library some 120 m square.

53. Rogatianus's name is preserved on an inscription that identifies the building as a library, *AE* 1908.12 (= *ILS* 9362). Rogatianus died before the structure was built, and the town took responsibility for erecting it. We do not know where the book collection came from.

54. My description depends upon the reports of Cagnat (1906) and Pfeiffer (1931), together with the comments of Strocka, in Strocka, Hoffmann, and Hiesel (2012), 170–72. I know of no full archaeological report on the site, but for further bibliography see Vössing (1994), 174, with n. 26. Pfeiffer (1931), 162, mistakenly says the library faces east.

55. Cagnat (1906), 17.

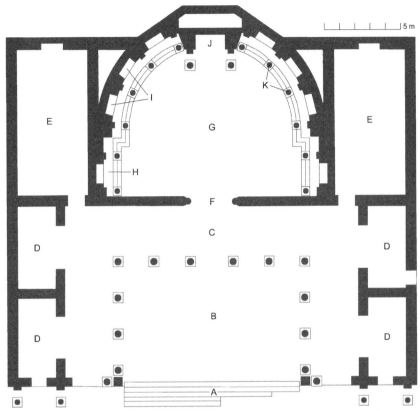

Figure 10. Plan of the library of Rogatianus in Timgad (Numidia), probably third century AD. The steps and entrance are on the west. The northeast corner (roughly room E) does not survive and has been restored here on an assumption of symmetry in the building's plan. Plan by Vincas P. Steponaitis, after Homer F. Pfeiffer (1931), 166, plate 16.

A. Steps from street level.

B. Courtyard (unroofed).

C. Roofed portico, extending around the north, east, and south sides of the courtyard.

D. Roofed rooms, 2.5 m deep, 5.5 m wide.

E. Roofed side rooms, approximately 4.5 m wide, 10.3 m deep. The entryways to these rooms had doors and could be closed.

F. Main entrance to library hall. The entrance could be closed and presumably locked.

G. Semicircular main hall (roofed), ca. 15 m wide at its widest and 10 m deep. There may have been chairs, tables, freestanding bookcases, statues, and other objects in this space, or it may have been left completely unencumbered.

H. Podium, 50 cm high, 60 cm deep, running continuously around the north, east, and south sides of the main hall except in front of podium J. It is approached by two low risers.

I. Wall niches, 1.25 m wide, 50 cm deep, estimated 2–2.5 m high. In these niches there were presumably closable wooden cabinets with shelves for book rolls.

J. Podium, 1.8 m wide, 1 m deep, presumably for a statue of a divinity or a human.

K. Columns. These seem to have been decorative and probably did not support an upper balcony.

wide and 50 cm deep; these were presumably fitted with wooden *armaria* with shelves for the storage of manuscripts. Between each pair of niches was an engaged pilaster, in front of which stood a limestone base supporting a column (K). The columns seem to have risen to a decorative entablature.[56] The west (entrance) wall presumably included one or more windows. The sill of the entrance door (F) contains dowel holes, and Pfeiffer argued that this door consisted of a metal grille divided into four sections, of which the outer two were stationary, while the inner two could be swung open.[57]

The theoretical maximum capacity of the Timgad library may be estimated using the same assumptions as those we used for the library of Celsus, but we must note that at Timgad there are eight wall niches, not ten; and that the height of the niches here is not known but might be slightly greater than in the library of Celsus, since the niches are slightly wider (1.25 m as opposed to 1.15 and 1.07 m). Thus there might have been space for nine shelves in each niche. On that assumption, the maximum capacity of the built-in *armaria* in the main hall of this library will be 5,184 rolls if we assume an average diameter per roll of 5 cm, or 3,240 rolls if we assume a diameter of 8 cm.[58] If we accept the thesis of Cagnat and Strocka—that there was an upper level of niches and bookcases—then the maximum capacity could be doubled to some 10,400 rolls. All of the same variables apply in this hall as in the library of Celsus.

The library hall at Timgad appears to form a coherent and inseparable part of a larger architectural complex.[59] What were the other elements in

56. Cagnat argued that the columns supported not just a decorative entablature, but an upper gallery with a second series of *armaria* in niches (ibid., 18–19). Strocka, in Strocka, Hoffmann, and Hiesel (2012), 172, concurred. There is, however, no archaeological support for a second floor; Pfeiffer (1931), 163, rejected the idea; and the existence of any upper floor remains quite uncertain.

57. Pfeiffer (1931), 163. As he points out, a metal grille would allow light in and provide for circulation of air. It would also, however, provide no protection against dust. Moreover, the door faced west and so would not admit much light during the better part of the day. Perhaps there was a window above the door, as Pfeiffer suggested, and there may have been windows in the upper part of the other walls, above the bookcases; this hall may have been similar to the reading room described by Pliny, with its windows that provided light at all hours of the day (Plin. *Ep.* 2.17.8).

58. The math: eight niches times nine shelves per niche = seventy-two shelves. For rolls of 5 cm, seventy-two rolls per shelf (the shelves being 1.20 m wide once we allow for the wooden sides of the *armarium*, and assuming rolls stacked three deep) times seventy-two shelves gives 5,184 book rolls. For rolls of 8 cm in diameter, forty-five rolls per shelf times seventy-two shelves gives 3,240 book rolls.

59. In general terms, this is not unusual. In Rome, several of the imperial libraries, and perhaps all of them, were subordinate parts of larger architectural complexes: the Apollo library, the library in the Portico of Octavia, and the library in the Temple of Peace, for example, all opened onto porticoes. But at Timgad, the library hall is itself the central feature, the focus of the architecture; it is not as though it simply opened onto a portico and there was a more important building, such as a temple, dominating the complex.

this complex used for? The four small rooms (D) opening onto the portico seem to have had no doors and so were not suitable for storage. If they had one or more windows, however, the light from these, combined with the light coming in through the large doors, would have made it possible on most days for people to read and copy texts in these rooms, while on cloudier days the portico itself might have provided sufficient light for reading and copying. The four rooms (D) may also have been used as spaces for meeting and discussion, whether centered on texts or not.[60]

The two larger rooms (E) could be closed and presumably locked. The east wall of the southern room seems to have had a niche about 40 cm deep, and Cagnat suggested that the niche was for the storage of book rolls, and that this pair of rooms may have had additional bookcases, freestanding and arranged in the open area of the room, so that they would have given the general appearance of the stacks in a modern library.[61] Cagnat's hypothesis has generally been accepted by subsequent scholars, and it is not difficult to imagine freestanding *armaria* out in the middle of the room, or *armaria* arranged along the walls, more or less as in room V in the Villa of the Papyri.[62] It is also possible that these rooms were workrooms, for staff or patrons or both, or small lecture halls for discussions or recitations; any of these functions might be combined with book storage in the form of, say, a row of *armaria* along one wall. We can, that is, suggest plausible uses for these rooms, some library-specific and some not, but we can prove nothing, since nothing of their contents has survived. What, apart from manuscripts and their storage facilities, might those contents have been? It is to that question that we turn next.

5.5. FURNITURE AND EQUIPMENT

What furniture and related equipment should we expect to find in a Roman library or book room? Chairs will certainly be needed, because Romans generally sat in chairs, sometimes on stools or benches, when they were

---

60. Strocka, in Strocka, Hoffmann, and Hiesel (2012), 169, suggested that the four small rooms could have served as classrooms, as spaces for formal recitations, or as workrooms for library staff.

61. Cagnat (1906), 19–20. The northern room has not survived, but it was probably identical to the corresponding room on the south.

62. Callmer (1944), 182, and Pfeiffer (1931), 164, both accepted Cagnat's suggestion. Strocka (1981), 317, did as well, though with some doubts. The small wall niches, however, were probably designed to hold statues rather than built-in bookcases. No certain library, including the main room here at Timgad, has book niches less than 50 cm deep. Here, at 40 cm deep, the niche would be just barely adequate for papyrus rolls of average size.

reading and studying.[63] Relief sculptures and other depictions almost universally show readers, whether they are men, women, or children, seated as they read, holding the papyrus roll in front of them. They do not sit at desks, but simply in chairs. The doctor in Figure 8 sits as he reads. He is close to his cabinet of books, but he has no table or desk. A woman in a stucco relief from Carthage sits reading a roll that is open in her lap; another, in a funerary monument from Rome, holds a text in her hand; children sit and read in school in an oft-reproduced sculpture from Nijmegen.[64] We know from anecdotes in Aulus Gellius that he and his friends would sit when they were in the library of the Temple of Trajan or the library of the Domus Tiberiana, reading and discussing rolls they found in the libraries' collections.[65] Two centuries earlier, Cicero came upon Cato the Younger seated in the library of Lucullus's villa; Cato sat as he read, surrounded by book rolls.[66]

Similarly, so far as we can tell, Romans who wanted to write in a papyrus roll ordinarily did so while seated in a chair; they would spread the roll out across their thighs and write on the part of the papyrus that was directly on top of one leg.[67] The evidence, all visual, is not extensive. A funerary cippus now in Strasbourg gives us a picture of a man, seated and writing in a papyrus roll, one end of which hangs over his knee and down his right leg; his left hand holds the unrolled part of the papyrus, and his right hand the pen.[68] A sarcophagus from the Via Appia, now in Berlin, includes four scenes. In one, a man is seated and holds a papyrus across his legs as he writes; in another, a young man sits in a chair and writes in a roll open in

63. They sometimes read while reclining on a couch: Plin. *Ep.* 5.5.5; Fronto *Ep.* 4.5.2; visual images in Marrou (1938), 121–29, nos. 130–50. As Small (1997), 166, rightly notes, however, reading on a couch (*lectulus*) was what one did at home. It is very unlikely that there were couches in municipal or imperial libraries, but they might have been present in the libraries of individuals, such as the semicircular reading room of Pliny's Laurentine villa.

64. There are many other scenes of men reading, sometimes by themselves (so Marrou [1938], 62–72, nos. 53–63), sometimes with others, including the Muses (Marrou [1938], 75–103, nos. 71–102). In these depictions, the book roll is open across the reader's lap, and there is no table. Women: Marrou (1938), 62, no. 52, and 75–77, no. 71 (with an image in Marrou's plate 3). These are domestic scenes, as Cavallo (2010), 226, noted, and no source clearly places women in any municipal or imperial library. The children from Nijmegen: Blanck (2008), 51, fig. 16.

65. Gell. *NA* 11.17.1: *Sedentibus forte nobis in bibliotheca templi Traiani* ("As we were sitting in the library of the Temple of Trajan"); 13.20.1: *Cum in domus Tiberianae bibliotheca sederemus* ("While we were sitting in the library of the Domus Tiberiana").

66. Cic. *Fin.* 3.2.7: *Marcum Catonem . . . vidi in bibliotheca sedentem, multis circumfusum Stoicorum libris.* ("I spotted Marcus Cato sitting in the library, surrounded by a great number of Stoic texts.")

67. Parássoglou (1979) is the basic study. See also Turner and Parsons (1987), 5–6; Small (1997), 150–55.

68. Parássoglou (1979), plate 2; Blanck (2008), 97, fig. 43. Marrou (1938), 152–53, no. 197, provides several scenes, one of which consists of one man dictating to another. The latter is seated and writing in his lap.

his lap.[69] As they wrote, Romans may have used a backing board to provide support, so that the point of the pen would not pierce the papyrus.[70]

A funerary relief, probably from Athens but Roman in date (Figure 11), shows a girl sitting on a stool and writing. In this case, she is writing not on a papyrus roll, but on wax tablets; a book roll she had perhaps been reading or copying earlier can be seen on a bookstand near her.[71] In other depictions of persons reading or writing, the reader is often seated in a substantial chair with a high back, as is our doctor in Figure 8; alternatively, one could sit on a stool, like the young girl in Figure 11. In sum: we will need chairs or stools wherever we expect people to read or write. In any substantial library—municipal, imperial, and even personal ones such as Pliny's—we would expect to find a number of chairs, stools, or both.

Were there desks, or more exactly tables that could serve as desks? No surviving Greek or Roman depiction shows a person reading from or studying a roll open on a table, and none shows a scribe writing in a book roll that rests on a table. Only one anecdote in literature known to me mentions a table in a library, and no details about that table are provided.[72] On the other hand, we do have a number of reliefs, as we have just seen, that show Romans writing not at desks but on book rolls or tablets that they hold in their laps, and this, rather than writing at a table, seems to have been the regular practice. Still, given the limited nature of our evidence, we cannot entirely rule out the possibility of tables used as desks.[73]

Whether or not there were large tables or desks, there may well have been small tables. A stone relief from Ostia shows two scribes sitting at low tables, *styli* in hand and wax tablets lying before them on the tables (Figure 12). Between the two scribes, a man declaims, and we may infer that they are transcribing his speech.[74] This is probably not a scene in a library, and

69. Parássoglou (1979), 11–12, with plates 4 and 5. Parássoglou provided three further examples and concluded (p. 14) that the Greeks and Romans did not use tables or writing desks.

70. Turner and Parsons (1987), 6.

71. Turner and Parsons (1987), 6, discuss this relief. It is of particular interest because the subject is a girl and a young one at that. Her exact age is lost in a lacuna, but she is about ten years old. Provenance unknown; date probably first or second century AD.

72. Apul. *Apol.* 53.8. Apuleius mentions a *mensa* in a room where books were kept, and at *Apol.* 55.3 he calls the room a *bybliotheca*. It was a personal collection, the property of Apuleius's friend Pontianus.

73. Small (1997), 150–55 and 162–67, deals with the topic of tables at length and argues that they were never used in libraries or for copying. Note, however, the cautious remarks of Nicholls (2011), 139, with n. 81. He is inclined to believe that scholars such as Galen did use tables. Large tables that could serve as desks certainly existed in the Roman world and were used in many contexts: Croom (2007), 89–94.

74. As Turner (1980) remarked in the notes to his plate 6, the blunt ends of the *styli* are readily

Figure 11. Marble relief of a young girl. Seated on a stool, she writes in tablets open on her lap. More or less in front of her is a stand with what may be a book holder and papyrus roll. British Museum, registration no. 1805,0703.187. Image © The Trustees of the British Museum, London.

Figure 12. Marble relief of a speaker, scribes writing at low desks, and an audience. The scribes write not in papyrus rolls but on wax tablets. From Ostia Antica, inv. no. 130 = ICCD inv. E 49915. Image © 2012 Istituto Centrale per il Catalogo e la Documentazione, Rome. Reproduction authorized by the Italian Ministry of Cultural Heritage and Activities, Central Institute for Cataloguing and Documentation.

it does not depict papyri, but it clearly shows that scribes did sometimes sit at a low table when they were writing. A low table or stand could also serve as a convenient surface for a scribe to place his equipment (extra reeds, knife, inkwell, sponge, and so on), and a painting from the tomb of Vestorius Priscus in Pompeii (Figure 13) shows two low round tables or stands used for exactly that purpose. On top of the table on the left are a wax tablet and either one papyrus roll partially unrolled or two rolls. On top of the other are a wax tablet, a pen in an inkpot, a partially opened roll, a cylin-

_____

visible, showing that the scribes are writing in wax tablets. Behind the scribes, the relief depicts several men gesticulating; presumably they are debating or discussing the speech.

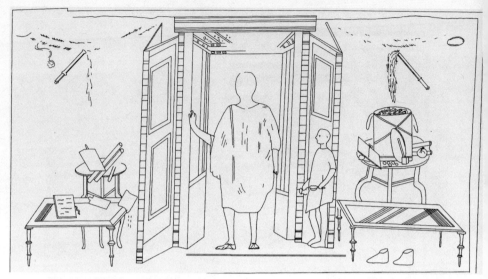

Figure 13. Drawing of a wall painting from the tomb of Vestorius Priscus, Pompeii, showing, at left and right, two round tables, each holding scribal equipment. From Rivista di Studi Pompeiani *VI (1993–94), 25; reproduced by permission of L'Erma di Bretschneider.*

drical book box with papyrus rolls in it, very much like the book box in our Figure 7, and other objects.[75]

    This is not a library scene, but rather, it seems, a domestic one; but it shows that, when a Roman thought of writing implements, he might think of accompanying small tables. To the bookcases and chairs with which we are furnishing our library we should probably add a number of low tables for the use of copyists or those studying manuscripts.

    People working with book rolls, whether readers, students, or copyists, may well have found it helpful to place the book roll in some kind of frame in order to protect it and hold it at a certain place in the roll. Martial (14.84) mentions an object made of fir wood, apparently a sort of box, that would keep the edges of a papyrus from fraying when it was in use.[76] Elizabeth

---

    75. Mols and Moormann (1993–94), 26–27, discuss the scene and identify the objects in it. The rectangular objects in the foreground seem to be not tables but beds. Croisille (2010), 69–70, also discusses this scene. Small tables or stands some 50 to 100 cm high are well attested in domestic contexts in Herculaneum. They could serve any number of purposes. See for examples Mols (1999), 170–81 (a catalog) and 49 (dimensions and use).

    76. *Ne toga barbatos faciat vel paenula libros, / haec abies chartis tempora longa dabit.* ("Lest your toga or cloak [chafe] your books and leave them frayed, this fir-wood [box] will provide a long life for your rolls.")

Knauer has called attention to a number of visual representations that may depict just such an object. One of them appears in our Figure 11: on top of the stand to the right of the girl is what appears to be a box-like object containing an open papyrus roll. Other such boxes appear in paintings from the Bay of Naples and in reliefs from Como in north Italy.[77] Another class of possible book-roll holders has been identified by Susan Wood; in this case, there is a framework that supports rods, and the papyrus could have been wound under and over the rods in such a way that it was held in place, keeping one or two columns of text readily visible. Made of ivory and highly decorated, these seem to be luxury items, and at least some of them were found in assemblages of women's objects.[78] Probably we should not supply the typical library or reading room with either sort of papyrus holder, but they may have been in use in private book collections.

The Scribe's Equipment[79]

The essential items were, of course, papyrus, pen, and ink. To copy a text, or to repair a damaged roll, one would need all or part of a papyrus roll or several rolls.[80] These might be rolls that were bought new from a dealer, or they might be rolls that already contained writing, generally documents but sometimes literary texts, and in that case the scribe would turn the roll over and use the blank side. In some cases, a library or owner might choose to reuse an old text already in his collection. Thus *P.Oxy.* 33.2659 is a book list that was written on the back of a Greek-to-Latin glossary. The glossary may have belonged to a library and been turned over to provide a roll for the creation of a new list of the holdings of the library.[81] Black ink, in the Roman period, was generally made of soot (often lampblack) mixed with

---

77. Knauer (1993), 25.

78. Wood (2001), with a reconstruction of one of the devices in use on p. 27. Luxury items: Wood (2001), 24–26. These objects have been taken as small looms by other scholars. See Berke in Schneider (1990), 272, or Christof (2010), 348–51. Wood's reconstruction seems to me to be more convincing, but it cannot be regarded as certain.

79. In this section, I use the term "scribe" in the widest possible sense of that term: any person, slave or free, professionally trained or not, who was involved in writing, copying, or correcting literary texts. I would not argue that scribal equipment was found in every private collection of book rolls, since copying and repairs could well be done by professional scribes outside the house.

80. Papyrus seems to have been sold as rolls, not as individual sheets. You could use the whole roll if you were copying an entire text; or you could cut off the amount you needed in order to repair the damaged section of a roll: Leach and Tait (2000), 230–38; Bülow-Jacobsen (2009), 19. Purchases of rolls are occasionally mentioned in documentary papyri: Turner and Parsons (1987), 6, n. 19.

81. See above, section 2.10. The Aurelius family reused part of their copy of Iulius Africanus's *Cestoi* to make a fresh copy of a will: above, section 4.8.

water and gum arabic.[82] The soot or other blackening agent was kept in solid form, probably in small blocks, and the scribe would begin his work by mixing just enough ink for the task at hand. Roman pens were generally made from reeds, which were sharpened to a point that was split to hold the ink. Bronze pens are also known.[83]

Other tools used by scribes are known from references in literary sources, especially a small group of poems in the *Greek Anthology*, from surviving examples, and from depictions in wall paintings.[84] They include a sharp knife to cut, split, and sharpen the point of the reed pen; a sponge to erase mistakes;[85] a ruler and a disk of lead, used to mark guidelines on the papyrus prior to copying;[86] an inkpot, generally a small jar, sometimes open and sometimes with a lid;[87] and pumice used perhaps to smooth the writing surface or to sharpen the pen or both.[88] A professional copyist would presumably have all of these items ready to hand in his workplace. Scholars, too, may have had sets of tools. When Galen set out to do some copying in the Palatine libraries, as we know he did, he presumably had one or more slave assistants, one of whom could carry the writing tools.[89] What we do not know is whether any libraries provided such materials. It is usually thought, probably correctly, that the staff of the imperial libraries did at least some copying, and they must have done repairs and maintenance. Perhaps there was a cabinet somewhere in each library with blank papyrus rolls and other supplies for the use of the staff. Most interesting in this regard is water, which was needed for mixing ink and wetting one's sponge. Did each user bring a vial of water for his own use, or did the library provide water? We do not know; but where there were scribes there must have been water.

82. Bülow-Jacobsen (2009), 18; for a full chemical analysis, see Leach and Tait (2000), 238–39. On red ink, which was sometimes used in headings: Leach and Tait (2000), 239.

83. Pens: Thompson (1912), 39–40; Cockle (1983), 150. Reed pens need to be resharpened frequently. Turner and Parsons (1987), 7, remark upon a manuscript in which it is clear that the scribe stopped to sharpen his pen every fifty lines or so.

84. The most important of the poems is *Anth. Pal.* 6.295. On this, and for an introduction to all of the relevant epigrams, see Gow and Page (1965), 467–69.

85. Thompson (1912), 43; Turner and Parsons (1987), 7.

86. Gow and Page (1965), 468; cf. Thompson (1912), 43.

87. Thompson (1912), 42. Inkpots of various sorts are depicted in Campanian wall paintings: Croisille (2010), figs. 3 and 9, with discussion on p. 74. See also Kenyon (1951), facing p. 72.

88. Gow and Page (1965), 469; Turner and Parsons (1987), 7. Pen, inkpot, book rolls, and wax tablets are all visible in the wall painting in Figure 13.

89. Galen talks about copying texts in one or another of the imperial libraries at *Ind.* 17 and 19. It is possible that he copied not onto papyrus but rather wax tablets, but since his goal was to acquire accurate permanent copies it seems likely that he was copying (or having his scribe copy) directly onto a papyrus roll.

Light

In a famous passage, Vitruvius states that sitting rooms (*cubicula*) and libraries (*bibliothecae*) "should face east, because the purpose they serve requires the morning light."[90] His concern with morning light seems to be reflected in the regulations for the library of Pantaenus in Athens, which was open only from dawn to noon, but in practice those who built libraries and those who used books seldom bothered to follow Vitruvius's advice.[91] There were other ways to secure adequate light.

In his Laurentine villa, Pliny the Younger tells us, the reading room, with its cabinet of books, had curved walls with windows so placed that sunlight shone through one or another of them all day long.[92] It is generally assumed, and surely correct, that large municipal libraries had generously sized windows. Our evidence is slight, because the walls of known library halls are seldom preserved to a height where there would have been windows, but there were certainly three large windows at Ephesus, and there were probably one or more windows at Timgad, where Pfeiffer plausibly restored a large window above the entrance door.[93] The windows in the library in the Sanctuary of Asclepius at Pergamum were apparently provided with sheets of thin-cut yellowish marble and alabaster to let light in while keeping rain and insects out.[94] Windows in libraries of all sorts may well have been made of panes of glass from the first century AD on: glass was relatively inexpensive, windowpanes could be produced quickly and easily, and glass would provide protection against rain, dust, and insects.[95] We should not assume that windows contained grille work rather than glass.

So far as we know, municipal and imperial libraries were not open for use in the evenings or at night. Individuals, however, might want to read or write during the hours of darkness, especially during the winter months, and numerous texts describe literary men assembling rolls, tablets, and other equipment before beginning nighttime work in their own book col-

90. Vitr. *De arch.* 6.4.1: *Ad orientem spectare debent, usus enim matutinum postulat lumen.*

91. The library of Pantaenus faced southwest, not east; the library at Timgad west; the library in the Sanctuary of Asclepius at Pergamum west; the library at Nysa south. Of the five libraries positively identified by inscriptions, only the library of Celsus in Ephesus faced east.

92. Plin. *Ep.* 2.17.8.

93. For Ephesus and Timgad, see above, section 5.4.

94. Deubner (1938), 43.

95. Harden (1961), 39–52, gives examples of Roman window glass and discusses the possible ways of manufacturing windowpanes. I have not found reports of glass in the excavations of known libraries, but glass can be overlooked because it fragments into tiny pieces.

lections. In the prefaces to their works, Pliny the Elder and Aulus Gellius make a point of mentioning the work, implicitly involving many texts, that they had done in the hours of darkness.[96] Seneca the Younger devoted part of the night to his work, and so did Pliny the Elder, at least from late August on through the winter months.[97] When the philosopher Athenodorus set out to spend the night in a haunted house, he prepared himself by assembling his wax tablets, *stilus*, and lamp.[98] The principal source of light after sunset must have been the oil lamp, as in Athenodorus's case, or more likely several lamps, and we may readily assume that such lamps and stands were part of the standard equipment of private book collections.[99]

Footstools and Ladders

The wall niches for built-in *armaria* in the library of Celsus were 2.55 m high. If we assume that the *armaria* filled the entire vertical space of the niches, the uppermost shelf in each *armarium* would have been about 2.2 m above the level of the podium on which the book seeker was standing. That is so high that most people would not have been able to handle the book rolls on the top shelf or shelves without risking damage to the rolls, and scholars have accordingly tended to assume that the persons removing rolls or reshelving them would have needed a stepladder or stool of some sort. This may well be right, and we might reasonably assume that any large, and some private, libraries had one or more such stools or stepladders.[100] We may also note here that, in his recent discussions of the libraries at Ephesus and Timgad, Volker Strocka argued for two and one upper galleries respectively, with each gallery providing access to an upper row of niches and bookcases. Since no trace of any stairs to upper floors has been found, Strocka suggested that the upper levels were accessed by means of

96. Plin. *HN praef.* 18; Gell. *NA praef.* 4 and 10.

97. Sen. *Ep.* 8.1; Plin. *Ep.* 3.5.8. The practice of nighttime reading and study (*lucubratio*) became a literary topos. Ker (2004) discusses these and other passages and places them within a cultural context.

98. Plin. *Ep.* 7.27.7: *Poscit pugillares, stilum, lumen.*

99. For examples of lamps and lamp stands, see Mattusch (2011), 106–7, or Ward-Perkins and Claridge (1978), 166, no. 132. Taller stands (about 1.3 m high) would stand on the floor; shorter ones (20 to 60 cm high) could be placed on a low table next to the scribe or reader. Candles were known and in use, but no evidence survives that connects them with libraries or book collections. The Romans seem to have found them more difficult to use than oil lamps: Forbes (1966), 134 and 139–40.

100. I have not, however, been able to find a Roman-era representation of a person using a stepladder. It is also possible, as Wendel (1974), 66, suggested, that the upper part of each niche held not shelves but a portrait bust. In that case no stool or ladder would be needed.

narrow ladders.[101] If this is correct, we may add ladders to our inventory of movable objects. Further, carrying papyrus rolls while climbing down or up a ladder would be awkward and potentially perilous for the rolls, so perhaps we should think in terms of baskets raised and lowered by ropes. The library personnel would climb up to the appropriate level, find the roll(s), put them in a *capsa, cista,* or the like, and lower the container to the floor of the reading room.[102]

The List of Books

As we saw above in chapter 2, many book collections and libraries had one or more book lists. These were not like modern catalogs, by which I mean a comprehensive list that included the author, the title, perhaps the subject, and some kind of identifying number for every book roll in the collection. Rather, the visitor to a Roman library might expect to find one or more papyrus rolls with a basic inventory of the contents of all or some part of the library, ordinarily organized by genre, then by author and title. Other modes of organization were possible as well—order of accession, for example— and might result in lists such as *P.Ross.Georg.* 1.22 (section 2.7), where the books appear to the modern reader to be listed in random order. The point of such a list was presumably to allow the visitor to scan it and determine if a given work was present, and if the collection was not huge, and the list not too long, no particular order was needed. It is possible that a given library had several lists, each devoted to a particular section of the collection. Thus in the Palatine libraries as described by Galen there were collections, evidently distinct and recognizable, known as the Callinia, Atticiana, and Peducaeana, and it is possible that a separate inventory was maintained for each of them.[103] Papyrus rolls or sheets containing book lists may, then, be added to our list of a library's standard equipment.

5.6. EMBELLISHMENTS AND ART

So far, we have been concerned with practical items, the things that made a book collection usable: storage, furniture, scribal equipment. Beyond the

---

101. Strocka, in Strocka, Hoffmann, and Hiesel (2012), 167–68, on Ephesus; 173 on Timgad.

102. Strocka did not discuss the problem of carrying rolls while climbing ladders. I know of no support for the scenario I propose; it is simply a suggestion to resolve the difficulties posed if we accept the thesis of ladders giving access to upper levels of bookcases. Alternatively, we might assume the niches in the upper levels were used for statues rather than book rolls.

103. Gal. *Ind.* 13.

necessities, collectors could create a beautiful space for their book rolls, embellishing it with some combination of marble, mosaics, stucco, paintings, and sculpture, none of which were, strictly speaking, necessary for the operation of the library. Benefactors, or their heirs or agents, sometimes tell us specifically, in an inscription, that they have provided funds for the embellishment of the library hall they created. The inscription recording Iulius Aquila's gift of a library at Ephesus tells us that Aquila provided funds for its decoration (κόσμος) and ornaments (ἀναθήματα, presumably statues), as well as its book rolls;[104] in Athens, Flavius Pantaenus gave his new library a collection of book rolls and its embellishments (κόσμος),[105] while Hadrian's library in Athens, according to Pausanias, had "rooms that had gilded roofs and alabaster and were adorned with statues and paintings."[106] A library at Volsinii in Italy, built by an unknown benefactor, was provided by its founder with not just books but statues as well.[107]

In a few cases, some or much of the decoration survives for us to see and admire. At Pergamum, a woman named Flavia Melitine had a library built in the Sanctuary of Asclepius. The floor was paved with colored marble, forming geometric patterns, the walls were covered in marble veneer, and a mosaic covered the wall of an apse in which was placed a statue dedicated to the emperor Hadrian, who was honored here as a god.[108] The library of Celsus in Ephesus was similar: its floor was of colored marble, and its walls were covered in marble veneer.[109] In the library at Timgad, in north Africa, the floor of the main hall was paved with simple white limestone, but many small fragments of colored marble were found during the excavation and had probably formed part of a decorative treatment of the walls of the room.[110] Several other buildings that are thought to have been libraries were similarly decorated. Thus the twin halls generally, and probably rightly, taken as the libraries of the deified Trajan in Rome had elegant floors with rectangles of gray granite defined by narrow strips of giallo antico (yellowish-brown) marble, walls veneered in multicolored marble,

---

104. *IK Ephesos* VII.2, no. 5113.

105. *SEG* 21.703. On the foundation of this library, see Perrin-Saminadayar (2010).

106. Paus. 1.18.9: οἰκήματα . . . ἐστιν ὀρόφῳ τε ἐπιχρύσῳ καὶ ἀλαβάστρῳ λίθῳ, πρὸς δὲ ἀγάλμασι κεκοσμημένα καὶ γραφαῖς. Note the verb: its root is κόσμος, as in the inscriptions from Athens and Ephesus.

107. *CIL* 11.2704b: *bybliothecam a solo / . . . [ornata?]mque libris et statuis.*

108. Wiegand (1932), 10–11, described the decorative elements and took them as a masterpiece of Pergamene marble work. We will return to the statue of Hadrian below.

109. Hueber (1997), 78 (walls), 80 (floor). In addition, the library at Ephesus had an elaborately decorated façade with many statues and inscriptions: Hueber (1997), 80–81; Sauron (2010).

110. Pfeiffer (1931), 161 (floor), 162 (colored marble).

and other types of marble in the columns and their capitals and bases.[111] Such halls must have been striking visually, and it was no doubt precisely such a visual impact that was intended.[112]

5.7. SCULPTURE

More informative, because invested with meaning, are the figurative images—sculptures and paintings—that Romans placed in their libraries. We have specific evidence of only some two dozen images, and sometimes we cannot tell if they were paintings or sculptures, but even this small sample reveals a remarkable variety of subjects and forms and allows us to infer a number of functions of the works of art.[113]

Most numerous seem to have been portraits of mortal men, whether heads, busts, or standing figures. These were sometimes writers of the past, sometimes living, contemporary authors.[114] Tacitus tells us that there were images of authors in the Apollo library on the Palatine, among them Cicero's contemporary Hortensius,[115] and the Tabula Hebana confirms that there were portraits of "men of outstanding talent" in this library.[116] From the scattered evidence—literary, archaeological, and epigraphical—for portraits, we can compile a list of such images. Past (that is, dead) writers known to have been represented in Roman libraries include Homer;[117] Epicurus;[118] Euphorion, Rhianus, and Parthenius (three Greek writers favored by Tiberius);[119] Hortensius, the orator; Titus Catius, an Epicurean philosopher;

---

111. Packer (1997), 125, with specifics on the surviving evidence at 450–54.

112. On Roman libraries as displays designed to impress, see Wendel (1974), 158; Fedeli (1989), 46–47; Nicholls (2013), especially 264.

113. In addition to the examples I will discuss, scholars have cited a number of other passages as evidence of portraits in libraries. Among them are Cic. *Att.* 4.10.1, a bust of Aristotle somewhere in Atticus's house; Plin. *Ep.* 3.78 (Silius Italicus had had many *imagines* in his villas); Mart. 9.47.1–3 (*imagines* of Democritus, Zeno, and Plato); and Juv. 2.4–7 (plaster cast of Chrysippus; portraits of Aristotle and Pittacus; an "original portrait" of Cleanthes). None of these can be assigned with certainty to a real library or reading room, although they do indicate what a Roman might expect to find in a library.

114. I deal with men who were emperors or members of the imperial family as a separate category below.

115. Orators in general: Tac. *Ann.* 2.83.3, *auctores eloquentiae*. Hortensius: Tac. *Ann.* 2.37.2, *Hortensii inter oratores sita imago*. If Hortensius was there, Cicero must have been, too.

116. *Viri illustris ingeni*, not necessarily literary men. A convenient text is in Crawford (1996), 519.

117. An over-life-size group of Homer, the *Iliad*, and the *Odyssey* (the latter two depicted as human figures) survives in fragmentary form and can confidently be assigned to the library of Pantaenus in Athens: Thompson and Wycherley (1972), 115.

118. Naples Museum, inv. 5470, from the Villa of the Papyri, Herculaneum, a small bronze about 10 cm high. Photograph: Mattusch (2005), 290, fig. 5.210.

119. Suet. *Tib.* 70.2; cf. Houston (2008), 255–59.

Cornelius Nepos, the biographer;[120] Livy the historian; and Vergil.[121] The writers who were alive at the time their portraits were placed in a library include the great scholar Terentius Varro; Martial, the poet; the second-century AD philosopher and rhetor Favorinus; and Sidonius Apollinaris, poet and administrator.[122] Dead or alive, you clearly did not need to belong to the canon of great authors to have your portrait placed in some library; it was necessary only that you be appreciated by some collector, town, or emperor. Homer and Vergil are in our list, to be sure, but few would place Titus Catius, Euphorion, Rhianus, Favorinus, or Sidonius in the first rank of ancient authors. There is no discernible correlation between the importance of the author and the type of collection he was placed in. In our sample, Homer and Favorinus were in municipal collections, Vergil and Titus Catius in (or intended for) private ones. Euphorion, Rhianus, Parthenius, and Sidonius were all in imperial libraries in Rome.

We also find images of the immortals in libraries. Cicero thought that statues of the Muses would be appropriate for a library,[123] and Juvenal lists book rolls, shelves, and a (statue of) Minerva as a coherent gift.[124] There was a statue of Apollo in the library on the Palatine.[125] Surely, though, by far the most remarkable statue of a god in any Roman library was the fifty-foot-high bronze statue of Apollo that Tiberius brought from Syracuse and set up in the library of the New Temple of Augustus.[126] It made good sense

120. Hortensius: Tac. *Ann.* 2.37.2. Catius and Nepos: Plin. *Ep.* 4.28. The portraits of Catius and Nepos were intended for the personal collection of Herennius Severus.

121. Caligula considered removing the portraits of Livy and Vergil from the imperial libraries in Rome (Suet. *Calig.* 34.2). Vergil, whose likeness was presumably in many libraries, is attested in a late antique personal collection, as we learn from a letter of an otherwise unknown Rusticus to Eucherius, Bishop of Lugdunum (modern Lyon). Text in Wotke (1894), 199. The letter is to be dated ca. AD 440.

122. Varro: Plin. *HN* 7.115. Martial: Mart. 9 *praef.*: his friend Stertinius Avitus wished to have a portrait of Martial in his library. Favorinus: Fav. *Corinthiaca* 8 (ca. AD 130). The speech has come down in the manuscripts of Dio Chrysostom (*Or.* 37), but is now assigned to Favorinus: Barigazzi (1966), 298. Sidonius: Sid. Apoll. *Epist.* 9.16.25–28.

123. Cic. *Fam.* 7.23.2.

124. Juv. 3.219. It is sometimes asserted that an image of Minerva was virtually obligatory in a Roman library. So, for example, Callmer (1944), 189; or Settis (1988), 59. That may be true, and Juvenal's statement supports it, but there seems to be no certain evidence of a Minerva in any specific Roman-era library. There was, of course, an Athena in one of the rooms assigned to the library of the Sanctuary of Athena at Pergamum: Strocka (2000), esp. 155.

125. Tabula Hebana (Crawford [1996], 519), lines 1–4: a *simulacrum Apollinis* that stood in its own [*fas*]*tigium*, which must have been a sort of aedicula or baldachin. Late sources would have us believe that this was a statue of Augustus in the guise of Apollo. Sources and discussion: Corbier (2006), 176. The Tabula Hebana, however, was contemporary with the statue and is explicit: this was a likeness of Apollo.

126. Plin. *HN* 34.43; Suet. *Tib.* 74. It was an ancient Greek statue, not originally designed for a library. Houston (2008), 250–52, discusses the sources and problems.

to place the image of a divinity in your library: it would honor the divinity, call the god's attention to your structure, and, if all went well, evoke divine favor.

Emperors too were honored, for obvious reasons: they might provide patronage and funding, and it was always a good idea to flatter them. We know of images of Augustus in the Apollo library,[127] Trajan in the municipal library at Prusa in Bithynia, and Hadrian in the library in the Sanctuary of Asclepius at Pergamum.[128] Members of the imperial family might also be so honored. In AD 19 images of the recently deceased Germanicus (the adopted son of Tiberius) and of Drusus, Germanicus's natural father, were erected in the Apollo library.[129] Of all of these, the most useful to us is the statue of Hadrian in Pergamum, because in this case, and only this one, we have part of the library hall, the dedicatory inscription, and the statue itself.[130] In this statue, Hadrian is over life-size (2.8 m) and nude. A cloak is flung over his left shoulder, he holds a scabbard in his left hand, and there is a cuirass, presumably a trophy, on the ground beside his right leg. The statue stood on a base with a simple inscription: "Fl(avia) Melitine (for) Hadrian the God."[131] It was erected during Hadrian's lifetime, but for most of its existence it will have represented a dead (eventually long dead) and deified emperor.[132] As the decades went by and memories of Hadrian faded, those who entered the library may have reacted to the statue in different ways. Even so, we can recover some of its significance. Clearly, the statue was intended to honor Hadrian as both emperor and god, and to call his attention and favor to the library and its city. Hadrian was a particularly apt choice, since he was himself an author and an encourager of scholarly activity.[133] The scabbard and trophy cuirass symbolize the military and political power of Hadrian and Rome, while the designation of him as "god" reminds the viewer of the surrounding locus of cult, namely the shrine of

127. Tac. *Ann.* 2.37.2, an *imago Augusti* that is mentioned in a scene set by Tacitus in AD 19. It is not clear if Tacitus had in mind an *imago clipeata* or a statue.

128. Trajan: Plin. *Ep.* 10.81.2 (AD 110 or 111). There may also have been one or two statues of Trajan in the library of Pantaenus in Athens: Shear (1973a), 175–76, and Shear (1973b), 404–5.

129. Tac. *Ann.* 2.83; Tabula Hebana in Crawford (1996), 519.

130. Wiegand (1932), 10–11; Deubner (1938), 40–43. The walls are preserved to a maximum height of about 2 m but can be partially restored. Found in many pieces, the statue has been restored and is nearly complete. For a photograph of the statue, see Deubner (1938), 41, fig. 32, or Petsalis-Diomidis (2010), 210, fig. 59.

131. Habicht (1969), 29–30, no. 6: θεὸν Ἀδριανόν / Φλ. Μελιτίνη.

132. Habicht (1969), 29–30, showed that the term θεός ("god") could be, and here was, used of an emperor who was alive at the time the statue was created. Cf. Hallett (2005), 225–30.

133. As was pointed out by Deubner (1938), 43.

Asclepius in which the library was situated.[134] Finally, the succinct inscription closely associates two names: Hadrian the god and Flavia Melitine. It demonstrated to all who read it, in particular the other leading citizens of Pergamum, that Flavia is or was a person to reckon with, someone whose name could appear on the same stone as that of Hadrian the god, and in letters just as large.[135] In short, this statue was not simply decorative. It set up a series of resonances—with the literature in the surrounding book rolls, with military and political power, and with cult and divinity—that included the library but also moved well beyond it. No doubt the works of art in many other libraries did the same.[136]

Portraits in libraries came in a surprising variety of shapes and sizes. There were, it seems, paintings, although no certain example of a painted portrait in a library survives.[137] Sculptures do survive. Some were in the form of an *imago clipeata*. These were portraits (generally, we may assume, in bronze) of men in relief, placed in the center of round, shield-shaped, fields. (*Clipeus* means shield.) They seem to have been suspended from the walls or from the top of a column, leaning forward at the top so that the portrait would be readily visible from below.[138] We hear of a series of them in the library at the Temple of Apollo in Rome, depicting outstanding orators and writers of earlier generations.[139] In the year AD 19, *imagines* of Germanicus, the recently deceased adopted son of Tiberius, and of Germanicus's father Drusus, were added to the collection already in the library. The choice of subjects and their placement could of course carry meaning, and Petrain has recently argued convincingly that the images placed in the Palatine library constituted not just literary statements, but, more importantly, political ones, and that they enabled the emperor to use the prestige of the literary tradition to enhance the prestige of the imperial family.[140]

---

134. Petsalis-Diomidis (2010), 171 and 212–16, discusses the combination of political and religious symbolism.

135. My thanks to James Rives, who pointed out the political function of the statue to me.

136. One other possible sculpture of an emperor in a library is a small ivory statuette of Septimius Severus, found in the area of the Templum Pacis and assigned to the library there by Meneghini (2010), 36–37. It was, however, found in a stratum dated to the sixth century.

137. A painting probably of the poet Philoxenus of Cythera was found in a room that might have included bookshelves in a house in Pompeii: Strocka (1993); Esposito (2008); nn. 27–29 above.

138. Some *imagines clipeatae* may have been in other materials. R. Lanciani uncovered what he took to be stucco *imagines* of authors in what may have been a private library on the Esquiline in Rome: Lanciani (1884), 48–49; cf. Clark (1909), 23; *CIL* 6.29828. There are, however, numerous problems: Guidobaldi (1986), 198.

139. Tac. *Ann.* 2.83.4: *auctores eloquentiae . . . veteres scriptores.*

140. Petrain (2013), 341–46, citing the portraits of Germanicus and his father Drusus. Drusus was by no means a distinguished literary figure.

Small bronze portrait heads or busts may have been common, although only one that can be assigned to a specific library seems to survive, namely a head of Epicurus from the Villa of the Papyri in Herculaneum.[141] There were no doubt marble heads and busts mounted on low pedestals or in the form of herms, which were columns about a meter high topped by a portrait head, in some or many libraries. As with bronze portraits, none seems to be known that can be securely associated with any particular book collection, but many marble portrait heads of literary figures have survived, and some of them may well have come from libraries or reading rooms.[142] We are told of full-length statues (thus Favorinus and Sidonius); the Hadrian in Pergamum is over life-size; larger yet is a group from the library of Pantaenus in Athens (Homer along with allegorical figures of the *Iliad* and the *Odyssey*); and there is finally the colossal Apollo from the Templum Novum library in Rome. All of this can be summed up succinctly: as you entered an unfamiliar room that contained a book collection, you would instantly recognize the nature of the room from the cabinets or boxes with their book rolls; but before entering the hall you could never be quite sure of the identity, style, or size of the sculptures you might find therein.

Representations in libraries of writers, scholars, and other great men served a number of purposes. By adding a statue or a painting, you could honor a god, an emperor, an author past or living, a friend, or an influential individual. Such honor was not necessarily disinterested. When the city of Corinth erected a statue of Favorinus in their library, they were no doubt aware that he was a friend of, and enjoyed access to, the emperor Hadrian.[143] That is, the image may have been a political statement, not a cultural one. Sometimes collectors just liked an author's works and wanted a visual image of him, as in the case of Tiberius's three favorite Greek authors and Stertinius Avitus's desire to put a likeness of Martial in his library.

It has occasionally been suggested that portraits of authors were used to help organize a collection and to make the organization clear to users.[144] A

141. See above, n. 118. A small bronze bust of the Stoic Chrysippus has been assigned to the library in the Temple of Peace by Papini (2005), 131–35, but the bust was found in a late antique stratum, and any association with the library must remain uncertain.

142. Zanker (1995) provides dozens of examples of marble heads and busts. Most are Roman copies of Greek portraits of the great classical authors, but Cicero (fig. 106) and Seneca (fig. 107) appear, along with numerous stylized "intellectuals": Zanker (1995), 197–99, with fig. 108. As Zanker noted, these portraits could have been displayed in a library, but they might also have been placed in other spaces dedicated to intellectual activity.

143. The city of Athens too erected a statue of Favorinus, but when the Athenians heard that he had quarreled with Hadrian and lost the emperor's favor, they destroyed the statue: Philostr. *VS* 1.8 490 (Favorinus).

144. So, for example, Fedeli (1989), 46, with n. 41 on p. 61; Meneghini (2010), 33.

bust of Homer resting atop an *armarium*, for example, could indicate that the *armarium* contained the Homeric poems, other epic poetry, or both. This is certainly possible, although I know of no ancient evidence to support it, but there would be practical problems. Not all of the portraits known to us could be used effectively as signs: some of the writers were obscure, and many of the portraits were added long after the library was first established and organized, so that they cannot have served to help in the original organization of the collection.[145] Many ancient authors, both Greek and Roman, wrote in several distinct genres. What would a bust of Ennius, for example, tell us about the contents of the *armarium* on which it stood? Ennius wrote epic, tragic drama, satire, and philosophy, all at some length. Moreover, there were some works that did not fit comfortably within the limits of any of the classical genres, including encyclopedic works, such as that of Pliny the Elder, and technical treatises. Would a bust of Frontinus, assuming you recognized it (or read its label), tell you that that part of the collection contained works on water, or on military tactics? And whose bust would we choose to show where we kept our fiction, which, as we saw above in chapters 2 and 4, was present in some collections? None of this rules out the use of portraits as signs for the classic genres and authors. But it does suggest two things: portraits would not be a very satisfactory way of displaying the organization of all of a book collection, although they might well highlight certain parts of it; and not all of the portraits we know of can have been used for this purpose.

5.8. CONCLUSION

If we needed a reminder that we should not approach ancient libraries with modern preconceptions, the statue of Hadrian in the library built and dedicated by Flavia Melitine would serve us well. Few persons today, as they enter a library, expect to find an over-life-size, fully nude statue of the ruler of their country facing them from a position of prominence across the hall. Just so: we must not assume that any other aspect of an ancient book collection or library can be predicted on the basis of what we know and take for granted. Instead, we must consider the evidence we have and what it implies.

Drawing on the evidence presented in this chapter, we can attempt, in our imaginations, to restore the interior appearance of the library of Celsus in Ephesus. I choose this library simply as an example, and several others

---

145. The portraits of Euphorion, Rhianus, Parthenius, Titus Catius, Cornelius Nepos, and Sidonius Apollinaris were all added decades or centuries after the library they stood in was first established.

would do as well. As we saw, the library of Celsus consisted essentially of a large box-like space. On the floor of that space, we will supply numerous stools and high-backed chairs where readers and copyists can sit, read, discuss, and copy. There are almost certainly low wooden tables, with tops a meter or so across, and on them are papyrus rolls and perhaps scribal equipment. There may be freestanding cabinets with doors for the permanent storage of part of the collection, and there may be boxes for the temporary or permanent storage of papyrus rolls. We should probably not assume the presence of large desk-like tables of the sort we use. On the podium facing the main entrance, there is a statue. It might be Minerva or some other divinity. It might be a nude Hadrian or other mortal figure. Here and there in the open space of the floor are other sculptural representations: heads and busts on cabinets, and perhaps life-size statues placed systematically in front of the columns that line the walls. It is possible that the room is somewhat cluttered. Along the walls are the bookcases, with doors, that contain the bulk of the library's collection of book rolls. A number of stepladders are available to help staff members reach the higher shelves. Light enters through the doors and the windows above them, but there may be lamp stands for use on dark days.

Such a picture can be scaled down or up to suit other collections. The reading room in Pliny's Laurentine villa, evidently intended for quiet reading of texts rather than for literary debate, may have had just a couple of chairs, and Pliny mentions just one bookcase. At the other end of the scale, the twin halls of the Trajan library in Rome were large enough for many chairs, cabinets, work spaces, conversations, and, not least, statues of prominent authors both ancient and, like Sidonius Apollinaris, living. No library survives with its equipment and furnishings intact, and we need not draw out this series of sketches. The reader has such evidence as there is.

These interiors, especially those furnished with works of art, were more than purely functional. Like the book rolls themselves, the rooms with their statuary could serve as cultural statements, attesting to the owner's taste and sophistication.[146] Sculptural figures could indicate and honor the favorite authors of the collector, preserve the memory of authors and other men both famous and obscure, suggest a connection between the god or person honored and the owner or donor of the collection, and attract divine or imperial attention. On the level of the imperial collections, the book rolls and the materials that accompanied them helped to convey the extent and

146. Vitr. *De arch*. 6.5.2 lists the library as one of the rooms in a private house that helps establish a man's status. Such rooms, he notes, should be given an appropriately magnificent appearance.

power of empire, as the Ptolemaic library at Alexandria had done earlier. These were, or could be, elaborate displays.

Despite this, we can imagine disharmonies as well. Lucian and Juvenal are bitterly critical of men who collect, respectively, fancy volumes and portraits of authors whose works the collectors cannot understand.[147] The cultural message here has been perverted by ignorant collectors.[148] We would like to know, but cannot, if there were other contradictions. Did some individuals have handsome volumes that they kept in disorderly, unpleasant spaces? Were there houses or villas containing magnificent art but manuscripts of poor quality? Or was there usually a correlation between the art and the content of the book rolls: did, for example, the owner of Grenfell and Hunt's second find, which was strong in early Greek poetry, have busts of lyric poets? No evidence is available to answer such questions.

Whatever the aesthetic value of the collection, it required attention: rolls must be rewound after use; torn rolls need to be repaired and worn-out volumes replaced; rolls must be shelved where they can be retrieved promptly; such art as there is in the reading room will need cleaning, and all equipment associated with the collection of volumes will need care and maintenance. And the persons who provided care for the volumes and works of art? It is to them that we turn in chapter 6.

147. Lucian *Ind.*; Juv. 2.1–5.
148. Rutledge (2012), 68, usefully notes that collecting art was considered a good thing except when it was used to exaggerate one's social status or create a false impression of oneself. In the context of book collections, this principle would apply to either portraits or book rolls.

6
Personnel and Their Activities

6.1. INTRODUCTION

Book rolls and equipment we have; it is time now to put people in our libraries. In this chapter, I will set out the evidence for the people who managed and maintained book collections and libraries, from owner to slave worker, and for their tasks and responsibilities. Our goal is to see how Roman libraries functioned and how collections of manuscripts, once assembled, were organized, maintained, and made usable.[1] Given this focus, we will be concerned primarily with relatively large collections, since small collections would need only occasional maintenance and, in most cases, no specific staff. Through his comments on his own and other libraries, Cicero gives us a useful first look at the management of Roman book collections and the personnel involved, so I will begin with him. Closely connected to Cicero's collections are two Augustan-era libraries, those in the Temple of Apollo and the Portico of Octavia.

6.2. BASICS: CICERO, THE LIBRARY IN THE TEMPLE OF APOLLO, AND THE LIBRARY IN THE PORTICO OF OCTAVIA

Cicero

In his letters, Cicero often refers to his book collections, to the tasks associated with them, and to the men who undertook those tasks. Sometimes explicitly, sometimes implicitly, he tells us who did what. We can distinguish at least three levels of activity.

The owner of a collection, of course, made the basic decisions concerning subject matter, budget, and quality. Cicero clearly hoped to acquire highly accurate texts. Writing to his brother Quintus in the fall of 54, he

---

1. I will not deal specifically or systematically with users of libraries—those who went to libraries to find and consult manuscripts and do scholarly work—but we will meet such individuals in passing, since they regularly interacted with the staff.

lamented the fact that it was difficult to find good manuscripts: "It's a time-consuming task, and it takes a very careful man. I know this myself: after a lot of effort I have accomplished nothing. I really don't know where to turn regarding the Latin texts; both copies that one has made [i.e., commissions] and [ready-made] copies that are on sale are full of errors."[2] We do not find Cicero explicitly defining the subject areas he wanted in his collection, but we can assume that he was interested in rhetoric and oratory (among other things), and he presumably had a broad general collection of Greek and Latin literature.[3] The owner would also be the person who accepted gifts and bequests, borrowed and lent manuscripts, and decided on major purchases.[4]

As Cicero remarked, however, assembling a good collection was hard work, and people of his rank were inclined to entrust the task to men who were both learned and in need of a salary: scholars, teachers, and other literary men. This emerges clearly from the events of 57–56 BC, just after Cicero's return from exile. His book collection had been damaged and in part destroyed or dispersed while he was away, and to repair and reorganize his collection he engaged the Greek scholar Tyrannio of Amisus.[5] In a letter of June 56, Cicero reported to Atticus on what had been done by then: "You will find [when you come to visit] that Tyrannio's organization (*dissignatio*) of my books is quite wonderful. What remains of them is far better than I had expected. Please also send me two of your book workers (*librarioli*) for Tyrannio to use as menders (*glutinatores*) and assistants in other matters, and tell them to bring a bit of parchment to make those labels (*indices*) that you Greeks call, I think, *sittybae*."[6] Not long after that letter, Cicero wrote

---

2. Cic. *QFr.* 3.5(5–7).6: *Res operosa est et hominis perdiligentis. Sentio ipse, qui in summo studio nihil adsequor. De Latinis vero quo me vertam nescio; ita mendose et scribuntur et veneunt.* Cf. *QFr.* 3.4.5, written a few weeks earlier: *Neque enim venalia sunt, quae quidem placeant.* ("For they aren't for sale, at least not the ones you would want.") Similarly, the collection represented by Grenfell and Hunt's first find (section 4.2 above) seems to have been assembled by a person who worked hard to obtain accurate texts. I use Shackleton Bailey's editions of the letters of Cicero and accept his dates of the letters.

3. For a full treatment of Cicero's book collections, see above all Dix (2013). He discusses the general nature of Cicero's collection, 221.

4. For these activities, see above, sections 1.5, 1.12, 1.6, and 1.11, respectively.

5. Tyrannio was a distinguished and experienced scholar: Christes (1979), 27–38; Johnson (2012). Cicero seems to have brought what remained of his collections together in his villa at Antium, and it would be there that Tyrannio worked on them: Dix (2013), 223.

6. Cic. *Att.* 4.4a.1: *Offendes dissignationem Tyrannionis mirificam librorum meorum, quorum reliquiae multo meliores sunt quam putaram. Et velim mihi mittas de tuis librariolis duos aliquos quibus Tyrannio utatur glutinatoribus, ad cetera administris iisque imperes ut sumant membranulam ex qua indices fiant, quos vos Graeci, ut opinor, σιττύβας appellatis.*

Atticus again: "Now that Tyrannio has organized (*disposuit*) my book rolls, it seems that my house has recovered its intelligence."[7]

From what Cicero says, we learn, or can infer, what Tyrannio did. He sorted and organized the collection (*dissignatio*; *disposuit*). If, as is likely, some of the volumes had been damaged and had no titles, he would have needed to identify them from such fragments as survived. He probably compiled an inventory and informed Cicero of what was damaged or missing, since Cicero was able quickly to assess what remained of his collections. Tyrannio also supervised the work of other men (*librarioli*; *glutinatores*), so he had administrative responsibilities as well as scholarly ones. When Cicero asked Atticus for men whom Tyrannio could "use as . . . assistants in other matters" (*ad cetera administri*), he did not specify what those "other matters" would be, but presumably they included mending damaged rolls and, if necessary, making entirely new copies of some works. One of Tyrannio's responsibilities was to oversee this work on repairs and copies.

Two years later, Cicero and his brother Quintus conferred on how to improve Quintus's library. On this occasion too Cicero hoped to find someone who could take on the difficult task of assessing the quality of manuscripts that were for sale and either buy or arrange for the copying of texts that Cicero and Quintus wanted. Cicero's first choice was again Tyrannio, and the second a certain Chrysippus, presumably a literate freedman of Cicero.[8] Later, in 46, one of Cicero's slaves, a man named Dionysius, seems to have had a supervisory role similar to Tyrannio's, since Cicero says that he had been "managing" the collection in Cicero's house on the Palatine.[9] The library work of these men—Tyrannio, Dionysius, and perhaps Chrysippus—constitutes a second level of activity.

A third level of work is that undertaken by the men who assisted Tyrannio, both the men whom Cicero calls *librarioli* and *glutinatores* and others who have no names or professional titles and whose very existence must be inferred from their activities. Cicero names two men, lent to him by Atti-

---

7. Cic. *Att.* 4.8.2: *Postea vero quam Tyrannio mihi libros disposuit, mens addita videtur meis aedibus.*

8. Cic. *QFr.* 3.4.5, discussing how to go about getting the volumes Quintus wanted: *Chrysippo tamen imperabo et cum Tyrannione loquar.* ("I will tell Chrysippus to work on it, and I'll speak to Tyrannio about it.") In a later letter, Cic. *QFr.* 3.5(5–7).6, we learn that Tyrannio has done nothing, and that Cicero still plans to talk to Chrysippus. We know little about Chrysippus. He may be identical with a Chrysippus who, although a literary man and trusted by Cicero, turned out to be a scoundrel (Cic. *Att.* 7.2.8, of 50 BC). See Shackleton Bailey (1965–70), ad loc.

9. Cic. *Fam.* 13.77.3. The verb used of Dionysius's activity is *tractare*, too general a term to be of much use to us. Dionysius later stole a number of Cicero's volumes and fled. See further below, section 6.7.

cus, and tells us several things they did: they made *sillyba*; they constructed *pegmata* (presumably shelves of some sort); and they painted the library, shelves and all.[10] As *glutinatores*, they presumably repaired manuscripts, not only pasting torn fragments together, but making new copies of missing sections and attaching them to what survived of the original manuscript.[11] Tyrannio will also have needed help in the form of physical labor: transporting book rolls, carrying book boxes from one place to another, and perhaps setting up portrait busts or other works of art. These tasks required no special training, and it is likely that Cicero simply assigned some of his own slaves to help Tyrannio do them.

We have, thus, three levels of work: the owner, making basic decisions; a literary person organizing and assessing the collection, appraising the quality of manuscripts, advising the owner, and overseeing other workers; and men who undertook the physical tasks, some of which were very simple, while others required training or expertise.

The Library in the Temple of Apollo

Republican practices, naturally enough, were by and large continued in the libraries of the early Empire. Augustus (when he was still Octavius) assembled what apparently was, or subsequently became, an exceptional collection of manuscripts, built a home for it within the sacred precinct of Apollo on the Palatine hill, and in 28 BC dedicated precinct, temple, and library all together.[12] He delegated the task of organizing the book rolls in this new library to a man named Pompeius Macer, about whom, unfortunately, we know nothing else for certain.[13] At some later time Augustus put

---

10. *Sillyba*: Cic. *Att.* 4.8.2: *Mirifica opera Dionysi et Menophili tui fuit. Nihil venustius quam illa tua pegmata, postquam sittybae libros illustrarunt.* ("The work of your Dionysius and Menophilus has been wonderful. Nothing [could be] more charming than those shelves (?) of yours, now that the *sillyba* have brightened them up.") The precise meaning of *pegmata* is not known. Painting: *Att.* 4.5.4: *Bibliothecam mihi tui pinxerunt cum structione et sittybis.* ("Your men have painted my library, along with the shelves [?] and *sillyba*.") The reading *cum structione*, a conjecture of Theodor Birt, is not certain.

11. The tasks and skills of *glutinatores* were essentially the same as those of copyists: Puglia (1996c).

12. Date: Cass. Dio 53.1.3. We are not told how Augustus acquired the volumes he put in the library.

13. Suetonius (*Iul.* 56.7) tells us about Macer, *cui* (i.e., *Pompeio Macro*) *ordinandas bibliothecas delegaverat* (*Augustus*). ("Augustus had entrusted the task of organizing the collections to him.") On the meaning of *ordinare* here, see Kaster (1995), 219–20. Macer has traditionally been taken as a son of Theophanes of Mytilene and a procurator of Asia. So, for example, Fehrle (1986), 75, with n. 23; the procurator is known from Strabo 13.2.3 C618. There are, however, problems in the identification, and White (1992), 214–15, argued that the two men are not one and the same. Bowie (2013), 245–46, and Wachtel in *PIR*², P 625, return to the usual view, but the matter cannot be regarded as settled.

one of his freedmen, Gaius Iulius Hyginus, in charge of the library. We do not know how long Hyginus served in this post, nor his exact responsibilities, but Suetonius tells us that, even while he was director of the library, Hyginus took on many students, and we know also that he was a scholar and prolific author, so his responsibilities as director cannot have been too onerous.[14] In addition to these two men, we have epigraphical evidence of slave assistants called *a bybliotheca Apollinis* (or some variation on that title), most of them datable to the Julio-Claudian period.[15] They are of interest both singly and as a group, and I list those who are known to us below, placing them in chronological order insofar as possible.[16]

Name	Title	Status	Reference
Callisth<e?>nes Ti(beri) Caesaris Aug(usti)	A bybliothece Latina Apollinis	Slave (of Tiberius)	*CIL* 6.5189
Diopithes	A bybliot(hece) Latina Apollinis	Slave (of Tiberius, it seems; brother of the preceding)	*CIL* 6.5189
Alexander G(ai) Caesaris Aug(usti) Germanici ser(vus) Pylaemenianus[17]	Ab bybliothece Graeca Templi Apollinis	Slave of Caligula, died aged thirty years	*CIL* 6.5188
Antiochus Ti(beri) Claudi Caesaris (servus)	A bibliotheca Latina Apollinis	Slave of Claudius	*CIL* 6.5884
Liberalis (?)	[A bibliotheca] Latina Apollinis	Slave? or freedman	*CIL* 6.5191

14. Suet. *Gram. et rhet.* 20: *Praefuit Palatinae bibliothecae, nec eo secius plurimos docuit.* Fehrle (1986), 77–81, discusses Hyginus's life and work and argues that he, not Macer, was the man who first organized the Palatine library. That is not likely given what Suetonius says of the two men. Of Macer, he uses the verb *ordinare* ("organize"); of Hyginus, *praeesse* ("be head of," implying that the institution was already in existence). See further Kaster (1995), 211, on the limited nature of Hyginus's responsibilities.

15. For the origin and syntax of the imperial titles in *a(b)* plus the ablative, see Väänänen (1977). The prepositional phrase in *a(b)* defines the sphere of activity of the individual and in our case means (worker) "in the library."

16. For a full discussion of this and related material, see Houston (2002), 142–46. No women *a bibliotheca* are known.

17. Alexander had probably belonged previously to Pylaemenes (a son of Amyntas, the client king of Galatia under Augustus) and had passed to Caligula by inheritance: *RE* 23.2.2107–8, s.v. Pylaimenes 5 (Stein).

Four of these five men were certainly imperial slaves, and the fifth, Liberalis (?), probably was too. They were divided into two groups, and only two: those who worked with the Latin collection on the one hand, and those, such as Alexander, who worked with the Greek collection on the other. This implies, as has often been noticed, that their tasks required literacy, and that these were not men who simply pasted sheets of papyrus together or did other menial tasks.[18] It is worth noting, however, that there are no further subdivisions of the groups. As we saw in chapter 2, book owners in the Roman era seem to have organized some book collections at least in part by genre, and it is thus possible to conceive of a slave who was in charge of all the works in a particular genre, such as history or epic poetry. No indications of any such subdivisions appear, however, and it is not at all likely that any were made. Nor are the library workers divided, so far as we can tell, between those who would deal with newly arrived texts, which would need to be sorted, listed, and put in appropriate shelves, and those who dealt with existing rolls, which would involve repairs, retrieval, and reshelving. None of this is surprising. I point it out simply to show that the division of men that *was* made—between the Greek and Latin collections—was not the only possible way the Romans might have done things.[19] It was a conscious, if obvious, choice, and it suggests that the collections were not so large nor so complex as to require specialists.

The Library in the Portico of Octavia

Augustus or his sister Octavia or both together built and opened a library in the Portico of Octavia within a few years of the completion of the Apollo library.[20] It was staffed and managed, so far as we can tell, in a way very similar to that of the Apollo library: the founder, Octavia, probably contributed the core collection of book rolls, and a distinguished scholar, Gaius

---

18. The assignment of workers to Latin or Greek sections should not be taken as evidence that the library consisted of two rooms. In the first century AD, the main part of the Apollo library almost certainly consisted of a single large hall: Iacopi and Tedone (2005/6), 352–57. Greek volumes might simply have been shelved in one section of the hall, Latin in another. For a full discussion of the possible divisions in Roman libraries, see Nicholls (2010).

19. Extensive specialization and subdivision of tasks can be observed in many areas of the imperial domestic service. Consider, for example, the emperor's clothes. We find men in charge of at least three distinct types of clothing: *scaenica* (outfits suitable to wear to the theater, *CIL* 6.10090); *gladiatoria* (suitable to observe gladiatorial combats, *CIL* 6.3756); and *venatoria* (hunting gear, *CIL* 8555). See Boulvert (1970), 176, for details and further examples. Specialist slaves, each one assigned to a specific genre of literature, would not be an anomaly in the imperial domestic service.

20. Building history: Dix and Houston (2006), 685–86. The opening of the Octavia library can be dated between 23 and 11 BC.

Melissus, was chosen to organize and set up the collection.[21] At a lower administrative or clerical level, we have evidence of five men *a bybliotheca* who were assigned to this library. Two worked in the Greek section, two in the Latin; the assignment of the fifth is not known.[22] All seem to date to the first century A D. Two are given further titles, *vilicus*, and were presumably supervisors of some sort, of either a physical space or a group of slave workers. We will return to these *vilici* below.

Two of the men *a bybliotheca* who were assigned to the Octavia library are called *servus publicus* or simply *publicus* on their inscriptions and thus did not belong to the *familia Caesaris* (that is, they were not owned by the emperor), but rather were the property of the Roman people.[23] It is possible that all of the lower-level staff of this library consisted of public slaves, and that, as Mommsen suggested, the library itself was considered a municipal ("städtisch") library rather than an imperial one.[24] So far as I can tell, however, this administrative distinction had absolutely no effect on the policies or practices of the library, and users would not have noticed any significant difference between it and the Apollo library or the other later imperial libraries.[25]

The parallels between the management of Cicero's collections and the organization of the Apollo and Octavia libraries, at least in their early years, are clear. An owner (Cicero; the emperor) makes basic decisions on what to include and where to house the collection. He engages a scholar (Tyrannio; Macer and Melissus) who can assess the quality of manuscripts, oversee repairs, and draw up a list of what the collection contains. The scholar supervises a number of workers. In Cicero's case, these include both unskilled slaves of his own and highly trained slaves borrowed from Atticus; in the case of the Augustan foundations, the staff consists of the emperor's domestic slaves with, it appears, some special training and a title, *a bybliotheca*. Under the scholar's supervision, the workers organize and subsequently maintain the library. There is collaboration and consultation at

21. Octavia as donor of book rolls: Dix and Houston (2006), 686–87. On Melissus's scholarly work, see Kaster (1995), 215–16. We do not know how long he was involved with the library. Fehrle (1986), 76–77, suggested that the Octavia library was organized by Pompeius Macer, not Melissus, who in that case would have been one of Macer's successors.

22. Greek section: *Philoxenus Iulian(us) public(us servus)*, CIL 6.2348; *Laryx* (?), CIL 6.4433. Latin section: *Hymnus Aurelianus*, CIL 6.4431; *Montanus Iulianus*, CIL 6.4435. Unknown: *Soterichus publicus (servus) Vestricianus*, CIL 6.5192. See on these men Houston (2002), especially 140–46 and 156–58.

23. For *servi publici* in general, see Halkin (1897).

24. Mommsen (1887), 330, n. 1.

25. Houston (2002), 156–58.

various levels, especially when a library is first being established or when it is being significantly upgraded. Cicero was in correspondence with Atticus, who could provide advice as well as trained workers; Cicero and Tyrannio consulted about the state of the collection and what Cicero wanted; Quintus relied on his brother for advice and assistance; Augustus and Macer were certainly in contact with one another; and Octavia and Augustus must have collaborated in ways that we cannot recover.[26] Once established, a library of ordinary size, such as Cicero's, may not have needed continuous care or a dedicated staff, and an owner could assign any of his slaves to the everyday tasks involved. On the imperial level, where we may assume larger collections, more users, and more wear and tear on the book rolls, dedicated staff would be needed. Hence the men *a bybliotheca*.

6.3. WHAT DID THE LOWER-LEVEL STAFF DO?

We have more to observe and learn about the imperial libraries, especially at the upper levels of the administration, but at this point it will be useful to explore what can be known or inferred concerning the tasks and responsibilities of the lower-level workers we have just met, men such as the *librarioli* who worked for Cicero and the slaves and freedmen in the imperial libraries. What exactly did these men do? Most of them were slaves, so they were usually taken for granted, and we seldom find them mentioned in written sources. I will therefore draw heavily, although not exclusively, on surviving papyri. As papyrologists have noted, we can find traces of the handiwork of copyists and library workers in papyri, and those traces, combined with a consideration of the practical necessities of the job, enable us to put together a list of the tasks that might be undertaken by our library workers.[27]

I will take most of my examples from papyri that we have seen in chapters 2 through 4, because many of these manuscripts have some claim to having been part of a book collection or library. It must be admitted at once that, while any particular task involving a book roll may have been carried out within the formal space of a library, it could also have been

---

26. Plut. *Marc.* 30.6; Cass. Dio 49.43.8; Suet. *Iul.* 56.7 mentions written instructions that Augustus sent to Macer. Cf. Dix and Houston (2006), 685.

27. In using papyri as evidence, I am adapting a methodology developed by Turner (1983), Puglia (1996c), and above all by Puglia in his two fascinating books on the care and maintenance of papyrus rolls, Puglia (1991) and (1997b). My list, however, also includes several tasks that do not involve work on papyri, such as control of access and the creation of lists. Related but not central to our concerns is the matter of professional scribal work in general, not limited to libraries. On that see most recently Mugridge (2010), 575–80.

done in rooms or work areas more or less distinct from the reading hall of a library, or in some room in a private dwelling, or in the workplace of a professional scribe. That is, we cannot prove that a given papyrus roll that shows clear signs of repair was repaired in a formal library. But it could have been; and our goal is simply to compile a list of those tasks that we know were carried out somewhere and that could have been done by one or more library workers.[28]

Procuring a Roll

If a text was to be copied, the obvious first step was to procure a roll of papyrus with at least one blank side. Newly made rolls could be purchased, of course, but there were different qualities of papyrus, and a discriminating collector might choose to assign a trained and experienced person to this task, or shop for papyrus himself.[29] Alternatively, a roll that contained a text on its recto could be turned over, and a new text could be copied on the verso. Perhaps the most interesting such opisthograph among the materials we have seen so far is the list of comedies (*P.Oxy.* 33.2659) written on the verso of a roll; on the recto was a Greek-Latin glossary (*P.Oxy.* 33.2660).[30] It is possible that the glossary belonged to a municipal or institutional library and was not much used, and that when the time came to draw up a new inventory of the collection, the librarians decided to use the back of the glossary for the inventory. If that is the scenario (which is very uncertain), we would have evidence of a specific task that was carried out by workers in this library.

When no entire roll was available, one could be created by pasting together a series of documents or sections from other rolls. Among the opisthographs found by Grenfell and Hunt in their first find, the roll containing the commentary on Thucydides, Book 2 (*P.Oxy.* 6.853) was created by pasting together at least three different documents.[31] The documents might be one's own, of course, but many of those that survive are official or public

---

28. References to papyri in this chapter will vary in format. Sometimes I will give *P.Oxy.* numbers, sometimes *MP*[3] or other numbers. I cite the papyri here in the same way as I cited them in chapters 2 through 4, so that the reader can readily find the earlier discussions of them.

29. On the production of new rolls: Turner (1980), 4–5.

30. This papyrus is discussed above (section 2.10) and is list 5 in appendix 1. Two other examples, both from the Breccia + GH3 collection: a comedy (*MP*[3] 2860) reused for notes or a treatise on rhetoric (*MP*[3] 2300), and an historical work (*MP*[3] 168.01) reused for a list of tachygraphic symbols (*MP*[3] 2776.5).

31. *P.Oxy.* 841 (Pindar's *Paeans*) was composed of at least two earlier documents. Puglia (1997b), 46–48, gives other examples of such composite rolls.

records.[32] We have in all of this activity several potential tasks for our library workers: acquiring new or used rolls; gathering documents that could be pasted together; doing any needed pasting. None of these tasks would ordinarily require specialized training.

Preparatory Work on Reused Papyrus

Sometimes documents or pieces of papyrus needed to be repaired or strengthened before a new text could be copied on the verso.[33] At least three of the manuscripts from Grenfell and Hunt's first find show signs of such work. Pindar's *Paeans* (first find, number 7, *P.Oxy.* 5.841) were written on a roll that was made from at least two documents. The documents themselves were in poor condition, so the weaker parts were cut out and the better parts pasted together. The resulting roll was trimmed to a uniform height.[34] This work probably did require a trained scribe.

Locating an Exemplar

Before a work could be copied, an exemplar of suitable quality would need to be found. This was presumably the task of the collector, although he or she could delegate it to a qualified person such as Tyrannio, and it was not always easy. I have discussed the possibilities and the problems above in sections 1.5 to 1.8, but we may note here that some of our papyri provide evidence of mistakes or gaps that were probably caused by the use of faulty exemplars and testify to the difficulty involved in finding reliable ones. From Grenfell and Hunt's first find, two manuscripts contain gaps that are probably due to reliance on damaged or illegible sections of text in the exemplars from which they were copied, and one of the manuscripts from their second find contains numerous uncorrected mistakes.[35]

---

32. We do not know how such official records came onto the market for reuse. Lama (1991), 86–87, surveys the various theories. There may have been a mechanism by which out-of-date administrative records were sold to merchants in used papyrus. Or, as Turner (1952a), 135, suggested, officials may have kept documents that were produced in the offices where they worked and used them later for the copying of texts.

33. Details and examples: Puglia (1996c), 48; Puglia (1997b), 43–48.

34. Puglia (1997b), 48. Two other examples from Grenfell and Hunt's first find: *P.Oxy.* 5.842 (the *Hellenica Oxyrhynchia*) was strengthened; *P.Oxy.* 7.1016 (Plato's *Phaedrus*) was cut down.

35. *P.Oxy.* 5.844, Isocrates, *Panegyricus* (on recto; at least three gaps, only two of which were successfully corrected). *P.Oxy.* 7.1016, Plato, *Phaedrus* (on verso; the scribe seems to have had problems reading the text he was copying). Satyrus's *Lives* (*MP³* 1456), from Grenfell and Hunt's second find, contains numerous mistakes. Presumably the owner was not concerned with accuracy.

Copying

Whether they were in-house copyists or professional scribes working in a commercial shop, copyists seem to have worked sometimes from dictation, sometimes from a written text. We do not know which was the more common procedure.[36] In terms of staff, what we need is a scribe who can write clearly and, where the scribe is working from dictation, both a reader whose pronunciation and phrasing help ensure accurate copies and a copyist who can spell correctly.

Correcting

As a copyist wrote, he might correct mistakes he made immediately, as he made them. Copies, once complete, were sometimes and perhaps often corrected by the original scribe, a proofreader (*diorthotes*), or both. In some cases, we find two or more correctors, and it is possible that when a third hand appears it is the hand not of a professional scribe involved in the production process, but rather of an owner, trying to make his text as accurate as possible, as we find Galen trying to do.[37] Surviving papyri show a wide variation in the number of correctors. Taking the sixteen manuscripts from Grenfell and Hunt's first find as a sample, we have one manuscript that contains no corrections at all, three with corrections by the original scribe only, five corrected by a *diorthotes* only, one with corrections by both the first and a second hand, and one that was corrected by the original scribe and two other hands.[38]

Of particular interest are those cases where a second exemplar was apparently used to correct the copy or to add variant readings. A second hand added numerous variant readings in one of the copies of Plato's *Phaedrus* from Grenfell and Hunt's first find (*P.Oxy.* 7.1017), apparently after a comparison of this copy with another exemplar.[39] In another papyrus, *P.Petaus* 30, we read about this process in action: the writer of the letter rented eight

---

36. The question has been much discussed. The most recent comprehensive treatment known to me is that of Yuen-Collingridge and Choat (2012), 827–30. See also above, section 3.7.

37. Gal. *Ind.* 14.

38. These are respectively nos. 16; 6, 12, and 13; 1, 2, 3, 9, and 10; 4; and 11 in the list of the first find above in chapter 4. Some corrections may have been made by the owner of the book roll; we would not always be able to distinguish those from corrections made by a *diorthotes*.

39. Similarly, two manuscripts from the Breccia + GH3 concentration contain readings that suggest the use of a second exemplar: *MP³* 1400.1 (Plato), and *MP³* 1509 (Thucydides, Book 1). It is possible that in some cases it was not consultation of a second exemplar, but simply the owner's or reader's intelligence, that suggested the correction.

manuscripts, apparently to use them to correct, or add variant readings to, copies of works he already owned (above, section 1.8). All of these manuscripts imply well-trained and attentive scribes and some sort of direction: someone was needed to decide on and distribute tasks.[40]

Repairs

Manuscripts could be dropped, torn, crammed carelessly into crowded shelves or containers, or simply worn out through use. Exposed to damp, they might become moldy, and their layers could stick together, as Galen complains (*Ind.* 19). Insect larvae might eat straight through a roll. Sometimes repairs were possible, and several types of repair are visible among the manuscripts we considered in chapters 2, 3, and 4.[41] In some cases, it was enough to paste strengthening strips along the damaged or weakened parts of a papyrus.[42] Other rolls, however, seem to have been torn right in two, with some columns of text being rendered unusable, and damage that severe naturally called for more extensive repairs, as can be seen in manuscripts from Herculaneum. One, a copy of Epicurus, *On Nature*, Book 25, was probably torn in two not long after it was first made, and part of it was recopied, either because the damaged sections were no longer usable or in order to improve the accuracy of the text. The two sections—part of the original roll, and the freshly copied columns—were then pasted together.[43] Similarly, a section of a book roll containing lives of Epicurean masters seems to have been damaged and cut out of its roll; the excised columns were then recopied, and the new copy was pasted in.[44] Sometimes we can see that the ends of rolls were replaced with fresh copies, and that implies that the ends of the original rolls had been damaged or destroyed.[45]

40. In passing, we may note that there seems to be no convincing evidence for the existence in the first three centuries AD of systematic, large-scale reproduction of texts in the imperial libraries in Rome. Galen makes it quite clear that the imperial staff did not make duplicate copies of some titles that were known to be rare and perhaps unique (*Ind.* 13). Some works apparently existed in only one copy and so vanished in the fire of AD 192. See further below, section 6.7.

41. There are many further examples and a systematic treatment of the topic in Puglia (1997b).

42. Thus *MP*³ 462 (Herodotus) from the Breccia + GH3 concentration. Also *MP*³ 1321 (guide to the works of Menander) and *MP*³ 1237 (Ibycus), both from Grenfell and Hunt's second find.

43. Puglia (1997b), 40–42.

44. Ibid., 42–43.

45. Henry (2010), xxv–xxvi. Note especially *P.Herc.* 1050, a copy of Philodemus's *On Death*. At a certain point, there is a clear change in both the hand and the width of the roll; perhaps no papyrus exactly matching the width of the original roll was available when repairs were needed.

Addition of Bibliographical Information

Did library staff write anything in the manuscripts that would help them organize, shelve, and retrieve the book rolls? In the papyri from Herculaneum and Oxyrhynchus that we have looked at, there is very little evidence that they did. A *sillybon* was added to a text of Bacchylides a generation or two after the text was written, and so not by the original scribe, but by an owner or by library staff.[46] Occasionally a *subscriptio* was added by a second hand, or information was added to a *subscriptio*, but these are probably cases of scribes replacing *subscriptiones* that had been damaged, rather than librarians creating an organizational system for the collection.[47] Similarly, at least five manuscripts from Herculaneum and eleven from Egypt have initial titles that are written in large, often calligraphic, letters, and usually in hands distinct from those of the main texts.[48] It is possible that the titles were added purely for aesthetic reasons, or to replace damaged titles, but it is also possible that librarians added them as part of a general restoration and upgrading of the collection.

On the negative side, no *sillybon*, no *subscriptio*, no book list on papyrus known to us includes anything like a call number, shelf number, or other locator. It is difficult to prove the absence of something, of course, but to judge from the surviving papyri, it is very unlikely that the addition of bibliographical information to manuscripts was one of the tasks demanded of Roman library personnel.[49]

46. *MP*³ 177 = no. 10 in Grenfell and Hunt's second find; above, section 4.10. Perhaps it replaced a *sillybon* that had been damaged or lost; and it could have been added by a dealer, not a collector or a member of the collector's staff. When Tyrannio restored Cicero's collection in 56, one of the tasks his assistants undertook was the manufacture and pasting on of *sillyba*, but we do not know if this was the first time the manuscripts had been given *sillyba*, or if earlier *sillyba* had been damaged during Cicero's exile (*Att.* 4.4a and 4.8).

47. In *PHerc.* 1414, a copy of Philodemus's *On Gratitude*, we find a *subscriptio* written by the original scribe, but then, in a second hand and somewhat later, additional information, including the number of papyrus sheets and columns in the roll. Delattre (2006), 48, suggested that this roll had been damaged and that the additional information was added as a check, to show that the repairs had restored the whole of the text.

48. List and discussion: Capasso (2001a). The manuscripts from Egypt with initial titles are treated fully by Caroli (2007).

49. Papyrologists have suggested that the number of columns or sheets of papyri—both of which appear in some *subscriptiones* and initial titles—could have helped a scribe who was about to begin copying a text. See, for example, Puglia (1997b), 109–11.

Inventories and Lists

It is clear from the surviving lists we saw in chapter 2 that it was common, although not necessarily universal, for owners to have staff members write out lists of the titles in their collections. We do not know precisely how this was done, but a simple method would be for one or two staff to work through a collection, shelf by shelf or box by box, and record for each roll the author, title, book number (if any), and, in some cases, the fact that a roll was an opisthograph.[50] In two of our lists, check marks to the left of entries seem to indicate a second inventory of some sort, presumably made at a later date.[51] One list has so many corrections, additions, and the like that it would seem to be a preliminary version; perhaps a cleaner version was made later.[52] Much work of this sort could be done by almost any literate staff member, since in most cases no decisions had to be made. The *subscriptio* (or *sillybon* or initial title, if present) could simply be copied, and the roll checked to see if it was an opisthograph. On the other hand, there might be problem manuscripts, rolls in which the author's name and the title were lacking or illegible or simply incorrect. In such cases, a scholar might be needed to identify what works the manuscript contained.[53]

Protecting the Manuscripts

Papyrus rolls needed protection from dust and larvae, among other things. In a letter of the third century AD, a doctor, away from home for an extended period, writes asking his wife or mother to take his medical treatises out of their place of storage and shake them out, presumably to rid them of dust and larvae.[54] This was probably a common task for library personnel. Some surviving papyri, including two from Grenfell and Hunt's second find, were treated with oil of cedar, an insecticide, to protect them against worms.[55]

---

50. In *P.Vars.* 5 verso = chapter 2, list 4, careful attention is paid to recording opisthographs.

51. *P.Ross.Georg.* 1.22 = chapter 2, list 2, lines 15 and 18. *P.Turner* 9 = chapter 2, list 8, lines 2, 3, and 5 to 15.

52. *P.Vars.* 5 verso = chapter 2, list 4.

53. One of the important tasks Tyrannio performed for Cicero in 56 BC may have been to identify the author and title of those rolls that had been damaged and no longer had an initial or final title. In the second century AD, Galen found some manuscripts in the Palatine libraries that were incorrectly labeled (*Ind.* 16). He could tell, he says, because neither the diction (λέξις) nor the thought (διάνοια) in them was characteristic of the authors they had been ascribed to.

54. *P.Ross.Georg.* 3.1.17–19; more detail above, chapter 5, n. 14.

55. *MP*³ 1237 (Ibycus) and *MP*³ 1495 (Theocritus). Oil of cedar as an insecticide: Puglia (1991), 40–42.

Control of Access

A staff member would be needed both to open a library in the morning and then to lock it up at closing time. For the library of Pantaenus in Athens, we have an explicit statement in the form of an inscription: "Open from the first hour to the sixth," that is, open from dawn until noon; staff members unlocked the doors early in the morning and closed them at midday.[56] At Timgad in North Africa, it was almost certainly possible to close and lock the main entrance.[57] Restricted access might be the rule even in a private house, for Cicero found it necessary to request that Atticus order his staff to allow Cicero access to Atticus's library, and in the second century AD Apuleius's friend Pontianus kept the room where he stored his books locked. It had to be opened by a servant (*promus librorum*) who had the key.[58]

Within the reading room of a large library, it is very likely that access to the bookcases and thus to the papyrus rolls was restricted to library personnel. Readers and scholars—those who wished to use the rolls—were not permitted to browse among the rolls. The evidence on this point is partly textual, partly archaeological. From anecdotes in Gellius and Fronto we learn that, at least in second-century Rome, manuscripts were brought by library personnel to the men who wanted to consult them.[59] In the remains of Roman-era libraries, as Strocka emphasizes repeatedly in his survey of library buildings, access to the bookcases and the rolls within them was apparently restricted. The bookcases were separated from the floor level by a podium; some shelves within the bookcases could only be reached with the help of a short ladder; and if there were upper levels of bookcases, access to them was provided by full ladders. All of this suggests that it was library personnel, not the scholars themselves, who fetched rolls and then returned them to the shelves.[60]

---

56. *SEG* 21.500.

57. Pfeiffer (1931), 163.

58. Atticus's library: Cic. *Att.* 4.14.1. Atticus's library may, of course, have been a special case. It is, however, startling to find that a man as eminent as Cicero, who was presumably well known to Atticus's household, might be denied access by them to the book collection. Pontianus's: Apul. *Apol.* 53.8.

59. Gell. *NA* 11.17; Gell. *NA* 13.20.1; Fronto *Ep.* 4.5. On these passages, see Houston (2004).

60. Strocka (2012), 168, discussing the library of Celsus in Ephesus, assumes that there were ladders to reach the second and third levels of bookcases, and argues that these ladders were only for the use of library personnel. On 172, he suggests that the book niches in the library at Timgad were made tall specifically to prevent readers from reaching the rolls by themselves. To reach the upper shelves, and perhaps even to have the cabinet unlocked, you would need the assistance of a staff member. It should be noted, however, that we do not know for sure how high the niches at Timgad were; the height is estimated from the width. Cf. ibid., 181 (supposed library in the Baths of Caracalla), 183

Housekeeping

Someone would need to keep floors, walls, and windows clean. Wooden cabinets and shelves might need preservative oils or repairs.[61] If mice or insect larvae infested the rolls, they would need to be eliminated, if they could be. Manuscripts needed to be protected against dampness and mildew.[62] Statues, busts, and other decorative elements all had to be kept clean and might need polishing. In an imperial villa certainly, and probably in many private villas as well, there were staff assigned specifically to maintain the statuary and other precious items throughout the villa, and we can assume that it was they, not the skilled scribal staff, who tended to the works of art in the library; but in smaller households those who worked with the manuscripts might be expected to maintain the book cabinets as well, along with any associated equipment or decoration.[63]

Any or all of these tasks, then, might be assigned to those members of a household who were expected to manage the manuscript collection, and in the great imperial libraries many such responsibilities fell to the men *a byb-liotheca*. We will need to keep in mind the potential activity in the library at this level—men moving around; bringing out book rolls from their cabinets, boxes, or other storage facilities; cleaning; working on repairs or copies; in short, some level of movement and noise—as we return now to consider the upper levels of library management.

6.4. THE EMPEROR'S COLLECTION

From the earliest years of the Roman Empire, the emperors owned a large and ever-growing collection of manuscripts, both Latin and Greek. We looked above at Augustus's first foundations, the Apollo and Octavia libraries. Both he and subsequent emperors evidently continued to acquire manuscripts, for they constructed a succession of individually named libraries to house the imperial collection. I turn now to the men who were

---

(library of Hadrian in Athens). In contrast, the library at Nysa had two wooden staircases leading to an upper level: ibid., 11.

61. Dust must have been a particular problem in dry climates, including north Africa and Egypt. Given this, we may wonder about Pfeiffer's assumption of an open-grille entrance door to the library in Timgad; it would be best to keep dust from blowing in in the first place.

62. Galen (*Ind.* 19) complains that the layers of papyrus in some rolls in the imperial library at Antium had become stuck to one another because of the damp conditions. See on this below, n. 129.

63. The staff of the imperial villa at Antium included an *a supellectile* and a *politor*, either or both of whom could have been given responsibility for maintaining the decorative elements in the Villa's library: *Fasti Antiates ministrorum domus Augustae, Insc.Ital.* 13.2, p. 207.

concerned with the management and administration of these libraries, beginning with the upper-level management and moving gradually down until we meet, once again, the men *a bybliotheca*.[64] Throughout, our questions are straightforward: how were the libraries administered, what responsibilities and tasks fell to each level of staff, and what significance did their administration and staffing have for the contents and users of the libraries?

The Emperor's Personal Involvement in the Libraries

The emperor was the owner of the collection, and in theory it would be he who made the choices concerning the subjects, authors, and titles he wanted in his collection. In practice, of course, most emperors will simply have accepted what their predecessors had done and appointed qualified men (whom we will meet shortly) to undertake the various tasks involved in acquiring and managing book rolls. We are occasionally reminded, however, of the potential for direct imperial action. If need arose, an emperor might intervene on a massive scale. Domitian sent an unknown but large number of scribes to Alexandria to obtain or make new copies of works that had been lost in a fire;[65] and every decision to build a new library building clearly involved imperial initiative. Sometimes, we are given anecdotes of emperors doing what we might call micromanaging. Augustus instructed Pompeius Macer not to allow the works that Julius Caesar had written as a youth to reach the hands of the public; presumably copies of them were to be kept, but locked away somewhere.[66] The works of Ovid were apparently *libelli non grati* in the imperial collections of Rome, on instructions from Augustus.[67] Tiberius ordered the works of three Greek poets—Euphorion, Rhianus, and Parthenius—to be added to the imperial libraries then in existence.[68]

---

64. I am concerned here with collections that were, at least in theory, made available to the general public. Libraries in imperial villas outside Rome may have been used by the emperor's family and friends, but we have no reason to believe that they were open to others on a regular basis, so they are not relevant here. The libraries known to us as open to the public are described in Callmer (1944); Dix and Houston (2006); and, in greater detail, Nicholls (forthcoming).

65. Suet. *Dom.* 20. This was probably the fire of AD 80.

66. Suet. *Iul.* 56.7.

67. Ovid represents the poems he wrote in exile as being refused entrance to the three great libraries then in existence (Apollo, Octavia, and Atrium Libertatis): Ov. *Tr.* 3.1.59–72. Analysis of the passage: Dix (1988).

68. Suet. *Tib.* 70.2; cf. Houston (2008), 255–59. Nicholls (2011), 140, n. 82, cites several further examples of emperors placing favorite works in the imperial libraries.

Commissioners of the Imperial Libraries in the City of Rome

Emperors, however, were busy men, and ordinarily they did not have the time to be involved in the day-to-day management of the imperial manuscript collection. From at least the time of Tiberius they therefore appointed men to oversee the collection on their behalf. These men were known, over the course of time, by a number of different titles—*supra bibliothecas omnes*, *a bibliothecis*, and *procurator bibliothecarum* are all attested—and in the discussion that follows I will, for convenience, use the English "commissioner" to refer to these men, rather than choosing any one of the titles the Romans used. We know the names and something of the careers of at least six such commissioners.[69] Unfortunately, no literary source, no anecdote, gives us even a fleeting glimpse of any of these men actually present, much less at work, in a library. What were their responsibilities? What did they do, from day to day? How, if at all, did they relate to and connect with the slaves *a bybliotheca*? We cannot provide definitive answers to these questions—the evidence is just not there—but the training, careers, and professional activities of these men enable us to draw some useful inferences about what they did and how they functioned.[70]

Ti(berius) Iulius Zoili f(ilius) Fab(ia tribu) Pappus. Known to us from an inscription of Aphrodisias in Asia Minor, Pappus was *comes* (adviser to or assistant of) the emperor Tiberius, and then "over (= in charge of) all the libraries of the emperors from Tiberius Caesar to Tiberius Claudius Caesar," that is, under Tiberius, Caligula, and Claudius, and from at latest AD 37 to at least 41.[71] No other positions are mentioned. The irregular nature of his library title, *supra bybliothecas omnes Augustorum*, suggests that he was the very first commissioner of all the libraries, and the need for such a com-

---

69. Other men have often been added to this group. They include Scirtus, an imperial freedman and *proc(urator) bybl(iothecarum)*, known from an inscription, *CIL* 10.1739; a certain Sextus mentioned by Martial, who seems to have had control over accessions in some library; and three equestrian procurators. I omit these men because they were by no means certainly commissioners of all the libraries and their careers are too problematic to serve as reliable evidence. See on them now Bowie (2013), 248–49 and 250 (Scirtus and Sextus respectively).

70. The official careers of these men and their various accomplishments have been studied repeatedly, and there is no need to include full discussions here. I deal only with matters that are relevant to our current concerns; for full treatments of the careers, the reader may consult Pflaum (1960–61) and the relevant articles in *RE* and *PIR*². Bowie (2013), 249–58, provides perceptive comments on the men, their careers, and their intellectual accomplishments.

71. *AE* 1960.26, republished with discussion by Panciera (1969): *Comes Ti. Caesaris Augusti; supr(a) bybliothecas omnes Augustorum ab Ti(berio) Caesare usque ad Ti(berium) Claudium Caesarem.* For *comes* as "adviser," see Panciera (1969), 113–14. On Pappus's family and career, see Smith (1993), 4–14.

missioner may have arisen when Tiberius decided to create a fourth imperial library, the one in the Templum Novum Divi Augusti.[72]

Dionysius, son of Glaucus, of Alexandria (Pflaum [1960–61], 111–12). Known from an entry in the *Suda*, s.v. Dionysios, D 1173 Adler: "A *grammaticus*; he was in charge of the libraries and he became head of the office of the emperor's correspondence and in charge of receiving, and responding to, embassies and legations."[73] Dionysius was first and foremost, then, a *grammaticus*, that is, a teacher and scholar. Later in this passage in the *Suda*, we learn that before he moved to Rome he was a student of the Stoic philosopher Chaeremon, whom he succeeded as head of a school or institute, probably but not certainly the Museum in Alexandria. We do not know exactly when Dionysius moved from Alexandria to Rome, nor precisely when he was commissioner of the libraries; the best we can do is date him in the second half of the first century A D.[74]

If the order of posts listed in the *Suda* can be trusted, Dionysius's very first administrative post was as commissioner of the libraries. The positions he held after that, whatever their exact titles, involved dealing largely or exclusively with written documents, but they may also suggest that Dionysius was a specialist in Greek affairs, or, as Pflaum put it, "chef du cabinet impérial pour les affaires grecques."

Gaius Suetonius Tranquillus (Pflaum [1960–61], 219–24). This is the imperial biographer. A badly damaged honorary inscription gives us most of his career: he was *flamen* of an unknown emperor or divinity; adlected *inter selectos* (that is, appointed) to the panel of equestrian jurors at Rome by Trajan;[75] *pontifex Volcanalis* in a town that cannot be identified; *a studiis*; *a bybliothecis*; and *ab epistulis* of Hadrian.[76] Of the numerous uncer-

---

72. Houston (2008), 250–54.

73. Γραμματικός: τῶν βιβλιοθηκῶν προύστη καὶ ἐπὶ τῶν ἐπιστολῶν καὶ πρεσβειῶν ἐγένετο καὶ ἀποκριμάτων. The exact Latin titles, and thus the precise English meanings, of the positions held by Dionysius are not certain, but seem to have been something like *a bibliothecis, ab epistulis et responsis ad legationes*, as suggested by Stein in *PIR*[2], D 103.

74. Chaeremon may have moved from Alexandria to Rome to serve as a tutor to Nero: Barrett (1996), 106–7. That would be in the 40s A D, and it would be about then that Dionysius became head of the school in Alexandria, and sometime later that he followed Chaeremon to Rome. Lewis (1981), 159, dated all of Dionysius's posts under Nero. Pflaum (1960–61), 112, suggested that Dionysius moved to Rome only in A D 70. In that case, his library post would have been under the Flavians.

75. All that survives on the stone of this adlection is -*NT*-, and, as Pflaum pointed out, the -*NT*- might be restored not as *[adlectus i]nt[er selectos]*, but as *[adlectus i]nt[er comites]*, which would mean that Suetonius was chosen to be one of the emperor's advisers. A man who was "adlected" was (to put it briefly) appointed to or chosen to be a member of a political or social group, such as a college of priests, or the Senate, or, as here, the jurors or imperial advisers. For the many types of adlection, see *Diz. Epig.* 1.411–22, s.v. *allectio*.

76. *AE* 1953, 73 (Hippo, in north Africa). There is a lacuna after *Volcanalis*, leaving space for some

tainties in this career, two are of particular interest to us. First, the date of Suetonius's library position, which (depending upon how the rest of his career is construed) may have been sometime before 122, perhaps in part under Trajan; or about ten years later.[77] In neither case do we know how long he served. Second, it has been suggested that Suetonius served as *a studiis* and *a bybliothecis* simultaneously, and that must be regarded as a real, if unprovable, possibility.[78]

Suetonius's official career was brief, three or four posts that in all likelihood occupied no more than a dozen years, and perhaps less. Before, during, and probably after his official career, he was active as a scholar, and he was a prolific writer and one of the leading Roman literary men of his day.[79] We may note also that Suetonius seems to have been a member of Hadrian's court and perhaps one of his advisers: he certainly served as *ab epistulis* under Hadrian, and an anecdote in the *Historia Augusta* about Suetonius's dismissal indicates that he was closely involved in affairs at court.[80]

Valerius Eudaemon (Pflaum [1960–61], 264–71). Valerius Eudaemon first comes to our attention at the time of Trajan's death and Hadrian's succession. He seems to have been in Cilicia with Hadrian when Trajan died (AD 117) and to have assisted Hadrian in the accession; and his first known official post, attested on two inscriptions, has been interpreted as showing that Hadrian immediately sent Eudaemon to Egypt to assume the financial administration there and help secure the wealth of the province for Hadrian.[81] We may date this post roughly in the period 117–120.[82] Eudaemon's next post, presumably in about 120–122, was his library position. He is the first commissioner known to have been called *procurator bibliothecarum*.

Following his term as commissioner of libraries, Eudaemon served as *ab epistulis Graecis* (assisting Hadrian with his correspondence in Greek) and

---

other post before *a studiis*. For an extended treatment of the inscription and of Suetonius's life and career, see Bradley (1991), 3701–32, with career on 3704–13.

77. Earlier chronology: Pflaum (1960–61), 223. Later: Lindsay (1994), 459–64.

78. See Van't Dack (1963), 183–84.

79. Full details: Sallmann (1997), 16–49. Suetonius's works included biographies and works on Greek and Roman antiquities, institutions, words, and (in Greek) insults. In the *Suda* Suetonius is defined first as a *grammaticus*, just as Dionysius is: *Suda*, s.v. Τράγκυλλος, T 895 Adler.

80. *SHA Hadr.* 11.3. Suetonius, at the time *ab epistulis*, and several other men were dismissed by Hadrian because of some indiscretion that involved Hadrian's wife Sabina.

81. Eudaemon in Cilicia: *SHA Hadr.* 15.3, calling him *conscius imperii*, which Birley (1997), 79, interprets as meaning "an accomplice in gaining the throne." The two inscriptions are *CIL* 3.431 and *IGRR* 3.1077.

82. Birley (1997), 79, reconstructs the sequence of events.

then in a long series of important procuratorships.[83] The *Historia Augusta* tells us that he fell out of favor with Hadrian late in Hadrian's reign, but he resumed his career under Antoninus Pius, serving as prefect of Egypt from 142 to 143 or 144.[84] All of Eudaemon's posts were in Rome or the Greek East, none was a military position, and most involved substantial financial responsibilities. Eudaemon worked closely with Hadrian as *ab epistulis Graecis*, and both of the anecdotes in the *Historia Augusta* indicate that he was a close associate of the emperor. We have no evidence that he was a scholar or a writer.

Lucius Iulius Vestinus (Pflaum [1960–61], 245–47). We know nothing about the early stages of Vestinus's career, but a Greek inscription from Rome, now lost, lists his senior posts: "High priest of Alexandria and of all Egypt, director of the Museum (at Alexandria), commissioner of the Latin and Greek libraries in Rome; *a studiis* of the emperor Hadrian; head of correspondence of the same emperor."[85] We cannot date the career or the library post exactly. Vestinus's last two positions, *a studiis* and *ab epistulis*, fell in Hadrian's principate, but whether early in the reign or later, with the library post ca. 130–35, we do not know.[86] We do know that Vestinus was a famous sophist and that he wrote several lexicographical works.[87] His posts *a studiis* and *ab epistulis*, both under Hadrian, indicate that he worked closely with that emperor for at least part of his career.

Lucius Volusius L(uci) f(ilius) Maecianus (Pflaum [1960–61], 333–36). Volusius Maecianus had a long and distinguished career in the imperial administration, was one of the outstanding jurists of his day, and served simultaneously as *a studiis* and *procurator bibliothecarum* early in the reign of Antoninus Pius, ca. 140–46.[88] Passing over his junior positions, we may consider the more senior ones, which all fall in the reign of Antoninus Pius. In chronological order, these are prefect of the imperial post; *a studiis*

---

83. He may also have been prefect of the grain supply: Pavis d'Escurac (1976), 341.

84. Falling out with Hadrian: *SHA Hadr.* 15.3. Prefect of Egypt: papyri, listed in Bastianini (1975), 289.

85. *IGUR* 1.62 (= *IGRR* 1.136), known only from a ninth-century copy which does not seem to have preserved the full text. The Latin equivalents of the Greek titles on the inscription are *Archiereus Alexandreiae omnisque Aegypti*; *curator Musei*; *a bibliothecis Latinis et Graecis Romae*; *a studiis Hadriani imperatoris*; *ab epistulis imperatoris eiusdem*.

86. Early date (immediately after Suetonius): Birley (1997), 142; later date, ca. AD 134: Pflaum (1960–61), 246. Bowie (2013), 253–55, provides an excellent discussion of Vestinus as literary figure and points out a previously unnoticed inscription from Smyrna that may well mention him.

87. *Suda* s.v. Οὐηστῖνος, O 835 Adler.

88. Career: known chiefly from *CIL* 14.5347 and *AE* 1955.179, both from Ostia. For additional sources, see Pavis d'Escurac (1976), 346–47.

and (at the same time) commissioner of the libraries; in charge of petitions and censuses (also simultaneously); member of the college of minor pontiffs (priests of equestrian rank); prefect of the grain supply; prefect of Egypt; jurisconsult; granted senatorial rank; prefect of the Treasury of Saturn; and chosen to become consul.[89] He was an *amicus principis* and member of the emperor's *consilium* under Pius and Marcus Aurelius.[90] Maecianus is the only man who was certainly *a studiis* and commissioner of libraries simultaneously, although Suetonius and Iulius Vestinus may have been. One of Marcus's teachers and a legal adviser to both Pius and Marcus,[91] Maecianus produced various legal treatises, among them fourteen books on the standing criminal courts and sixteen on bequests.[92]

6.5. THE COMMISSIONERS OF THE IMPERIAL LIBRARIES

I begin with some things that are not found in these careers. No senator or man of senatorial rank is known to have been involved in the library administration at any time, at any level. No emperor, so far as we know, thought fit to appoint a *curator bibliothecarum*, parallel to the senatorial *curatores* of public works, of roads, or of the bed and banks of the Tiber, nor were young senators ever assigned to assist in the libraries at a lower level. This should not be taken as a sign that the libraries were considered unimportant, for equestrians were certainly entrusted with some crucial administrative posts. They controlled the grain supply, governed Egypt, and commanded the praetorian cohorts, all posts critical to the stability of the imperial system. Rather, the absence of senators in the libraries suggests that, in the Roman mind, these libraries were intended not so much for the use of people in general as for the internal working of the administration. The post *a bibliothecis* is parallel to, and sometimes associated directly with, other important Palatine posts, such as the *a studiis*, the *ab epistulis*, and the *a libellis*, none of which provided a service used directly by the

---

89. *Praefectus vehiculorum; a studiis et procurator bibliothecarum; a libellis et censibus; pontifex minor; praefectus annonae; praefectus Aegypti; iuris consultus;* adlected into the Senate; *praefectus aerari Saturni; consul designatus.* The adlection into the Senate is not mentioned in the inscription but can be inferred from his position as prefect of the Treasury of Saturn, since only senators could hold that prefectureship. (For adlections, see n. 75 above.) Maecianus's prefectureship in Egypt can be dated in 161: Bastianini (1975), 295. We do not know if he lived to be consul.

90. *Dig.* 37.14.17 *praef.* (Ulpian).

91. *SHA Marc.* 3.6; Honoré (1994), 16, for Maecianus as Marcus's teacher. For his work as adviser, note Honoré (1994), 18–19.

92. Sallmann (1997), 131–33.

general public, but all of which were important to the internal functioning of the principate.[93]

Only one of the commissioners is known to have held a military position when he was young (Maecianus, prefect of a cohort); it is possible that Suetonius, Vestinus, or Eudaemon held one or more of the preliminary equestrian military posts, although in no case is this probable. Nor do the men who were appointed as library commissioners seem to have been made governors of equestrian provinces, such as Noricum or the Mauretanias.[94] No known commissioner of libraries ever served as either commander of a fleet (*praefectus classis*) or praetorian prefect. These are not military men.

Commissioners and Finances

Men of equestrian rank were often appointed to positions requiring financial expertise, but that is not true of our subgroup of library commissioners. Only one of the six known commissioners had a career that involved a succession of financial positions. This is Valerius Eudaemon, who was in Egypt, probably in an administrative and financial post, before he became *procurator bibliothecarum*, and then served as financial procurator in at least three Eastern provinces after his library post. Two other library commissioners—Vestinus and Maecianus—held administrative posts that would have involved some financial responsibilities, but as a group the commissioners of libraries known to us do not seem to have been particularly experienced in financial affairs.

There is good reason for this: library commissioners did not need financial experience or expertise. To be sure, there must have been ongoing expenses in the libraries—for papyrus, ink, paste, equipment including stools, chairs, carrying cases, and the like—but these are minor matters, not likely to result in complicated bookkeeping.[95] In addition, the commissioners of libraries had no staff to assist them with financial affairs. We do not find, in any library context, any of the slave or freedman staff who are so charac-

93. Cf. Pflaum (1950), 253–54, on the salaries given these officials. He took all of them as ducenarian.

94. At least two, Eudaemon and Maecianus, became prefects of Egypt. That, however, was a special appointment, not an ordinary provincial governorship. It could be entrusted only to a highly competent man whose loyalty to the emperor could be taken for granted.

95. Maintenance of the buildings themselves was probably the responsibility of the *fiscus* or was financed through the private resources of the emperor: Kolb (1993), 134. An entirely new building would be funded, we must assume, by the emperor. The library commissioner may well have played an important role, though, in the decision to build.

teristic of financial and administrative offices in other areas of the imperial administration: there are no *dispensatores* (cash handlers), *rationales* (accountants), *tabularii* (secretaries), or the like. The library commissioners were not, so far as we can tell, the heads of administrative offices.[96]

How then were library expenses handled? Frontinus tells us that imperial slaves who worked on the aqueducts (*aquae*) received their subsistence allowances (*commoda*), supplies (specifically, lead for water pipes), and funds for other necessities from the *fiscus*, so that the bookkeeping and cash management will have been done by the *fiscus*, not by the personnel of the *aquae*. This was almost certainly true of the libraries as well.[97] Our commissioners, then, did not direct and oversee the work of a financial office; rather, part of their job will have been to communicate by letter, by messenger, or in person with appropriate persons in the imperial administration in order to arrange for the purchase and delivery of supplies and equipment. Given that their needs were limited and their expenses relatively small, this cannot have been difficult.

Commissioners as Advisers

There are several indications that the library commissioner was an important member of the emperor's inner circle of advisers. First, the commissioners were paid well: Volusius Maecianus certainly, and other second-century commissioners probably, were paid two hundred thousand sesterces per year, the second-highest equestrian salary in the Roman administration.[98] Second, even though the post of library commissioner was sometimes the very first administrative position these men held, they were by no

96. Cf. Houston (2002), 152–54. No source, epigraphical, legal, or literary, ever mentions a *ratio bibliothecarum* (which would, if it existed, be the Roman term for the administrative office of the libraries).

97. Frontin. *Aq.* 118. I use the term *fiscus* because Frontinus does. It is a useful way of referring to all of the funds available for imperial projects, whatever title those funds might be given. In practical terms, *fiscus* probably meant, for our librarians, the *ratio castrensis* (central Palatine administrative and financial establishment) in the first century, and the *patrimonium* or *res privata* or both from some point in the second century. On this matter, see Kolb (1993), 134. For the *ratio castrensis* as a central administrative and financial office, see Boulvert (1970), 164–78. For the *res privata* in connection with libraries, note the problematic third-century inscription *CIL* 6.2132: *proc(urator) rat(ionum) summ(arum) privatarum bibliothecarum Augusti n(ostri)*, in which the libraries may be associated with the *rationes privatae*. If that is the case, funding for the libraries would seem to come from the personal resources of the emperors. See, however, Bowie (2013), 259, n. 110, for an alternative interpretation of this inscription.

98. Pflaum (1960–61), 1023. We know too little about the first-century commissioners to be able to determine their salaries.

means young and inexperienced when they came to it. Pappus was probably fifty to sixty years old, and had for some years been an adviser or assistant of Tiberius;[99] Dionysius and Suetonius were both established scholars before they became commissioner;[100] Vestinus was an eminent scholar who served as director of the library in Alexandria before moving to Rome; and Maecianus held five lower-level equestrian posts, at least four of them quite unusual and implying imperial favor, before taking the positions of *a studiis* and *procurator bibliothecarum*, which he held simultaneously.[101] Third, as we saw above, the post *a bibliothecis* is comparable, in terms of its perceived importance in the administration, to other Palatine posts, such as the *a studiis* and *ab epistulis*, both of which were held by men who worked directly with the emperor. Finally, the commissioners often were close advisers or associates of the emperor, sometimes even before they acceded to the library post. Pappus was *comes Tiberi*, Eudaemon *conscius imperi*; Suetonius was perhaps all too closely connected to life at court; Maecianus was *amicus principis* and one of Marcus Aurelius's teachers. The commissioners of libraries, then, seem to have been highly valued by the emperors, so we should try to gauge what library-related services they could have provided to warrant their generous salaries and position at court.

Commissioners who were scholars—and that would be most of those known to us—could advise the emperor on matters both large and small that pertained to the imperial book collection. If a large collection of manuscripts passed to the emperor through bequest, marriage, or confiscation, how should it be handled? Should it be kept intact, should it be divided among existing libraries, or should it be shelved among the volumes already in one of the libraries? Might an entire new library building be needed? The commissioner could help the emperor sort through the problems and possible solutions.

On a simpler level, the commissioners might provide the kind of advice Cicero seems to have wanted from Tyrannio and Chrysippus: guidance on the strengths and weaknesses of the existing collection; recommendations on works or authors to be acquired; and assessments of the accuracy

99. Smith (1993), 4–14, and in particular 8, argues that Pappus was born about 25 or 30 BC, and he was put in charge of the libraries probably in the 30s AD.

100. Dionysius, like his teacher Chaeremon, came to Rome only after making his reputation in Alexandria. Trajan granted Suetonius the *ius trium liberorum* ca. 112, or some years before he became commissioner, at least in part in recognition of his erudition (Plin. *Ep.* 10.94, 95).

101. On Maecianus's earlier posts and their unusual nature, see Pflaum (1960–61), 334. Particularly telling was his post as secretary for petitions to Antoninus Pius while Hadrian was still alive. Clearly he was, at least at that time, a close associate of Pius.

and authenticity of particular manuscripts.[102] If an emperor had special requests—works or authors to be acquired or discarded or never allowed in—it might fall to the commissioner to see that his wishes were carried out.[103] The commissioner could help the emperor on questions the answers to which could be found in books, such as matters of history, law, grammar, technology, or science,[104] and since libraries then as now sometimes housed archival materials, there might be questions of precedent or constitutional matters that the commissioners could help with. These men were intelligent; they read widely and had a broad range of knowledge; and they could be relied on (because of their position) to be available in Rome, so they would be useful as a source of ideas and a sounding board for proposals.[105]

6.6. THE COMMISSIONER AND THE SLAVES *A BYBLIOTHECA*

Thus far, we have considered ways in which the commissioner of libraries might have interacted with, and some of the services he could have provided for, the emperor. There is, however, a second aspect of the commissioner's job. He was, after all, an administrator as well as an adviser, and somehow he must have communicated policy decisions to the imperial and public slaves who worked in the libraries, that is, to the men *a bybliotheca* whom we looked at earlier. In practice, how might this have been done? In theory, the emperor could have appointed lower-level equestrians, perhaps young men at the very beginning of their careers, as directors of the individual libraries, and those men could have provided a link between the commissioner of all libraries and the slave staff in the individual libraries.[106] In sup-

---

102. Cicero and his advisers: above, section 6.2. Such advice would be especially helpful when the emperor was rebuilding a collection that had been destroyed in a fire, as we know Domitian did.

103. Caligula came close to banishing the works of Vergil and Livy from all the libraries (Suet. *Calig.* 34.2). The commissioner of libraries at that time was Pappus, and we might guess that Pappus played a role in dissuading Caligula from pursuing this policy. Given Caligula's unpredictable temper, that may well have been a touchy matter.

104. In so doing the *a bibliothecis* may seem much like the *a studiis*, for whose duties see Wallace-Hadrill (1983), 83–86. This may help explain why three of the known library commissioners served also as *a studiis*. For the kinds of assistance Republican-era library owners needed when they were involved in research, see Horsfall (1995), 53.

105. It is worth noting that the Roman emperors do not seem to have tried to rival the library at Alexandria in their appointments. While the men chosen as commissioner were generally scholars, and some of them excellent, they were not necessarily the equal of Eratosthenes, or even the most outstanding scholars and scientists of their own day, such as Ptolemy the geographer and the physician Galen.

106. There were subprocurators, *adiutores*, and the like in other areas of the imperial administration. Examples: *subcurator operum publicorum*, Pflaum (1960–61), 1028; *adiutor praefecti annonae*, Pflaum (1960–61), 1030.

port of such a thesis, we know of three men who may have been directors of individual libraries. Gaius Annius Postumus was perhaps procurator of the Templum Divi Traiani library under Hadrian;[107] Baebius Aurelius Iuncinus was a sexagenarian (and thus low-ranking) *procurator bibliothecarum* (i.e., *Graecae et Latinae?*);[108] and Titus Aelius Largus is attested as *proc(urator) Aug(usti) bybliothecaru[m]* on an inscription that probably dates from late in the second or early in the third century AD.[109] The exact responsibilities of each of these men are uncertain, however, and both Postumus and Iuncinus have also been taken as commissioners of all the libraries. To omit the details (which are more relevant to the history of the imperial administration than to our present concerns), there is no reason to believe that there were equestrian directors in each library on a regular basis, although the emperor may occasionally have appointed men as directors in response to specific circumstances and needs.[110]

Still, there must have been some mechanism for the transmission of policy decisions and orders from the emperor and his commissioner to the slave staff in the several libraries. If libraries were not ordinarily directed by procurators of equestrian rank, who might have provided this contact and organized the work in each library? Several of the men *a bybliotheca* known to us are called *vilicus*, and perhaps it was the *vilici*—one for the Greek and the other for the Latin collection—who served as supervisors in the individual libraries. The title itself suggests a position of real though limited authority, because we know that *vilici* served as managers in other contexts: they were sometimes responsible for a particular building or structure, and sometimes in charge of a group of slaves, to whom they would presumably distribute the tasks that needed to be done.[111] The *vilicus a byblio-*

107. *CIL* 14.5352 (Ostia): *proc(urator) bibliothecarum divi Traiani*, implying director of the (Greek and Latin) libraries at the Templum Divi Traiani. But he is also known from *CIL* 8.20684 (Saldae in Mauretania) as *[p]roc(urator) Aug(usti) a bybliothecis*; and that implies that he was commissioner of all the libraries. Further discussion in Pflaum (1960–61), 316–19; Bowie (2013), 250–51. I take Postumus as most likely a director of the Trajan library, appointed by Hadrian for a specific term or task now lost to us, but the matter cannot be resolved conclusively.

108. *CIL* 10.7580, from late in the second century. "Sexagenarian" here means that he was paid 60,000 sesterces per year, the lowest level of pay for equestrians in the imperial administration. Iuncinus's title is ambiguous and has been variously interpreted. That he was procurator of all libraries seems unlikely given his youth and salary; and that he was director of a single library is unlikely given that no library is named on his inscription, which is otherwise quite detailed.

109. *CIL* 14.2916.

110. Systematic review of the evidence: Houston (2002), 168–72. Iulius Africanus states that he was appointed by the emperor for a specific task in connection with the library *in Pantheo*: *Cestoi*, fragment of Book 18 (= Vieillefond [1970], 284–91).

111. Carlsen (1995), 27–55.

theca might have been responsible for the book collection, stacks, and other slave personnel in a given library, although not for the maintenance of the library buildings themselves. Perhaps it was they who controlled access to the libraries, maintained the collection through the assignments they gave to the other slaves, and met with and assisted users, or gave orders to others to assist them. The *vilici*, in short, may have served as the means of communication between emperor or commissioner on the one hand and slaves *a bybliotheca* on the other.

We have now moved down the ladder of control in the imperial collections, from emperor, through the commissioners he appointed, to possible supervisors in individual libraries, and finally to the men *a bybliotheca*. Several further things need to be said about the last, for they must have been the personnel most commonly encountered in the imperial libraries. The slaves *a bybliotheca* were in many respects a privileged group. As members of the *familia Caesaris* or as *servi publici*, and not just ordinary household slaves, they enjoyed a certain status. Their jobs and lives were relatively stable and secure: they had a place to live, clothing, and food; they had the right to a *peculium* and could make legally valid wills.[112] The very term *a bybliotheca* suggests a title rather than the description of a menial task (such as *glutinator*, which we will come to below). Above all, working in a library might well provide occasional access to important men, and serving such men efficiently could lead to tips, gifts, and favors returned.[113]

In addition to the men *a bybliotheca*, it is possible that there were other workers in the imperial libraries, because there is epigraphical evidence for four *glutinatores* in the context of imperial villas outside of Rome, and some of the many *librarii* known from inscriptions could have worked in libraries or been assigned to libraries as need arose.[114] Similarly, slaves and freedmen of various sorts—*anagnostae* (readers), *tabularii* (messengers), and others—were probably assigned by Cicero and Atticus to work in their

112. Status: Weaver (1972), 5. Food and other perquisites: Boulvert (1974), 114. In general on *servi publici* and their benefits: Halkin (1897), 130–35.

113. The young Marcus Aurelius used the Apollo library and expected his teacher, the famous scholar Fronto, to use the library in the Domus Tiberiana: Fronto *Ep.* 4.5.2. The celebrated physician Galen haunted the libraries of Rome and must have dealt with the staff frequently.

114. Slave *glutinatores* in the imperial villa at Antium: *Insc.Ital.* 13.2, p. 205 (AD 38). A slave *glutinator* of Tiberius, perhaps from a villa on the Bay of Naples: *CIL* 10.1735. A *glutinator* probably in an imperial villa at Tusculum: *Insc.Ital.* 13.1, p. 302. For *librarii*, see *Diz.Epig.* s.v. *librarius*, 960–61 (R. F. Rossi). There are uncertainties: no *librarius* attested in an inscription is ever explicitly assigned to a library; and we cannot be sure that the *glutinatores* we hear of in inscriptions worked on book rolls, because the words *gluten* and *glutinum* were used not only for "library paste" but also for "carpenter's glue" and other adhesives (Plin. *HN* 16.225–26 and 33.94).

libraries from time to time.[115] In the case of the imperial libraries, however, the evidence is so slim that we can draw no firm conclusions.

We do not know how many men worked in the imperial libraries of Rome. Were there just two men in each library at a time, one for the Greek and the other for the Latin collection? Were there two men *a bybliotheca* plus other, untitled, slaves assigned to help them on an occasional basis? Or were there numerous workers in each library? On this matter, there is no direct evidence for the early Empire, but in late antiquity, the emperor Valens issued an edict specifying that the imperial library in Constantinople should have seven scribes (*antiquarii*), four for Greek and three for Latin. The scribes, Valens specified, were to occupy themselves both in creating new codices and in repairing old ones, and other men (*condicionales*) were to be found and assigned to other tasks (*bibliothecae custodia*) in the library;[116] those tasks presumably included the various nonscribal tasks I outlined above. We cannot know how many new codices Valens hoped would be created, but the figure of seven scribes is helpful: there is not just one scribe, and there are not dozens of them. Some such number—seven or thereabouts—seems reasonable for established libraries in Rome of the first two centuries AD as well, but we cannot be more precise than that.[117]

Inscriptions that mention men *a bybliotheca* do not appear after the time of Hadrian.[118] We do not know why this is so, but it is possible that at a certain point the emperors regularized the staffing of the libraries, appointing not domestic slaves but administrative personnel. These could well have continued to be members of the *familia Caesaris*, but their titles might have changed, or they might have been given no titles at all.[119] In a similar development, the evidence concerning the upper levels of the administration

---

115. So Dix (1986), 135.

116. *Cod. Theod.* 14.9.2, an edict of AD 372: *Antiquarios ad bibliothecae codices componendos vel pro vetustate reparandos quattuor Graecos et tres Latinos scribendi peritos iubemus . . . ad eiusdem bibliothecae custodiam condicionalibus et requirendis et protinus adponendis.* Each such worker was to be given a suitable subsistence allowance.

117. Lenski (2002), 269, with n. 34, following Janin and Vanderspoel, suggested that seven scribes were needed because the library had been founded only about ten years earlier and so still had only a limited collection. Julian, however, had given all of his books to the library when he founded it, and Valens's scribes were to be employed not just in making new codices, but in repairing old ones. The number of scribes, seven, does not seem to be large enough to turn out great numbers of new manuscripts.

118. The latest known is a *vilicus* [*a byblio*]*theca* known from a dedicatory inscription dated AD 126, *CIL* 6.8744.

119. For the distinction between domestic and administrative personnel in the *familia Caesaris*, see Weaver (1972), 5–7. Weaver originally took all of the men *a bybliotheca* to be administrative, but at a later point saw them as domestic: Houston (2002), 150–51, with n. 19.

becomes more difficult to interpret after the time of Antoninus Pius, and there may have been significant changes. The evidence, however, does not allow us to make confident inferences concerning the internal workings of the imperial libraries and is therefore not considered here.[120]

6.7. TROUBLES IN THE LIBRARIES

So far, we have considered libraries and the staff in them in normal times, when things were going well. But things could and did go awry. As we have seen, readers might tear rolls while reading them, and staff could damage them by placing them on their shelves or in their containers carelessly. We have seen evidence of this sort of damage, both direct (rolls that have been torn and repaired) and indirect (gaps in texts that imply faulty or damaged exemplars). In this section, I will explore a number of additional problems. Some of them are less obvious, some are potentially more harmful, and some could be disastrous.

When an owner or visitor requested a manuscript, one of the staff would need to retrieve it from its cabinet or from storage.[121] This was not always a straightforward or easy task. Collections were often and perhaps regularly organized by genre and then alphabetically by author and title, but there could be complications. At the Villa of the Papyri, for example, certain multivolume works had titles—*On Vices* was one, *Epitome of Characters and Lives* another—but individual books within them had their own titles (or what we might call subtitles), too. *On Flattery* was Book 1 of *On Vices*, *On Frank Speech* apparently one of the books in the *Epitome of Characters and Lives*.[122] How was a roll that had both a general title (*On Vices*, for example) and its own subtitle (*On Flattery*) assigned a place when it was shelved or stored? Which title would determine the roll's position in the stacks, *Vices* or *Flattery*?[123] In the lists we examined in chapter 2, we found no subtitles, but the number of books in a work was often indicated. Similarly, in the final and initial titles of manuscripts from the Villa of the Papyri, the book number seems always to be included when a work consists of more than one book, whereas subtitles are rare and not consistently

---

120. Summary comments concerning these later administrators: Houston (2002), 170–72; Bowie (2013), 258.

121. In the case of small personal collections, the owner himself may have done the shelving and retrieving, but the problems that could arise would be more or less the same.

122. References and additional examples will be found above in section 3.3.

123. In this case, as it happens, there would be little difference, because the Greek words both begin with the letter kappa, but that would seldom be the case.

entered.[124] Subtitles, that is, do not seem to have been regarded as essential, whereas the book number was. It seems likely, then, that book rolls in the Villa were arranged by the title of the comprehensive work—*On Vices*, *Epitome of Characters*, and so on—and then by book number, with the subtitle ignored in the shelving process. Whatever the usual practice, though, an inattentive slave, reading a subtitle instead of the title of the whole work, might easily put a roll on the wrong shelf.

Similarly, opisthographs and rolls containing more than one work might cause problems. In the list of mostly Platonic dialogues in *PSI Laur.* inv. 19662 verso (chapter 2, list 7), we find, it seems, one roll containing both a *Parmenides* and an *Anacharsis* (line 7), and another (line 11) that contained *Hippiases* 2 and *Eudemus*. The only known *Anacharsis* is by Lucian, not Plato, and the *Eudemus* is by Aristotle. It would appear that a decision was made in each case to privilege the Platonic text, since that is the one listed first; but that leaves the *Anacharsis* and *Eudemus* in a kind of limbo: they were listed, and presumably shelved, with works by Plato, not with other works by Lucian and Aristotle respectively. To find these works, one would need to read through the whole book list, or perhaps a staff member would simply remember where they were. Book rolls, in short, could cause difficulties for anyone trying to sort and classify them. Someone working with the collection would need to make decisions, and other staff members, both then and later, would need to be aware of those decisions.[125]

Another set of potential problems is suggested by Galen's statement that certain specific materials within the libraries on the Palatine—ones that he calls the Callinia, Atticiana, and Peducaeana—were destroyed in the fire of AD 192.[126] It is possible that these materials were separated out from the general Palatine collection and shelved as coherent and identifiable sub-collections.[127] If that is the case, then there were at least two major systems

124. In *PHerc.* 1008 and *PHerc.* 1424, for example, the overall title is given in the *subscriptio*, but the title of the individual book is not. See above, section 3.3, with n. 28.

125. It is useful to recall that some manuscripts were opisthographs as we try to understand anecdotes related by Aulus Gellius. In *NA* 13.20.1, Gellius tells how he and his friends were brought a book roll that contained, to their surprise, works by a certain M. Cato Nepos. The cause of their surprise? Perhaps the slave attendant simply brought out the wrong book roll; or perhaps the book roll contained more than one work, both the one they requested and the works by Cato Nepos. My thanks to Kerr Houston for the latter suggestion.

126. *Ind.* 13. On these collections, presumably named after the men who either had the copies in them made or collected the manuscripts, see above, introduction, n. 32 and associated text; on the text of Galen, see Stramaglia (2011), 120–21.

127. So Nicholls (2011), 133. I agree with him, but it remains possible that these volumes were not stored together as identifiable collections, but scattered through the whole collection and identifiable by some sort of notation in the manuscripts or their *sillyba*.

of classifying manuscripts in use in the Palatine collections: by genre and author; and by named collection. This would present a challenge to any staff member(s) who tried to compile an inventory of the Palatine collection. Were these rolls—those in the Atticiana, say—listed along with all the other book rolls in a single list, with their special status noted in the list? Or was there a separate list for each of the named collections? If they were stored separately, a slave sent to fetch a book roll would need to know where that collection was to be found, and the slave who shelved the roll would need to know, too, or the manuscript might be misshelved and, at least temporarily, lost.[128]

Not all staff were competent and responsible. Galen tells us that, when he visited the imperial library at Antium in order to make copies of certain texts, he found that some rolls had deteriorated seriously due to dampness. The staff had evidently not taken proper care of the book rolls. Worse, when he returned to the Antium collection some twenty-five years later, he found that many of the rolls were now completely useless: the dampness had seeped into the papyrus rolls and caused the layers to stick to one another so that they could not be unrolled (*Ind.* 17–19).[129] This, Galen says, was due to the incompetence or carelessness of several successive groups of staff. He was, needless to say, outraged at the mistreatment of the book rolls, and, if what he says is true, it is a serious indictment of the imperial slaves and freedmen who were in charge of the library at Antium. As Enzo Puglia put it, the most important function of library staff was to unroll and shake out the volumes from time to time; but here in the imperial villa at Antium we find a whole collection that for many years had not been maintained in even the most minimal of ways.[130]

128. There is a possibility that parts of the Palatine collections were stored not in the main hall within the precinct of Apollo, but rather in storerooms (*apothecae*) in the imperial warehouses at the foot and along the flanks of the Palatine: Tucci (2013), 293–96. This is an attractive suggestion. It would help explain why Galen pays so much attention to the destruction of warehouses in the fire (e.g., at *Ind.* 18); and we saw above in chapter 2 hints that collections were sometimes divided between two separate places of storage.

129. The passage is corrupt in the manuscript, creating two main problems: what library or libraries did Galen have in mind, and what exactly happened to it or them? Boudon-Millot and Jouanna (2010), xxii–xxviii and 71–73, provided a text that limited the libraries to ones in Rome and argued that there was damage due not just to the fire, but also to thefts by staff members. I follow the suggestions of Puglia (2011); he in turn accepted the arguments of Jones (2009), 393–97; Stramaglia (2011), 132–35; and Roselli (2010), 146, with n. 87. Together, they argue that one of the libraries Galen used was in the imperial villa at Antium, that it was that library (and not one in Rome) that had suffered from dampness, and that the text does not say that staff had stolen items, but that the staff at Antium had been in charge, year after year, as the manuscripts deteriorated due to the damp.

130. Puglia (2011), 59–60.

As valuable objects, book rolls were an obvious target of theft and needed to be guarded carefully. Galen tells us that he and at least one other scholar rented storerooms in the imperial warehouses near the Palatine in good part because the warehouses also contained imperial archives and were consequently guarded by soldiers.[131] The fourth-century orator Libanius had a copy of Thucydides of which he was particularly fond. It was small, in fine script, and he was in the habit of carrying it to his lectures, but, he tells us, thieves broke into his house and stole it.[132] Dismayed, Libanius asked his friends to watch for it, and eventually one of them recognized it in the hands of a student, who had bought it secondhand.[133] Thus it made its way back to Libanius. Whole libraries could disappear. In the fourth century (to make a long story short), a certain Bishop George was killed and his books were stolen.[134] The emperor Julian hoped to recover the books and recommended that George's slave scribe (νοτάριος) be put in charge of identifying the thieves and recovering the book rolls.[135] Presumably, Julian expected that the scribe would be familiar with the collection, and that his familiarity with it might help in the recovery of the manuscripts.[136]

Thefts by staff, or enabled by staff, are attested as well. Workers in libraries had ready access to the rolls, and in the normal course of events they would be seen taking book rolls for repairs or for the owner's use, and they would not arouse suspicion if they removed a roll from its shelf or container. And, of course, they would be well aware of which were the most valuable manuscripts. In 46 BC, Cicero wrote to Sulpicius Rufus, who was at that time propraetor in Illyricum, to ask for Sulpicius's help in apprehending one of his slaves: "My slave Dionysius, who has been managing my book collection—which is worth quite a lot—stole a large number of manuscripts and then, when he thought he would probably be caught, he fled. He is in your province."[137] This was theft by a member of the library staff, perhaps the very person who at that time was in charge of Cicero's library.[138] Writ-

---

131. *Ind.* 8–10. The warehouses were also considered safe from fire.

132. Lib. *Or.* 1.148–50, a dramatic story. It is not clear if they stole other books as well.

133. The theft of books, with the possibility of selling them as motive, is incidentally an argument in support of an active trade in old books, though not necessarily of used books generally.

134. Library: Julian. *Ep.* 106 (Bidez). Death of George: Amm. Marc. 22.11.3–10. For date, discussion, and further details: Caltabiano (1991), 249, n. 5, on *Ep.* 58.

135. Julian. *Ep.* 106, to Porphyrius, a financial official, and 107, to Ecdicius. The Greek verb that I render "stolen" is ἀφαιρέω. For the two men, see Caltabiano (1991), 45 (Ecdicius) and 52 (Porphyrius).

136. The scribe might also have been able to identify the thieves, if they had been staff in the library.

137. Cic. *Fam.* 13.77.3: *Dionysius, servus meus, qui meam bibliothecen multorum nummorum tractavit, cum multos libros surripuisset nec se impune laturum putaret, aufugit. Is est in provincia tua.*

138. What Cicero meant by *tractavit* is not clear. Dionysius may have been in charge of the collection; or perhaps *tractavit* here means simply "worked on."

ing in the 140s AD, the young Marcus Aurelius told his teacher Fronto that Fronto would need to give the *bibliothecarius* of the library in the Domus Tiberiana some money if he wished to obtain a certain book. The implication is that the *bibliothecarius* is bribable.[139]

It is perhaps in this context of theft and untrustworthy staff that we may best understand the famous inscription from the library of Pantaenus in Athens, in which the staff collectively aver that "books shall not be taken out, for we have sworn an oath."[140] A similar prohibition against removing books from a library is found in a Hellenistic inscription from Rhodes. The inscription, not yet fully published, preserved a public decree that forbade the removal of books.[141] Line 7 of the inscription includes the rule, "It shall not be permitted to anyone to take the books out" (τὰ βυβλία . . . μηθενὶ ἐξέστω ἐκφέρειν ἔξω). In both libraries, we might posit a desire to have staff promise, on oath if necessary, that they would not let anyone remove a book.[142]

If the library staff was not diligent and honest, book rolls could, it seems, be subject to mistreatment by visitors to the library. Users might simply take pen and ink and write in the manuscripts. Galen, for example, complained that users had sometimes altered manuscripts in the Palatine libraries in order to make them conform to their own theories.[143]

Fire, obviously, was a constant and terrible danger. A major fire in the city of Rome, such as the great fire of AD 64, would probably destroy not only imperial libraries, but also thousands of book rolls that were in the possession of private individuals whose houses were burned.[144] In his account of the fire of 64, Tacitus describes the path it took and the sections of the city it destroyed. These included parts of eleven of the fourteen Augustan regions of Rome and many of the areas where the grand houses of wealthy families stood. It is entirely reasonable to assume that many of the larger houses, and perhaps some of the apartments in *insulae* (tenements), con-

139. Fronto *Ep.* 4.5.2; cf. Houston (2004), 10–11. One might consider the money a tip, but Marcus implies that it is not optional: a bribe rather than a tip.

140. *SEG* 21.500.

141. Papachristodoulou (1986), 268.

142. We do not know if users of libraries had, or could obtain, borrowing privileges. Galen's new treatise refers to his working on books in the imperial libraries, but never to his removing a book from them, so at least in that case borrowing seems not to have been permitted. Different libraries, however, may have had different rules.

143. Zadorojnyi (2013), 391–93, provides the texts and an excellent elucidation of them.

144. Of imperial libraries, the only one certainly destroyed in the fire of 64 was the library in the Portico of Octavia (Cass. Dio 66.24). For the imperial libraries in fires of the first century AD, see Dix and Houston (2006), 693–95. Boudon-Millot and Jouanna (2010), xxii–xxviii, deal with the fire of AD 192.

tained book collections large or small. The damage to the literary patrimony of Rome must have been substantial.[145]

There was little that staff could do to control a fire in a library once it began, but there were steps that collectors or staff could take ahead of time to prevent or minimize damage. Galen says that he kept some of his personal collection of book rolls in a storeroom in one of the imperial warehouses in part because it seemed safe from fire.[146] Perhaps more importantly, staff would ordinarily be capable of creating duplicate copies and would have the facilities to do so; and those duplicates could be stored in other houses, villas, or libraries. We might have assumed that this was one of the tasks of the imperial slaves who were assigned to the libraries, but Galen states that a significant number of works in the Palatine libraries were unique and not, he says, to be found anywhere else (*Ind.* 13). Can it be true that no copies of such works had been made and distributed to one or more of the libraries elsewhere in the city, or to one of the imperial villas outside the city?[147] If so, it is stunning to find the men responsible for the imperial libraries—the emperors and their commissioners—content with unique copies of works in a city where fires were common and the total destruction by fire of large libraries was a known phenomenon.

6.8. CONCLUSION

Emperor, advisers and scholars, skilled and unskilled library workers: all can be traced, in varying degrees of detail and in connection with activities suitable to their rank, in the private book collections and imperial libraries of Rome. We can assume that similar administrative and managerial structures were to be found in municipal libraries throughout the Greco-Roman world, although specific evidence outside of the city of Rome is scarce.[148] When Iulius Aquila Polemaeanus set up a municipal library in Ephesus in honor of his father, Celsus Polemaeanus, he left an endowment of twenty-five thousand denarii for the maintenance of the library, specifying that

145. So Gal. *Comp.Med.Gen.* 1.1 (13.362 Kühn): not only his own, but the book rolls of many others (ἑτέρων τε πολλῶν), were destroyed in the fire of AD 192.

146. *Ind.* 8: the only wood in the warehouses, Galen says, is in the doors.

147. In addition to the villa at Antium, we know that the Villa of Hadrian at Tibur (Tivoli) had a library, and presumably most or all of the imperial villas did.

148. It would not be a coincidence if there were similarities in the structures of library staff over both time and space. Hellenistic Greek handbooks on library management seem to have included advice both on what titles to own and on the organization of the rolls in the available physical space. The scholar Varro wrote three books *de bibliothecis* that may have made the specialist Greek literature available to Latin readers. Otranto (2000), xi, gives a useful summary and references.

some of the income was to be used to provide library staff (προσμένοντες), presumably public slaves.[149] Similarly, Pliny the Younger created a library in his hometown of Comum and left an endowment of one hundred thousand sesterces for its upkeep (*in tutelam bybliothecae*); we may assume that this included funds for staff.[150] As we learned in chapters 3 and 4, coherent bodies of book rolls might continue to exist for long periods of time, in some cases for centuries. In chapter 4, we came across one collection that included book rolls of consistently high quality, and others that revealed the collector's interest in obtaining accurate copies. The intelligence and professional skills of those who tended such collections, despite the problems and occasional negligence or malfeasance we have just outlined, are revealed in the quality and long survival of such collections.

149. *IK Ephesos* VII.2, no. 5113, lines 6–11.

150. *CIL* 5.5262 (= *ILS* 2927). The sum of one hundred thousand sesterces is exactly the same as Aquila's twenty-five thousand denarii. Dix (1996), 95–97, discusses the amount and projected income of Pliny's endowment.

Conclusion

If we return now to the questions we posed in the introduction about ancient book collections—how they were formed, what they contained, how they reflected their owners' tastes, what quality of book rolls was to be found in them, and the like—we will find that we can suggest a range of responses to our questions. The range is wide, but it is not infinite. We have a significant body of evidence, grounded in surviving parts of Roman book collections, that provides us with a set of possibilities and establishes realistic limits for any Roman book collection. We know a good deal about the contents of book collections, the condition and ages of the manuscripts in them, the ways in which collections developed and grew, the conditions under which they were maintained, the idiosyncrasies of collectors, and many other matters. It is my hope that the materials assembled in this book will enable the reader to recreate, in her or his own mind, a variety of Roman book collections small or large, set within more or less clearly defined physical spaces and supplemented with appropriate equipment, furniture, and persons. This book is, of course, a beginning, not in any sense an end. There will be mistakes to correct, omissions to note. New discoveries will change observations and inferences. Readers will note flaws in logic or disagree with interpretations.[1] All of this will help to move the field forward. To that end, it may be useful here, at the end of this study, to outline briefly the principal aspects of the collections we have analyzed, note recurring characteristics, and consider some of the implications of the material.

THE EVIDENCE

We have several types of evidence. First, there are eight ancient lists of books preserved in papyri from Egypt, each of which seems to represent the holdings of part or all of an ancient book collection. These are presented and analyzed in chapter 2, and the Greek texts of five of them are in appendix 1. Second, there is the material from the Villa of the Papyri in Hercula-

---

1. I have avoided using the evidence to take up questions of literacy, literary culture, and related areas of study in order to avoid circular reasoning. It is my hope that scholars who are interested in those questions will find material in this volume that will be useful to them.

neum (chapter 3 and appendix 2). Third, we have analyzed five groups of papyri from the Egyptian city of Oxyrhynchus, each of them representing a different ancient collection (chapter 4). Finally, there is literary, archaeological, and epigraphical evidence that sheds light on the equipment, decoration, and staffing of book collections; those materials are presented in chapters 5 and 6.

SIZES AND STORAGE

The collections that we can identify using this evidence range in size from a few dozen to several thousand rolls (2.14).[2] The partially preserved book rolls from the Villa of the Papyri probably number somewhere around eight hundred volumes, although estimates vary widely (3.5). By our standards, of course, these are small collections, but in a preindustrial context a collection such as the one in the Villa of the Papyri is very substantial. There is no indication in our evidence of particularly large collections numbering tens of thousands of volumes.[3] The storage facilities needed for the collections dealt with in this book must have been as diverse as the collections themselves, ranging from portable boxes, to cabinets with several shelves, to entire rooms with cabinets set into their walls (5.2–5.4). The presence of permanent shelving by no means rules out the use, at the same time and in the same rooms, of boxes or cases of various sizes and shapes. A box could help keep a specific work or set of rolls together.[4]

FAMILIAR PHENOMENA

Many aspects of collections familiar to modern readers can be traced in ancient ones as well. We often find duplicate copies of works or, on the other hand, gaps in collections and incomplete works. Odd items that were perhaps gifts or book rolls acquired on a whim sometimes appear in what are otherwise coherent collections.[5] Within a given collection, book rolls may

2. In the conclusion, I provide cross-references in this shortened form (2.14 = chapter 2, section 14).

3. It would be reasonable to assume that the imperial collection in Rome, which was spread through several library buildings, numbered in the tens, and possibly hundreds, of thousands. Cf. Dix and Houston (2006), 708–9. I see no reason to accept the claim of the author of the life of Gordian II (*SHA Gord.* 18.2) that Serenus Sammonicus accumulated sixty-two thousand volumes.

4. It may be that some book rolls in the imperial collection were stored on a permanent basis in storerooms (*apothecae*) in the imperial warehouses that lined the Via Sacra and the lower slopes of the Palatine. See Tucci (2013), 295.

5. List 1 (*P.Vindob.* inv. G 39966, column 2; section 2.6) provides examples. The collection represented by this list may have had duplicate copies of Hesiod's *Catalog*, Book 5; it lacked Books 4, 5,

vary in physical quality, from cheaply produced to elegant and sturdy, but each collection tends to have volumes that are for the most part consistent in terms of quality.

BUILDING A COLLECTION

It is sometimes possible to follow the processes involved in the creation of collections. The single most important step—and the most difficult one— was to locate one or more exemplars of the text that one wanted and to assess their relative qualities. Several problems might arise. Some texts were very rare, hard to find, or even unique. Galen laments the loss, in the fire of AD 192, of manuscripts that existed in only one copy, so far as he knew.[6] Even if a work was relatively common, it might be difficult to locate a reliable text of it that one could use, and finding a second copy to correct one's principal exemplar would be an additional challenge (6.3, "Correcting"). Some available texts were forgeries (1.9), and Galen complained of his own texts being copied with minor changes and distributed under someone else's name.[7]

Much the most common problem was careless copying. Every manuscript was handmade and unique, so every manuscript was either more or less accurate than all others, not identical to any of them. There were no guarantees of quality. We almost never find information in a manuscript that tells us who made the copy, or when and where it was made, or what exemplar had been used to make it.[8] Thus it fell to the collector or his agent to judge if a given text was not a fake but genuine, and, assuming it was genuine, if it was accurate enough to warrant inclusion in his collection (1.8, 1.9). Such critical judgments were necessary whether the collector wanted

---

and 9 of a lexicon; its holdings in poetry were conservative (Homer, Hesiod, and Callimachus), but in prose it had a number of unusual works, including one and perhaps two copies of the otherwise unknown *Peri epimones*.

6. *Ind.* 13.

7. Gal. *Lib.Prop. praef.* 6–7 (= Boudon-Millot [2007a], 135). Zetzel (1973), 239–43, gives examples of scholarly readers in the second century who were fooled by forgeries.

8. Some manuscripts may have been marked (truthfully or not) as having been made by copyists, or in scribal workshops, that were reputed to be especially reliable. A medieval manuscript of Demosthenes includes, at the end of one of Demosthenes's speeches, the claim that it had been "checked against two of the Attician manuscripts" (Dem. *Or.* 11 *subscriptio* = Dilts [2002], 148); the statement had presumably been copied at some point from a papyrus roll along with the speeches themselves. Similarly, Lucian, in his satire *The Ignorant Book Collector*, can conceive of manuscripts that were somehow marked as having been done by, or perhaps owned by, Callinus or Atticus; thus they would have been particularly valuable (and, we presume, accurate). Exactly what this mark was is a puzzle, since the surviving examples of titles and *sillyba* do not provide any indication of the scribe, nor of the time or place of copying.

to make his own copy or was seeking to buy an existing copy. The imperial libraries in Rome played a crucial role in this context, because they served both as a source of texts that might be difficult to find and, even more importantly, as a source of particularly accurate copies.[9]

Copies could be made by dictation, that is, with one scribe writing down what another one read aloud, but the evidence suggests that copies were often, and probably most often, made by a scribe who read the exemplar himself, then wrote what he had read (3.7, 6.3). The scribe might be the collector himself, but that would be rare; more often, he would be a slave trained as a scribe, or a professional scribe outside the collector's house. There are strong indications of the use of large numbers of professional copyists who were not working in-house, even in the case of the Villa of the Papyri (3.7, 3.8, 4.7; summarized in 4.13).

LIFE HISTORIES OF COLLECTIONS

Once assembled, a collection would remain more or less intact for some period of time. Can we tell how long? In some cases, we can trace the continued existence of at least the core of a collection over two or more generations. The concentration I call Breccia + GH3 probably, but not certainly, belonged to the family of a man named Sarapion. It included volumes copied at various times over the course of about a century, and the essential core volumes in it may well have passed down from one generation to the next, probably with some volumes being discarded and others added (4.5–4.7). The collection represented by Grenfell and Hunt's second find may have originated in the late second century AD, continued to grow for a generation or two, and then been kept but not further developed for as much as a century before being discarded ca. 400 (4.10). At the Villa of the Papyri in Herculaneum, the surviving manuscripts of the works of Philodemus seem to have been copied, in most cases, in the middle third of the first century BC (not necessarily in Herculaneum); most scholars have argued that they then remained together, relatively neglected, until the time of the eruption of Vesuvius more than a century later (3.10). Galen, writing in the late second century AD, speaks of collections within the Palatine libraries

9. In this respect, the imperial collection in Rome played a role similar to the one the library of Alexandria had played in Hellenistic times. We need not assume that the imperial manuscripts were perfect. Galen talks about working hard to make error-free copies from some of the rolls he found in the imperial collection, and he clearly found some mistakes in them (*Ind.* 14). But he also mentions specific subgroups that were known to be particularly accurate (*Ind.* 13).

that may in his day have been more than two hundred years old (1.11; 5.5; Galen, *Ind.* 13). In sum, several ancient collections, and particular parts of other collections, can be shown to have existed as coherent wholes for more than a century, and in some cases a good deal longer.

THE LIFE SPAN OF A BOOK ROLL

The identification of such collections, and of the manuscripts within them, provides new evidence on an old question: how long did a papyrus roll last? The evidence from our collections indicates that a usable lifetime of about 100 to 125 years was common and can reasonably be considered the norm; a small but significant number of manuscripts were still usable some 300 years after they were first created; and on rare occasions a manuscript might last, it seems, for half a millennium (3.9 and 4.13).

STORAGE

The individual manuscripts thus acquired could be stored, until they became too numerous, in any one of several types of container (5.2). Small collections could grow into large ones over time, but they might also change hands through sale, say, or inheritance, and be absorbed into a larger collection. In at least some cases they may have kept a kind of identity even after being assimilated in this way: within the imperial collection, Galen could name certain groups of manuscripts—the Atticiana and others—which he knew consisted of particularly accurate copies.[10]

COLLECTORS' INTERESTS

The collections that resulted from these processes regularly reveal at least some of the interests and priorities of the collector. The collection represented by Grenfell and Hunt's first find implies a keen interest in the events and history of the late fifth and early fourth centuries BC (4.3). Three of our collections center on philosophy (broadly defined): the collection from the Villa of the Papyri (chapter 3), list 2 (2.7), and list 4 (2.9). At least two contain substantial numbers of opisthographs and so may suggest collectors

---

10. *Ind.* 13. These may have been kept as discrete collections (section 6.7), or simply be manuscripts, spread through the Palatine collections, that were marked as "Atticiana" or by some other appropriate word. It is worth noting that Galen assumes that his correspondent will know what he is referring to when he mentions these collections. Whatever they were, serious readers knew about them.

interested in keeping costs low: list 4 (2.9) and Grenfell and Hunt's first find. In the latter, the collector seems to have aimed at accuracy and not to have been much concerned about the beauty or elegance of his book rolls (4.3). Grenfell and Hunt's second find contains a very high percentage of manuscripts of poets, especially but not exclusively early lyric (4.9, 4.11), and a strikingly high number of its manuscripts contain commentary in the form of annotations (4.11). List 5 contains names of writers of comedy and no others and may be all that survives of the list of titles in a large municipal or institutional library (2.10). One of our collections consists of the professional papers of an astrologer (4.12), and list 1 includes very standard poetry—Homer, Hesiod, and Callimachus—but recherché prose, some of it otherwise unknown to us (2.6). The collection I call Breccia + GH 3, finally, is the only collection in this group that certainly contains a wide and representative sample of classic Greek literature; it is nicely balanced, with no emphasis on any particular field, and it includes annotated texts and commentaries, indicating that it is not just a collection designed to impress, but a collection to be read and studied (4.6).

The collectors who are implied by the lists and concentrations of books constitute a broadly consistent class of readers who are interested in serious literature and concerned to obtain accurate copies, often furnished with explanatory annotations, as well as commentaries, lexicons, and other materials that would help them study and understand what they were reading. In general, the collectors seem to be wealthy enough to secure what they want, but they are often happy to save money by reusing old papyri. Most demonstrate a wide-ranging curiosity. Some are assembling professional collections, most have particular preferences, and many include a few surprising or obscure titles in their collections.

SHELVING AND RETRIEVING IN
THE ABSENCE OF CATALOGS

Roman book collections had no catalogs in our sense of the term, that is, a comprehensive list that included author, title, subject, and some kind of identifying catalog or call number for every roll in the collection. The *sillyba*, *subscriptiones*, and initial titles provide author, title, and book number, but in surviving examples of all of these there is never any equivalent to our call number (2.4, 3.8). We must assume that those three items of identification (author, title, book number), plus the language (Greek or Latin) and probably the genre of the work, were used to sort and organize the collection and to store and retrieve the manuscripts. It is not likely that the statues and busts that were present in libraries served as a readily recognized means of guiding the user to the items he sought (5.7).

In his *De indolentia*, Galen says that he had found some items in the Palatine collections that were not included in "what are called the *pinakes*," as well as some items that were listed in the *pinakes* but were not (or no longer) to be found in the collection.[11] We do not know for sure what Galen meant by *pinakes*.[12] Jacques Jouanna, in his commentary on the *De indolentia*, argued that these were the bibliographical works that had originated in the library of Alexandria, such as the *Pinakes* of Callimachus; they provided information about a given author's life and listed his works.[13] Matthew Nicholls has suggested another possibility: Galen's *pinakes* were the lists that Andronicus and Tyrannio made, in the first century BC, of the collection of Aristotle's works that Sulla had brought to Italy.[14] Both suggestions are attractive, but the *pinakes* mentioned by Galen may simply have been lists such as we saw in chapter 1. Galen would then be saying that he had found some works (rare and so worth noting) in the Palatine collections that were not listed, and he had sought some works, also rare, that were in the list(s) but could not be found in the Palatine libraries.

STAFF, COMPETENCE, AND CONFUSION

The lack of comprehensive catalogs had a number of consequences. First is the importance of the (slave) staff, especially in larger libraries. In one's own personal collection, if it had no more than a few hundred volumes, it would be easy enough to recall which box or set of shelves held Euripides, and which the *Institutiones* of Gaius. But if one visited another person's library, or went to a municipal library that had several thousand rolls, it might not be immediately apparent how the rolls were organized, and reading *sillyba* would quickly become tiresome. In this case, we can reasonably assume that there was a staff member, ordinarily a slave, and that it was his job to serve as a kind of human catalog, to know how things were arranged and to fetch promptly whatever rolls were required (6.3). Under such conditions, we might expect occasional confusion, and not surprisingly there

---

11. *Ind.*17: τινὰ δὲ ἐν ἐκείνοις [sc. πίναξι] γεγραμμένα μέν, μὴ φαινόμενα δ' αὐτά.

12. He uses the word twice. The first occurrence, in *Ind.* 16, is in a difficult passage where the meaning of the word ἔξωθεν, if that is the correct reading, is not clear. No completely convincing suggestion has been made for this passage, and it is best for now not to use it as evidence for the nature of the *pinakes*.

13. Boudon-Millot and Jouanna (2010), 63–64.

14. Nicholls (2011), 135.

are indications of it (6.7). Sometimes difficulties in finding or identifying specific texts appear in anecdotes in literature,[15] and sometimes they may be reflected in lists of book rolls, as when an odd title such as *Peri epimones* shows up twice in one list (2.6), or an otherwise impeccable list of comedies includes three probable repetitions within the space of eleven lines (2.10). The discrepancy between the *pinakes* consulted by Galen and the books he was able to find in the Palatine library may have been due in part to careless shelving. Nor need we be surprised to find a certain amount of disorder. Latin texts sometimes seem to have been commingled with Greek, for we find them listed among Greek titles (2.8, 3.4, 4.6), and here and there one finds indications that documents and works of literature could be stored together (2.8).[16] Stray materials—a glossary of tachygraphic symbols (4.6), an encomium on the fig (4.9), and numerous others—turn up among the more standard book rolls in the collections from Oxyrhynchus.[17]

SOME FUNCTIONS OF COLLECTIONS

A book collection could serve any one of a variety of purposes. It might be a professional tool, such as the astrologer's collection (4.12). Several collections could have been used by scholars or teachers in their teaching, their own studies, or both; these would include the philosophical collection from Memphis (2.7), the texts from the Villa of the Papyri, and Grenfell and Hunt's second find (4.9, 4.11). Collectors often furnished the rooms in which they stored their book collections with works of art, and an ensemble of handsome book rolls, art, and expensive building materials might be used to impress one's friends and visitors. Given their often ruinous state of preservation, it is difficult to identify surviving collections of book rolls that might have been gathered specifically because they were handsome, but at least one of our collections (Breccia + GH3, 4.7) contained enough

---

15. For example: Gell. *NA* 11.17 and 13.20.

16. Thus the probable commingling of literary texts and records of the Sarapion family (section 4.5), and the late antique mix of documents and literary texts that belonged to Dioscorus of Aphrodito and were perhaps stored together in a single ceramic container: MacCoull (1988), 2–5. We must not exaggerate here: Turner noted that it is rare for literary texts to be found within archives of documents. He also pointed out, however, that such mixing of types of material may originally have been more common than now appears, because the provenance of many literary papyri is unknown and they may have been found among documents: Turner (1980), 77–78.

17. Disorder can show up in the book lists, too: note *P.Vars.* 5 verso, with its lines crammed into too-small spaces, sections marked by great looping parentheses, and counts and recounts (section 2.9).

high-quality manuscripts that it would have made an impressive display.[18] An important function of all collections must have been to provide exemplars that could be copied by friends, acquaintances, or friends of friends.

USES OF THE IMPERIAL COLLECTION

If we consider not personal collections or collections in general, but specifically the great imperial collection in Rome, we find a similar mix of functions. The evidence we have indicates that the emperor's collection, housed in a series of purpose-built halls, was not, at least in origin, regarded as providing a public service in the way that the roads or the aqueducts did (6.5). Rather, the imperial collection and the numerous buildings that housed it were intended to serve other purposes. They enhanced the prestige of Rome and the emperor; even people who walked by a library could look in and see the great collections of papyrus rolls, with all the learning and culture they implied. The imperial libraries housed materials that could serve as a resource for the emperor and his agents. Some people did go to these libraries to read and discuss texts, as we know from Gellius, but we need not imagine either that book rolls could be removed from the libraries or that throngs of ordinary citizens went to them on a regular basis.[19] Above all, the imperial collection was the source of last resort for rare or particularly accurate copies of works in both Greek and Latin, and the most important function of these unusually large and well-stocked collections may well have been to provide exemplars that could be copied. That is what Galen used them for, more than anything else.

THE VILLA OF THE PAPYRI

The collection of book rolls from the Villa of the Papyri has been the object of study for a quarter of a millennium now, but particularly rapid and sometimes spectacular advances have been made within the last forty years. The patient and often brilliant work of many papyrologists, and the development of new tools and techniques, have provided much new information: hands and scribes have been identified, and titles of texts—exact or approxi-

---

18. It was also a collection in which the collector was clearly concerned with accuracy, so providing an impressive display was definitely not its only function.

19. I agree with the general conclusions of Piacente (2011), 40–49, if not with all of the details, and with Nicholls (2011), 129 and 137.

mate, depending upon the nature of the evidence—have been determined through the reading of *subscriptiones* or the analysis of contents. In recent editions of texts from the Villa, papyrologists have provided careful descriptions of the physical condition of rolls as well as the texts themselves.[20] All of this makes possible a far more comprehensive analysis of the Villa collection, in library-historical terms, than was possible even as recently as 1970.

SIZE AND CONTENTS OF THE VILLA COLLECTION

The collection, as we know it, probably numbered some six hundred to one thousand book rolls (3.5), most of them in Greek, but with a significant number, perhaps sixty to eighty rolls, in Latin (3.4). More than half of the texts that have been identified so far are treatises by Philodemus of Gadara on topics of importance to Epicureans (ethics, aesthetics, mathematics, but not metaphysics). At present, about thirty-four titles by Philodemus are known or can be inferred from the contents of the manuscripts; in some cases, we know that Philodemus wrote multivolume works (*On Vices*, for example) that included single books with their own titles (*On Flattery*, one book roll in *On Vices*). In addition to the many works by Philodemus, the Villa very probably had at least one copy of each of the thirty-seven books of Epicurus's *On Nature*; of these, copies of eight different books have been found, with some duplicates and, in one case, three copies of a given book. The Villa also included important collections of works by Demetrius of Laco (some nine separate treatises) and at least six other Greek authors, including the Stoic Chrysippus (3.3; appendix 2).

PHILODEMUS AND THE VILLA

Papyrologists date most of the copies of the works of Philodemus to the middle part of the first century BC on paleographical grounds. Several of the authors represented in the Villa lived before Philodemus, and some of their manuscripts—notably those of Epicurus—have been dated to the second and even the third century BC. How and when all of the volumes came to the Villa is not clear. As Guglielmo Cavallo suggested, Philodemus may have brought some of the earlier works with him when he moved, in about 70 BC, from Greece to Italy; but it is also possible that the collection was assembled, in whole or in part, by a Roman, and that it then attracted the

---

20. The series La Scuola di Epicuro, published by Bibliopolis in Naples, provides texts with translations, commentaries, and careful descriptions of the physical properties of the manuscripts.

attention of Philodemus (3.10).[21] Recent work by archaeologists suggests that the Villa may not have been built until the 40s or 30s BC, and it has generally been thought that Philodemus died around 40 or sometime in the 30s BC. It is thus possible that Philodemus did not live at the Villa most of the time he was in Italy, if he lived there at all. Perhaps he worked mostly in Rome, the collection being transferred to the Villa late in his life or after his death.

THE VILLA DOES NOT SEEM TO HAVE BEEN, OR TO HAVE CONTAINED, A SCRIPTORIUM

The manuscripts of Philodemus's works were copied by at least twenty-one different scribes and probably many more, and that fact, together with the presence of stichometric counts in many of the manuscripts, suggests that a significant percentage of the manuscripts were not copied by in-house slave or freedman scribes, but by professional scribes who were commissioned to do the work (3.11). The large numbers of copyists involved may also suggest that many of the manuscripts of Philodemus's works were copied not in Campania, but in Rome, where there were substantial numbers of professional scribes (3.10). I know of no convincing evidence of an in-house scriptorium intended to generate copies of the works of Philodemus or other Epicurean writers.[22]

CONTENTS OF THE VILLA COLLECTION

The contents of the Villa collection are interesting for at least two further reasons. First, the collection as known so far contains none of Philodemus's poetry, although poetry is what he was best known for in antiquity (3.6).[23] Second, there is very little overlap between the non-Philodemean works present in the Villa collection and those cited by Philodemus in his treatises. We may perhaps infer that, if Philodemus was the person who assembled the collection, he did not do so with his own research needs in mind (3.6).

---

21. One of the manuscripts of Epicurus's *On Nature* seems not to have entered the Villa's collection until well into the first century BC and was probably not brought to Italy by Philodemus: Houston (2013), 192–93.

22. None of the works of Philodemus made it into the manuscript tradition. They may have been scarce. If that was the case, it would be an argument against a scriptorium in the Villa turning out multiple copies of Philodemus's works. It would not be a decisive argument, though, because his works may simply have been of no interest to the copyists of late antiquity.

23. Much of Philodemus's treatise *On Poems* does survive, however.

In the Villa, most volumes that we know of seem to have been stored in a single room (Weber's room V), but several dozen book rolls were found in boxes in other rooms, and such boxes might conceivably have been in use as permanent storage facilities. Some book rolls seem to have been found in small stacks on the floor of some rooms (3.2); this may reflect the disarray and confusion at the time of the eruption of Vesuvius.

BOOK ROLLS IN PERIL

Book collections in the Roman world faced a number of dangers (6.7). Fire, or a volcano, could destroy them utterly. Damp could render them unusable. Dust and the larvae of insects might damage them, and so might careless or heavy use over a long period of time (6.3). The incompetence or dishonesty of staff could lead to the deterioration or loss of book rolls (6.7). Occasionally a collection seems to have contained an incomplete copy of some work, perhaps indicating that the archetype was damaged, or that the collector had had difficulty in finding reliable archetypes (1.6–1.8; 4.3). Loss of interest in a collection on the part of successive owners may be expected and perhaps can be seen in some of our collections (4.7).[24] And, of course, there was the arrival of the codex: by the fourth century AD, the book rolls and collections we have identified and analyzed were in some sense obsolete. As copies of the works they contained became available in codex form, the old rolls could be discarded or ignored. Fortunately, some traces of Roman collections of papyrus book rolls have survived. Lists of books, concentrations of discarded rolls, the collection from the Villa of the Papyri, references in literature, and inscriptions: all help us recover the book collections of ancient Rome.

---

24. Note also the collection of the Aurelius family (section 4.8). Their copy of Iulius Africanus's *Cestoi* was turned over and reused when it was not more than fifty years old.

Lists of Books on Papyrus

Greek Texts, English Translations, and Commentary

I present in this appendix the Greek texts and English translations of the five book lists that are discussed in chapter 2. In presenting the Greek texts, I use the Leiden system of conventional signs to indicate the status of the letters in the papyrus. The ones used here are as follows:[1]

Letters about the reading of which there is genuine doubt are marked by an underdot.	Αἰλιαν
Illegible letters the approximate number of which is known are indicated by periods.	.....
Missing letters the approximate number of which is known are indicated by periods enclosed in square brackets.	[.....]
Missing letters the number of which is not known are indicated by square brackets.	] or [ ] or [
Letters restored by the editor are enclosed in square brackets.	[᾿Επ]ιγράμ[ματα]
Letters omitted by the scribe and supplied by the editor are enclosed in angle brackets.	Καλ<λ>ιμάχου
Completions of abbreviated words are enclosed in parentheses.	Καλλιμά(χου)
Letters or words wrongly added by the scribe and deleted by the editor are enclosed in curly brackets.	πολιτεία{ς}
Erasures by the scribe are enclosed in double square brackets.	[[ρμ]]
Letters written by the scribe slightly higher than the other letters in the line are enclosed in single opening and closing quotation marks.	`μ´

In the English translation, I use conventional titles where they exist (Aristophanes's *Peace*, for example); where they do not, I transliterate names of authors and titles using the spelling in the index of Lesky (1966) as a model. In general, I do not indicate the state of preservation of the Greek text in the English translation and instead print a text that represents what can be reasonably reconstructed of the Greek text. I do include some of the stray letters. Some notes and comments on matters relevant to this study

---

1. Adapted from Schubert (2009), 203; he provides a full explanation of the system. The Greek texts I give are provided for the reader's convenience and should not be used as the basis for scholarly research. For that, the reader should use the original publications of the several papyri.

follow the texts, but I do not present or discuss all of the problems in the texts, for which the reader should consult the editions and scholarly works cited.

1. *P.Vindob.* inv. G 39966, column 2 = Otranto number 3,
column 2 = *MP*³ 2089.1 = *CPP* 0347; probably from the Arsinoite nome,
mid-first century AD; now in Vienna (Figure 2)

This list was written on a sheet of papyrus, 37.3 cm wide, that was created by gluing together at least two documents and using the blank back of the resulting sheet as a writing surface. The sheet contains two book lists, this one and *P.Vindob.* inv. G 39966, column 1 (our list 6); the two lists are separated by a blank space of about 20 cm. They were written in the same hand, and, it seems, at about the same time.[2] We seem to have both the beginning and the ending of column 2. Text based on Puglia (1998), 83.

GREEK TEXT

1 [.] . [......] Ὁμήρο[υ Ἰλιά(δος) α β γ δ ε ζ η θ ι κ λ μ ν]
   ξ ο π [ρ σ τ] υ φ χ ψ ω | Ὀδυσ(σείας) ἀ [β γ δ ε ζ η θ ι] κ λ μ ν
   ξ ο π ρ ọ τ υ φ χ ψ ω γ δ Ἡσιόδọṵ [Γυν]αικῶ(ν)
   α β ε ε θεογ`ο΄(νία) Ἔργ`α΄ καὶ Ἡ`μ΄(έραι) Καλ<λ>ιμά(χου)
5 Αἰτί`ω΄(ν) α . [.] Ὕμ(νοι) [Ἐπ]ιγράμ[ματα]
   Ἑκάλη   Ἐγλογαὶ ῥητ[ορ] ...
   δώρ`ο΄(υ) Λẹ[ξε]ων [α] β γ ζ η θ [κ] λ μ ν
   Διονυσί[ο]ṵ ...`.΄ [...] . `μ΄ Αἰλιạṿ[οῦ ...] ...
   δ ...... δισ .[...] β δ η .. δ. [   ] Πẹ-
10 ρὶ ἐπιμ[ονῆ]ς.

   Αἰσχίνους Κατὰ Κṭ[η]σιφῶν`τ΄(ος) .αṭο[
   ρίου Περὶ ἐπιμονῆς Δημọσθέν[ου]ς
   Περὶ τοῦ στεφάνου

ENGLISH TRANSLATION

1 (?   ) Homer's [*Iliad* 1 2 3 4 5 6 7 8 9 10 11 12 13]
   14 15 16 [17 18 19] 20 21 22 23 24; *Odyssey* 1 [2 3 4 5 6 7 8 9] 10 11 12 13
   14 15 16 17 18 19 20 21 22 23 24 3 4; Hesiod's (*Catalog of*) *Women*
   1 2 5 5; *Theogony, Works and Days*; Callimachus's
5 *Aetia* 1 (?), *Hymns, Epigrams,*
   Hecale.   Selections from (or *of?*) *the Orators* (or *Rhetoricians?*) ...
   (?)dorus's *Lexicon* [1] 2 3 6 7 8 [10] 11 12 13;
   Dionysius's (?); ... m(?); Aelianus's (?),
   d ..... dis . [...] 2 4 7 d .... *On*

---

2. The two lists are generally printed together with continuous line count, as though they were a single list. They seem, however, to be two separate lists, either of two distinct collections of books or of one collection that changed considerably between the first and second times it was inventoried.

10   *Epimone.*

Aeschines's *Against Ctesiphon;* .ato
riou (?), *On Epimone*; Demosthenes's
14   *On the Crown*

NOTES AND COMMENTS

Letters of the alphabet that I translate as numbers are marked by macrons in this papyrus. In some of our other papyri, the fact that a letter is being used as a number is indicated by an acute accent to the right of the letter.

Line 1. This line begins with a lacuna long enough for about a dozen letters. I print the Greek text as in Puglia (1998), 83, but in the English translation I simply leave a space of a dozen letters within parentheses.

Lines 1–3. Most of the book numbers of the *Iliad* are lost in a lacuna, so we cannot know if the collection included them all or not. After Book 24 (omega) of the *Odyssey*, in line 3, one sees the numbers gamma and delta (i.e., 3 and 4), clearly out of sequence. Various explanations are possible. Perhaps the collection contained two copies of Books 3 and 4; or perhaps these books were overlooked during the initial inventory, then added here at the end when the compiler of the list came upon them later. Robert Babcock has suggested a third scenario, based on similar out-of-sequence numbers in medieval Latin manuscripts: the numbers gamma and delta may apply not to the *Odyssey*, but to Hesiod's *Catalog of Women*, which follows. In this case, the compiler would have left a space between Book 24 of the *Odyssey* and Hesiod, recorded the books of Hesiod's *Catalog*, and proceeded to Hesiod's *Theogony*. At some subsequent point, he would have come across Books 3 and 4 of Hesiod's *Catalog* and, seeking a place to record those books, put them in line 3, in the space he had earlier left blank.

Lines 3–4. It is not clear which books of Hesiod's *Catalog of Women* the collection included; the numbers 1, 2, and 5 can be read, but 3 and 4 cannot. There are two epsilons (fives), so it is possible that the collection included two copies of Book 5, but the first epsilon lacks a macron above it and so was perhaps not a number. Sijpesteijn and Worp (1974), 330, took it as a mistake. Puglia (1998), 81, took it as the numeral 5. If Puglia is correct, then this collection had two copies of Book 5 of the *Catalog*.

Line 6. Puglia (1998), 81–82, followed by Otranto (2000), 13–14, took the open space after *Hecale* as indicating a change of author. Otranto noted that all of the works before this space are poetry, while all of the works that follow it are or could be prose, and in particular works related to rhetoric. That being the case, the title that follows the space, "Selections from the Orators," might have been intended by the compiler of the list as a sort of subheading. Puglia (1998), 82, took the Ἐγλογαὶ Ῥητ[όρων] not as a subheading, but as part of the title of a work, perhaps an anthology of selections from speeches (adding λόγων) or a lexicon (adding λέξεων). Subheadings are rare in these lists, so it is probably best to take the Ἐγλογαὶ Ῥητ[όρων] as an anthology of some sort.[3]

3. Selections of a given genre were certainly in circulation. Another example, a "selection of Socratic letters," appears in our list 2, column 1, lines 1–2.

Lines 6-7. The missing end of line 6 contained the first syllable(s) of the name of the author whose name ends in -δώρο(υ) at the beginning of line 7; thus the name could have been Apollodorus, Diodorus, Theodorus, or any one of many others. This author's work, perhaps λέξεις, or a lexicon of some sort, consisted of at least thirteen books, since the book numbers that survive include the number nu (13). Alternatively, we might read Ἀ[πολλο]/δώρο(υ) Πε[ρὶ θε]ῶν, as a reader for the University of North Carolina Press has suggested to me.[4] In that case, the author would be Apollodorus of Athens, who wrote a work *On the Gods* in twenty-four books, as we know from a citation in Philodemus's *On Piety*: *P.Herc.* 1428 (fragment 5), cited in Jacoby, *FGrHist* 244 F 103 = T 9; cf. Obbink (1996), 17.

Line 8. The author's name Ailianos (Aelianus) is very uncertain. Sijpesteijn and Worp (1974), 330, noted that one could possibly read Αἰ[ο]λίδαι (Ae[o]lidae) instead. Neither Dionysius nor Aelianus (if that is the correct reading) can be identified, and the titles of their works that were listed here cannot be recovered.

Lines 9-10. *Peri epimones.* It is not clear what this title means. It appears twice in this list, here and in line 13. Sijpesteijn and Worp (1974), 330-31, pointed out that *epimone*, when used in a rhetorical context, refers to a figure of speech that consists of "persisting with a particular point," and that it is possible that some rhetorician wrote a treatise on this topic. They also noted, however, that *epimone* can mean "residence," and that the *On Epimone* listed in line 13 may thus be a speech by an unknown orator that dealt with residence in exile.[5] Finally, it is also possible that the *Peri epimones* was a philosophical treatise on the subject of endurance or persistence, the meaning of the word at Plato, *Cratylus* 395A. In that case, however, we would have two speeches separated by a philosophical work in our inventory.

Line 12. After the title *Against Ctesiphon* are three letters, probably ατο. It is not possible to complete the name or title of which they were a part.

2. *P.Ross.Georg.* 1.22 = Otranto number 15 = *MP*³ 2089 = *CPP* 0385;
Memphis, first half of the third century AD; now in the National Library of Russia,
St. Petersburg, inv. no. *P.Graec.* 1.13 (Figure 3)

A single piece of papyrus, 9.6 cm wide and 12 cm high, contains parts of two columns containing the names of authors, all but three of them in the genitive case, followed by titles. The papyrus is broken on all four sides, so we do not know how long the list was. The left-hand column is missing the first two or three letters in each line. Of the right-hand column, only the beginnings—about five letters—of each line survive, so in that column we can reconstruct most of the authors' names but have no titles at all. In column 2, lines 15 and 18 are preceded by forward slash marks. The papyrus is written on

---

4. Everything between -δώρο(υ) and the number β ("2") is lost in a lacuna, except for tiny traces of letters that could be Πε . . . ων.

5. Aeschines lost the case he argued in the speech *Against Ctesiphon*, mentioned in the previous line, and as a result was compelled to go into exile.

one side only, in a cursive that is dated on paleographical grounds to the first half of the third century ᴀᴅ.[6] Text based on Linguiti in *CPF* I.1*, 87–89.

GREEK TEXT

Column 1	Column 2
1 [..].εϲτίου Σωκ[ρα]τικῶν ἐπιϲτο[λῶν]	Ἀπίων[ος
συναγωγαί	
[ἐ]ν οἰκίᾳ	
[..]γυϲταλλυου Ἀντιοχέως .[..].	
5 [..] Δάφνην κ(αὶ) πιουσαιεσ..πρ(οσ).ᾳ..	
[..]πον καὶ Κλυμένη	
[Ἀρι]στοτέλους Περὶ ἀρετῆς	
[Πο]σειδωνίου ἐκ τ(ῆς) α' Περὶ ὀργῆς	..ϙ..
[Θε]οδᾶ Κεφάλαια	
10 [Θε]οφράστου Περὶ σωφροσύνης	Θεοφρ[άστου
[Δίω]νος Περὶ ἀπιστίας	Ἱππίου[
[Ἀρισ]τοτέλους Ἀθηναίων πολ[ι-]	Διογεν[
τεία{ς}	
[Κρί]των Σωκρ[ατ]ιϙός	
15 [Ν]ιγρίνου Ἀπ[ο]λογίαι	/ Αἰλίου [
[Διογ]ένους Περὶ ἀλυπίας	
..... ς Δια[λ]έξε[ις] πρὸς Τυρίους	Εὐκρι[
....ς	/ Ἀρχιμ[ήδους
[Σί]μων Σω[κ]ρα[τι]κός	Χρυσίπ[που
20 [Χρ]υ[σ]ίππ[ου Τέχνης λόγων κ]α[ὶ] τ[ρό-]	
πων α'	Χρυσ[ίππου
Ἀριστοτέλους Πολιτεία Νεοπο[λιτῶν]	Ἀριστο[τέλους
Κέβης Σωκρατικός	− − −
[.....]ε.ους Περὶ τῶν δέκᾳ τ[.....	
− − −	

ENGLISH TRANSLATION

Column 1	Column 2
1 *Collections of Letters of the Socratics*	Apion's
of (?)estius	
In the house (?)	
(?)gustalluos of Antioch's (?)	*(About eight lines are lost here.)*

6. Linguiti, *CPF* I.1*, pp. 85–93, provides an extensive commentary on this papyrus. It may be that the papyrus can be dated specifically to the period ᴀᴅ 222–238: Linguiti in *CPF* I.1*, p. 86, summarizing the observations of Zündel and Häberlin.

Column 1	Column 2
5 (?) daphne and (?) piousaies pr(?) a	
(?)pos (?) and Clymene	
Aristotle's *On Virtue*	
Posidonius's *On Anger*, selection(s) from Book 1	..k..
Theodas's *Basic Principles* (of medicine)	
10 Theophrastus's *On Wisdom*	Theophrastus's
Dio's *On Distrust*	Hippias's
Aristotle's *Constitution of the*	Diogen[?]
Athenians	*(Two lines are lost.)*
Crito, a Socratic	
15 Nigrinus's *Apologies*	Aelius's
Diogenes's *On Avoiding Grief*	
(?)s's *Discourses to the Tyrians*	Eucri(?)
(t?)elos (?)	Archim(edes's ?)
Simon, a Socratic	Chrysippus's
20 Chrysippus's *Handbook of Arguments and Modes*,	
Book 1	Chrysippus's
Aristotle's *Constitution of the Neapolitans*	Aristotle's
Cebes, a Socratic	
... e . ous, *On the Ten T*(?)	

NOTES AND COMMENTS

Column 1, lines 1–2. A collection of some two dozen letters that purported to be written by students and friends of Socrates has survived in manuscript form. Almost all are thought to be spurious compositions of the second century AD, and we learn from the reference in this papyrus that there was more than one such collection circulating in antiquity. The -estius is presumably the man who assembled the selection of letters present in this book collection. See further Linguiti, *CPF* I.1*, 89–90.

Line 3. The papyrus reads [?]νοικια. Some scholars have taken this as a single word, [ἐ]νοίκια, meaning "rental receipts." Others take it as [ἐ]ν οἰκίᾳ, "in the house," and assume that it is a subheading in the list that marks a new section, namely that of book rolls stored in the owner's house. Linguiti, *CPF* I.1*, 90, questioned where else book rolls might have been stored, but we now know that Galen kept books both in his house (κατὰ τὴν οἰκίαν) and, at least temporarily, in a storeroom (ἀποθήκη): Galen, *Ind.* 10. The reading of line 3 remains uncertain.

Lines 4–6. The reading is very uncertain. The name Clymene (line 6) and possible name Daphne (line 5) suggest a work or works of fiction, and the author's name may be hidden in line 4. Otranto (2000), 83, noted that there was a famous town Daphne near Antioch and suggested that lines 4 and 5 may refer to some part of a geographical work. A reader for the University of North Carolina Press points out that [..]γυσταλλυου may conceal the name of an individual (presumably from Antioch), and that he might have been the owner of the house mentioned in line 3. In the right half of line 5, it is not clear where words begin and end, so I have (arbitrarily) printed the sigmas as ordinary (nonfinal) sigmas.

Line 7. This appears to be the pseudo-Aristotelian work elsewhere called *On Virtue and Vices*, which was written sometime in the first century BC or the first century AD. See Otranto (2000), 84, with n. 13.

Line 11. Dio is Dio of Prusa, also known as Dio Chrysostom, active in the first and early second centuries AD. This essay is also known as Speech 74 in the collected speeches of Dio; in modern editions, it is some twelve to fourteen pages long.

Line 14. Crito here, Simon in 1.19, and Cebes in 1.23 are all in the nominative, and they are the only names in the nominative in this list. All three are followed by "Socratic." Given their case, they should perhaps be taken as titles, with the "Socratic" indicating that they are dialogues (so Linguiti, *CPF* I.1*, 91). More likely, however, they are the names of authors and put in the nominative because all of their works were included in the book roll present in the collection. As Otranto (2000), 85, noted, we know from Diogenes Laertius that Socrates's friend Crito wrote seventeen dialogues that filled one book roll; another friend, Simon, took notes on Socrates's conversations and wrote thirty-three dialogues, all of which fit in one book roll; and a certain Cebes wrote three dialogues (Diog. Laert. 2.121, 122, and 125, respectively). Cebes's three dialogues might easily have fit in one book roll. I take Crito, Simon, and Cebes all as authors, although some doubt persists.

Line 15. It is not known who this Nigrinus was, and perhaps the name should be restored not as Nigrinus but as Peregrinus. See Otranto (2000), 85–86.

Line 16. This is almost certainly Diogenes of Babylonia, a Stoic and student of Chrysippus. He lived roughly from 240 to 150 BC.

Line 18. Linguiti, *CPF* I.1*, 92, considers the letters in this line "indecipherable." The reading is very difficult, and none of the letters is certain, but Otranto (2000), 81 and 86, follows several earlier editors in reading [τ]έλος. If it is the Greek word τέλος, it might mean "the end," that is of this section of the list, or "in sum," or perhaps "conclusion." None of these seems especially apt, since the list continues after this with both form and content identical to what has gone before, so far as can be told.

Column 2, line 1. This might be the Apion, an eminent literary scholar from Alexandria, who is known from Josephus's *Against Apion*. If so, he can be dated to the first century AD.

Line 15. Suggestions for Aelius include Aelius Aristides and Aelius Herodianus. See Linguiti, *CPF* I.1*, 93. The gentilicium Aelius almost certainly indicates a writer of Roman imperial date.

Line 18. This Archimedes might be the famous mathematician of the third century BC, but later authors of this name are known as well.

   3. *P.Jena* inv. 267 = *P.Turner* 39 = Otranto number 14 = *MP*³ 2090.1;
   Apollinopolis Magna, early third century AD; now in Jena (Figure 4)

Three fragments of papyrus, two of which are very small, contain part of what appears to be an inventory of items including both book rolls and domestic objects. There are lacunae of uncertain length, we almost certainly do not have the beginning of the inventory, and we may not have the ending either. Text based on Otranto (2000), but I include the two small fragments as lines 1 to 5.

GREEK TEXT

1   *(One or more lines lost.)*
   ] τόμοι β´
      (One or more lines lost.)
   ]κτηνο`θ´
5   ] . α

   — — —

   [....] .....Φιλήμονο(ς) λ[
   Ἐρατοσθ(ένους) Εἰς τὸν ἐν τῇ Ἰλ[ιάδι
10   Πλάτωνο(ς) λέξεις
   Τὸ εἰς τὰ ἔπη Πρείσκου.[
   Τὸ ἐγκώμιο(ν) Ῥούφο(υ) εἰς ο[
   ἀναγραφὴ σαλαρίο(υ)
   ἀναγραφὴ τῶν ἐν Διοσ[πόλ(ει)
   (About two lines left blank here.)

15   κελλάρια καταλυ *(vacat)*
   μαχαίριον ὁλοσίδ(ηρον)[
   ἀγγεῖα κασσιτέρ[ι]ν[α

ENGLISH TRANSLATION

1   *(One or more lines lost.)*
   2 volumes
   (One or more lines lost.)
   ktenoth
5   (?) a

   (At least two lines lost.)
   (Lacuna of about eight letters.) Philemon's *L*(?)
   Eratosthenes's *On the (?) in the Iliad*
10   *Lexicon of Plato*
   Commentary (?) on the epic (?) poetry of Priscus
   Rufus's *Encomium on (?)*
   Register of payment
   Register of the inhabitants (?) of Dios[polis]
   (About two lines left blank.)

15 storerooms (or containers?) disassembled (? or detached? or in the lodging?)
    iron knife
    tin containers

NOTES AND COMMENTS

Lines 1–5. These lines are contained in two very small fragments. Their placement with respect to the single larger fragment of lines 8 to 18 is not known.

Line 4. The surviving letters are κτηvoθ (= ktenoth). The final theta is raised above the line, as can be seen in figure 4; that probably indicates that the word is abbreviated at this point. Puglia (2000), 193, suggested ἕ]κτη vóθ(η), "sixth, spurious," and interpreted this as meaning that the work, whatever it was, was divided into six parts or books, the sixth of which was marked as a forgery.

Line 8. Several Philemons are known. One was an important writer of New Comedy. Another, a grammarian, wrote a work entitled *Attic Lexicon*. If that is the work referred to, we might restore λ[έξεις] here. See further Otranto (2000), 75.

Line 10. This might be the famous philosopher Plato, but there was also a playwright named Plato.

Line 11. Priscus cannot be identified. G. Poethke, in editing the papyrus, noted that two poets of that name are cited as contemporaries by Ovid, *Pont.* 4.16.10, in a context that implies epic poetry. The name in any case is a Roman name, and Priscus's poetry was probably in Latin.

Line 15. *Cellarion* is a loan word from Latin, and it can refer in Latin, as in Greek, to a wide range of containers, from jars (*P.Oxy.* 4.741.12, second century AD) to storerooms (*P.Oxy.* 16.1851, sixth-seventh century). Puglia takes it as referring to a piece of furniture designed to hold book rolls, perhaps simple shelves that could be hung on walls (Puglia [2000], 195–96).[7] This is an attractive hypothesis, but it is by no means certain, given the range of possible meanings of *cellarion*, and the *cellaria* could be taken rather as storerooms, in which the items that follow in the list, including the tin containers, were to be found.

Lines 16 and 17. These lines appear to be indented one or two spaces.

4. *P.Vars. 5* verso = Otranto number 17 = *MP*³ 2088 = *CPP* 0387;
Arsinoite nome, third century AD; now in Warsaw (Figure 5)

A tall, thin strip of papyrus, 31 cm high by 6 cm wide, contains a highly fragmentary list of authors and works written on the verso of a census list. There are margins of 1.6 cm at the top and 7.9 cm at the bottom, and much or most of the first nineteen lines on the left has been lost. The papyrus presents many problems of reading and interpretation. These have been discussed in detail by papyrologists; the principal treatments are Manteuffel (1933, the editio princeps); Manfredi, Andorlini, and Linguiti in *CPF* I.1*, 99–105; Puglia (1996a) on lines 1–22; Puglia (1997a) on lines 22 bis to 36; and Otranto

---

7. This allows him to suggest that the word following *cellaria* can be completed as καταλυόμενα, "disassembled." Poethke (1981), 165, took the *cellaria* generally as "cabinets" or "containers."

number 17. I comment here briefly on the format of the text but do not provide a full commentary. Text based on Otranto (2000) except as noted in the comments.

GREEK TEXT

1	]..[	
	] Γεμείνου	α'
	] Διογένο(υς) Βαβυλω(νίου)	α'
	] .	γ'
5	Σ]ωκρατικοῦ	α'
	]	β'
	]	θ'
	]	α'
	Ζήνωνος] Ταρσέως	ε'
10	Ζήνωνος Κ]ιτιέως	γ'
	] . Ἱεροκλέους	θ' (ὀπιστόγρ[(αφα)
	] . ε ..	κθ' (ὦν ὀπιστό[γρ(αφα)
	]ου	ζ'
	]	α'
15	]	λβ'
	]	α'
	]	ιγ' (ὦν ὀπισ[τόγρ(αφα)
	] [[ρμβ]]	
	φι]λοσόφων	ρμβ'
20	ὦν ὀ]πιστόγρ(αφα) Γλαύκωνο(ς)	α')
21	]ους θ' Ξενοφῶντο(ς)	β')
22	]Χρυσίππου α' γ(ίνεται)	ιδ')
22 bis	] (ὀπιστόγρ(αφα)	)
23	]υς β' Θεσσαλο(ῦ)	α'
24	] .. θ' [[α]] (ὀπιστόγρ(αφα)	
25	]κο νάρθηξ α'	
26	[ι]γ	
26a	(ὦν ἐν ὀπιστογρ(άφω) Ἐρασιστ[ράτου	
26b	(Θεμίσωνο(ς) θ'	
27	]υτο τὰ προκ(είμενα)	
28	] σορ '	
29	]ὦν ὀπιστό[γρ(αφα) μς')	
30	τῶ]ν προκειμένων	
	] .. καὶ ἕτερα	
	] . νο φιλοσόφου αυα.ε..	
	] . Ἁρποκρατίωνο(ς) ...	
	].ρτου	
35	]..	
	].. ξθ'	

ENGLISH TRANSLATION

	(?)	
	Geminus's	1
	Diogenes the Babylonian's	1
	(?)	3
5	Socraticus's	1
	(?)	2
	(?)	9
	(?)	1
	(?) Zeno (?) of Tarsus's	5
10	(?) Zeno (?) of Citium's	3
	(?) Hierocles's	9 (opisthogr(aphs))
	(?) e..	29 (of which ? are opisthographs)
	(?)ou	7
	(?)	1
15	(?)	32
	(?)	1
		13 (of which ? are opisthographs)
	(?) [[142]]	
	of philosophers	142
20	opisthogr(aphs) Glaucon's	1
21	(?)ous 9 Xenophon's	2 (*or* 3)
22	(?) Chrysippus's 1 adds up to (?)	14
22 bis	(?) (opisthogr(aphs))	
23	(?)ys 2 Thessalus's	1
24	(?) ... 9 [[1]] (opisthogr(aphs))	
25	(?)co narthex	1
26	[1]3(?)	
26a	(of which in opisthogr(aph) Erasistratus's	
26b	(?) Themison's	9
27	(?)uto the ones that are here (?)	
	(?) 296	
	(?) of which 46 (are) opisthographs	
30	of those present	
	(?) and (the) others	
	(?)no(?) philosopher's ana.e.	
	Harpocration's	
	(?)rtus's	
35	(?)	
	(?) 59	

NOTES AND COMMENTS

Line 1. Puglia (1996a), 29, supplies the name Glaucon and reconstructs this line as "Glaucon, Book 1, opisthograph."

Line 5. Puglia (1996a), 29, supplies the name Euclides before Socraticus.

Line 12. Puglia (1996a), 29, reads [Ξενοφόν]το(ς), "Xenophon's."

Lines 18 and 24. The numbers enclosed within double square brackets were crossed out on the papyrus.

Lines 20–22 are enclosed at the right within large looping parentheses that partially encircle the text in those lines on both the top and the bottom. Similarly, lines 26a and 26b are partially encircled by large parentheses at the left; these too extend over and above the lines. In each case, there were presumably corresponding parentheses at the opposite ends of the lines. These large encircling marks are indicated in the Greek text here by regular parentheses. The first part of line 20, in the lacuna, is the suggestion of Puglia (1996a), 29.

Line 21. Most editors have read a beta (i.e., the number 2) at the right end of the line, but Puglia (1996a) believed he could also read a gamma (= 3) just to the right of the beta, and suggested that the beta was written by mistake, then corrected to gamma but not crossed out.

Line 22. The letter gamma is almost certainly an abbreviation for γίνεται, or "adds up to."

Line 25. The first part of this line cannot be read or restored with any confidence.

Line 26. The remains of this line—a gamma (so Manteuffel [1933], 370, and Puglia [1997a], 133) or a tau and omicron (*CPF* I.1* 102, and Otranto [2000], 99)—stand alone, to the left of lines 26a and 26b. Puglia (1997a), 133, restored an iota before the gamma to give the number 13.

Lines 26a and 26b are written in letters somewhat smaller than the letters in other lines, so that the two lines fit in the space of a single line. They are indented slightly, and the indentation provides a space for line 26 to their left. A single tall parenthesis encloses them on the left; I represent that here with a normal parenthesis to the left of each line.

Line 28 consists of a number, sigma (= 200) plus koppa (=90) plus digamma (=6). The koppa and digamma are both uncertain.

Line 29. The parenthesis at the right end of this line is in the papyrus, not an editorial addition. It may indicate the conclusion of a particular section of the list.

5. *P.Oxy.* 33.2659 = Otranto number 6 = *MP*³ 2087.1 = *CPP* 0336;
Oxyrhynchus, second century AD; now in Oxford (Figure 6)

Two fragments of papyrus can be combined to give us much of two columns of what seems to have been a long inventory of titles. There is a gap of approximately twelve lines in the middle of column 1, and another of one or two lines in the middle of column 2. The list is written on the verso of a Greek-to-Latin glossary dated to the first or early second century AD.[8] The surviving portion of the book list presents the names of

---

8. The word list was published as *P.Oxy.* 33.2660.

ten writers of comedy arranged in alphabetical order; an eleventh name can be supplied at the beginning. The names are in the genitive case, and the name of each author is followed by the titles of one or more of his works, generally in single-letter alphabetical order.[9] The authors' names are in ecthesis, that is, they extend two or three spaces to the left of the column of titles. The contents of the list are as follows.[10] Text from Otranto (2000).

Column 1, Greek	*Column 1, English*
1 Μοιχοί	*Lechers*
Σ]απφώ	*Sappho*
Ἀπο]λλωνίου	Apollonius's:
].[.]επίκλητος	(?)epicletus
5 Ἀπολ]λωφάνους	Apollophanes's:
Δα]λίς	*Dalis*
Κρ]ῆτες	*Cretes*
Ἀραρό]τος	Ararus's:
Ἄδ]ωνις	*Adonis*
10 Παρ]θενὶς ἢ Καμπά-	*Parthenis*, or *Campa-*
λι`ο´(ς)	*lius*
]ν...[	(?)n...(?)
Ἀριστο]φάνους	Aristophanes's:
Αἰο]λοσίκων	*Aeolosicon*
15 Ἀμ]φιάρ[εω]ς	*Amphiaraus*
— — —	
(About a dozen lines are lost here.)	
27 Δράματα ἢ Κ]έν`τ´(αυρος)	*Dramata* or *Centaur*
Διόνυσος] Ναυαγ`ό´(ς)	*Dionysus Nauagus*
Εἰρήνη]	*Peace*
30 Ἐκκλησ]ιάζουσαι	*Ecclesiazusae*
Ἥρωες]	*Heroes*
Θεσμο]φορ[ιά]ζουσαι [	*Thesmophoriazusae*
Ἱππ]εῖς	*Knights*
Κώ]καλος	*Cocalus*
35 Λυσ]ιστράτη	*Lysistrata*
Νε]φέλαι β'	*Clouds 2*
Ὁλκ]άδες	*Holcades*

9. With one exception, the authors' names are set out not just in single-letter alphabetical order, but in absolute alphabetical order. The one exception is in column 2, lines 10–12, where Diocles precedes Dinolochos.

10. The line numbers differ here from those given in Otranto (2000) and other publications because I do not indicate the two different fragments of the papyrus. Each fragment contains part of column 1 and part of column 2. Violation in alphabetical order in the English is caused by the transliteration of the Greek alphabet into English letters.

Column 1, Greek	Column 1, English
Ὄρν]ιθες	*Birds*
Προ]άγων	*Proagon*
40　Πλ]οῦτ[ο]ς α′	*Plutus 1*
Ποίησι]ς	*Poiesis*
Πολύ]ειδος	*Polyidus*
Σκηνὰ]ς Καταλαμ‵β′ (ἄνουσαι)	*Scenas Catalambanusae*
Σφῆκ]ες	*Spheces*
45　Τελμη]σσεῖς	*Telmesseis*
Τριφά]λης	*Triphales*
Φοίνισ]σαι	*Phoenissae*
Ὧραι]	*Horae* (?)
........]νους	...]*nous*
50　......].	
......].	

Column 2, Greek	Column 2, English
1　Ἀρχίπ[που	Archippus's:
Ἀμφι[τρύων	*Amphitryon*
Ἡρακλ[ῆς Γαμῶν	*Heracles Gamon*
Ῥείνω[ν	*Rheinon*
5　Αὐτοκρ[άτους	Autocrates's:
Τυμπα[νισταί	*Tympanistae*
Δημητρ[ίου	Demetrius's:
Διονύσου [γοναί	*Dionysus's (Children* ?)
Σικελία	*Sicelia*
10　Διοκλέο[υς	Diocles's:
Θάλατ[τα	*Thalatta*
Δινολόχου	Dinolochus's:
Ἰατρός	*Iatrus*
Κίρκα ἤ .[	*Circe* or ?
15　Λευ[κα]ρ[ίων	*Leucarion*
Μήδεια	*Medea*
Μελέαγ[ρος	*Meleager*
Οἰνεύς	*Oeneus*
Ὀρέστη[ς	*Orestes*
20　....].σ.[	(?) *s* (?)
.....].[	
(*Two or three lines are lost here.*)	
..[	
[	
25　Τήλεφ[ος	*Telephus*
Φόλος	*Pholus*

Column 2, Greek	Column 2, English
(Two lines are lost here.)	
ε[	*e (?)*
..[	
Ἐπιχάρμ[ου	Epicharmus's:
30 Ἀταλάν[ται	*Atalantae*
Ἀγρωστε[ῖνος	*Agrostinus*
Ἄμυκος	*Amycus*
Ἀλκυονε[ύς	*Alcyoneus*
Ἀντάνω[ρ	*Antanor*
35 Ἁρπαγα[	*Harpaga(e?)*
Βούσειρ[ις	*Busiris*
Ἁρπαγα.[	*Harpaga(e?)*
Γᾶ καὶ Θ[άλασσα	*Ge and Thalassa*
Γηραιά[	*Geraia(?)*
40 Δεξα.[	*Dexa(?)*
Διόνυσο[ι	*Dionysoi*
Διόνυσ[	*Dionys(?)*
Δίκτυες[	*Dictyes*
Ἐπινίκ[ιος	*Epinicius*
45 Ἐπινίκ.[ος	*Epinic(ius?)*
[	
Ἐλπὶς [ἡ Πλοῦτος	*Elpis or Plutus*
Ἥβας [Γάμος	*Hebas Gamos*

NOTES AND COMMENTS

This papyrus contains the names of writers of Old Comedy, with one writer, Ararus, who is usually now assigned to Middle Comedy; and following the name of each writer, we have titles of works by that writer, arranged in alphabetical order. For discussions of the individual playwrights and titles of plays, see Rea (1966), the commentary on *P.Oxy.* 33.2659 (also by Rea), and Otranto (2000), 32–38.

Column 1, line 1. Before the first title, we can supply the name of the playwright Amipsias. Both the *Lechers* (*Moechi*) and the *Sappho* are known from other sources, as are other titles by Amipsias.

Checklist of Books in the Collection of the Villa of the Papyri

I present here a checklist of the certain and probable titles so far identified in the Villa's collection. Greek works appear first, Latin second. In each case, works by identified authors precede those by unknown authors (incerti). Wherever possible, I provide an English-language title that is in current use, but where none such exists I have provided my own translations. I list the works alphabetically by author and then by title, using the English titles as the basis for alphabetizing, and ignoring initial prepositions such as "on" and "against" and the word "the." In column 2 I give the total number of books known or thought to have been in each work, and in column 3 I give the number of books of the work known to have been in the Villa's collection. Finally, I add, in column 4, the *P.Herc.* number and the Greek version of the title as it appears in the *subscriptio* or the initial title, or as it has been reconstructed by conjecture by modern scholars. Conjectures are indicated by square brackets. I do not include underdots. It goes without saying that this list is subject to change as papyrologists identify additional works and learn more about those rolls that have already been identified.

I do not attempt to list or identify all of the *P.Herc.* fragments. Rather, I try to include the titles (exact or approximate) of those works that are attested in the collection. In short, this is a study of the book collection, not of the papyrus fragments.

The basis for this list is Gigante's *Catalogo* (Gigante [1979]). More recent titles and information on the manuscripts come from Delattre (2007), 1:xlviii–lii (works of Philodemus, alphabetical by Greek title); Delattre (2006), 137–41 (works of Philodemus, organized by subject); and Houston (2013), 197–208 (works by authors other than Philodemus).[1] A plus sign indicates that two fragments certainly or probably come from the same original roll; an "and" between two *P.Herc.* numbers indicates two separate copies of the same book.

---

1. Much further information on the fragments assigned to works of Philodemus is available in Dorandi (1990a).

GREEK AUTHORS AND WORKS

Author and Title	Number of Books in the Work	Number of Books Attested in the Villa	P.Herc. Number and Greek or Latin Version of Title
Carneiscus			
Philistas	At least 2	1 (Book 2)	*P.Herc.* 1027. Φιλίστας
Chrysippus			
On the Elements of Propositions	At least 1	1	*P.Herc.* 1380. [Πε]ρὶ τῶν [σ]τοιχείων [τ]ῶν λεγομένων[2]
On Foresight	At least 2	2 (Books 1, 2)	*P.Herc.* 1421, 1038. Περὶ προνοίας
Problems of Logic	At least 1	1	*P.Herc.* 307. Λογικῶ[ν] ζητ[η]μ[άτων]
Colotes			
Against Plato's *Euthydemus*	At least 1	1	*P.Herc.* 1032. Πρὸς τ[ὸ]ν Π[λά]των[ος] Εὐθύδημον
Against Plato's *Lysis*	At least 1	1	*P.Herc.* 208. Πρὸς τὸν Πλάτωνος Λύσιν
Demetrius Laco			
On the Aporiae of Polyaenus	At least 5	2 (Books 1, 5)	*P.Herc.* 1258, 1429. Πρὸς τὰς Πολυαίνου ἀπορίας[3]
On the Form of the Divine (?)	At least 1	1	*P.Herc.* 1055. Greek title unknown
On Geometry	At least 1	1	*P.Herc.* 1061. Περὶ γεωμετρίας
On Music	At least 1	1	*P.Herc.* 233 + 860; cf. Janko 2008, 32–35. [Περὶ μουσικῆς]
On Poems	At least 2	2 (Books 1, 2)	*P.Herc.* 188, 1014. Περὶ ποιημάτ[ω]ν
Protreptic to a Student of Philosophy (?)	1	1	*P.Herc.* 831. Greek title unknown[4]
Rhetoric (?)	At least 1	1	*P.Herc.* 128. Greek title unknown
On the Size of the Sun (?)	At least 1	1	*P.Herc.* 1013. Greek title unknown
On Some Topics for Discussion Concerning the Manner of Life	At least 1	1	*P.Herc.* 1006. Περί τινων συζητηθέντων κατὰ δίαιταν

2. Title from Del Mastro (2005a). Exactly how to translate the Greek is not certain. Del Mastro (2005a), 65, provides a "generic" translation, "parti degli enunciati."

3. *P.Herc.* 1258 has a longer but lacunose version of the title.

4. *P.Herc.* 831 was assigned to Demetrius Laco by Philippson (1943); cf. Parisi (2012), 112, n. 4.

Author and Title	Number of Books in the Work	Number of Books Attested in the Villa	P.Herc. *Number and Greek or Latin Version of Title*
Textual and Critical Problems in Epicurus (?)	At least 1	1	*P.Herc.* 1012. Greek title unknown

Epicurus

Echelaus	At least 1	1	*P.Herc.* 566. Ἐχέλαος[5]
On Nature	37	8 (Books 2, 11, 14, 15, 21, 25, 28, 34)[6]	*P.Herc.* 1149 + 993, 1783 + 1691 + 1010, 154, 1042, 1148, 1151, 362, 1191, 1420 + 1056, 419, 459, 697, 1634, 1479 + 1417, 1431. Περὶ φύσεως

Metrodorus of Lampsacus

On Wealth	At least 1	1	*P.Herc.* 200. Περὶ π[λο]ύτου
Against the Dialecticians or Against the Sophists	At least 1	1	*P.Herc.* 255 + 418 + 1084 + 1091 + 1112. Πρὸς τοὺς (?)

Philodemus

Against Demonstration (?), from Zeno's lectures	At least 3	1 (Book 3)	*P.Herc.* 1389. Κατ[ὰ τῆς] ἀ[ποδ]εί[ξ]εως ἐκ τῶν Ζήνωνος σχολῶν
On Anger[7]	At least 1	1	*P.Herc.* 182. [Πε]ρὶ ὀργῆς
On Arrogance[8]	At least 1	1	*P.Herc.* 1008. Περὶ κακιῶν ι′; probably Περὶ ὑπερηφανίας
On Avarice (?)[9]	At least 1	1	*P.Herc.* 253, 415, 465, 896, 1090, and 1613 (?). Περὶ φιλαργυρίας?

5. Del Mastro (2011–12) has read this title, below Epicurus's name in the genitive, at the end of the final column in *P.Herc.* 566, but almost nothing else of this papyrus can be read. The work is not otherwise attested, and nothing is known of Echelaus.

6. There are at least two copies each of Books 2 and 11 and at least three copies of Book 25. Many fragments have been assigned to the *On Nature*, but not to any particular book. For the identification of *P.Herc.* 362 as Book 21, see Del Mastro (2012a).

7. We learn from its *subscriptio* that *On Anger* probably formed part of a larger work, but the title of the larger work is not preserved. Scholars have posited a multivolume *On the Passions*, to which *On Anger* might be assigned; see further Delattre (2006), 88, or Capasso (2010b), 97.

8. This manuscript was Book 10 in the multivolume work *On Vices and the Opposing Virtues*. The subtitle, *On Arrogance*, does not appear in the *subscriptio* of this roll. We know, however, of a roll described by Winckelmann that seems to have had an initial title including the letters φανίας. That roll, long thought lost, is probably the initial part of *P.Herc.* 1008: Indelli (2010), 325.

9. The title of this book is inferred from its contents. It almost certainly was one of the subsections of *On Vices*, which is probably to be restored in the initial title of *P.Herc.* 253. See Capasso (2010b), 102–4. Several uncertainties remain.

Author and Title	Number of Books in the Work	Number of Books Attested in the Villa	P.Herc. *Number and Greek or Latin Version of Title*
On Calumny[10]	At least 1	1	*P.Herc.Paris.* 2. Perhaps Περὶ διαβολῆς
On Choices and Avoidances (? a.k.a. Ethica Comparetti)	At least 1	1	*P.Herc.* 1251. Greek title unknown[11]
On Conversation	At least 1	1	*P.Herc.* 873. Περὶ ὁμιλίας
On Death[12]	At least 4	1 (Book 4)	*P.Herc.* 1050. Περὶ θανάτου
On the Eleatics and Abderites (?)[13]	At least 1	1	*P.Herc.* 327; cf. Cavalieri (2002).
On Envy (?)[14]	At least 1	1	*P.Herc.* 1678. Greek title unknown
Epicurean Ethics (?)	At least 1	1	*P.Herc.* 346. Greek title unknown
On Epicurus	At least 2	2 (Book 2 and another)	*P.Herc.* 1289, 1232, 118a.[15] Περὶ Ἐπικούρου
On Flattery[16]	Probably 2	2	*P.Herc.* 222 + 1675 (Book 1), 1457 (Book 2), et al. Περὶ κολακείας
On Frank Speech[17]	1	1	*P.Herc.* 1471. Περὶ παρρ[η]σίας
On the Gods	At least 3	At least 2 (Books 1, 3)	*P.Herc.* 26, 152 + 157 columns 10–15. Περὶ θεῶν

10. This manuscript was one of the parts of the multivolume work *On Vices and the Opposing Virtues*. For the reconstruction of the title, see Monet (2011).

11. The title of this work is not attested and must be inferred. Gigante (1979), 291–92, suggested Περὶ αἱρέσεων καὶ φυγῶν.

12. Henry (2010) is a new edition of this text. It is securely identified by its end title: Henry (2010), 94–95. *P.Herc.* 807 was tentatively assigned to *On Death* by Crönert (1906), 114, n. 515, and may contain parts of one of the other rolls: Henry (2010), xv, n. 18; cf. Giuliano (2009).

13. This manuscript was one part of Philodemus's multivolume work on the history of the philosophical schools, known collectively as the Σύνταξις τῶν φιλοσόφων. The exact Greek title of this particular part is not known.

14. Tepedino Guerra (1985) takes this work as part of a multivolume work *On Passions*. It could conceivably have been one of the books in *On Vices and the Opposing Virtues*.

15. *P.Herc.* 1232 and 1289 are securely assigned to Philodemus by their *subscriptiones*. *P.Herc.* 118a may be by Philodemus or some other author, and may be on Epicurus or on the Epicurean school. See Militello (1997), 82–83. Dorandi (1980) suggested that *P.Herc.* 1780, on Epicurus's Garden, may also have been a part of the history of the Epicureans.

16. The initial title of *P.Herc.* 222 gives us the title of this book—Περὶ κολακείας—and tells us that it was the first book (not the seventh, as earlier scholars had thought) of the larger work *On Vices*: Angeli (1994), 76–78. Capasso (2010b), 101, lists the other fragments to be assigned to this roll and notes that *P.Herc.* 1675, with a double *subscriptio*, formed the end of the roll. Capasso argues that the second book (*P.Herc.* 1457) dealt with vices similar to or associated with flattery. *P.Herc.* 1457 has both an initial title and a *subscriptio* that assign the roll to the *On Vices* but provide no subtitle.

17. We know from the *subscriptio* of *P.Herc.* 1471 that *On Frank Speech* is one book in the multivolume work *Epitome of Characters and Lives from Zeno's Lectures*.

Author and Title	Number of Books in the Work	Number of Books Attested in the Villa	P.Herc. *Number and Greek or Latin Version of Title*
On the Good King According to Homer	At least 1	1	*P.Herc.* 1507. Περὶ τοῦ καθ' Ὅμ[ηρ]ον ἀγα[θοῦ] βασ[ιλέως]
On Gratitude[18]	At least 1	1	*P.Herc.* 1414. Π[ερὶ χ]άριτος
On Household Management[19]	At least 1	1	*P.Herc.* 1424. [Περὶ οἰκονομίας]
On the Lectures (?) of Zeno	At least 3	1 (Book 3)	*P.Herc.* 1003. Περ[ὶ τ]ῶν Ζ[ή]νων[ος σχολῶν]
Life of Philonides[20]	At least 1	1	*P.Herc.* 1044. Greek title unknown
Life of Socrates (?)[21]	At least 1	1 (probably in two copies)	*P.Herc.* 558 and 495.[22] Greek title unknown
On the Manner of Life and Character (?)	At least 2	1 (Book 1)	*P.Herc.* 168. [.... Περὶ βί]ω[ν καὶ] ἠθ[ῶν]
On Music	At least 4	1 (Book 4)	*P.Herc.* 1497 et al. Περὶ μουσικῆς
On Phenomena and Inferences	At least 3	1 (Book 3)	*P.Herc.* 1065. Περὶ [φαινομένων? καὶ] σ[ημε]ιώσεων[23]
On Piety	At least 1	1	*P.Herc.* 1098, 1088, 1428, et al.[24] Περὶ εὐσεβείας
On Plato and the Academy[25]	At least 1	2 copies	*P.Herc.* 1021, 164. Greek title unknown
On Poems	5	5	*P.Herc.* 207, 1425 et al., 1538, 466 et al., 1074b et al., 1087 + 1403.[26] Περὶ ποιημάτων

18. This title may have been one of the parts of the multivolume work *On Vices and the Opposing Virtues*, but Delattre (2006), 137, and (2007), xlviii, assigned it rather to the *(Epitome) of Characters and Lives*.

19. English translation from Sider (2005), 111, n. 167. The *subscriptio* tells us that this is Book 9 in the multivolume work *On Vices and the Opposing Virtues*, but the title *On Household Management* (or, as it is sometimes rendered, *On Thrift*) must be inferred from the contents.

20. It is likely, but not certain, that it was Philodemus who wrote the life of Philonides preserved in *P.Herc.* 1044. See De Sanctis (2009), 107–9.

21. For the title and content, see Gallo (2002), 61–62. Giuliano (2001) suggested *History of Socrates and His School*.

22. For these papyri as two copies of the same work: Baldassarri, cited by Gallo (2002), 59–60; cf. Giuliano (2001).

23. This title is particularly uncertain. Delattre (2007), li, for example, provides a substantially different restoration.

24. Obbink (1996) is an edition of Part One of this work. Obbink (1996), 64, listed the constituent papyri, which seem all to have come from a single roll: Janko (2000), 114, with n. 7. According to Janko, the roll was an estimated 23.1 m long.

25. This is one of the books in the multivolume work called the *Syntaxis*, or history of the philosophical schools. *P.Herc.* 1021 seems to be notes, excerpts, and early drafts of short sections: Cavallo (1984), 14–17; cf. Capasso (2000), 21–24, and Dorandi (2007), 40–42.

26. Janko (2000) and Janko (2011) gather and publish the fragments of Books 1 and 3–4, respectively. The copy of *On Poems*, Book 5, in *P.Herc.* 1538 was divided into two rolls. *P.Herc.* 1538 is the

Author and Title	Number of Books in the Work	Number of Books Attested in the Villa	P.Herc. Number and Greek or Latin Version of Title
On the Pythagoreans (?)[27]	At least 1	1	*P.Herc.* 1508. Greek title unknown.
On Rhetoric	10 (?)	More than 5 (Books 1, 2, 3, 4, 7, 8?, 10?)	*P.Herc.* 1427 + 234 and 1619; 1674 and 1672; 1506 and 1426; 1423, 1007 + 1673, 1004, 1015 + 832, 1078 + 1080; plus many other fragments.[28] Περὶ ῥητορικῆς
To His School Companions (?)	5	1 (Book 1?)	*P.Herc.* 1005.[29] Πρὸς τοὺς (?)
On Sensations (?)	At least 1	1	*P.Herc.* 19 + 698. Greek title unknown
Sketches of Epicureans[30]	At least 1	2 copies	*P.Herc.* 1418, 239a + 1787 (and 310 and 474?). Πε[ρὶ] τῶν [.] Ἐπικ[ο]ύ[ρου τε] καί τινων ἄλλω[ν] πραγματεῖαι μνημ[άτων?]
On the Stoics[31]	At least 1	3 copies	*P.Herc.* 339, 155, 1018. Περὶ τῶν Στωικῶν
On Wealth	At least 2	1 (Book 1)	*P.Herc.* 163. Περὶ πλούτου

Polystratus

Author and Title	Number of Books in the Work	Number of Books Attested in the Villa	P.Herc. Number and Greek or Latin Version of Title
Against Irrational Doubters[32]	At least 1	1	*P.Herc.* 336 + 1150. Περὶ ἀλόγου καταφρονήσεως, οἱ δ' ἐπιγράφουσιν Πρὸς τοὺς ἀλόγως καταθρασυνομένους τῶν ἐν τοῖς πολλοῖς δοξαζομένων
On Philosophy	At least 2	1 (Book 1)	*P.Herc.* 1520. Περὶ φιλοσοφίας

---

second of the two; so far as I know, the first has not been identified yet. Janko (2000), 12–13, provides a table of the fragments and books to which they should probably be assigned.

27. This title is quite uncertain: Cavalieri (2002).

28. At least two of the books of the *On Rhetoric* are present in duplicate copies: Book 2, *P.Herc.* 1674 and 1672 ; Book 3, *P.Herc.* 1506 and 1426. *P.Herc.* 1004 probably contains a fragment of Book 7: Del Mastro (2012b). For the fragments of Book 4, see Fimiani (2012). Many uncertainties remain.

29. For the number of books in this work, see Del Mastro (2002), 247. Del Mastro (2002), 245, n. 4, summarizes the suggestions that have been made to complete the title.

30. This work is often called *Memorie Epicuree* in the modern literature. For the content, hand, and date of *P.Herc.* 239a + 1787, see Janko (2008), 42–43. He suggests that *P.Herc.* 310 and 474 may belong to the same roll as 239a + 1787. *P.Herc.* 1418 is a second copy.

31. This is one of the books in the multivolume work called the *Syntaxis*, or history of the philosophical schools. *P.Herc.* 339 may be a provisional draft, *P.Herc.* 155 the finished product.

32. For the unusually long title in Greek, see above, section 3.8. It may be not Polystratus's title for the work, but added by a copyist.

Author and Title	Number of Books in the Work	Number of Books Attested in the Villa	P.Herc. *Number and Greek or Latin Version of Title*
Zeno of Sidon			
Response to the *On Geometric Proofs* of Craterus[33]	At least 1	1	*P.Herc.* 1533. Πρὸς τὸ Κρατεροῦ Πρὸς τὸ περὶ τῶν γεωμετρικῶν ἀποδείξεων
Uncertain authors (Greek)			
Treatise on Poverty and Wealth[34]	At least 1	1	*P.Herc.* 1570. Greek title unknown
Passages from a series of Epicurean works	At least 1	1	*P.Herc.* 1111. Title unknown
On the Friends of Epicurus[35]	At least 1	1	*P.Herc.* 176. Title unknown
Final Illness of an Epicurean	At least 1	1	*P.Herc.* 1041. Title unknown
On Physics?	At least 1	1	*P.Herc.* 439. Title unknown
On Ethics?	At least 1	1	*P.Herc.* 1696. Title unknown

Latin Works[36]

Description of the Work	Number of Books in the Work	Number of Books Attested in the Villa	P.Herc. *Number and Latin Title*
Poem (epic?); the surviving fragment describes the Battle of Actium	At least 1	1	*P.Herc.* 817 + 399. Title unknown[37]
Oration addressed to the emperor (?)	At least 1	1	*P.Herc.* 1067. Title unknown
Oration, probably judicial	At least 1	1	*P.Herc.* 1475. Title unknown
Oration, probably political	At least 1	1	*P.Herc.* 238a. Title unknown
Verse, perhaps epic?	At least 1	1	*P.Herc.* 395.[38]
Prose, perhaps history?	At least 1	1	*P.Herc.* 863.[39]

33. The title is not easy to translate. Kleve and Del Mastro (2000), 153, render it into Italian as "A Cratero 'Contro il libro sulle dimostrazioni di geometria.'"

34. For the subject and text, see Ponczoch (2009). This may well be by Philodemus and is perhaps another book of *On Wealth* known from *P.Herc.* 163: Armstrong and Ponczoch (2011).

35. Longo Auricchio (2008), 198, restores the title as *Sugli amici di Epicuro.*

36. I include here only those *P.Herc.* fragments where something of the nature of the text can be known. For a survey of what survives on other Latin fragments, see Ammirati (2010), 10–13.

37. This papyrus has been given a modern title, *De bello Actiaco.*

38. Kleve (1989 and 2007) identified *P.Herc.* 395, as well as the fragments *P.Herc.* 1829–31, as coming from Lucretius's *De rerum natura.* This is not correct: Capasso (2011), 63–86. *P.Herc.* 395 does, however, seem to contain fragments of verse. See Beer (2009), 75–77.

39. Radiciotti (2009), 114: this fragment may contain a *subscriptio* mentioning the eighth book of some work.

Catalog of Manuscripts in the Breccia + GH3 Find

I list here the papyri found by Evaristo Breccia in the Kôm Ali el Gamman in 1932, combined with those from Grenfell and Hunt's third find. Items are arranged in order of their *MP³* number. We have only fragments of each of the works named in column 1, not the entire work or book; but in all cases I presume the roll originally contained the entire work or book. In column 2, all dates are AD, and scribe numbers refer to the numbers assigned by Johnson (2004), 61–65. In column 3, I do not mention standard additions to the text, such as accent marks, the correction of spelling mistakes, and common punctuation such as the *paragraphus*. I do mention anything that seems unusual or worthy of notice. In column 4, items that are known only from their publication in *P.Oxy.* volume 17 are marked by an asterisk. The list consists of three parts: Identifiable Works in Greek; Greek Adespota; and Texts in Latin.

I omit from this catalog a codex that contained several works by Philo, although I included it in my earlier publication of this concentration.[1] The two largest surviving sections of it were published by Grenfell and Hunt as *P.Oxy.* 9.1173 and 11.1356, and neither of those volumes is known to have included any materials from the third find. It would appear that a few small fragments became detached from the codex and came to rest near the concentration I call Breccia + GH3, but are not a part of that concentration.

---

1. Houston (2007), 343.

Author and Work	Century; Scribe If Known	Condition of Manuscript; Repairs, Marginalia, Opisthograph, etc.	MP³ Number
IDENTIFIABLE WORKS IN GREEK			
Aeschylus, *Dictyulci*	2nd; scribe A3	Stichometric mark, a theta (= 800), opposite column 2, line 2, of *P.Oxy.* 18.2161	26
Aeschylus, *Glaucus Potnieus*	2nd; scribe A3		28
Aeschylus, *Myrmidons*[2]	2nd; scribe A3		33
Aeschylus, *Myrmidons* (?)	2nd; scribe A10	One paraphrase in a second hand[3]	34
Aeschylus, *Niobe*	2nd; scribe A3		36
Aristophanes, *Thesmophoria-zusae*	2nd	In *PSI* 11.1194, fragment 6, *subscriptio* and possible stichometric count: [Αριστοφαν]ους / [Θεσμοφορι]-αζουσαι / [?]ΧΗΠΙ[4]	154
A work on Hellenistic history, possibly by Arrian[5]	2nd	Each column was numbered. The second surviving column was number 82 (ΠΒ). This text is on the recto; on the verso, in a more recent hand, is part of a glossary of shorthand symbols (= *MP³* 2776.5, below).	168.01
Callimachus, *Aetia*, prologue to Book 1 and fragments from uncertain books	1st half of 2nd century	Four marginal annotations survive, all probably paraphrases and in a second hand.[6]	195
Callimachus, *Aetia*, Book 1	2nd		*PSI* 11.1217 B[7]

2. This manuscript includes *P.Oxy.* 18.2163 and *PSI* 15.1472, the latter of which was destroyed in World War II. For the connection between the two fragments, and the assignment of them to the collection represented by Breccia + GH3, see Bartoletti (1966), 121–23, and Ciampi (2009), 148.

3. Date of manuscript: Cavallo (2008), 95. Annotation: McNamee (2007), 131.

4. Nothing else survives on this fragment, so we cannot tell where the *subscriptio* stood in relation to the column. Vitelli, commenting on *PSI* 11.1194, noted that the last line of the *subscriptio* (fragment 6) may be a number (that is, a stichometric count), but that the reading is very uncertain.

5. What survives deals with the time of the successors of Alexander. Bosworth (1978), 228–29, argued that it is a fragment from Arrian's *History of the Successors*.

6. McNamee (2007), 220–21.

7. *MP³* includes this fragment along with the others listed under *MP³*195. *PSI* 11.1217A, fragment 2, lines 1–8, however, contain the same text as *PSI* 11.1217B, lines 6–13, so the two fragments must represent two different copies of the same poem. They are in two different hands.

Author and Work	Century; Scribe If Known	Condition of Manuscript; Repairs, Marginalia, Opisthograph, etc.	MP³ Number
Commentary on Callimachus, *Aetia*, Book 1	2nd?[8]	Format: a line is given in ecthesis, then there are comments, including explanations of terms and names. Many abbreviations.	196
Callimachus, *Aetia*, Book 2	2nd	Extensive annotations, from one to four lines long, all in hand of original scribe. Contents: metaphrases; etymologies of place names; explanation of a festival.[9]	206*
Callimachus, *Aetia*, Book 3	2nd half of 2nd century		207.2 and 207.21[10]
Callimachus, *Aetia*, Books 3 and 4	1st or 2nd		207.4
Callimachus, *Iambi, Lyrica*, et al.	1st or 2nd[11]	One annotation, a metaphrase[12]	222
Cratinus, *Ploutoi*	2nd		253
Demosthenes, *Olynthiac 3*	Late 1st or 2nd[13]	Subtitle below final column: ολυνθια[...], followed by a margin of 8 cm	259
Demosthenes, *Against Leptines*	2nd		301
Demosthenes, *Against Androtion*	2nd, perhaps late[14]	Perhaps the same copyist as the one who did Isocrates, *On the Peace* (*PSI* 11.1199 = MP³ 1271), q.v. below[15]	309
Demosthenes, *Against Aphobus*	2nd; scribe A8		326

8. The date is from Bastianini (2006), 152, but it is not certain, and others have suggested dates as early as the first century and as late as the third. Bastianini notes that the hand is informal and rapid.

9. McNamee (2007), 228–31.

10. *MP³* noted that these two papyri probably both come from the same roll. For further confirmation of that, see Ciampi (2009), 148 and 150: we now know that *P.Oxy.* 18.2173 (= *MP³* 207.2) was found by Grenfell and Hunt in their fifth season at Oxyrhynchus, so it may well have been part of the third find.

11. First century: Vitelli, ad *PSI* 11.1216. Second: Lobel, ad *P.Oxy.* 18.2171.

12. McNamee (2007), 234. The note was added by a second hand.

13. Second century: Vitelli, ad *PSI* 11.1205. Late first century: Manfredi, ad *PSI Congr.XVII* 11 (*PSI* inv. 2018).

14. Date: Cavallo (2008), 109.

15. Dörrie, ad *PSI* 11.1199, noted the similarity of hands.

Author and Work	Century; Scribe If Known	Condition of Manuscript; Repairs, Marginalia, Opisthograph, etc.	MP³ Number
Euphorion, *Thrax* and *Hippomedon Maior*[16]	2nd; scribe A5	Numerous annotations in the intercolumnar spaces. On *Thrax*, fragment B, four are by a second hand, one by a third. Most are on matters of fact, such as city names.[17]	371
Commentary, probably on a work by Euphorion[18]	Early 2nd	Format: lemmata in ecthesis, followed by comments	374*
Eupolis, *Prospaltioi* (?)	2nd[19]		377
Euripides, *Phoenissae*	2nd		423
Euripides, *Alcmaeon*[20]	2nd; scribe A24	Annotations in a second hand. One might be a stage direction.[21]	431[22]
Herodotus, Book 1	2nd	Strengthening strips of papyrus on back[23]	462*
Herodotus, Book 1	3rd		464*
Herodotus, Book 8	1st half of 2nd century		481*
Hesiod, *Works and Days*	3rd, probably 1st half		490*
Hesiod, *Theogony*	2nd, middle of century		492*
Hesiod, *Theogony*	2nd or 3rd; scribe B3	*Subscriptio*: ΗΣΙΟΔΟΥ / ΘΕΟΓΟΝΙΑ[24]	493.2

16. These are the two poems attested. The roll may have contained others as well.

17. McNamee (2007), 250–51.

18. Nature of the work and author whose work is commented on: Lloyd-Jones and Parsons (1983), 218. The commentary may be on a poem called the *Chiliades*, which was written in the third century BC and attacked people who owed money to the poet.

19. Date: Cavallo (2008), 95. Cavallo noted this and similar scripts as particularly handsome.

20. Euripides wrote two plays about Alcmaeon. It is not known which of the two these fragments belong to.

21. McNamee (2007), 257.

22. MP³ 431.1 (= *P.Oxy.* 45.3215, fragment 1) may well be another fragment from this same roll. The hand and format are identical, according to Lobel, ad *P.Oxy.* 45.3215; but, as Lobel noted, the marginal annotations in MP³ 431 (= *PSI* 13.1302) and MP³ 431.1 (= *P.Oxy.* 45.3215, fragment 1) are in two different hands. It is possible, of course, that more than one person added notes to the one manuscript. The provenance of *P.Oxy.* 45.3215, fragment 1, cannot be established. See further Kannicht in *TrGF* 5.2.948–9.

23. Cursive writing is visible on the strips. For the repair: Puglia (1997b), 32–33.

24. On the *subscriptio*, see Schironi (2010), 156–57, in particular the detail photograph on 157. As

Author and Work	Century; Scribe If Known	Condition of Manuscript; Repairs, Marginalia, Opisthograph, etc.	MP³ Number
Hesiod, *Catalog of Women*	2nd		516.4
Homer, *Iliad* 6	2nd, probably 1st half		792
Homer, *Iliad* 6	2nd or 3rd	On the verso; the recto contains administrative accounts. The end of Book 6 is marked by a *coronis* with *paragraphus*.[25]	795
Homer, *Iliad* 9	1st or, less likely, 2nd		848
Homer, *Iliad* 9	2nd	Hand similar to but not the same as that of *MP³* 848.	849
Homer, *Iliad* 10	2nd or 3rd	On the verso; the recto contains administrative accounts of the 2nd half of the 2nd century. The end of Book 10 is marked by a *coronis*, *paragraphus*, and *subscriptio*: ιλιαδος / κ.[26]	852.02
Homer, *Iliad* 23 and 24	2nd, probably 2nd half	Two fragments, *PSI* 11.1189 and *PSI* 14.1379. The latter contains fragments of *Iliad* 23, the former of *Iliad* 24. Perhaps from two separate rolls.	1008
Homer, *Odyssey* 5	2nd or 3rd		1060
Homer, *Odyssey* 16	2nd		1124
Isocrates, *To Nicocles*	2nd half of 1st century[27]		1253
Isocrates, *On the Peace*	2nd; perhaps by same scribe as 309		1271
Lysias, *Epitaphius*	2nd or early 3rd; scribe A8		1291

Schironi points out, we cannot tell if this was the end of this roll, or if another work, such as *Works and Days*, followed.

25. Schironi (2010), 152–53, discusses the *coronis* and *paragraphus*. Because of the fragmentary state of the papyrus, we do not know if there was an end title as well.

26. Schironi (2010), 154–55. The elegant script and format of *MP³* 795 (*Iliad* 6) and *MP³* 852.02 (*Iliad* 10), both written on the verso of documents, led Lama (1991), 97, to suggest that the two manuscripts had belonged to one person.

27. For the date: Messeri Savorelli and Tempesta, *CPF* I.2, 21.19 (p. 444).

Author and Work	Century; Scribe If Known	Condition of Manuscript; Repairs, Marginalia, Opisthograph, etc.	MP³ Number
Phlegon, *Chronica* (?)[28]	Late 2nd		1348*
Pindar, *Olympian* 2	Late 2nd	Two scribes. The original scribe was replaced by another somewhere in the 7 lines lost between lines 46 and 54 of column 2.	1353*
Plato, *Phaedrus*	2nd, probably 2nd half	Corrections that seem to be based on a second archetype[29]	1400.1
Plato, *Gorgias*	2nd	Annotations in a second hand. One, at the top of a column, may summarize the text in the column below.[30]	1414
Plato, *Timaeus*	2nd		1426
Sappho, Book 2	Late 1st or early 2nd;[31] scribe A6	*Subscriptio*: Σαπφο[ῦς μελῶν] / Β Marginal notes refer to a column lost at the left. At least five separate notes on about twelve lines of text, all in the hand of the original scribe.[32]	1448*
Sophocles, *Ajax*	Late 2nd or early 3rd		1461*
Sophocles, *Oedipus Rex*	2nd	Four marginal notes, all in a second hand. One explains a custom, another points out the similarity of some lines to others at the beginning of the play.[33] Two provide paraphrases.	1466 = *PSI* 11.1192 and *P.Oxy.* 18.2180[34]

28. Phlegon of Tralles was a freedman of Hadrian. Among his compositions was an historical summary that seems to have been organized by Olympiads, as is the material in this fragment.

29. Hunt, ad *P.Oxy.* 17.2102: the manuscript was "subjected to a revision whereby a number of readings have been brought in from another source."

30. The suggestion is that of McNamee (2007), 351.

31. Date: Turner (1973), 22.

32. The content of the annotations is uncertain. McNamee (2007), 355–56, takes two of them as possibly metaphrases, the other two as perhaps explanations (of a proverb, for example).

33. For the annotations, see McNamee (2007), 363. Apropos of the note on line 197, she suggests that "the unusual disjointedness of the note suggests it may have been captured in haste during an oral lecture."

34. Barrett (2007), 369, argued that *PSI* 11.1192 and *P.Oxy.* 18.2180 are not from the same roll. If he is correct, then the collection would seem to have had two copies of the *Oedipus Rex*. Barrett noted

Author and Work	Century; Scribe If Known	Condition of Manuscript; Repairs, Marginalia, Opisthograph, etc.	MP³ Number
Sophocles, *Scyrii?* or *Nauplius?*[35]	Late 2nd or early 3rd; scribe A24		1478*
Sophron, mime(s) about women[36]	1st	Lectional marks were added by the original scribe and may have been intended to help in oral reading.	1482
Thucydides, Book 1	3rd or 2nd; scribe A33	The corrector was probably checking the text against a second exemplar: Haslam ad *P.Oxy.* 57.3882.	1509
Xenophon, *Anabasis* 6	3rd or 2nd		1542
Xenophon, *Cyropaedia* 1	Late 2nd?[37]		1545*[38]
Xenophon, *Hellenica*, 5 and 6	Late 1st or 2nd	The fragments presumably come from two separate rolls but are all by one scribe.	1555[39]

that *P.Oxy.* 18.2180 is an elegant roll: each column contains exactly 20 lines, and there are ample upper and lower margins of at least 4 cm.

35. For the title *Scyrii*: Pfeiffer (1933). *Nauplius* was the suggestion of Gilbert Murray, cited by Hunt, ad *P.Oxy.* 17.2077.

36. In one of the surviving fragments, a ritual is in progress. For its subject and a possible connection with a mime by Sophron called *The Women Who Say They Are Expelling the Goddess*, see Hordern (2004), 127–28.

37. Cavallo (1967), 65, suggested a fourth-century date. If he is correct, this manuscript (*P.Oxy.* 17.2101) is not likely to have been part of Grenfell and Hunt's third find, which was found commingled with third-century documents. Turner, however, cited by Paap, ad *P.Oxy.* 36.2750, suggested that *P.Oxy.* 17.2101 (= *MP³* 1545) and *P.Oxy.* 36.2750 (= *MP³* 1544.1) are from the same roll, which he seems to have dated in the late second century.

38. *MP³* 1544.1 (= *P.Oxy.* 36.2750), containing the beginning of Book 1 of Xenophon's *Cyropaedia*, may belong to this same roll. See previous note.

39. It is not certain that all of the fragments listed in *MP³* belong to the Breccia + GH3 concentration. The fragments are published as *PSI* 11.1197, *PSI Congr.XVII* 8 (both found by Breccia in 1932), and *P.Oxy.* 2.226. The last was published in 1899, and so cannot have been found within their "third find," since that did not occur until the 1905–6 season. It was presumably found by Grenfell and Hunt during their survey at Oxyrhynchus in 1897. How are we to explain the presence of fragments of the same work copied by the same scribe but discovered, some in 1897 and others in 1932? We might guess that Grenfell and Hunt found the fragments that became *P.Oxy.* 2.226 in the Kôm Ali el-Gamman (the mound where they found the third find), since they describe surveying the whole site in 1897 and taking samples here and there. Or perhaps, when the Xenophon text was thrown out, some fragments of it were carried by the wind from one part of the dump to another.

Author and Work	Century; Scribe If Known	Condition of Manuscript; Repairs, Marginalia, Opisthograph, etc.	MP³ Number
GREEK ADESPOTA			
A comedy	2nd		1636
A comedy	2nd		1637
Commentary on choral lyric, probably Pindar[40]	2nd; scribe A5	Format: a line is given in ecthesis, then there are comments. In one case, the comment is thirteen lines long.	1949
Sophron (?)[41]	2nd		1981
Socratic-style dialogue[42]	Late 1st or early 2nd		2098
Glossary	2nd	Entries beginning with the letter alpha survive. Words are alphabetized to two letters. Format: a word is given, then there is an example of its use drawn from some prose source.[43]	2120*
A work on stories or proverbs[44]	2nd		2298
Notes on rhetoric[45]	3rd	On verso. The recto contains a commentary on a comedy (= MP³ 2860, below).	2300*
Oration delivered before an emperor[46]	2nd or 3rd		2522

40. For Pindar as the author of the lines commented on, see Lavecchia (1996).

41. For the tentative assignment of this small fragment to Sophron, see Hordern (2002). Hordern characterizes the script as a "small, elegant uncial."

42. The dialogue was probably written in the fourth century BC. It seems to be cast in the form of a discussion between an oligarch and a partisan of democracy, with the former dominating. See Gigante (1949) and Merkelbach (1949).

43. The glossary was highly selective, containing very few words: Esposito (2005), 79. No principle of selection has been identified.

44. The fragment deals with types of story or perhaps proverbs. It may be part of a larger rhetorical work, a short treatment of the topic, or part of an introduction to a collection of proverbs.

45. First taken as possibly part of a formal treatise, this fragment more likely consists of notes taken during a lecture or class: the notes seem to be a series of observations, not part of a coherent argument. See Cribiore (2001), 144, and, with additional arguments, McNamee (2007), 20.

46. The speech is in defense of a certain Didymus. Bolelli, ad *PSI* 11.1222, points out that it is simple in style and so does not seem to be a rhetorical exercise. Implicitly, then, he takes it as a real speech of unknown date.

Author and Work	Century; Scribe If Known	Condition of Manuscript; Repairs, Marginalia, Opisthograph, etc.	MP³ Number
Novel about Ninus[47]	2nd half of 1st century	A professionally written copy, with punctuation to aid the reader. Columns follow Maas's Law.[48] Each column has fifty lines of text, and there seems to have been an attempt to economize on papyrus.[49]	2617
Narrative, perhaps from a comic novel called the novel of Panionis[50]	2nd, middle or somewhat later	Professional but informal copy, with punctuation to aid the reader	2625 and 2625.01
List of words with their tachygraphic equivalents	3rd, probably 2nd half	On verso. The recto is the Hellenistic history *MP³* 168.01, above. Format: words listed in alphabetical order. The tachygraphic symbol of each word is entered to the left of the word.[51]	2776.5
Commentary on a comedy[52]	2nd half of 2nd century	On recto. On the verso are notes on rhetoric (*MP³* 2300, above). Format: lemmata in ecthesis.	2860*

47. For this novel, see Stephens and Winkler (1995), 23–71. The text has been republished several times, most recently by Bastianini (2010), with a full textual commentary.

48. Bastianini (2010), 280.

49. The physical properties of this roll are well described by Del Corso (2010), 247 and 253. He would date it to about the middle of the first century AD, and he notes that it was certainly copied by a professional scribe.

50. *MP³* 2625 (= *PSI* 11.1220); *MP³* 2625.01 (= *P.Oxy.* 71.4811). The two fragments are in the same hand. They may come from the same roll, from two different rolls of the same work, or two different works. Del Corso (2010), 257–58, takes them as coming from two rolls of a single work, the novel of Panionis, and I follow him here. Parsons (2010), noting that one fragment (*MP³* 2625.01) deals with someone named Panionis, the other (*MP³* 2625) with someone named Staphylus, discusses how they might both have fit into one and the same novel. On the Staphylus fragment see also Stephens and Winkler (1995), 429–31. It may yet turn out to be from a separate work.

51. The surviving fragment contains nouns, verbs, and adjectives drawn from various contexts and may well have been used in the course of training a student in tachygraphy. See further Menci, ad *PSI Congr.XX* 4.

52. Luppe (1978–79), 245, and others have suggested that the commentary was on an Old Comedy, but no specific author can be identified.

Author and Work	Century; Scribe If Known	Condition of Manuscript; Repairs, Marginalia, Opisthograph, etc.	MP³ Number
TEXTS IN LATIN			
Gaius, *Institutiones*, Book 4	Probably ca. 200[53]	Columns numbered, perhaps by a second hand. Possibly a copy made for the copier's personal use.[54]	2954*
A work dealing with actions of Servius Tullius[55]	2nd	Words are generally separated by interpuncts	2999*

53. Dated to the third century by Hunt in *P.Oxy.* 17.2103; second or third by Lowe, *CLA Suppl.* no. 1716; ca. AD 200 by Seider (1981), 46.

54. Seider (1981), 45–46, pointed out that this manuscript was copied within some fifty years of the composition of the work by Gaius. He noted also that the copyist wrote in a hand experienced in document writing, rather than in a book hand, and suggested that it may have been a personal copy, not one made by a professional scribe.

55. The work seems not to have been a narrative. Hunt, ad *P.Oxy.* 17.2088, suggests that it may have been an antiquarian work, not a history.

Bibliography

Adler, Ada. 1928–38. *Suidae Lexicon.* 5 vols. Leipzig.

Affleck, M. 2013. "Priests, Patrons and Playwrights: Libraries in Rome before 168 BC." In *Ancient Libraries,* ed. König, Oikonomopoulou, and Woolf, 124–36.

Alexander, M. C. 1990. *Trials in the Late Roman Republic, 149 BC to 50 BC.* Toronto, Buffalo, and London.

Algra, K. A., M. H. Koenen, and P. H. Schrijvers, eds. 1997. *Lucretius and His Intellectual Background: Proceedings of the Colloquium, Amsterdam, 26–28 June 1996.* Amsterdam.

Ambaglio, D. 1983. "La dedica delle opere letterarie antiche fino all'età dei Flavi." In *Saggi di letteratura e storiografia antiche,* ed. Ambaglio, Asheri, and Magnino, 7–52.

Ambaglio, D., D. Asheri, and D. Magnino, eds. 1983. *Saggi di letteratura e storiografia antiche.* Biblioteca di Athenaeum, 2. Como.

Ammirati, S. 2010. *Bibliologia e codicologia del libro latino antico.* Diss. Università degli studi Roma Tre, 26 April 2010. Online at http://handle.net/2307/574.

Andorlini, I., ed. 2004. *Testi medici su papiro: Atti del Seminario di studio (Firenze, 3–4 giugno 2002).* Florence.

Andorlini, I., et al., eds. 2001. *Atti del XXII Congresso internazionale di papirologia, Firenze, 23–29 agosto 1998.* 3 vols. Florence.

Angeli, A. 1994. "Lo svolgimento dei papiri carbonizzati." In Capasso, *Il rotolo librario,* 36–104.

Antoni, A. 2007. "Nouvelles lectures dans le *PHerc.* 1384." In *Proceedings of the 24th International Congress of Papyrology,* ed. Frösén, Purola, and Salmenkivi, 43–52.

———. 2012. "Le *PHerc.* 1384: Édition critique." *CErc.* 42: 17–94.

Antoni, A., and G. Dorival. 2007. "Il *P.Herc.* 1384: Una nuova ipotesi di attribuzione." *CErc.* 37: 103–9.

Antoni, A., G. Arrighetti, et al., eds. 2010. *Miscellanea papyrologica Herculanensia.* Vol. 1. Pisa and Rome.

Armstrong, D., and J. A. Ponczoch. 2011. "[Philodemus] *On Wealth* (*PHerc.* 1570 Cols. VI–XX, Pcc. 4–6a): New Fragments of Empedocles, Menander, and Epicurus." *CErc.* 41: 97–138.

Assante, M. G. 2008. "Per un riesame del *P.Herc.* 1006 (Demetrio Lacone, *Alcune ricerche comuni sul modo di vita*)." *CErc.* 38: 109–60.

[Auctores varii]. 1966. *Atti dell'XI Congresso internazionale di papirologia, Milano, 2–8 settembre 1965.* Milan.

[Auctores varii]. 1982. *La regione sotterrata dal Vesuvio: Studi e prospettive. Atti del Convegno internazionale, 11–15 novembre 1979.* Naples.

[Auctores varii]. 1984. *Atti del XVII Congresso internazionale di papirologia (Napoli, 19–26 maggio 1983).* Naples.

Auvray-Assayas, C., and D. Delattre, eds. 2001. *Cicéron et Philodème: La polémique en philosophie*. Paris.

Bagnall, R. S. 1992. "An Owner of Literary Papyri." *CPh* 87: 137–40.

———. 2002. "Alexandria: Library of Dreams." *PAPhS* 146: 348–62.

———, ed. 2009. *The Oxford Handbook of Papyrology*. Oxford.

Bagnall, R. S., B. W. Frier, and I. C. Rutherford. 1997. *The Census Register P.Oxy. 984: The Reverse of Pindar's Paeans*. Papyrologica Bruxellensia, no. 29. Brussels.

Bardong, K. 1942. "Beiträge zur Hippokrates- und Galenforschung." *Nachrichten von der Akademie der Wissenschaften in Göttingen, Philologisch-Historische Klasse*, 7: 577–640.

Barigazzi, A. 1966. *Favorino di Arelate, Opere: Introduzione, testo critico e commento*. Florence.

Barrett, A. A. 1996. *Agrippina: Sex, Power, and Politics in the Early Empire*. New Haven and London.

Barrett, W. S. 2007. "New Identifications in *P.Oxy*. 2180 (Sophocles, *Oedipus Tyrannus*)." In *W. S. Barrett: Greek Lyric, Tragedy and Textual Criticism*, ed. West, 368–85.

Barron, J. P. 1969. "Ibycus: To Polycrates." *BICS* 16: 119–49.

Bartoletti, V. 1966. "Un frammento dei 'Myrmidones' di Eschilo." In *Essays in Honor of C. Bradford Welles*, ed. Samuel, 121–23.

Bassi, D. 1909. "La sticometria nei papiri ercolanesi." *RFIC* 37: 321–63 and 481–515.

Bastianini, G. 1975. "Lista dei prefetti d'Egitto dal 30a al 299p." *ZPE* 17: 263–328.

———. 2006. "Considerazioni sulle *Diegeseis* fiorentine (PSI XI 1219)." In *Callimaco: Cent'anni di papiri*, ed. Bastianini and Casanova, 149–66.

———. 2010. "PSI XIII 1305, *Romanzo di Nino*." In *I papiri del romanzo antico*, ed. Bastianini and Casanova, 279–88.

Bastianini, G., and A. Casanova, eds. 2006. *Callimaco: Cent'anni di papiri. Atti del Convegno internazionale di studi, Firenze, 9–10 Giugno 2005*. Florence.

———. 2010. *I papiri del romanzo antico: Atti del Convegno internazionale di studi, Firenze, 11–12 giugno 2009*. Florence.

Beer, B. 2009. "Lukrez in Herkulaneum?—Beitrag zu einer Edition von PHerc. 395." *ZPE* 168: 71–82.

Bell, H. I., and W. E. Crum. 1925. "A Greek-Coptic Glossary." *Aegyptus* 6: 177–226.

Berti, M., and V. Costa. 2010. *La Biblioteca di Alessandria: Storia di un paradiso perduto*. Tivoli.

Bilik, R. 1998. "Stammen P.Oxy. XI 1364 + LII 3647 und XV 1797 aus der Ἀλήθεια des Antiphon?" *Tyche* 13: 29–49.

Bingen, J., and G. Nachtergael, eds. 1978. *Actes du XVe Congrès international de papyrologie*. Part 1. Papyrologica Bruxellensia 16. Brussels.

Birley, A. R. 1997. *Hadrian: The Restless Emperor*. London.

Birt, T. 1907. *Die Buchrolle in der Kunst: Archäologisch-antiquarische Untersuchungen zum antiken Buchwesen*. Leipzig.

Blanchard, A., ed. 1989. *Les débuts du codex: Actes de la journée d'étude organisée à Paris les 3 et 4 juillet 1985 par l'Institut de papyrologie de la Sorbonne et l'Institut de recherche et d'histoire des textes*. Bibliologia 9. Turnhout (Belgium).

Blanck, H. 2008. *Il libro nel mondo antico*. Translated, with additions and revisions, by Rosa Otranto. Bari. Originally published as *Das Buch in der Antike* (Munich, 1992).

Blank, D. 1998. "Versionen oder Zwillinge? Zu den Handschriften der ersten Bücher von Philodems *Rhetorik*." In *Editing Texts—Texte Edieren*, ed. Most, 123–40.

Bollansée, J. 1999. *Hermippos of Smyrna and His Biographical Writings: A Reappraisal*. Leuven.

Bona, F. 1960. "Sul concetto di manubiae e sulla responsabilità del magistrato in ordine alla preda." *SDHI* 26: 105–75.

Bosworth, A. B. 1978. "Eumenes, Neoptolemus and *PSI* XII 1284." *GRBS* 19: 227–37.

Boudon-Millot, V. 2007a. *Galien, Tome I: Introduction générale, Sur l'ordre de ses propres livres, Sur ses propres livres, Que l'excellent médecin est aussi philosophe*. Paris.

———. 2007b. "Un traité perdu de Galien miraculeusement retrouvé, le *Sur l'inutilité de se chagriner*: Texte grec et traduction française." In *La science médicale antique*, ed. Boudon-Millot, Guardasole, and Magdelaine, 72–123.

Boudon-Millot, V., A. Guardasole, and C. Magdelaine, eds. 2007. *La science médicale antique: Nouveaux regards. Études réunies en l'honneur de Jacques Jouanna*. Paris.

Boudon-Millot, V., and J. Jouanna. 2010. *Galien, Tome IV: Ne pas se chagriner. Texte établi et traduit*. Paris.

Boudon-Millot, V., and A. Pietrobelli. 2005. "De l'arabe au grec: Un nouveau témoin du texte de Galien (le *Vlatadon* 14)." *CRAI*: 497–534.

Boulvert, G. 1970. *Esclaves et affranchis imperiaux sous le haut-empire romain: Rôle politique et administratif*. Naples.

———. 1974. *Domestique et fonctionnaire sous le Haut-Empire romain: La condition de l'affranchi et de l'esclave du prince*. Centre de recherches d'histoire ancienne, vol. 9. Paris.

Bowie, E. 2013. "Libraries for the Caesars." In *Ancient Libraries*, ed. König, Oikonomopoulou, and Woolf, 237–60.

Bowman, A. K., R. Coles, et al., eds. 2007. *Oxyrhynchus: A City and Its Texts*. London.

Bradley, K. R. 1991. "The Imperial Ideal in Suetonius' 'Caesares.'" *ANRW* 2.33.5: 3701–32.

Braun, E., ed. 1953. *Die Bibliothek*. Forschungen in Ephesos, Bd. 5, Heft 1. Vienna.

Buchwald, J. A., ed. 2012. *A Master of Science History: Essays in Honor of Charles Coulston Gillispie*. Archimedes 30. Dordrecht.

Budde, E. G. 1940. *Armarium und Κιβωτός: Ein Beitrag zur Geschichte des antiken Mobiliars*. Würzburg-Aumühle.

Bülow-Jacobsen, A. 2009. "Writing Materials in the Ancient World." In *The Oxford Handbook of Papyrology*, ed. Bagnall, 3–29.

Burzachechi, M. 1963. "Ricerche epigrafiche sulle antiche biblioteche del mondo greco." *RAL* 18: 75–96.

Cagnat, R. 1906. *Les bibliothèques municipales dans l'Empire romain*. Extract from the *Mémoires de l'Académie des inscriptions et belles-lettres*, vol. 38, part 1.

Calderini, A. 1922. "Di un nuovo testo biografico nei papiri di Ossirinco (POxy. XV. 1800)." *RIL* 55: 261–66.

Callmer, C. 1944. "Antike Bibliotheken." *Opuscula Archaeologica* 3: 145–93.

Caltabiano, M. 1991. *L'epistolario di Giuliano Imperatore: Saggio storico, traduzione, note e testo in appendice.* Naples.

Cambiano, G., L. Canfora, and D. Lanza. 1993. *Lo spazio letterario della Grecia antica.* Vol. 1, *La Produzione e la circolazione del testo.* Part 2, *L'Ellenismo.* Rome.

Camodeca, G. 2002. "Per una riedizione dell'archivio ercolanese di L. Venidius Ennychus." *CErc.* 32: 257–80.

Canfora, L. 1993. "La Biblioteca e il Museo." In *Lo spazio letterario della Grecia antica,* ed. Cambiano, Canfora, and Lanza, 1.2: 11–29.

Canfora, L., and R. Pintaudi. 2004–5. "Frammento di orazione giudiziaria (*P.Cair.* J.E. 47991)." *APapyrol.* 16–17: 9–18.

Capasso, M. 1982a. "Il saggio infallibile (PHerc. 1020 col. I)." In [Auctores varii], *La regione sotterrata da Vesuvio,* 455–70.

———. 1982b. *Trattato etico epicureo (P.Herc. 346): Edizione, traduzione e commento.* Naples.

———. 1988. *Carneisco, Il secondo libro del* Filista *(P.Herc. 1027).* Naples.

———. 1989. "Primo Supplemento al *Catalogo dei Papiri Ercolanesi.*" *CErc.* 19: 193–264.

———. 1990. "Le tavolette della Villa ercolanese dei Papiri." *CErc.* 20: 83–6.

———. 1991. *Manuale di papirologia ercolanese.* Galatina.

———. 1992. "Le tavolette della Villa dei Papiri ad Ercolano." In *Les tablettes à écrire,* ed. Lalou, 221–30.

———, ed. 1994. *Il rotolo librario: Fabbricazione, restauro, organizzazione interna.* Papyrologica Lupiensia 3. Lecce.

———. 1995. "Marco Ottavio e la Villa dei Papiri di Ercolano." *Eikasmos* 6: 183–89.

———. 1996. *Atti del V Seminario internazionale di papirologia.* Papyrologica Lupiensia 4. Galatina.

———, ed. 1997a. *Bicentenario della morte di Antonio Piaggio: Raccolta di studi.* Papyrologica Lupiensia 5. Galatina.

———, ed. 1997b. *Ricerche di papirologia letteraria e documentaria.* Papyrologica Lupiensia 6. Galatina.

———. 2000. "I papiri ercolanesi opistografi." In *Atti del V Convegno nazionale di egittologia e papirologia,* ed. Russo, 5–25.

———. 2001a. "Tre titoli iniziali interni in papiri ercolanesi." In *Atti del XXII Congresso internazionale di papirologia,* ed. Andorlini et al., 177–86.

———. 2001b. "Les livres sur la flatterie dans le *De vitiis* de Philodème." In *Cicéron et Philodème,* ed. Auvray-Assayas and Delattre, 179–94.

———, ed. 2002. *Dal restauro dei materiali allo studio dei testi: Aspetti della ricerca papirologica.* Papyrologica Lupiensia 11. Galatina.

———, ed. 2004. *Da Ercolano all'Egitto: Ricerche varie di papirologia.* Vol. 4. Papyrologica Lupiensia 12. Galatina.

———. 2007. "I rotoli ercolanesi: Da libri a carboni e da carboni a libri." In *Akten des 23. Internationalen Papyrologenkongresses,* ed. Palme, 73–77.

———. 2010a. "Per una ricostruzione del *De vitiis* di Filodemo." In *Proceedings of the 25th International Congress of Papyrology*, ed. Gagos, 97–104.

———. 2010b. "Who Lived in the Villa of the Papyri at Herculaneum—A Settled Question?" In *The Villa of the Papyri at Herculaneum*, ed. Zarmakoupi, 89–113.

———. 2011. *Les papyrus latins d'Herculanum: Découverte, consistance, contenu.* Cahiers du CeDoPaL, no. 6. Liège.

Capasso, M., and T. Dorandi. 1979. "*P.Herc.* 1696 e 1822." *CErc.* 9: 37–45.

Carlsen, J. 1995. *Vilici and Roman Estate Managers until AD 284.* Rome.

Caroli, M. 2007. *Il titolo iniziale nel rotolo librario greco-egizio: Con un catalogo delle testimonianze iconografiche greche e di area Vesuviana.* Bari.

Casanova, G. 2001. "Biblioteca: Conservazione e trasporto dei libri." *Aegyptus* 81: 219–41.

Casson, L., and M. Price, eds. 1981. *Coins, Culture and History in the Ancient World: Numismatic and Other Studies in Honor of Bluma L. Trell.* Detroit.

Cavalieri, M. C. 2002. "La 'rassegna dei filosofi' di Filodemo: Scuola eleatica ed abderita (PHerc 327) e scuola pitagorica (PHerc 1508)?" In *Dal restauro dei materiali allo studio dei testi*, ed. Capasso, 17–53.

———. 2010. "Per una nuova edizione dell'*Index Stoicorum* di Filodemo (*P.Herc.* 1018)." In *Proceedings of the 25th International Congress of Papyrology*, ed. Gagos, 121–30.

Cavallo, G. 1967. *Ricerche sulla maiuscola biblica.* Florence.

———. 1983. *Libri scritture scribi a Ercolano: Introduzione allo studio dei materiali greci.* Naples.

———. 1984. "I rotoli di Ercolano come prodotti scritti: Quattro riflessioni." *S&C* 8: 5–30.

———, ed. 1989a. *Le biblioteche nel mondo antico e medievale.* 2nd ed. Rome and Bari.

———. 1989b. "Codice e storia dei testi greci antichi: Qualche riflessione sulla fase primitiva del fenomeno." In *Les débuts du codex*, ed. Blanchard, 169–80.

———, ed. 1992. *Libri, editori e pubblico nel mondo antico: Guida storica e critica.* Rome and Bari.

———. 2008. *La scrittura greca e latina dei papiri: Una introduzione.* Pisa and Rome.

———. 2010. "Donne e cultura scritta nel mondo romano da Cesare ad Adriano." In *Neronia VIII*, ed. Perrin, 216–26.

Celentano, M. S., ed. 2003. *Ars/Techne: Il manuale tecnico nelle civiltà greca e romana. Atti del Convegno internazionale, Università G. d'Annunzio di Chieti-Pescara, 29–30 ottobre 2001.* Alessandria.

Chappuis, C. 1868. *Fragments des ouvrages de M. Terentius Varron intitulés Logistorici, Hebdomades vel de imaginibus, De forma philosophiae, recueillis, mis en ordre, accompagnés d'introduction et de notes.* Paris.

Christes, J. 1979. *Sklaven und Freigelassene als Grammatiker und Philologen im antiken Rom.* Forschungen zur antiken Sklaverei 10. Wiesbaden.

Christof, E. 2010. "Römische Elfenbeintäfelchen und kleinformatige Webtechniken." *MDAI(R)* 116: 343–61.

Churchill, J. B. 1999. *"Ex qua quod vellent facerent*: Roman Magistrates' Authority over *Praeda* and *Manubiae.*" *TAPhA* 129: 85–116.

Ciampi, A. 2009. "I *kimân* di Ossirinco: Abu Teir e Ali el-Gammân." *Comunicazioni dell'Istituto papirologico "G. Vitelli"* 8: 123–54.

Clark, J. W. 1909. *The Care of Books*. Cambridge.

Clausen, W. V. 1956. *A. Persi Flacci Saturarum liber: Accedit vita*. Oxford.

Coates, V. C. G., and J. L. Seydl, eds. 2007. *Antiquity Recovered: The Legacy of Pompeii and Herculaneum*. Los Angeles.

Cockle, W. E. H. 1983. "Restoring and Conserving Papyri." *BICS* 38: 147–65.

———. 1987. *Euripides, Hypsipyle: Text and Annotation Based on a Re-examination of the Papyri*. Rome.

Coqueugniot, G. 2007. "Coffre, casier, et armoire: La Kibôtos et le mobilier des archives et des bibliothèques grecques." *RA* 44: 293–304.

———. 2013. "Where Was the Royal Library of Pergamum? An Institution Found and Lost Again." In *Ancient Libraries*, ed. König, Oikonomopoulou, and Woolf, 109–23.

Coquin, R.-G. 1975. "Le catalogue de la bibliothèque du couvent de Saint-Élie 'du rocher' (ostracon IFAO 13315)." *BIAO* 75: 207–39.

Corbier, M. 2006. *Donner à voir, donner à lire: Mémoire et communication dans la Rome ancienne*. Paris.

Costabile, F. 1984. "Opere di oratoria politica e giudiziaria nella biblioteca della Villa dei Papiri: i *P.Herc.* latini 1067 e 1475." In [Auctores varii], *Atti del XVII Congresso internazionale di papirologia*, 590–606.

Courtney, E. 1980. *A Commentary on the Satires of Juvenal*. London.

Crawford, M. H. 1996. *Roman Statutes*. 2 vols. London.

Cribiore, R. 2001. *Gymnastics of the Mind: Greek Education in Hellenistic and Roman Egypt*. Princeton and Oxford.

Crisci, E. 1999. "I più antichi libri greci: Note bibliologiche e paleografiche su rotoli papiracei del IV-III sec. a.C." *S&C* 23: 29–62.

Croisille, J.-M. 2010. "L'instrumentum scriptorium dans la peinture romaine." In *Neronia VIII*, ed. Perrin, 63–78.

Crönert, W. 1906. *Kolotes und Menedemos, Texte und Untersuchungen zur Philosophen- und Literaturgeschichte*. Photographic reprint, 1965. Amsterdam.

Croom, A. M. 2007. *Roman Furniture*. Stroud (Gloucestershire).

Crum, W. E. 1893. *Coptic Manuscripts Brought from the Fayyum by W. M. Flinders Petrie*. London.

D'Alessio, G. B. 1997. "Pindar's *Prosodia* and the Classification of Pindaric Papyrus Fragments." *ZPE* 118: 23–60.

Daly, L. W. 1967. *Contributions to a History of Alphabetization in Antiquity and the Middle Ages*. Brussels.

D'Arms, J. H. 1970. *Romans on the Bay of Naples: A Social and Cultural Study of the Villas and Their Owners from 150 B.C. to A.D. 400*. Cambridge (Mass.).

Daroca, F. J., and M. de la Paz López Martínez. 2010. "Communauté épicurienne et communication épistolaire: Lettres de femmes selon le *PHerc.* 176. La correspondance de Batis." In *Miscellanea papyrologica Herculanensia*, ed. Antoni and Arrighetti, 21–36.

De Lacy, P., and E. De Lacy. 1978. *Philodemus: On Methods of Inference*. Naples.

Delattre, D. 1996. "Les mentions de titres d'oeuvres dans les livres de Philodème." *CErc*. 26: 143–68.

———. 1997. "Les titres des oeuvres philosophiques de l'épicurien Philodème de Gadara et des ouvrages qu'il cite." In *Titres et articulations du texte dans les oeuvres antiques*, ed. Fredouille, Goulet-Cazé, et al., 105–26.

———. 2006. *La Villa des Papyrus et les rouleaux d'Herculanum: La bibliothèque de Philodème*. Liège.

———. 2007. *Philodème de Gadara, Sur la musique: Livre IV*. 2 vols. Paris.

———. 2009. "Le sage épicurien face à la colère et à l'ivresse: Une lecture renouvelée du *De ira* de Philodème." *CErc*. 39: 71–88.

Del Corso, L. 2006. "Lo 'stile severo' nei P.Oxy.: Una lista." *Aegyptus* 86: 81–106.

———. 2010. "Il romanzo greco a Ossirinco e i suoi lettori: Osservazioni paleografiche, bibliologiche, storico-culturali." In *I papiri del romanzo antico*, ed. Bastianini and Casanova, 247–77.

Del Francia Barocas, L., ed. 1998. *Antinoe cent'anni dopo: Catalogo della mostra, Firenze, Palazzo Medici Riccardi, 10 luglio-10 novembre 1998*. Florence.

Del Franco, F., ed. 1994. *Storia poesia e pensiero nel mondo antico: Studi in onore di Marcello Gigante*. Naples.

Del Mastro, G. 2000. "Secondo Supplemento al Catalogo dei papiri ercolanesi." *CErc*. 30: 157–242.

———. 2002. "La subscriptio del *P.Herc*. 1005 e altri titoli in caratteri distintivi nei papiri ercolanesi." *CErc*. 32: 245–56.

———. 2003. "Osservazioni sulle *subscriptiones* dei *P.Herc*. 163 e 209." *CErc*. 33: 323–29.

———. 2005a. "Il *P.Herc*. 1380: Crisippo, *Opera logica*." *CErc*. 35: 61–70.

———. 2005b. "Riflessioni sui papiri latini ercolanesi." *CErc*. 35: 183–94.

———. 2009. "Osservazioni bibliologiche e paleografiche su alcuni papiri ercolanesi." *CErc*. 39: 283–300.

———. 2010a. "Papiri ercolanesi vergati da più mani." *S&T* 8: 3–66.

———. 2010b. "La *subscriptio* del *PHerc*. 168 (Filodemo, *opus incertum, hypomnematikon*)." In *Miscellanea papyrologica Herculanensia*, ed. Antoni, Arrighetti, et al., 137–45.

———. 2011. "*PHerc*. 1416, cr 5: Tre pezzi del papiro *Sul tempo* (*PHerc*. 1413)." *CErc*. 41: 27–32.

———. 2011–12. "Il PHerc 566: L'Echelao di Epicuro." *Papyrologica Lupiensia* 20–21: 19–24.

———. 2012a. "A proposito del ΠΕΡΙ ΦΥΣΕΩΣ di Epicuro: Il XXI libro e un nuovo papiro (PHerc. 362 e 560)." *Lexicon Philosophicum* 1 (Pre-issue abstract). Online at http://www.project-agora.eu/pre-print-of-1st-issue-of-lexicon.

———. 2012b. "Il *PHerc*. 1004: Filodemo, De rhetorica VII." *ZPE* 182: 131–33.

———. 2012c. "ΜΕΓΑ ΒΙΒΛΙΟΝ: Galeno e la lunghezza dei libri (ΠΕΡΙ ΑΛΥΠΙΑΣ 28)." In *Studi sul "De indolentia" di Galeno*, ed. Manetti, 33–61.

Del Mastro, G., and G. Leone. 2010. *"Addenda* e *subtrahenda* al *PHerc.* 1010 (Epicuro, *Sulla natura*, libro II)." In *Miscellanea papyrologica Herculanensia*, ed. Antoni, Arrighetti, et al., 315–35.

De Sanctis, D. 2009. "Il filosofo e il re: Osservazioni sulla *Vita Philonidis* (*P.Herc.* 1044)." *CErc.* 39: 107–18.

De Simone, A. 2010. "Rediscovering the Villa of the Papyri." In *The Villa of the Papyri at Herculaneum*, ed. Zarmakoupi, 1–20.

De Simone, A., and F. Ruffo. 2002. "Ercolano 1996–1998: Lo scavo della Villa dei Papiri." *CErc.* 32: 325–44.

———. 2003. "Ercolano e la Villa dei Papyri alla luce dei nuovi scavi." *CErc.* 33: 279–311.

Deubner, O. 1938. *Das Asklepieion von Pergamon: Kurze vorläufige Beschreibung.* Berlin.

Diels, H. 1916. *Philodemos über die Götter: Erstes und drittes Buch. Griechischer Text und Erläuterung [von] Hermann Alexander Diels.* 3 vols. in 1. Leipzig, 1970. Photographic reprint from *Abhandlungen der Königlich Preussischen Akademie der Wissenschaften, philosophisch-historische Klasse*, Jahrgang 1915, Nr. 7; Jahrgang 1916, Nr. 4; and Jahrgang 1916, Nr. 6.

Dilts, M. R. 2002. *Demosthenis Orationes.* Vol. 1. Oxford.

Dix, T. K. 1986. *Private and Public Libraries at Rome in the First Century B.C.: A Preliminary Study in the History of Roman Libraries.* Ph.D. diss., University of Michigan.

———. 1988. "Ovid Strikes Out: Tristia 3.1 and the First Public Libraries at Rome." *The Augustan Age* 8: 27–35.

———. 1994. "'Public Libraries' in Ancient Rome: Ideology and Reality." *Libraries & Culture* 29: 282–96.

———. 1996. "Pliny's Library at Comum." *Libraries & Culture* 31: 85–102.

———. 2000. "The Library of Lucullus." *Athenaeum* 88: 441–64.

———. 2004. "Aristotle's 'Peripatetic' Library." In *Lost Libraries*, ed. Raven, 58–74.

———. 2013. "'Beware of Promising Your Library to Anyone': Assembling a Private Library at Rome." In *Ancient Libraries*, ed. König, Oikonomopoulou, and Woolf, 209–34.

Dix, T. K., and G. W. Houston. 2006. "Public Libraries in the City of Rome from the Augustan Age to the Time of Diocletian." *MEFRA* 118: 671–717.

Dognini, C. 2000. "Il P. Oxy. 1612 e il culto di Cesare in Bitinia." *RIL* 134: 115–24.

Dorandi, T. 1980. "La rassegna dei filosofi di Filodemo." *RAAN* 55: 31–49.

———. 1984. "Sillyboi." *S&C* 8: 185–99.

———. 1990a. "Filodemo: Gli orientamenti della ricerca attuale." *ANRW* 2.36.4: 2328–68.

———. 1990b. "Per una ricomposizione dello scritto di Filodemo sulla Retorica." *ZPE* 82: 59–87.

———. 1994. "Marginalia papirologica 4: Etichette e *sillyboi*." In *Il rotolo librario*, ed. Capasso, 227–33.

———. 1997. "Lucrèce et les Épicuriens de Campanie." In *Lucretius and His Intellectual Background*, ed. Algra, Koenen, and Schrijvers, 35–48.

———. 2007. *Nell'officina dei classici: Come lavoravano gli autori antichi*. Rome.

Dorival, G. 2008. "L'attribution à Chrysippe de Soles du traité conservé dans le papyrus d'Herculanum 1384: Un nouvel argument décisif?" In *Epiphania: Études orientales, grecques et latines*, ed. Oudot and Poli, 423–27.

Esposito, D. 2008. "Filosseno, il Ciclope e Sesto Pompeo: Programmi figurativi e 'propaganda' politica nelle domus dell'aristocrazia pompeiana della tarda età repubblicana." *JDAI* 123: 51–99.

Esposito, E. 2005. "P.Oxy. XVII 2087 e una citazione dal Περὶ δικαιοσύνης di Aristotele." *ZPE* 154: 79–85.

Falivene, M. R. 2003. "A scuola nell'Egitto tolemaico: Testi dalla 'biblioteca' di Al Hiba." In *Ars/Techne*, ed. Celentano, 43–49.

Fearn, D. 2007. *Bacchylides: Politics, Performance, Poetic Tradition*. Oxford.

Fedeli, P. 1989. "Biblioteche private e pubbliche a Roma e nel mondo romano." In *Le biblioteche nel mondo antico e medievale*, ed. Cavallo, 29–64.

Fehrle, R. 1986. *Das Bibliothekswesen im alten Rom: Voraussetzungen, Bedingungen, Anfänge*. Freiburg im Breisgau.

Fimiani, M. 2012. "I papiri del IV libro della *Retorica* di Filodemo: Segni, correzioni e caratteristiche bibliologiche (*PHerc*. 1423, 1673/1007 e relative scorze)." *CErc.* 42: 121–88.

Forbes, R. J. 1966. *Studies in Ancient Technology*. Vol. 6, *Heat and Heating. Refrigeration. Light*. Leiden.

Fournet, J.-L. 1999. *Hellénisme dans l'Égypte du VIe siècle: La bibliothèque et l'oeuvre de Dioscore d'Aphrodité*. Mélanges de l'Institut français d'archéologie orientale 115. 2 vols. Cairo.

Frank, T., ed. 1940. *An Economic Survey of Ancient Rome*. Vol. 5, *Rome and Italy of the Empire*. Baltimore.

Fraser, P. M. 1972. *Ptolemaic Alexandria*. 3 vols. Oxford.

Fredouille, J.-C., M.-O. Goulet-Cazé, et al., eds. 1997. *Titres et articulations du texte dans les oeuvres antiques: Actes du Colloque international de Chantilly, 13–15 décembre 1994*. Paris.

Frischer, B. 1991. *Shifting Paradigms: New Approaches to Horace's "Ars poetica."* Atlanta.

Frösén, J., T. Purola, and E. Salmenkivi, eds. 2007. *Proceedings of the 24th International Congress of Papyrology, Helsinki, 1–7 August, 2004*. Helsinki.

Funghi, M. S., and G. Messeri Savorelli. 1992a. "Lo 'scriba di Pindaro' e le biblioteche di Ossirinco." *SCO* 42: 43–62.

———. 1992b. "Note papirologiche e paleografiche." *Tyche* 7: 75–88.

Gagos, T., ed. 2010. *Proceedings of the 25th International Congress of Papyrology, Ann Arbor, July 29–August 4, 2007*. American Studies in Papyrology. Ann Arbor.

Gallavotti, C. 1940. "La custodia dei papiri nella Villa suburbana Ercolanese." *Bollettino del Reale istituto di patologia del libro* 18: 53–63.

Gallo, I. 2002. "Una trattazione biografica di Socrate nei papiri ercolanesi." *SIFC* 20: 59–62.

Gianotti, G. F. 1973. "Mito ed encomio: Il carme di Ibico in onore di Policrate." *RFIC* 101: 401–10.

Giardina, A., ed. 1986. *Società romana e impero tardoantico.* Vol. 2, *Roma: Politica, economia, paesaggio urbano.* Rome and Bari.

Gigante, M. 1949. "Ancora sul frammento fiorentino di un dialogo politico." *Aegyptus* 29: 51–55.

———. 1979. *Catalogo dei papiri ercolanesi.* Naples.

———. 1988. "Atakta VIII." *CErc.* 18: 59–63.

———. 1995. *Philodemus in Italy: The Books from Herculaneum.* Trans. by Dirk Obbink. Ann Arbor.

Gigante, M., and M. Capasso. 1989. "Il ritorno di Virgilio a Ercolano." *SIFC* 7: 3–6.

Giuliano, F. M. 2001. "*PHerc.* 495–*PHerc.* 558 (Filodemo, *Storia di Socrate e della sua scuola?*): Edizione, commento, questioni compositive e attributive." *CErc.* 31: 37–79.

Giuliano, L. 2009. "*P.Herc.* 807: [Filodemo, *De morte*, libro incerto]." *CErc.* 39: 207–80.

Gottschalk, H. B. 1987. "Aristotelian Philosophy in the Roman World from the Time of Cicero to the End of the Second Century AD." *ANRW* 2.36.2: 1079–1174.

Gow, A. S. F., and D. L. Page. 1965. *The Greek Anthology: Hellenistic Epigrams.* 2 vols. Cambridge.

Grafton, A., and M. H. Williams. 2006. *Christianity and the Transformation of the Book: Origen, Eusebius, and the Library of Caesarea.* Cambridge (Mass.).

Graser, E. R. 1940. "The Edict of Diocletian on Maximum Prices." In *An Economic Survey of Ancient Rome,* ed. Frank, 5: 305–421.

Griffin, M., and J. Barnes, eds. 1989. *Philosophia Togata: Essays on Philosophy and Roman Society.* Oxford.

Guidobaldi, F. 1986. "L'edilizia abitativa unifamiliare nella Roma tardoantica." In *Società romana e impero tardoantico,* ed. Giardina, 2: 166–237.

Guidobaldi, M. P. 2010. "Arredi di lusso in legno e avorio da Ercolano: Le nuove scoperte della Villa dei Papiri." *Lanx* 6: 63–99.

Guidobaldi, M. P., and D. Esposito. 2009. "Le nuove ricerche archeologiche nella Villa dei Papiri di Ercolano." *CErc.* 39: 331–70.

Habicht, C. 1969. *Die Inschriften des Asklepieions.* Altertümer von Pergamon, Bd. 8.3. Berlin.

Halkin, L. 1897. *Les esclaves publics chez les romains.* Brussels. Photographic reprint, 1965. Rome.

Hallett, C. H. 2005. *The Roman Nude: Heroic Portrait Statuary 200 B.C.–A.D. 300.* Oxford.

Hammerstaedt, J. 1992. "Der Schlussteil von Philodems drittem Buch über Rhetorik." *CErc.* 22: 9–117.

Hanson, A. E. 2004. "A Title Tag: PCtYBR inv. 4006." In *Testi medici su papiro,* ed. Andorlini, 209–19.

Harden, D. B. 1961. "Domestic Window-Glass: Roman, Saxon and Medieval." In *Studies in Building History,* ed. Jope, 39–63.

Harrauer, H. 1995. "Bücher in Papyri." In *Flores litterarum Ioanni Marte sexagenario oblati,* ed. Lang, 59–77.

Hein, C. 1985. *Definition und Einteilung der Philosophie: Von der Spätantiken Einleitungsliteratur zur Arabischen Enzyklopädie.* Frankfurt am Main.

Henry, W. B. 2009. "New Light on Philodemus, *On Death.*" *CErc.* 39: 89–102.

——. 2010. *Philodemus, "On Death": Translated with an Introduction and Notes.* Leiden and Boston.

Hinard, F. 1985. *Les proscriptions de la Rome républicaine.* Rome.

Hirschfeld, Y. 2004. *Qumran in Context: Reassessing the Archaeological Evidence.* Peabody (Mass.).

Hoepfner, W., ed. 2002a. *Antike Bibliotheken.* Mainz am Rhein.

——. 2002b. "Die Celsus-Bibliothek in Ephesos: Eine kaiserzeitliche Bibliothek mit zentralem Lesesaal." In *Antike Bibliotheken*, ed. Hoepfner, 123–26.

Holford-Strevens, L. 1988. *Aulus Gellius.* Chapel Hill.

Holtz, L. 1997. "Titre et incipit." In *Titres et articulations du texte dans les oeuvres antiques*, ed. Fredouille, Goulet-Cazé, et al., 469–89.

Honoré, T. 1994. *Emperors and Lawyers.* Oxford.

Horak, U. 1992. *Illuminierte Papyri, Pergamente und Papiere.* Vol. 1. Pegasus Oriens, 1. Vienna.

Hordern, J. 2002. "Sophron, fr. 171, and Theocritus 15." *ZPE* 140: 1–2.

——. 2004. *Sophron's Mimes: Text, Translation, and Commentary.* Oxford.

Horsfall, N. 1993. "Empty Shelves on the Palatine." *G&R* 40: 58–67.

——. 1995. "Rome without Spectacles." *G&R* 42: 49–56.

Houston, G. W. 2002. "The Slave and Freedman Personnel of Public Libraries in Ancient Rome." *TAPhA* 132: 139–76.

——. 2003. "Galen, His Books, and the Horrea Piperataria at Rome." *MAAR* 48: 45–51.

——. 2004. "How Did You Get Hold of a Book in a Roman Library? Three Second-Century Scenarios." *CB* 80: 5–13.

——. 2007. "Grenfell, Hunt, Breccia, and the Book Collections of Oxyrhynchus." *GRBS* 47: 327–59.

——. 2008. "Tiberius and the Libraries: Public Book Collections and Library Buildings in the Early Roman Empire." *Libraries & the Cultural Record* 43: 247–69.

——. 2009. "Papyrological Evidence for Book Collections and Libraries in the Roman Empire." In *Ancient Literacies*, ed. Johnson and Parker, 233–67.

——. 2013. "The Non-Philodemus Book Collection in the Villa of the Papyri." In *Ancient Libraries*, ed. König, Oikonomopoulou, and Woolf, 183–208.

Hueber, F. 1997. *Ephesos: Gebaute Geschichte.* Mainz am Rhein.

Hunt, A. S., and J. Johnson. 1930. *Two Theocritus Papyri.* London.

Husson, G. 1983. "Un sens méconnu de ΘΥΡΙΣ et de fenestra." *JJP* 19: 155–62.

Iacopi, I., and G. Tedone. 2005/2006. "Bibliotheca e Porticus ad Apollinis." *MDAI(R)* 112: 351–78.

Iddeng, J. W. 2006. "*Publica aut peri!* The Releasing and Distribution of Roman Books." *SO* 81: 58–84.

Indelli, G. 1978. *Polistrato, Sul disprezzo irrazionale delle opinioni popolari: Edizione, traduzione, e commento.* Naples.

——. 1988. *Filodemo, L'ira: Edizione, traduzione, e commento.* Naples.

————. 2010. "Le colonne I-X 10 di *P.Herc.* 1008 (Filodemo, *I vizi*, libro X)." In
   Proceedings of the 25th International Congress of Papyrology, ed. Gagos, 323–33.

Jackson, R. 1988. *Doctors and Diseases in the Roman Empire*. Norman (Okla.) and
   London.

Jacob, C. 2013. "Fragments of a History of Ancient Libraries." In *Ancient Libraries*,
   ed. König, Oikonomopoulou, and Woolf, 57–81.

Janko, R. 2000. *Philodemus: "On Poems," Book 1. Edited with Introduction,
   Translation and Commentary*. Oxford.

————. 2002. "The Herculaneum Library: Some Recent Developments." *EClás* 44:
   25–41.

————. 2008. "New Fragments of Epicurus, Metrodorus, Demetrius Laco,
   Philodemus, the *Carmen de bello Actiaco* and Other Texts in Oxonian *Disegni* of
   1788–1792." *CErc.* 38: 5–95.

————. 2011. *Philodemus, "On Poems," Books 3–4, with the Fragments of Aristotle
   "On Poets": Edited with Introduction, Translation, and Commentary*. Oxford.

Johnson, J. de M. 1914. "Antinoë and Its Papyri: Excavation by the Graeco-Roman
   Branch, 1913–14." *JEA* 1: 168–81.

Johnson, L. L. 1984. "The Hellenistic and Roman Library: Studies Pertaining to Their
   Architectural Form." Ph.D. diss., Brown University.

Johnson, W. A. 2004. *Bookrolls and Scribes in Oxyrhynchus*. Toronto.

————. 2009. "The Ancient Book." In *The Oxford Handbook of Papyrology*, ed.
   Bagnall, 256–81.

————. 2010. *Readers and Reading Culture in the High Roman Empire: A Study of
   Elite Communities*. New York.

————. 2012. "Cicero and Tyrannio: *Mens addita videtur meis aedibus* (*Ad Atticum*
   4.8.2)." *CW* 105: 471–77.

Johnson, W. A., and H. N. Parker, eds. 2009. *Ancient Literacies: The Culture of
   Reading in Greece and Rome*. Oxford.

Jones, A. 1999. *Astronomical Papyri from Oxyrhynchus (P.Oxy. 4133–4300a)*.
   Philadelphia.

Jones, C. P. 2009. "Books and Libraries in a Newly-Discovered Treatise of Galen."
   JRA 22: 390–97.

Jope, E. M., ed. 1961. *Studies in Building History: Essays in Recognition of the Work
   of B. H. St. J. O'Neil*. London.

Kaster, R. A. 1995. *C. Suetonius Tranquillus: "De Grammaticis et Rhetoribus." Edited
   with a Translation, Introduction, and Commentary*. Oxford.

Kenyon, F. G. 1892. *Aristotle on the Constitution of Athens*. 3rd rev. ed. Oxford.

————. 1951. *Books and Readers in Ancient Greece and Rome*. Oxford.

Ker, J. 2004. "Nocturnal Writers in Imperial Rome: The Culture of *lucubratio*." *CPh*
   99: 209–42.

Kleberg, T. 1992. "Commercio librario ed editoria nel mondo antico." In *Libri, editori
   e pubblico nel mondo antico*, ed. Cavallo, 25–80.

Kleve, K. 1989. "Lucretius in Herculaneum." *CErc.* 19: 5–27.

————. 1990. "Ennius in Herculaneum." *CErc.* 20: 5–16.

———. 1994. "An Approach to the Latin Papyri from Herculaneum." In *Storia poesia e pensiero nel mondo antico,* ed. Del Franco, 313–20.

———. 1996. "How to Read an Illegible Papyrus: Towards an Edition of *P.Herc.* 78, Caecilius Statius, *Obolostates sive Faenerator.*" *CErc.* 26: 5–14.

———. 2007. "Lucretius' Book II in P.Herc. 395." In *Akten des 23. Internationalen Papyrologenkongresses,* ed. Palme, 347–54.

———. 2009. "Futile Criticism." *CErc.* 39: 281–82.

———. 2012. "The Puzzle Picture of Lucretius: A Thriller from Herculaneum." In *A Master of Science History,* ed. Buchwald, 63–78.

Kleve, K., and G. Del Mastro. 2000. "Il *P.Herc.* 1533: Zenone Sidonio *A Cratero.*" *CErc.* 30: 149–56.

Knauer, E. R. 1993. "Roman Wall Paintings from Boscotrecase: Three Studies in the Relationship between Writing and Painting." *MMJ* 28: 13–46.

Kolb, A. 1993. *Die kaiserliche Bauverwaltung in der Stadt Rom: Geschichte und Aufbau der cura operum publicorum unter dem Prinzipat.* Stuttgart.

König, J., K. Oikonomopoulou, and G. Woolf, eds. 2013. *Ancient Libraries.* Cambridge.

Konstan, D., D. Clay, C. E. Glad, J. C. Thom, and J. Ware. 1998. *Philodemus, "On Frank Criticism": Introduction, Translation, and Notes.* Atlanta.

Körte, A. 1923. "Die Zeitbestimmung von Hypereides' Rede für Lykophron." *Hermes* 58: 230–37.

Krüger, J. 1990. *Oxyrhynchos in der Kaiserzeit: Studien zur Topographie und Literaturrezeption.* Frankfurt am Main, New York, and Paris.

Krumeich, R., N. Pechstein, and B. Seidensticker, eds. 1999. *Das griechische Satyrspiel.* Darmstadt.

Lalou, É., ed. 1992. *Les tablettes à écrire de l'antiquité à l'époque moderne.* Turnhout (Belgium).

Lama, M. 1991. "Aspetti di tecnica libraria ad Ossirinco: Copie letterarie su rotoli documentari." *Aegyptus* 71: 55–120.

Lamedica, A. 1985. "Il P.Oxy. 1800 e le forme della biografia greca." *SIFC* 78: 55–75.

Lanciani, R. 1884. "Supplementi al volume VI del *Corpus inscriptionum Latinarum.*" *BCAR* 12: 39–60.

Lang, H. W., ed. 1995. *Flores litterarum Ioanni Marte sexagenario oblati: Wissenschaft in der Bibliothek.* Vienna, Cologne, and Weimar.

Laursen, S. 1987. "Epicurus, *On Nature* Book XXV." *CErc.* 17: 77–78.

———. 1995. "The Early Parts of Epicurus, *On Nature,* 25th Book." *CErc.* 25: 5–109.

Lavecchia, S. 1996. "P.Oxy. 2622 e il 'Secondo Ditirambo' di Pindaro." *ZPE* 110: 1–26.

Leach, B., and J. Tait. 2000. "Papyrus." In *Ancient Egyptian Materials and Technology,* ed. Nicholson and Shaw, 227–53.

Lenski, N. E. 2002. *Failure of Empire: Valens and the Roman State in the Fourth Century A.D.* Berkeley.

Lentini, G. 2007. "P.Oxy. XV 1788: Alceo o Saffo?" In *Akten des 23. Internationalen Papyrologenkongresses,* ed. Palme, 387–91.

Leone, G. 1984. "Epicuro, *Della natura,* libro XIV." *CErc.* 14: 17–107.

———. 2002. "Epicuro, *Della natura*, libro XXXIV (*P.Herc.* 1431)." *CErc.* 32: 7–135.

———. 2005. "Per la ricostruzione dei *P.Herc.* 1149/993 e 1010 (Epicuro, *Della natura*, libro II)." *CErc.* 35: 15–25.

———. 2012. *Epicuro: Sulla natura libro II. Edizione, traduzione e commento.* La Scuola di Epicuro, vol. 18. Naples.

Lesky, A. 1966. *A History of Greek Literature.* Trans. by James Willis and Cornelis de Heer. New York.

Lewis, N. 1981. "Literati in the Service of Roman Emperors: Politics before Culture." In *Coins, Culture, and History in the Ancient World,* ed. Casson and Price, 149–66.

Lindsay, H. 1994. "Suetonius as *ab epistulis* to Hadrian and the Early History of the Imperial Correspondence." *Historia* 43: 454–68.

Lloyd-Jones, H., and P. Parsons. 1983. *Supplementum Hellenisticum.* Berlin and New York.

Lobel, E., and D. Page. 1955. *Poetarum Lesbiorum fragmenta.* Oxford.

Longo Auricchio, F. 1996. "Nuovi elementi per la ricostruzione della *Retorica* di Filodemo." *CErc.* 26: 169–71.

———. 2008. "La biblioteca ercolanese." *A&R,* Ser. 2, 2: 190–209.

Longo Auricchio, F., and M. Capasso. 1987. "I rotoli della Villa ercolanese: Dislocazione e ritrovamento." *CErc.* 17: 37–47.

Lowe, E. A. 1938. *Codices Latini antiquiores.* Part 3, *Italy: Ancona-Novara.* Oxford.

Luppe, W. 1978–79. "Bemerkungen zu einem Komiker-Kommentar: P.Oxy. 2086r." *MCr* 13–14: 245–49.

MacCoull, L. S. B. 1988. *Dioscorus of Aphrodito: His Work and His World.* Berkeley, Los Angeles, and London.

Magness, J. 2002. *The Archaeology of Qumran and the Dead Sea Scrolls.* Grand Rapids and Cambridge.

Maiuri, A. 1925. *Nuova silloge epigrafica di Rodi e Cos.* Florence.

Mandilaras, B. G., ed. 1988. *Proceedings of the XVIII International Congress of Papyrology, Athens, 25–31 May 1986.* Athens.

Manetti, D., ed. 2012. *Studi sul "De indolentia" di Galeno.* Biblioteca di "Galenos," Contributi alla ricerca sui testi medici antichi, 4. Pisa and Rome.

Manfredi, M. 1983. "Opistografo." *PP* 38: 44–54.

Manteuffel, G. 1933. "De novo quodam librorum inventario (Pap. Varsov. N. 5)." *Aegyptus* 13: 367–73.

Marganne, M.-H. 2004. "Le médecin, la trousse et le livre dans le monde gréco-romain." In *Da Ercolano all'Egitto,* ed. Capasso, 4: 115–30.

Marrou, H.-I. 1938. *ΜΟΥΣΙΚΟΣ ΑΝΗΡ: Étude sur les scènes de la vie intellectuelle figurant sur les monuments funéraires romains.* Grenoble. Photographic reprint with additions, 1964. Rome.

Marshall, A. J. 1976. "Library Resources and Creative Writing at Rome." *Phoenix* 30: 252–64.

Mastino, A., and P. Ruggeri, eds. 1994. *L'Africa romana: Atti del X Convegno di studio. Oristano, 11–13 dicembre 1992.* Sassari.

Mattusch, Carol C. 2005. *The Villa dei Papiri at Herculaneum: Life and Afterlife of a Sculpture Collection.* Los Angeles.

————. 2011. *Johann Joachim Winckelmann: Letter and Report on the Discoveries at Herculaneum*. Los Angeles.

McDonnell, M. 1996. "Writing, Copying, and Autograph Manuscripts in Ancient Rome." *CQ* 46: 469–91.

McIlwaine, I. C. 1988. *Herculaneum: A Guide to the Printed Sources*. 2 vols. Naples.

McKechnie, P. R., and S. J. Kern. 1988. *Hellenica Oxyrhynchia*. Warminster.

McNamee, K. 2001. "A Plato Papyrus with Shorthand Marginalia." *GRBS* 42: 97–116.

————. 2007. *Annotations in Greek and Latin Texts from Egypt*. American Studies in Papyrology, no. 45. New Haven.

McNamee, K., and M. L. Jacovides. 2003. "Annotations to the Speech of the Muses (Plato *Republic* 546 b-c)." *ZPE* 144: 31–50.

Medda, E. 2003. *Lysiae In Hippothersem, In Theomnestum et fragmenta ex incertis orationibus (P. Oxy. XIII 1606)*. Florence.

Meiggs, R. 1973. *Roman Ostia*. 2nd ed. Oxford.

Menci, G. 1998. "I papiri letterari 'sacri' e 'profani' di Antinoe." In *Antinoe cent'anni dopo*, ed. Del Francia Barocas, 49–55.

Meneghini, R. 2010. "Le biblioteche pubbliche di Roma nell'alto impero." In *Neronia VIII*, ed. Perrin, 32–40.

Merkelbach, R. 1949. "Politischer Dialog in einem Florentiner Papyrus." *Aegyptus* 29: 56–58.

Miles, M. M. 2008. *Art as Plunder: The Ancient Origins of Debate about Cultural Property*. Cambridge and New York.

Militello, C. 1997. *Filodemo: Memorie epicuree (P.Herc. 1418 e 310). Edizione, traduzione e commento*. Naples.

Millar, F. 1977. *The Emperor in the Roman World*. Ithaca.

Millot, C. 1977. "Epicure, *De la nature*, livre XV." *CErc*. 7: 9–39.

Modrzejewski, J. M. 2011. *Droit et justice dans le monde grec et hellénistique*. Warsaw.

Moioli, M. L. 1987. "La famiglia di Sarapion alias Apollonianus stratego dei nomi Arsinoites ed Hermopolites." *Acme* 40: 123–36.

Mols, S. T. A. M. 1999. *Wooden Furniture in Herculaneum: Form, Technique and Function*. Amsterdam.

Mols, S. T. A. M., and E. M. Moormann. 1993–94. "*Ex parvo crevit*: Proposta per una lettura iconografica della Tomba di Vestorius Priscus fuori Porta Vesuvio a Pompei." *RSP* 6: 15–52.

Mommsen, T. 1880. "Inschriftbüsten. 1. Aus Herculaneum." *Archäologische Zeitung* 38: 32–6.

————. 1887. *Römisches Staatsrecht*. Vol. 1. 3rd ed. Leipzig.

Monet, A. 2001. "La *Flatterie* de Philodème et l'organisation des *Vices*: Réponse à Mario Capasso." In *Cicéron et Philodème*, ed. Auvray-Assayas and Delattre, 195–202.

————. 2011. "Heurts [*sic*] et bonheurs de la colonne N du *PHerc. Paris*. 2." *CErc*. 41: 93–96.

Montevecchi, O. 1973. *La papirologia*. Turin.

Most, G. W., ed. 1998. *Editing Texts — Texte Edieren*. Göttingen.

Muecke, F. 1993. Review of Frischer, *Shifting Paradigms: New Approaches to Horace's "Ars poetica."* *JRS* 83: 213–14.

Mugridge, A. 2010. "Writing and Writers in Antiquity: Two 'Spectra' in Greek Handwriting." In *Proceedings of the 25th International Congress of Papyrology*, ed. Gagos, 573–80.

Nesselrath, H.-G. 1990. *Die attische Mittlere Komödie: Ihre Stellung in der antiken Literaturkritik und Literaturgeschichte*. Berlin and New York.

Nicholls, M. 2010. "*Bibliotheca Latina Graecaque*: On the Possible Division of Roman Public Libraries by Language." In *Neronia VIII*, ed. Perrin, 11–21.

———. 2011. "Galen and Libraries in the *Peri Alupias*." *JRS* 101: 123–42.

———. 2013. "Roman Libraries as Public Buildings in the Cities of the Empire." In *Ancient Libraries*, ed. König, Oikonomopoulou, and Woolf, 261–76.

———. Forthcoming. *Roman Public Libraries*. Oxford.

Nicholson, P. T., and I. Shaw, eds. 2000. *Ancient Egyptian Materials and Technology*. Cambridge.

Obbink, D. 1996. *Philodemus: "On Piety," Part 1. Critical Text with Commentary*. Oxford.

Ohly, K. 1924. "Die Stichometrie der Herkulanischen Rollen." *APF* 7: 190–220.

Otranto, R. 2000. *Antiche liste di libri su papiro*. Rome.

Oudot, E., and F. Poli, eds. 2008. *Epiphania: Études orientales, grecques et latines offertes à Aline Pourkier*. Nancy.

Packer, J. E. 1997. *The Forum of Trajan in Rome: A Study of the Monuments*. Berkeley.

Page, D. L. 1951. "Ibycus' Poem in Honour of Polycrates." *Aegyptus* 31: 158–72.

Palme, B., ed. 2007. *Akten des 23. Internationalen Papyrologenkongresses: Wien, 22.-28. Juli 2001*. Vienna.

Panciera, S. 1969. "Miscellanea Epigrafica IV." *Epigraphica* 31: 104–20.

Papachristodoulou, I. X. 1986. "Νέα στοιχεία γιὰ βιβλιοθῆκες στὴν ἀρχαία Ρόδο: Ἐπιγραφὴ σχετικὴ μὲ τὴ βιβλιοθήκη τοῦ ἀρχ. Γυμνασίου." *Δωδεκανησίακα Χρονικά* 11: 265–71.

Papini, M. 2005. "Filosofi 'in miniatura': Il Crisippo dal *templum Pacis*." *BCAR* 106: 125–35.

Parássoglou, G. M. 1974. "A Book Illuminator in Byzantine Egypt." *Byzantion* 44: 362–66.

———. 1979. "Δεξια χειρ και γόνυ [*sic*]: Some Thoughts on the Postures of the Ancient Greeks and Romans When Writing on Papyrus Rolls." *S&C* 3: 5–21.

Parisi, A. 2012. "Osservazioni sul lessico del *PHerc*. 831 (Demetrio Lacone, *Opus incertum*)." *CErc*. 42: 111–20.

Parsons, P. 1989. Review of Cavallo, *Libri scritture scribi a Ercolano*. CR 103: 358–60.

———. 2007. "Copyists of Oxyrhynchus." In *Oxyrhynchus: A City and Its Texts*, ed. Bowman, Coles, et al., 262–70.

———. 2010. "Panionis and the Culture of Culture (P.Oxy. LXXI 4811)." In *I papiri del romanzo antico*, ed. Bastianini and Casanova, 43–49.

Parsons, P. J., and J. R. Rea, eds. 1981. *Papyri Greek & Egyptian Edited by Various Hands in Honour of Eric Gardner Turner on the Occasion of His Seventieth Birthday*. Egypt Exploration Society, Graeco-Roman Memoirs, 68. London.

Pavis D'Escurac, H. 1976. *La préfecture de l'annone: Service administratif impérial d'Auguste à Constantin*. Rome.

Pendrick, G. J. 2002. *Antiphon the Sophist: The Fragments. Edited with Introduction, Translation and Commentary.* Cambridge.

Perrin, Y., ed. 2010. *Neronia VIII: Bibliothèques, livres et culture écrite dans l'empire romain de César à Hadrien. Actes du VIIIe Colloque international de la SIEN (Paris, 2–4 octobre 2008).* Brussels.

Perrin-Saminadayar, É. 2010. "Bibliothèques publiques et bibliothèques privées athéniennes (Ier siècle av. J.-C.—IIe siècle ap. J.-C.): Le statut de la bibliothèque de Pantainos." In *Neronia VIII,* ed. Perrin, 227–35.

Petersen, E. 1900. "Der Sarkophag eines Arztes." *MDAI(R)* 15: 171–76.

Petrain, D. 2013. "Visual Supplementation and Metonymy in the Roman Public Library." In *Ancient Libraries,* ed. König, Oikonomopoulou, and Woolf, 332–46.

Petsalis-Diomidis, A. 2010. *Truly Beyond Wonders: Aelius Aristides and the Cult of Asklepios.* Oxford.

Pfeiffer, H. F. 1931. "The Roman Library at Timgad." *MAAR* 9: 157–65.

Pfeiffer, R. 1933. "Die ΣΚΥΡΙΟΙ des Sophokles." *Philologus* 88: 1–15.

Pflaum, H.-G. 1950. *Les procurateurs équestres sous le Haut-Empire romain.* Paris.

———. 1960–61. *Les carrières procuratoriennes équestres sous le Haut-Empire romain.* 4 vols. Paris.

Philippson, R. 1943. "Papyrus Herculanensis 831." *AJPh* 64: 148–62.

Piacente, L. 2011. "Sul prestito librario nell'antica Roma." *S&T* 9: 35–51.

Pintaudi, R. 2006. "Un'etichetta di rotolo documentario." *CE* 81: 205–6.

Poethke, G. 1981. "Inventarliste." In *Papyri Greek & Egyptian,* ed. Parsons and Rea, 163–66.

Ponczoch, J. A. 2009. "*P.Herc.* 1570: A Treatise on Poverty and Wealth." *CErc.* 39: 141–59.

Porter, J. I. 2007. "Hearing Voices: The Herculaneum Papyri and Classical Scholarship." In *Antiquity Recovered,* ed. Coates and Seydl, 95–113.

Puglia, E. 1991. *Il libro offeso: Insetti carticoli e roditori nelle biblioteche antiche.* Naples.

———. 1993. "Frammenti da *P.Herc.* 1158." *CErc.* 23: 29–65.

———. 1996a. "A proposito dell'elenco di libri conservato in PVars. 5 *verso.*" *ZPE* 111: 27–30.

———. 1996b. "Il catalogo di un fondo librario di Ossirinco del III d.C. (PSILaur. inv. 19662)." *ZPE* 113: 51–65.

———. 1996c. "Fra *glutinatores* e scribi." In *Atti del V Seminario internazionale di papirologia,* ed. Capasso, 45–52.

———. 1997a. "Ancora sull'elenco di libri tràdito da PVars. 5 *verso.*" In *Bicentenario della morte di Antonio Piaggio,* ed. M. Capasso, 129–35.

———. 1997b. *La cura del libro nel mondo antico: Guasti e restauri del rotolo di papiro.* Naples.

———. 1997c. "Note bibliologiche e sticometriche." *ZPE* 119: 123–27.

———. 1997d. "La soscrizione del libro XXVIII *Sulla natura* di Epicuro (PHerc 1479/1417)." In *Ricerche di papirologia letteraria e documentaria,* ed. Capasso, 101–6.

———. 1998. "Gli inventari librari di PVindob. Gr. 39966." *ZPE* 123: 78–86.

———. 2000. "Un fondo librario coi suoi accessori (*P.Turner* 39)." In *Atti del V Convegno nazionale di egittologia e papirologia,* ed. Russo, 191–98.

———. 2011. "La rovina dei libri di Anzio nel *De indolentia* di Galeno." *S&T* 9: 53–62.

Radiciotti, P. 1998. "Osservazioni paleografiche sui papiri latini di Ercolano." *S&C* 22: 353–70.

———. 2009. "Ercolano: Papiri latini in una biblioteca greca." *Studi di egittologia e di papirologia* 6: 103–14. Online at LIBRAweb, http://www.libraweb.net/.

Raven, J. 2004. *Lost Libraries: The Destruction of Great Book Collections since Antiquity.* Basingstoke and New York.

Rawson, E. 1985. *Intellectual Life in the Late Roman Republic.* Baltimore.

Rea, J. 1966. "List of Comic Poets and their Plays." In [Auctores varii], *Atti dell'XI Congresso internazionale di papirologia,* 209–17.

Richter, G. M. A. 1966. *The Furniture of the Greeks, Etruscans and Romans.* London.

Rispoli, G. 1988. "Correzioni, varianti, glosse e scoli nei papiri ercolanesi." In *Proceedings of the XVIII International Congress of Papyrology,* ed. Mandilaras, 309–20.

Roberts, C. H. 1981. "Menander, *Thais.*" In *Papyri Greek & Egyptian,* ed. Parsons and Rea, 30.

Roberts, C. H., and T. C. Skeat. 1983. *The Birth of the Codex.* London and New York.

Robinson, J. M., ed. 1996. *The Nag Hammadi Library in English: Translated and Introduced by Members of the Coptic Gnostic Library Project.* 4th rev. ed. Leiden.

Rolandi, G., A. Paone, et al. 2007. "The 79 AD Eruption of Somma: The Relationship between the Date of the Eruption and the Southeast Tephra Dispersion." *Journal of Volcanology and Geothermal Research* 169: 87–98. Online at ScienceDirect .com, http://www.journals.elsevier.com/journal-of-volcanology-and-geothermal -research/.

Romeo, C. 1988. *Demetrio Lacone: La Poesia* (PHerc. *188 e 1014*). *Edizione, traduzione e commento.* Naples.

Roselli, A. 2010. "Libri e biblioteche a Roma al tempo di Galeno: La testimonianza del *de indolentia.*" *Galenos* 4: 127–48.

Rothschild, C. K., and T. W. Thompson. 2012. "Galen's *On the Avoidance of Grief*: The Question of a Library at Antium." *CPh* 107: 131–45.

Rowlandson, J. L. 1987. "*P. Oxy.* XLII 3047, VII 1044, and the Land Tax in Kind." *ZPE* 67: 283–91.

Russo, S., ed. 2000. *Atti del V Convegno nazionale di egittologia e papirologia: Firenze, 10–12 dicembre 1999.* Florence.

Rutherford, I. 2001. *Pindar's "Paeans": A Reading of the Fragments with a Survey of the Genre.* Oxford.

Rutledge, S. H. 2001. *Imperial Inquisitions: Prosecutors and Informants from Tiberius to Domitian.* London and New York.

———. 2012. *Ancient Rome as a Museum: Power, Identity, and the Culture of Collecting.* Oxford.

Sallmann, K. 1997. *Die Literatur des Umbruchs: Von der römischen zur christlichen Literatur, 117 bis 284 n. Chr.* Handbuch der Altertumswissenschaft, Abt. 8, Bd. 4. Munich.

Samuel, A. E., ed. 1966. *Essays in Honor of C. Bradford Welles*. American Studies in Papyrology, no. 1. New Haven.

Santoro, M. 2000. *[Demetrio Lacone] [La Forma di Dio] (P.Herc. 1055): Edizione, traduzione e commento*. Naples.

Sauron, G. 2010. "La bibliothèque de Celsus à Éphèse: Étude de sémantique architecturale et décorative." In *Neronia VIII*, ed. Perrin, 374–85.

Sbordone, F. 1976. *Ricerche sui papiri ercolanesi*. Vol. 2. Naples.

Schironi, F. 2009. *From Alexandria to Babylon: Near Eastern Languages and Hellenistic Erudition in the Oxyrhynchus Glossary (P.Oxy. 1802 + 4812)*. Berlin and New York.

———. 2010. *TO ΜΕΓΑ ΒΙΒΛΙΟΝ: Book-ends, End-titles, and Coronides in Papyri with Hexametric Poetry*. Durham (N.C.).

Schneider, B. 1990. "Zwei römische Elfenbeinplatten mit mythologischen Szenen." *KJ* 23: 255–72.

Schorn, S. 2004. *Satyros aus Kallatis: Sammlung der Fragmente mit Kommentar*. Basel.

Schubert, P. 2009. "Editing a Papyrus." In *The Oxford Handbook of Papyrology*, ed. Bagnall, 197–215.

———, ed. 2012. *Actes du 26e Congrès international de papyrologie: Genève, 16–21 août 2010*. Recherches et rencontres, 30. Geneva.

Sedley, D. 1989. "Philosophical Allegiance in the Greco-Roman World." In *Philosophia Togata*, ed. Griffin and Barnes, 97–119.

Segre, M. 1935. "Epigraphica I: Catalogo di libri da Rodi." *RFIC* 63: 214–22.

Seider, R. 1981. *Paläographie der lateinischen Papyri*. Vol. 2.2.2. Stuttgart.

Settis, S. 1988. *La Colonna Traiana*. Turin.

Sève, M. 2010. "Dimensions des livres et locaux de conservation dans les bibliothèques antiques." In *Neronia VIII*, ed. Perrin, 22–31.

Shackleton Bailey, D. R. 1965–70. *Cicero's Letters to Atticus*. 7 vols. Cambridge.

———. 1977. *Cicero: Epistulae Ad Familiares*. 2 vols. Cambridge and New York.

———. 1980. *Cicero: Epistulae Ad Quintum Fratrem Et M. Brutum*. Cambridge and New York.

Shatzman, I. 1972. "The Roman General's Authority over Booty." *Historia* 21: 177–205.

Shear, T. L., Jr. 1973a. "The Athenian Agora: Excavations of 1971." *Hesperia* 42: 121–79.

———. 1973b. "The Athenian Agora: Excavations of 1972." *Hesperia* 42: 359–407.

Sider, D. 1997. *The Epigrams of Philodemos: Introduction, Text, and Commentary*. Oxford.

———. 2005. *The Library of the Villa dei Papiri at Herculaneum*. Los Angeles.

Sijpesteijn, P. J., and K. A. Worp. 1974. "Literary and Semi-Literary Papyri from the Vienna Papyrus Collection." *CE* 49: 309–31.

Small, J. P. 1997. *Wax Tablets of the Mind: Cognitive Studies of Memory and Literacy in Classical Antiquity*. London and New York.

Smith, R. R. R. 1993. *The Monument of C. Julius Zoilos*. Mainz am Rhein.

Speyer, W. 1971. *Die literarische Fälschung im heidnischen und christlichen Altertum: Ein Versuch ihrer Deutung*. Munich.

Spinelli, E. 1986. "Metrodoro contro i Dialettici?" *CErc*. 16: 29–43.

Starr, R. J. 1990. "The Used-Book Trade in the Roman World." *Phoenix* 44: 148–57.

Stephens, S. A. 1985. "The Ancient Title of the *Ad Demonicum*." *YClS* 28: 5–8.

Stephens, S. A., and J. J. Winkler. 1995. *Ancient Greek Novels: The Fragments. Introduction, Text, Translation, and Commentary.* Princeton.

Stramaglia, A. 2011. "Libri perduti per sempre: Galeno, *De indolentia* 13; 16; 17–19." *RFIC* 139: 118–47.

Strocka, V. M. 1981. "Römische Bibliotheken." *Gymnasium* 88: 298–329.

———. 1993. "Pompeji VI 17,41: Ein Haus mit Privatbibliothek." *MDAI(R)* 100: 321–51.

———. 2000. "Noch einmal zur Bibliothek von Pergamon." *AA*: 155–65.

———. 2012. "Der stadtrömische Bibliothekstypus." In *Die Bibliothek von Nysa*, ed. Strocka, Hoffmann, and Hiesel, 167–84.

Strocka, V. M., S. Hoffmann, and G. Hiesel. 2012. *Die Bibliothek von Nysa am Mäander.* Forschungen in Nysa am Mäander, Bd. 2. Darmstadt and Mainz.

Tepedino Guerra, A. 1985. "Il PHerc. 1678: Filodemo sull'invidia?" *CErc.* 15: 113–25.

———. 1991. *Polieno, Frammenti: Edizione, traduzione e commento.* Naples.

———. 1992. "Metrodoro 'Contro i Dialettici'?" *CErc.* 22: 119–22.

———. 2008. "Un frammento di Metrodoro di Lampsaco in Filodemo (*P.Herc. 57*, col. 3)." *CErc.* 38: 103–8.

Thompson, E. M. 1912. *An Introduction to Greek and Latin Palaeography.* Oxford.

Thompson, H. A., and R. E. Wycherley. 1972. *The Agora of Athens: The History, Shape and Uses of an Ancient City Center.* The Athenian Agora, vol. 14. Princeton.

Tov, E. 2002. *The Texts from the Judaean Desert: Indices and an Introduction to the Discoveries in the Judaean Desert Series.* Oxford.

Tsouna, V. 2007. *The Ethics of Philodemus.* Oxford.

———. 2012. *Philodemus: "On Property Management." Translated with an Introduction and Notes.* Atlanta.

Tucci, P. L. 2008. "Galen's Storeroom, Rome's Libraries, and the Fire of A.D. 192." *JRA* 21: 133–49.

———. 2013. "Flavian Libraries in the City of Rome." In *Ancient Libraries*, ed. König, Oikonomopoulou, and Woolf, 277–311.

Turner, E. G. 1952a. "Oxyrhynchus and Its Papyri." *G&R* 21: 127–37.

———. 1952b. "Roman Oxyrhynchus." *JEA* 38: 78–93.

———. 1973. *The Papyrologist at Work.* Durham (N.C.).

———. 1978. "The Terms Recto and Verso: The Anatomy of the Papyrus Roll." In *Actes du XVe Congrès international de papyrologie*, ed. Bingen and Nachtergael, 1–71.

———. 1980. *Greek Papyri: An Introduction.* 2nd ed. Oxford.

———. 1983. "Sniffing Glue." *CErc.* 13: 7–14.

Turner, E. G., and P. J. Parsons. 1987. *Greek Manuscripts of the Ancient World.* 2nd ed., revised and enlarged by Peter J. Parsons. London.

Väänänen, V. 1977. *Ab epistulis . . . ad sanctum Petrum: Formules prépositionnelles latines étudiées dans leur contexte social.* Annales Academiae Scientiarum Fennicae, Ser. B, 197. Helsinki.

Van Haelst, J. 1989. "Les origines du codex." In *Les débuts du codex*, ed. Blanchard, 13–35.

Van't Dack, E. 1963. "A studiis, a bybliothecis." *Historia* 12: 177–84.

Vieillefond, J.-R. 1970. *Les "Cestes" de Julius Africanus: Étude sur l'ensemble des fragments avec édition, traduction et commentaires.* Florence.

Vössing, K. 1994. "Die öffentlichen Bibliotheken in Africa." In *L'Africa romana,* ed. Mastino and Ruggeri, 169–83.

Wallace-Hadrill, A. 1983. *Suetonius: The Scholar and His Caesars.* New Haven.

Ward-Perkins, J., and A. Claridge. 1978. *Pompeii A.D. 79.* New York.

Weaver, P. R. C. 1972. *Familia Caesaris: A Social Study of the Emperor's Freedmen and Slaves.* Cambridge.

Wendel, C. 1974. *Kleine Schriften zum antiken Buch- und Bibliothekswesen.* Cologne.

West, M. L., ed. 2007. *W. S. Barrett: Greek Lyric, Tragedy, and Textual Criticism. Collected Papers.* Oxford.

White, L. M. 2009. "Ordering the Fragments of *P.Herc.* 1471: A New Hypothesis." *CErc.* 39: 29–70.

White, P. 1992. "'Pompeius Macer' and Ovid." *CQ* 42: 210–18.

———. 2009. "Bookshops in the Literary Culture of Rome." In *Ancient Literacies,* ed. Johnson and Parker, 268–87.

Wiegand, T. 1932. "Zweiter Bericht über die Ausgrabungen in Pergamon 1928–32: Das Asklepieion." *Abhandlungen der Königlich Preussischen Akademie der Wissenschaften, Philosophisch-historische Klasse,* Jahrgang 1932, Nr. 5. Berlin.

Wilberg, W. 1908. "Die Fassade der Bibliothek in Ephesus." *JOeAI* 11: 118–35.

———. 1953. "Das Gebäude." In *Die Bibliothek,* ed. Braun, 1–42.

Wilke, C. 1914. *Philodemi De ira liber.* Leipzig.

Wood, S. 2001. "Literacy and Luxury in the Early Empire: A Papyrus-Roll Winder from Pompeii." *MAAR* 46: 23–40.

Wotke, C. 1894. *Sancti Eucherii Lugdunensis [opera], accedunt epistulae ab Saluiano et Hilario et Rustico ad Eucherium datae.* Corpus Scriptorum Ecclesiasticorum Latinorum, vol. 31. Vienna, Prague, and Leipzig.

Youtie, L. C. 1976. "A Terminus Post Quem for the Oxyrhynchus Phaedrus." *ZPE* 21: 14.

Yuen-Collingridge, R., and M. Choat. 2012. "The Copyist at Work: Scribal Practice in Duplicate Documents." In *Actes du 26e Congrès international de papyrologie,* ed. Schubert, 827–34.

Zadorojnyi, A. V. 2013. "Libraries and Paideia in the Second Sophistic: Plutarch and Galen." In *Ancient Libraries,* ed. König, Oikonomopoulou, and Woolf, 377–400.

Zanker, P. 1995. *Die Maske des Sokrates: Das Bild des Intellektuellen in der antiken Kunst.* Munich.

Zarmakoupi, M., ed. 2010. *The Villa of the Papyri at Herculaneum: Archaeology, Reception, and Digital Reconstruction.* New York.

Zetzel, J. E. G. 1973. "*Emendaui ad Tironem*: Some Notes on Classical Scholarship in the Second Century A.D." *HSPh* 77: 225–43.

Index of Ancient Sources

The index does not include the appendices.

General Index

The index does not include the appendices.

Lamar Cecil, *Wilhelm II: Prince and Emperor, 1859–1900* (1989).

Carolyn Merchant, *Ecological Revolutions: Nature, Gender, and Science in New England* (1989).

Gladys Engel Lang and Kurt Lang, *Etched in Memory: The Building and Survival of Artistic Reputation* (1990).

Howard Jones, *Union in Peril: The Crisis over British Intervention in the Civil War* (1992).

Robert L. Dorman, *Revolt of the Provinces: The Regionalist Movement in America* (1993).

Peter N. Stearns, *Meaning Over Memory: Recasting the Teaching of Culture and History* (1993).

Thomas Wolfe, *The Good Child's River*, edited with an introduction by Suzanne Stutman (1994).

Warren A. Nord, *Religion and American Education: Rethinking a National Dilemma* (1995).

David E. Whisnant, *Rascally Signs in Sacred Places: The Politics of Culture in Nicaragua* (1995).

Lamar Cecil, *Wilhelm II: Emperor and Exile, 1900–1941* (1996).

Jonathan Hartlyn, *The Struggle for Democratic Politics in the Dominican Republic* (1998).

Louis A. Pérez Jr., *On Becoming Cuban: Identity, Nationality, and Culture* (1999).

Yaakov Ariel, *Evangelizing the Chosen People: Missions to the Jews in America, 1880–2000* (2000).

Philip F. Gura, *C. F. Martin and His Guitars, 1796–1873* (2003).

Louis A. Pérez Jr., *To Die in Cuba: Suicide and Society* (2005).

Peter Filene, *The Joy of Teaching: A Practical Guide for New College Instructors* (2005).

John Charles Boger and Gary Orfield, eds., *School Resegregation: Must the South Turn Back?* (2005).

Jock Lauterer, *Community Journalism: Relentlessly Local* (2006).

Michael H. Hunt, *The American Ascendancy: How the United States Gained and Wielded Global Dominance* (2007).

Michael Lienesch, *In the Beginning: Fundamentalism, the Scopes Trial, and the Making of the Antievolution Movement* (2007).

Eric L. Muller, *American Inquisition: The Hunt for Japanese American Disloyalty in World War II* (2007).

John McGowan, *American Liberalism: An Interpretation for Our Time* (2007).

Nortin M. Hadler, M.D., *Worried Sick: A Prescription for Health in an Overtreated America* (2008).

William Ferris, *Give My Poor Heart Ease: Voices of the Mississippi Blues* (2009).

Colin A. Palmer, *Cheddi Jagan and the Politics of Power: British Guiana's Struggle for Independence* (2010).

W. Fitzhugh Brundage, *Beyond Blackface: African Americans and the Creation of American Mass Culture, 1890–1930* (2011).

Michael H. Hunt and Steven I. Levine, *Arc of Empire: America's Wars in Asia from the Philippines to Vietnam* (2012).

Nortin M. Hadler, M.D., *The Citizen Patient: Reforming Health Care for the Sake of the Patient, Not the System* (2013).

Louis A. Pérez Jr., *The Structure of Cuban History: Meanings and Purpose of the Past* (2013).

Jennifer Thigpen, *Island Queens and Mission Wives: How Gender and Empire Remade Hawai'i's Pacific World* (2014).

George W. Houston, *Inside Roman Libraries: Book Collections and Their Management in Antiquity* (2014).